Peter Gibson

Monarchy and the Royal Family

A Guide for Everyman

Monarchy and the Royal Family

A Guide for Everyman

by

Graham and Heather Fisher

ROBERT HALE · LONDON

© *Graham and Heather Fisher 1979*
First published in Great Britain 1979

ISBN 0 7091 7814 X

Robert Hale Limited
Clerkenwell House
Clerkenwell Green
London, EC1

Printed in Great Britain by
REDWOOD BURN LIMITED
Trowbridge & Esher

Contents

Illustrations

CREDITS

By courtesy of Somerset Herald of Arms, 1; Central Press, 2; Radio Times Hulton Picture Library, 3; by Gracious Permission of Her Majesty The Queen, 4, 35c, 35d, 45, 46, 47, 48, 66, 68; A. F. Kersting, 5, 9, 40, 41, 42, 43, 69; Syndication International Ltd, 6, 12, 14, 15, 16, 18, 19, 20, 22, 25, 26, 28, 29, 31, 32, 34, 38, 39, 49, 50, 53, 54, 55, 56, 58, 59, 63, 64, 65, 67, 70, 71, 72, 73, 76, 77, 78, 79, 81; British Tourist Authority, 8; Camera Press Ltd, 10, 11, 17, 23, 44, 51, 57, 60, 61; Fox Photos Ltd, 13; Keystone Press Agency, 21; Mary Evans Picture Library, 24, 27; Popperfoto, 30, 52; The Press Association Ltd, 33, 62; The Ashmolean Museum, Oxford, 35a; National Portrait Gallery, 35b; Pitkin Pictorials Ltd, 36; Public Record Office, 37; British Railways Board, 75; Rolls-Royce, 7; National Railway Museum, York, Crown Copyright, 74; by Gracious Permission of Queen Elizabeth, The Queen Mother, 80.

Acknowledgements

This book is the distillation of more than twenty-five years' research. Too many people have helped us during that period for us to list them all here. However, we would like to tender our thanks to those who have helped to resolve knotty queries or with additional research during the twelve months or so it has taken actually to compile the book. In particular, our gratitude is due to Mrs Michael Wall, CVO, and others of the Buckingham Palace Press secretariat; Mr Michael Oswald, royal studs' manager; the late Sir Norman Hartnell; Mr Geoffrey Wakeford, author of *Thirty Years A Queen*; Mr Brian E. Smith, author of *Royal Daimlers*; Mr Raymond J. Fullagar; Mr M. Keene; Mr Dennis Miller-Williams (Rolls-Royce Motors); Mr T. S. Preston (British Rail); and last, but by no means least, Miss J. Barratt and others of the staff of Bromley Central Library.

G. AND H. FISHER,

Keston Park,
Kent.

Introduction

There seems no logical reason why a reference book should not be also entertainingly readable and we have tried to make this one so. As a work of reference, it is crammed with names, dates and answers to the sort of questions people so constantly ask about the Royal Family. As a book to be read, provided it is read in the right order, it tells the story of Britain's monarchs from the early Saxon kings to Queen Elizabeth II.

For use as a reference book, there is an alphabetical contents list, from Arms (the royal coat thereof) to Yacht (HMY *Britannia*). As far as possible, we have employed names and titles in popular use, Prince Charles instead of Prince of Wales, Prince Philip instead of Duke of Edinburgh, Trooping the Colour instead of the Queen's Birthday Parade, and so on. Similarly, except where it is part of an actual name (as in Royal Lodge), we have avoided the use of the word "royal" in devising the alphabetical sequence. So details of the royal yacht are to be found under Yacht and those of the royal train under Train. However, if you cannot immediately find what you are seeking in alphabetical sequence, there is a detailed and comprehensive index.

While many people will perhaps wish to use the book only as a work of reference or dip into it here and there, reading whatever catches their eye and takes their fancy, others would perhaps prefer to read it as the story of Monarchy and the Royal Family. To aid them, we have worked out a suggested reading order which follows this Introduction.

Suggested Reading Order

(arranged as a continuous narrative)

A

ARMS

The royal coat of arms of Queen Elizabeth II had its origin in the painted battle-shields of the ancient Saxons. It was on the shield of Alfred the Great that the now traditional English lion first made its appearance. By Norman times King Alfred's painted lion had become two golden lions (though they were known in those days as leopards). Richard the Lionheart added the third, though his mother, Eleanor of Aquitaine, also appears to have sported a triple lion device. In the days of Edward III, because of Edward's claim to the throne of France, England's lions were obliged to share their quarters of the shield with the French fleur-de-lis, and it was not until 1801 that the French device was finally removed.

Long before then, when James VI of Scotland became also James I of England, the Scottish lion was introduced into the second quarter of the shield. The Irish harp was introduced into the third quarter at the same time, though Ireland had in fact been a kingdom since the days of Henry VIII.

In heraldic terms, the royal arms are described as follows: 1st and 4th quarters – *gules*, three lions passant guardant in pale *or*, 2nd quarter – *or*, a lion rampant within a double tressure flory counterflory *gules*; 3rd quarter – *azure*, a harp *or* stringed *argent*; the whole encircled with the Garter.

Wales is not included because it is a principality, not a kingdom. As a principality its arms are separately borne by the Prince of Wales (*see* Prince Charles *and* Princes of Wales).

The Garter which encircles the shield, together with its motto, *Honi soit qui mal y pense* (Shame on him who thinks evil of it), comes down from the days of Edward III (*see* Order of the Garter), who was rather more chivalrous to the ladies of the court than ever he was to the Scots. The motto beneath the shield, *Dieu et mon droit,* is a heritage from Henry V, whose longbows defeated the French at Agincourt, while the lion crest remembers the kingly crest once worn on the helmet of Richard the Lionheart.

1

When seen in their full glory the royal arms are supported by a golden lion, "rampant guardant" in heraldic terms, and a silver unicorn. The silver unicorn, representing Scotland, was brought in, as was the Scottish lion on the shield itself, at the time of the union of England and Scotland. It replaced the Tudor greyhound which was one of the supporters of the royal arms of Henry VII; the other was a Welsh dragon. Other monarchs have favoured other supporters, among them a bull, a bear, an antelope, an eagle and a swan.

ASCOT

Thanks to the patronage of successive monarchs, Royal Ascot, held annually in June, is arguably the world's most famous race meeting, as renowned for its display of feminine fripperies and outrageous hats as for the quality of the racing.

The royal connection with Ascot dates from the days of stout Queen Anne, who loved racing but found a long trek to Newmarket too tiring for her. She was driving out from Windsor Castle one day when it occurred to her that Ascot Heath, so closely adjoining the castle, was ideal for racing. "This would really stretch a racehorse," she commented, knowledgeably.

It cost her slightly over £1,000 to lay out a course and the first race was run on an August Saturday in 1711 for a plate valued at £100 given by the Queen. Subsequent monarchs, notably George III and George IV, maintained royal interest and it was George IV who instituted the royal procession along the course which is now an Ascot tradition. Queen Victoria was less enthused by the whole business and once cautioned her son, the future Edward VII, against going to Ascot too often.

Queen Elizabeth II does not share her great-great-grandmother's inhibitions and Royal Ascot is a hardy annual in her social calendar. Under a private Act of Parliament passed in the reign of her grandfather, King George V, Ascot is run these days by a board of trustees known as the Ascot Authority. The Queen draws no rent and receives none of the profits. These, under the terms of her grandfather's Act, are ploughed back into prize-money, improvements and amenities "to further and promote the welfare and prosperity of Ascot Races".

But if it brings her no profits, Ascot does reward her with a great deal of personal pleasure. Each day of the meeting finds her in the royal box, flanked by upwards of thirty relatives and friends she has invited to her house party at Windsor (*see* Windsor Castle). To supplement the racing, she lays on a varied programme of activities for her guests. They can go riding with her in Windsor Great Park. There is tennis and swimming for those who prefer. Jigsaw puzzles and books abound if wet.

All this is in the morning, of course, with an early lunch leaving good time to change for the races . . . the ladies into billowing gowns, the cost of which is a secret between them and their dressmakers, the men into the striped trousers, tight waistcoats and cutaway coats which are the modern version of the hunting clothes worn by the Regency bucks. Then it is off in a procession of cars to Duke's-lane where the party transfers into Ascot landaus drawn by the famous Windsor Greys (*see* Coaches and Carriages) for the traditional cavalcade along the course to the royal box, where the Queen, if she has a horse running that day, will superstitiously finger a star of lighter wood inlaid into the mahogany stairpost.

The Queen and Prince Philip head the procession in company with the Master of the Horse. The Queen Mother, Princess Margaret, Prince Charles, Princess Anne and others of the family share the remaining landaus with other members of the house party, each of whom has an opportunity to take part in the procession on at least one day.

To see the Queen at Ascot – or at any other race meeting, come to that – is to glimpse a very different woman from the emotionally controlled monarch of other public occasions. She will hop excitedly from one foot to the other, pounding the woodwork of the box with a white-gloved hand in the thrill of a close finish. If one of her own horses is running (*see* Racing and Horses), she has even been known to shout instructions at her jockey as the royal colours flash past her. Nor is she content to remain in the royal box, but frequently treks to the paddock to inspect the horses as they parade for the next race. She does not bet, though she and her house guests will sometimes organize a small private sweepstake among themselves.

Prince Philip is less enthused by the racing scene and will sometimes retire quietly to the rear of the royal box to watch cricket on television.

The owner of the horse winning the major event of the day is usually invited to join the Queen and her friends in the royal box for afternoon tea, cucumber sandwiches and cake accompanied by a choice of iced coffee or tea (Indian or China). The day's racing over, the Queen and her guests return to Windsor Castle to change for dinner, with drinks beforehand. Around this time of day a liveried page traditionally tours the castle with a container of smouldering lavender, a hangover from the days when something had to be done to counteract the combined smells of cooking and bad drains.

Dinner is served in the state dining-room. Dining-table and sideboards glitter with gold, footmen and pages parade in their semi-state liveries, and a string band from the Brigade of Guards dispenses soothing music. After dinner, there may be a film show in the Throne Room, with the guests sitting on folding chairs, or the huge Persian carpet in the Crimson Drawing-Room may be rolled back for dancing.

B

BALMORAL

Queen Elizabeth II, like her great-great-grandmother before her, looks upon Balmoral as her "favourite spot". Favourite not only because of its picture-postcard setting, but also because its present-day 80,000 acres in the heart of the Scottish Highlands, some 480 miles north of London, afford her a combination of privacy and freedom such as she can find nowhere else. It is to Balmoral that she heads with her family each August for the long summer vacation.

The Royal Family's love affair with the Highlands started with the coming of the railways. Scotland was suddenly more accessible and Queen Victoria went there with Prince Albert in 1842. She was enraptured by what she saw. So enraptured that six years later she and Albert took a four-year lease on Balmoral House, a country mansion and estate of some 17,400 acres, six miles from Ballater. "A pretty little castle in the old Scotch style," the Queen noted in her journal.

She wore a dress of satin tartan when she stayed there in 1848. Albert and the boys donned kilts. While Albert stalked stags or shot ptarmigan, the Queen sketched. They fished together for trout in Loch Muick. They were back again the following year . . . and so began the royal pattern which has continued since. Albert learned Gaelic while the Queen and the children took lessons in Scottish dancing. Sir Edwin Landseer was brought north to capture their happiness in oils.

When the lease on Balmoral House ran out, they decided to buy the place. It cost them £31,500 out of the quarter-million left to Queen Victoria by the eccentric John Camden Nield. Not content with that, Albert conceived the idea of building the present turreted and castellated castle, a cross between a German *Schloss* and the Highland stronghold of a clan chieftain. It was built by William Smith of Aberdeen, the cornerstone being laid in 1853 and work completed in 1855. Victoria's son, the future Edward VII, did not much care for it and nicknamed it "The Highland barn of a thousand draughts".

The ghosts of Victoria and Albert still dominate Balmoral today. Subsequent royal owners have been reluctant to change the red and grey Balmoral tartan of the carpets which Prince Albert designed, or even the wallpaper embossed with the VRI cypher (I for *Imperatrix*) of Queen Victoria. A marble statue of Albert in full Highland regalia stands beneath the tattered standards of Scottish regiments in the entrance hall, and in almost every room are other echoes of Victorian times . . . the maple and pine furniture which Albert also designed, Parian marble candelabra carved in the form of Highland chieftains, mounted ram's heads which once served to hold snuff and, in one of the dressing-rooms, a frieze of fading Victorian family snapshots taken when photography was in its infancy.

Each year, as soon as they reach Balmoral, Elizabeth II and her family lose no time in "going native". Philip dons a kilt while the Queen slips into a tartan skirt worn with a tweed jacket. She has a choice of three tartans, Royal Stewart, Hunting Stewart and the red and grey Balmoral tartan which her great-great-grandfather designed.

Royal holiday pursuits have changed little since Queen Victoria's day. There is sailing and fishing on Loch Muick and picnics on the moors. There are horses to ride, grouse to shoot, deer to stalk. The Queen was nineteen when she first went stalking at Balmoral. World War II had not long ended and a shortage of clothing coupons prevented her buying suitable clothing. So she borrowed a pair of her father's plus-fours. Margaret thought them "unfeminine", but the elder sister found them so practical that she has continued to wear something similar, plus-fours or knickerbockers, ever since. She is a first-class shot with a hunting rifle and has bagged her share of stags, usually those which require culling because they are unfit to breed.

Royal holiday life still follows the traditions of the Scottish lairds. Each morning the Queen's piper paces up and down outside the castle, skirling traditional airs. Each evening, following dinner, a small contingent of pipers parades round the dining-table, pipes going full blast. There is usually a visit to the Highland Games at Braemar, which Queen Victoria confided to her journal was "a poor affair", and the Gillies' Ball, which Victoria and Albert initiated, is still one of the high spots of the royal stay. The Queen and Prince Philip invariably head the opening march in the castle ballroom before separating, as do others of the family, to join sets composed of gillies, their wives, other servants and soldiers from the guard of honour for a lively eightsome reel and other dances. Prince Philip, in the early days of his marriage to the then Princess Elizabeth, knew nothing of Scottish dancing and, on their first visit to Scotland, was reluctantly obliged to stand on the sidelines while someone else partnered his wife. He promptly took lessons and today dances as to the manner born. As for the Queen, she gets quite caught up in the fervour of Scottish dancing and is not beyond giving vent to traditional yells which punctuated some of the dances.

BANQUETS

The Queen herself was once heard to say, with evident satisfaction, that
the banquets she gives at Buckingham Palace to honour other monarchs or presidents paying state visits to Britain always "run like clockwork". That they do so is due in no small measure to a system of
miniature "traffic lights" discreetly hidden among the banked flowers
which decorate the palace ballroom on such occasions. The "traffic
lights" are operated by the Palace Steward. Standing behind the
Queen, he takes his cue from her, though no signal passes between
them. He can see for himself when she is ready for each course and
when she has finished it. He operates the lights accordingly, amber as a
signal for servants to take up positions, green for them to start serving or
clearing. In this way, each course is served to the scores of guests at
exactly the same moment that it is placed before the Queen herself and
her guest of honour.

Weeks of preparation involving dozens of servants contribute to the
success of a state banquet. What is known as the "royal gold" (though
much of it is silver gilt) is brought out of storage to be cleaned and bur-
nished with soft brushes and chamois leathers by the Yeoman of the
Gold and his assistants. The extent of the job can be gauged from the
fact that the collection weighs around five tons with some of the table
centres so massive that it requires four men to lift and position them. To
prevent damage to smaller items, knives and forks, plates and salvers,
they are carried to and from the ballroom in leather buckets.

It takes twenty housemaids to dust and polish the vast ballroom (*see*
Buckingham Palace). Damask table-cloths, some of them more than a
century old, are brought out of storage in the basement linen room and
taken up to the ballroom on wheeled trolleys to cover the main dining-
table and some nineteen extensions. The distance between each place
setting is carefully checked with a measuring stick to ensure that everything is precisely aligned. The cutlery is gold; the candelabra (made by
Paul Storr and John Bridges) are silver gilt. The plates too, some of
them dating back to Charles II, are silver gilt. The dessert china includes Worcester and Rockingham services dating back to William IV,
apple-green and turquoise Sèvres porcelain from the days of Louis XV
and a Minton service made for Queen Victoria.

On the day of the actual banquet the palace's residential staff is sup-
plemented with temporaries, as many as 150 of them hired through an
employment agency to act as extra footmen, chefs, kitchen porters.
State liveries are brought out from the moth-proof steel boxes in which
they are stored in the palace basement. Royal pages wear black and
gold tunics with black knee breeches, white stockings and black pumps.

Footmen wear tunics of scarlet and gold with scarlet knee breeches. But neither pages nor footmen are any longer required to "powder" their hair. It was always a messy business, involving the application of flour and starch to a wet, soapy head, and all except a few die-hard traditionalists were thoroughly delighted when Prince Philip, regarding it as "unmanly", persuaded his wife to put a stop to it.

Masses of flowers, roses, lilies and orchids, are entwined with purple grapes to decorate the corners of the ballroom, rising in banks perhaps eight feet high. More flowers fill the silver-gilt bases set between the candelabra on the tables. But those immediately in front of the Queen on the main table are short-stemmed, floating in a low bowl, so that she can be clearly seen.

Immediately prior to a banquet, before she goes to change, the Queen always visits the ballroom to check the place settings and décor for herself, walking round the tables, pausing here and there to deliver a brief word of thanks to those responsible.

Her entrance into the ballroom on the night of the banquet is regal in the extreme. Wearing a lavishly embroidered state gown, its bodice slashed by the blue ribbon of the Garter (*see* Order of the Garter), jewels from her fabulous personal collection (*see* Jewellery) shimmering at her throat, ears and wrists, usually also wearing shoes with three-inch heels to lend her additional height, she makes her entrance with two courtiers in tailcoats and knee breeches walking backwards in front of her (no easy task) while guests stand to attention and a band from the Guards Division plays the National Anthem.

Outside the ballroom, food for the dozens of guests is already on its way up from the kitchens, two flights of stairs below, hot courses being kept warm in heated cupboards in an adjacent room Downstairs in the kitchens ten servants brace themselves for the washing up to come, a task which necessarily continues well after the last guest has departed. As each item is washed and dried, the Yeoman of the Gold, the Yeoman of the Silver and the Yeoman of the Glass and China Pantry check it off in their record books. Seldom is anything lost or broken, though there was one occasion when a gold fork was found to be missing. A long and meticulous search finally brought it to light again. It had been inadvertently dropped into one of the huge bins in which the waste food is dumped.

BIRTHS AND BIRTHDAYS

Queen Elizabeth II has two birthdays, her real one on April 21 – she was born in 1926 – and her official one, a Saturday in June (usually the second Saturday). June in the hope that the weather will be fine for the

Birthday Parade (*see* Trooping the Colour) with which the occasion is celebrated and a Saturday so that London's weekday traffic is not disrupted.

Other birth-dates:

Prince Philip: 10 June, 1921

Prince Charles: 14 November, 1948

Prince Andrew: 19 February, 1960

Prince Edward: 10 March, 1964

Princess Anne: 15 August, 1950

Mark Phillips: 22 September, 1948

Peter Phillips: (Princess Anne's son): 15 November, 1977

Queen Mother: 4 August, 1900

Princess Margaret: 21 August, 1930

Earl of Snowdon: 7 March, 1930

Viscount Linley (Princess Margaret's son): 3 November, 1961

Lady Sarah Armstrong-Jones (Princess Margaret's daughter): 1 May, 1964

Princess Alice, Duchess of Gloucester: 25 December, 1901

Duke of Gloucester: 26 August, 1944

Duchess of Gloucester: 20 June, 1946

Earl of Ulster (Duke of Gloucester's son): 24 October, 1974

Lady Davina Windsor (Duke of Gloucester's daughter): 20 November, 1977

Duke of Kent: 9 October, 1935

Duchess of Kent: 22 February, 1933

Earl of St Andrews (Duke of Kent's son): 26 June, 1962

Lady Helen Windsor (Duke of Kent's daughter): 28 April, 1964

Lord Nicholas Windsor (Duke of Kent's son): 25 July, 1970

Princess Alexandra: 25 December, 1936

The Hon. Angus Ogilvy: 14 September, 1928

James Ogilvy (Princess Alexandra's son): 29 February, 1964

Marina Ogilvy (Princess Alexandra's daughter): 31 July, 1966

Prince Michael of Kent: 4 July, 1942

Lord Frederick Windsor (Prince Michael's son): 6 April, 1979

Earl of Harewood: 7 February, 1923

Viscount Lascelles (Earl of Harewood's son): 21 October, 1950

James Lascelles (Earl of Harewood's son): 5 October, 1953

Robert Lascelles (Earl of Harewood's son): 14 February, 1955

Mark Lascelles (Earl of Harewood's son): 5 July, 1964

Gerald Lascelles (Earl of Harewood's brother): 21 August, 1924

Henry Lascelles (Gerald Lascelles's son): 19 May, 1953

Princess Alice, Countess of Athlone: 25 February, 1883

Earl Mountbatten of Burma: 25 June, 1900

Duchess of Windsor: 18 June, 1896

BUCKINGHAM PALACE

Prince Philip once referred to the Queen and himself as "living over the shop". And so, in a sense, they do; in a second-floor apartment above offices in which typewriters chatter and telephones ring constantly.

Buckingham Palace today (*see* Palaces) has several functions. It serves as a workaday home for the Queen and her husband; acts as a hostel for some of their many servants; affords offices in which secretaries, typists and telephonists, accountants and clerks work as cogs in the wheels of monarchy; and provides more than one suite of magnificent state rooms in which the Queen can play host to foreign monarchs and presidents, Commonwealth heads of state, ambassadors, High Commissioners and Governors-General. Though it is not only the top brass who go there. Lesser mortals are also invited from time to time, mainly for investitures (*see* Honours and Investitures) and garden parties (*see* Garden Parties), to say nothing of the ordinary youngsters who go there to receive the "golds" for which they have qualified in Philip's Duke of Edinburgh Award Scheme designed to encourage a spirit of enterprise and adventure in young people.

Originally known as The Queen's House, and before that as Buckingham House (royal servants still sometimes refer to it rather irreverently as "Buck House"), the palace stands on the site of what was once a disreputable pleasure garden and before that a mulberry orchard. It was Scottish James I who conceived the mulberry scheme with the idea of breeding silkworms and thus launching a new British industry. So he bought four acres of land for £935 and planted them with 10,000 mulberry trees. Unfortunately, he picked the wrong type of tree, the experiment failed and the mulberry orchard passed into other hands.

A lord named Goring built himself a house on the site, but with the end of the Civil War the silkworm sheds were turned into wine booths and eating places and the area degenerated into a pleasure garden frequented by prostitutes and the young rakes who consorted with them. Then in 1702 the Duke of Buckingham acquired the site, rebuilt Goring's original house as a red-brick mansion which hc called Buckingham House. On his death, house and land passed to his wife, the bastard daughter of James II, and from her to Buckingham's bastard son, Charles Herbert. Herbert changed his name to Sheffield and promptly sold the place for £21,000 to George III, who renamed it The Queen's House in honour of his wife. Twelve of their children were born there, including the son who became William IV and the prince who fathered Queen Victoria.

It was another son, their eldest, the Prince Regent who later became George IV, having already spent a fortune on the Royal Pavilion at Brighton, who conceived the idea to turning The Queen's House into a royal palace. He also had the idea of turning Windsor Castle into an English-style Versailles (*see* Windsor Castle). Parliament, which should have known better, agreed to let him do so. A ceiling of £200,000 was placed on the work, but neither George nor his designer, John Nash, took any notice of that. Nine years after work first started, with up to one thousand workmen toiling away, the job was still not done and the cost had already escalated to three times the original figure. In the end, the work went on so long that the Prince, now King, died without ever moving in.

Considerably embarrassed by all this, as he had been by the lavishness of his brother's coronation, William IV said the new palace was "too ornate" for him and asked the Government to take it off his hands. It would make a fine parliament building, he suggested; failing that, a barracks. But Parliament wanted nothing to do with it and, reluctantly, with the help of a new architect, Edward Blore, William set about finishing it. The final cost was slightly less than one million pounds and William, like his brother, never lived in it.

Queen Victoria did. She moved in on the twenty-third day of her reign at the age of eighteen. It has been the home of the Royal Family and the seat of monarchy ever since.

In those days Victoria was not the black-clad widow of later life. She was young and vivacious, and, following her marriage to Prince Albert, many a ball and concert was held in the new palace. But the births of successive children at a rate of almost one a year soon had her complaining that the place was not big enough for a growing family. Parliament thereupon sold the Royal Pavilion at Brighton and voted another £150,000 out of the proceeds to give Buckingham Palace a fourth wing. It was also arranged for the state rooms to be furnished with fire-places, mirrors and suchlike shipped up from Brighton. Edward Blore was again given the job of designing the new wing, together with a ballroom and kitchens beneath. To make way at the front, the Marble Arch, which Nash had designed as a main entrance for George IV, was taken down and rebuilt in its present position at the north-east corner of Hyde Park.

The new wing was completed in time for Queen Victoria to stand on the balcony and watch her troops march off to the Crimean War, the start of a royal tradition of balcony appearances which still continues.

With the death of her beloved Albert, Victoria deserted the palace – and public life – for the solitude of Osborne, on the Isle of Wight, and Balmoral (*see* Balmoral). Again the palace languished and it was left to Edward VII to bring life back to it with a spate of entertaining. He also set about modernizing the place, replacing gas lighting with electricity; improving the plumbing. Displaying a considerable passion for cleanliness, he equipped some of the dressing-rooms with as many as three wash-basins, one for the hands, one for the face and one for cleaning the teeth. He paid less attention to the exterior of the palace and by the time George V succeeded to the throne Blore's new wing was already beginning to crumble under the combined attack of English weather and London smoke. As a result, Sir Aston Webb was called in and in 1913 it was refaced with 5,757 tons of Portland stone. The gates and railings which front the palace were erected at the same time while, inside, Queen Mary set about restoring the state apartments to the grandeur envisaged by the Prince Regent.

While the exterior has remained unchanged since then, modernization of the interior has continued from time to time. George VI converted the old conservatory into a swimming pool for his daughters. The installation of central heating has done away with the need for ten men to be employed lighting fires each day. Elevators, heated trolleys and electric hotplates have come to the aid of servants having to convey food all the way from the kitchens to the Royal Family's private dining-room. For all this, Buckingham Palace remains a vast, ungainly and largely sunless building.

Successive royal occupants have seldom had a good word to say about it. Edward VII called it "a sepulchre". George V grumbled that he would like to pull it down and move to Kensington Palace. The Duke of Windsor, as Edward VIII, complained of the "dank, musty smell". George VI, in the days before central heating, termed it "an icebox", and Elizabeth II, when she became Queen, wanted to continue to live at Clarence House (*see* Clarence House). But Prime Minister Winston Churchill disapproved.

Viewed from the air today, the palace forms a hollow square around its central courtyard. It has been said that it has six hundred rooms, but it depends on what you class as a "room". Take away closets (some of which, admittedly, are as big as an average room), enclosed corridors and suchlike, and the number shrinks to nearer the three hundred mark. In many ways, Buckingham Palace is not unlike a small village, with its own police station, fire station, telephone exchange and post office. Elizabeth II, when she first went there as a small girl, was surprised to find postmen tramping the red-carpeted corridors delivering mail from room to room. And though it has no pub, the palace does have its own "club" where staff can relax over a quiet drink and which serves also as a village store selling tea, coffee, biscuits and fruit. There is a sick-bay with a resident nurse. It has its own filling station, its own smithy, its own workshops for electrical, plumbing and furniture maintenance.

The Royal Family's private apartment is on what is known in Britain as the first floor and in America as the second floor of the north wing, its windows overlooking that part of the gardens which flanks Constitution Hill. It consists of about a dozen rooms with communicating doors. Focal point of the apartment is the sitting-room, a long, lofty, bay-windowed room which also doubles as the Queen's study. Here, at a Chippendale desk inherited from her father, surrounded by family photographs including one of a youthfully bearded Prince Philip, she works away daily at the contents of her Boxes. Here, of an evening, shoes off to ease her feet if she has done a public walkabout that day, she sits on a sofa with her feet up to watch television or tackle a crossword. The sofa and matching armchairs flank a marble fire-place. Close to the fire-place is a handsome Hepplewhite cabinet which was a wedding gift from forty-seven members of the Royal Family. A portrait of the Queen, painted in the days when she was still a young princess, hangs on one wall, balancing the gilt-framed mirror suspended above the porcelain cockerels which strut on the mantelpiece. It is a comfortably cluttered room, often fragrant with the scent of carnations, the Queen's favourite flower, in which the homeliness of family life as represented by snoozing corgis and their water-bowl near one of the doors contrasts with the authority of the leather-covered despatch box which stands on a side table alongside the desk.

Communicating doors lead to the family's private dining-room on one side and to the royal bedroom on the other. Like most of the other rooms, the bedroom is spacious and high-ceilinged, lighted by tall windows. Filmy draperies suspended from a gilded crown frame the bed-head. From the bedroom another door leads into the Queen's dressing-room and, beyond that, to her bathroom. Philip's bathroom adjoins and from the internal corridor which serves both bathrooms a door leads to Philip's dressing-room.

On the other side of the sitting-room a door leads through to the dining-room with its oval-shaped table which can be extended to seat ten if there are friends or relatives to dinner (*see* Meals). Just around the corner from the dining-room, at the rear of the palace, is the audience room in which the Queen receives the prime minister and others. At the other end of the apartment corridor, and also linked by communicating doors, are Prince Philip's study and the sitting-room which doubles as his audience room. With its control panel enabling him to stop or start his tape recorder at will, swivel the television set to a different angle, close or open the curtains, Philip's study tends to present a more businesslike appearance than the Queen's sitting-room; streamlined and functional, it is lower-ceilinged than most of the palace rooms because of the false ceiling he had installed soon after he and the Queen took over.

The state rooms are mainly in the west wing, overlooking the gardens to the rear, accessible through the *porte-cochère* of the Grand Entrance. Inevitably, a building as vast as Buckingham Palace has many doors. The Grand Entrance, where state visitors are formally welcomed and from which the Queen departs on state occasions, is the most important one. For more informal departures the Queen usually uses the garden entrance in the north wing. Prince Philip prefers to come and go by what is still known as the King's Door. It was suggested to Elizabeth, when she first came to the throne, that she should rename it the Queen's Door, but she has kept it unchanged. At the front of the palace, on one side, is the Privy Purse Door, used by members of the Household and those calling on official business. Also at the front, on the other side, is the Visitors' Door, inside which is housed the visitors' book, waiting to be signed by those who observe the old custom of calling to pay their respects at times when there is a birth, illness or death in the family. Just round the corner, in Buckingham Palace Road, is the Trade Door where groceries and meat, milk and vegetables, are delivered.

Beyond the Grand Entrance is the Marble Hall on to which open a number of semi-state rooms. The Bow Room takes its name from the deep bow windows overlooking the gardens. Adjoining it is the 1844 Drawing-Room, so named because it was occupied in that year by the visiting Tsar of Russia; the 1855 Drawing-Room which takes its name from a similar visit paid by Napoleon III; and the Belgian Suite, named after King Leopold of the Belgians who so often occupied it. The Queen and Prince Philip occupied this suite in the early days of her monarchy, while waiting for the Queen Mother to move out to Clarence House. Later, the Queen moved briefly back into it for the births of Prince Andrew and Prince Edward. These days it is usually used to accommodate foreign monarchs and presidents paying state visits to Britain.

At the top of the Grand Staircase is the Picture Gallery, forming a central corridor 150 feet long from which massive mirror-glass doors lead to the various state rooms: the Throne Room in which the young Victoria declared her intention of marrying Albert; the State Dining-Room with its table which can be extended to 80 feet; the Ballroom; the Music Room, its domed and gold-encrusted ceiling making it a fit setting for royal christenings; the Blue, Green and White Drawing-Rooms. Smallest of the state rooms is the Royal Closet. It is here that the Queen and her entourage assemble on formal occasions, a touch of a spring causing one of the china cabinets and the mirror above it in the adjoining White Drawing-Room to swing back like a door for the royal party to make its entrance.

The Throne Room (*see* Throne) is as regal as its name, 65 feet long, its white walls trimmed with gold, carpet, curtains and canopy in crimson.

The Ballroom which Queen Victoria had added to the palace is even more majestic than the Throne Room and certainly vaster, 123 feet long, 60 feet wide and 45 feet high.

On the same floor, in the east wing at the front of the palace, is what is known as the Principal Corridor. Some twenty feet wide, it is even longer than the Picture Gallery at 240 feet, its length divided into the appearance of separate rooms by mirror-glass doors. It is from the middle of the three rooms so formed that the Queen walks out on to the palace balcony.

The 39-acre garden at the rear of the palace was landscaped for George IV by William Aiton. He cleared the area which is now the lawn (a mixture, incidentally, of Bent grasses, smooth-stalked meadow grass, rye grass, dog's tail grass and camomile), joined two ponds to form the present lake, created the southern mound and planted it with a screen of trees. Today, the gardens with their birds and butterflies, wild duck and flamingoes, form a quiet oasis in the very heart of London. With its rose beds and 170 yards of herbaceous border, its camellias and magnolias, it is in many ways a typically English garden. It boasts no statues or fountains, though it does have two bronze cranes which Edward VII brought back from India and the huge Waterloo Vase which Louis XVIII presented to the Prince Regent. Most of all it has trees, plane and beech, holly, chestnut and silver birch, together with a few more unusual ones like maple, swamp cypress and the Chinese tree of heaven. And still there, linking the present with the past, is one of James I's original mulberry trees.

ARMS. The royal coat of arms. ASCOT. One of the world's most prestigious race meetings. The Queen, Prince Philip and Prince Charles ride along the course in a landau drawn by the famous Windsor Greys during the Royal Meeting, 1978. BALMORAL. First visited by royalty in 1842 when Queen Victoria went there with Prince Albert, though they did not build today's castle until 1853-55.

BANQUETS. The magnificent ballroom at Buckingham Palace, set out for a state banquet. BUCKINGHAM PALACE. Originally known as The Queen's House, Buckingham Palace stands on the site of what was once a mulberry orchard.

BUCKINGHAM PALACE. The White Drawing-Room. CARS. The Queen's Rolls-Royce Phantom VI State Limousine, presented to Her Majesty in 1978 by the Society of Motor Manufacturers and Traders.

CASTLE OF MEY. The Castle of Mey, originally known as Barrogill Castle, stands on the craggy coastline of the Pentland Firth, Caithness. CHEVENING. Chevening – the seventeenth-century Palladian mansion which is now the country home of Prince Charles. CHANGING THE GUARD. The changing the guard at Buckingham Palace – a great favourite with the tourists.

CLARENCE HOUSE. Named after the Duke of Clarence (later William IV), Clarence House is the London residence of the Queen Mother.

COACHES AND CARRIAGES. The Gold State Coach which dates from the days of George III.

CORONATION. The Coronation of Queen Elizabeth II in Westminster Abbey, 1953.

CROWN JEWELS. Among the priceless collection of Crown Jewels are (*above left*) St Edward's Crown, the Orb, the Rod with Dove, the Sceptre with Cross, the Ring and (*below left*) the Ampulla and the Anointing Spoon.

DOGS. Prince Charles with his labrador Harvey at Balmoral, and the Queen with some of the royal corgis.

DUKE AND DUCHESS OF GLOUCESTER. *Above left:* The Duke and Duchess of Gloucester at Heathrow, en route for Australia, February 1979. DUKE AND DUCHESS OF KENT. *Above right:* The Duke and Duchess of Kent willing Virginia Wade to victory against Holland's Betty Stove, Wimbledon, July 1977. DUKE AND DUCHESS OF WINDSOR. *Below left:* The Instrument of Abdication as witnessed by the Dukes of York, Gloucester and Kent. *Below right:* The Duke and Duchess of Windsor are welcomed by Hitler during their controversial visit to Nazi Germany in 1937.

INSTRUMENT OF ABDICATION

I, Edward the Eighth, of Great Britain, Ireland, and the British Dominions beyond the Seas, King, Emperor of India, do hereby declare My irrevocable determination to renounce the Throne for Myself and for My descendants, and My desire that effect should be given to this Instrument of Abdication immediately.

In token whereof I have hereunto set My hand this tenth day of December, nineteen hundred and thirty six, in the presence of the witnesses whose signatures are subscribed.

SIGNED AT
FORT BELVEDERE
IN THE PRESENCE
OF

EARL MOUNTBATTEN OF BURMA. Prince Charles, "Uncle Dickie" and Prince Philip pictured together at a polo match, April 1978. FLYING. The Queen and Prince Philip step off the Concorde that flew them to the oil-rich desert state of Kuwait during their historic tour of the Middle East in 1979. The Queen is the first reigning British monarch to have set foot on Arab soil.

CARS

To mark her 1977 Silver Jubilee, the Society of Motor Manufacturers and Traders subscribed £60,000 to build Queen Elizabeth II a new Rolls Royce to go with the other four already garaged in the royal mews. Built by the Mulliner Park Ward division, the new Rolls – a Phantom VI Special limousine – was somewhat delayed by an industrial dispute and not actually delivered until March of the following year. But it was well worth waiting for.

Finished in black over royal claret, the new royal Rolls is 19 feet 10 inches long, 6 feet 7 inches wide and 6 feet 1 inch high. To fit the available space on the royal yacht, it can be shortened by nine inches in a matter of minutes by removing the front and rear bumpers. It has a V8 engine of 6.75 litres, a three-speed torque converter automatic transmission, an electronic ignition system and centralized door locking. Brakes are of the drum type, operated by two independent power-boosted circuits with additional mechanical linkage to the rear brakes.

So that the Queen can be plainly seen, there is a transparent dome embracing the rear roof quarters and a transparent roof to the rear compartment. A detachable cover with a smaller rear window affords privacy when required while the sliding cover for the transparent rear roof can be operated electrically. The rear compartment is illuminated fluorescently and the rear seat, upholstered in pale blue, is four inches higher than normal. The rear carpet is mountain blue and there are blue lambswool rugs.

The wide central armrest in the rear compartment contains a radio, a cassette player and a dictating machine. In place of the usual cocktail cabinet, there is a clock and a compartment for tapes, one of which is a selection of military music chosen by the Queen herself. In the side armrests and the adjacent sills are controls for the interior lighting, air-conditioning, reading lamps, windows and sliding glass partition. While neither the Queen nor Philip smoke, ashtrays and cigar lighters are mounted on the rear side sills. There are separate air-conditioning systems to front and rear compartments, and the front, which is

15

trimmed in dark blue hide with matching carpet and black rubber mats, also has its own radio.

The Spirit of Ecstasy fitted to the car on delivery was in the kneeling posture, echoing the Silver Dawn and Wraith models of the 1950s. However, for state occasions the Queen uses her own St George and the Dragon mascot. Only one small point disappointed the Queen when she first saw the car. It had rectangular wing mirrors, while she would have preferred round ones. It took some hunting to find round mirrors, out of fashion at the present day, but they were finally found and fitted.

The Queen's great-grandfather, Edward VII, was the first of the Royals to use a car. He bought his first in 1900 while still Prince of Wales. It was a two-cylinder, 6 h.p. Daimler with a four-seater open body built by Hooper & Co., painted in chocolate and black picked out in red, and can be seen today in the museum at Sandingham. The first time he used it a groom rode in front on horseback. But the car quickly overtook the horse, and the groom was ordered back to the stables. By the time he took over the throne the following year Edward had a fleet of three Daimlers, including a 14-seater "beaters' car" which was rather like a small bus. When he was driven from Buckingham Palace on October 19, 1904, to inspect the Woolwich Garrison it was the first time a car was used for a royal public occasion.

Like every car-owning family, the Queen's great-grandparents appear to have had arguments over cars. Queen Alexandra had a two-seater Columbia electric car with tiller steering. But this was suitable only for the private roads of the Sandringham estate and she wanted a proper car of her own, she said. When she didn't get one, she borrowed a friend's. Finally, her husband relented and bought her a Wolseley. Queen Alexandra enjoyed motoring, though she was quick to poke her chauffeur in the back with her parasol as a signal to slow down on bends. Her husband, by contrast, was constantly shouting "Faster, faster" as his car dashed along at speeds up to 50 m.p.h. This worried royal aides so much that the King's chauffeur was secretly instructed that he must slacken speed as soon as he could do so without the King noticing.

As a diplomatic gesture to Germany and France, Edward also bought three successive Mercedes and a Renault landaulette for foreign travel, but Daimler remained the official state car. For something like half a century the Daimler marque was virtually synonymous with the Royal Family. Both as Prince of Wales and King, George V had a succession of Hooper-bodied Daimlers, as well as a Pullman limousine seating eleven people which Offord & Sons built specially for the Delhi Durbar, and for his Silver Jubilee in 1935 he acquired two special Daimler Double-Sixes. George VI, though he drove a Lanchester as Duke of York, continued the Daimler tradition when he succeeded to the throne and by the close of his reign there were four Daimler 5½-litre straight-eight landaulettes and a 1937 straight-eight shooting brake in the royal garages.

As a princess, Elizabeth II had a 2½-litre Daimler saloon which her father bought her for her eighteenth birthday and a Hooper-bodied Daimler limousine – registration: HRH 1 – which was a wedding gift to her and Prince Philip. She inherited her father's state Daimlers along with the throne and also used Daimler all-weather cars upon occasion, including her 1953-4 world tour. The royal standard was mounted on the wing and in Australia so many disappeared into the pockets of souvenir hunters that a fresh batch had to be flown out from London. As well as Daimlers, Elizabeth continued to use the Rolls Royce Phantom IV (of which only eighteen were built) with H. J. Mulliner limousine coachwork which she had also had as a princess and in 1954 she acquired another Phantom IV, this time with a Hooper landaulette body. In 1960 and 1961 two more Rolls Royces – Phantom Vs with Park Ward limousine coachwork – replaced the last of the Daimlers.

However, the Queen Mother, though she also has a Mulliner Park Ward Phantom V Rolls Royce landaulette, has continued the family link with Daimler with a Hooper-bodied 4½-litre limousine (NLT 1) built in 1955 and a Vanden Plas DS420 which was acquired in 1970.

It was a coachbuilt Vanden Plas Princess (NGN 2), one of two kept in stock when the model ended and supplied to the royal mews in 1969, in which Princess Anne and her husband were travelling in March, 1974, when they were held up at gunpoint in an attempt to kidnap the princess (*see* Princess Anne and Mark Phillips). Princess Anne was chauffeur-driven that night. On less formal occasions she frequently drives her own car, having been stopped several times for speeding, and has passed the special test necessary to qualify for a heavy goods licence, which enables her to drive her own horse-box.

The Queen learned to drive during a war-time stint in the Auxiliary Territorial Service. The car her father gave her as an eighteenth birthday present had the registration number JGY 280, a number which, out of affection for her father, she has had transferred to successive royal cars ever since. Though she rarely drives in London, she does so frequently at Windsor, Balmoral and Sandringham. It was at Sandringham, out driving one winter, that she became trapped in a snow drift. She was forced to abandon her car and plough through deepening snow to the nearest house in order to telephone for help.

CASTLE OF MEY

Seeking temporary seclusion in the aftermath of her husband's death, the Queen Mother went to stay with her old friend, Lady Vyner, at her home in the far north of Scotland. While there, driving one day between Thurso and John o' Groats, she spied the near-ruined Castle of Mey, perched like a fortress on the craggy coastline of the Pentland Firth. Built of local sandstone in the sixteenth century by the 4th and 5th Earls of Caithness, and known in those days as Barrogill Castle, it had been unoccupied for years when the Queen Mother first saw it. It was riddled with damp, its stonework cracked and the roof in danger of collapse, while the two-acre garden was much the same sort of tangled wilderness as that of Royal Lodge had been when she and her husband took it over in the 1930s. To the Queen Mother it represented a challenge – and a challenge was exactly what she needed to occupy her mind at that time.

She bought it on impulse from the Earl of Caithness, together with the sporting rights over several hundred acres of adjacent moorland, and set about restoring it. Essential repairs were carried out, new plumbing, lighting and central heating installed. It was redecorated and the garden brought under control. The Queen Mother scoured antique shops for suitable items of furniture, among them a Queen Anne bureau, a Chinese Chippendale mirror, a Victorian *gros-point* stool and a nineteenth-century Brussels carpet. She bought local landscapes to hang on the walls. Taking the Queen Mother's Scottish connections as his motif, Sir Martin Charteris, the Queen's private secretary, designed and cast a new bronze interior for the non-functional fire-place in the dining-room, while Stephen Gooden R.A. designed the tapestry of the Queen Mother's coat of arms – it took three girls of the Edinburgh Tapestry Co. three years to embroider it – which hangs opposite.

It is to the renamed Castle of Mey that the Queen Mother retreats each year following her birthday on August 4 though "retreat" has ceased to be the operative word. She takes a considerable retinue of aides and servants with her; has friends to stay. Her brother, Sir David Bowes-Lyon, was a frequent visitor until his death in 1961. A keen gardener, the Queen Mother enjoys nothing so much as a daily walk round the restored garden, stone-walled to protect it from that devastating sea wind known locally as "the sworp". Open to the public on three days of the year (in July and August), it is an all-purpose garden with fruit, vegetables and herbs (including myrtle grown from a cutting of the bush which supplied Queen Victoria's wedding bouquet), a herbaceous border and a border of the appropriately-named Elizabeth of Glamis (*see* Queen Elizabeth, the Queen Mother) floribunda.

Like all the best castles, Mey is reputed to be haunted. The Green Lady is said to be the ghost of Lady Fanny Sinclair, daughter of the 13th Earl of Caithness. She haunts one of the bedrooms in the tower, from the window of which poor Fanny flung herself when she was brought back and locked in after eloping with one of her father's servants.

CHANGING THE GUARD

Although the responsibility for guarding members of the Royal Family is undertaken these days by specially-trained police bodyguards, Buckingham Palace still has its foot-stamping, butt-thumping sentries and its morning ritual of changing the guard. But these days it is the sentries who require protecting from London's annual invasion of tourists. At the outset of Queen Elizabeth II's reign they were posted outside the palace railings where pretty girls ogled them while their boy friends took photographs, small boys marched behind them in danger of being trampled underfoot when a sentry did a smart about-turn, and crowds milled round them with people saying things designed to make stiff upper lips quiver or bring a blush to a sentry's cheeks. Finally, in the summer of 1959, the Guards struck back – or did they? As Guardsman Victor Footer, of the 3rd Battalion, Coldstream Guards, took a smart pace forward, there was a yelp of anguish from a hovering American tourist. Guardsman Footer, she complained, had kicked her. "Not intentionally," he protested in defence. Nevertheless, he was sentenced to ten days' confinement to barracks.

The ogling and teasing continued. Another tourist made a grab at a sentry's rifle. A small boy was struck on the head with a rifle butt as a sentry about-turned. Finally, on October 17, 1959, the Guards, who once helped to vanquish Napoleon, surrendered the narrow strip of pavement they had held outside the palace for more than a century and moved their sentry boxes back into the forecourt. All these years later the Guards have become accustomed to being protected by the palace railings at the same time that they themselves are guarding the palace, but at the time their surrender was as embarrassing as that never-to-be-forgotten occasion when a raw young officer, determined to march his men across a crowded junction without breaking step, directed them down the stone steps of what he took to be a subway – and ended up invading a ladies' lavatory.

Just as the mounted regiments of the Household Cavalry have the privilege of forming the Sovereign's Escort for state processions, so the foot regiments of the Guards Division have the privilege of sentry duty at Buckingham Palace, though occasionally other troops, such as the Gurkhas, are invited to take over. The ceremony of changing the guard takes place every morning in the palace forecourt, weekends included, from April to August and every other morning from September to

March. Sentries change every two hours. Almost imperceptible signals enable them to maintain their reputation for precision. A single out-stretched finger while marching to and fro means "I am going to halt", two fingers mean "I am going to salute", and all fingers outstretched mean "I am going to present arms".

The five regiments of foot guards are distinguishable from one another when mounting guard at the palace – or anywhere else – by their plumes and buttons.

The Grenadiers have single buttons evenly spaced and white plumes on the left of their bearskins. They are the senior regiment, their history dating from 1656 when they were first raised in Bruges to serve the exiled Charles II as the Royal Regiment of Foot Guards. It was in 1815, when they threw back the Grenadiers of the French Old Guard at Waterloo, that the name Grenadier was added. Queen Elizabeth II's first official appointment, as a young princess, was as honorary Colonel of the Grenadier Guards and on her sixteenth birthday they marched past her at war-time Windsor while she took the salute in a pleated skirt and woollen jacket. The Grenadiers have held a special place in her af-fections ever since and years later, when two guardsmen were caught pilfering from Buckingham Palace, she reacted indignantly to a sugges-tion that they might be Grenadiers.

"Certainly not," she said. "Grenadiers would never do such a thing."

The Coldstream Guards, named after the Scottish village from which General Monck led them into England to help restore the Stuarts to the throne in 1660, wear their buttons in groups of two and have a red plume on the right of their bearskins.

The Scots Guards, formed in 1877, have their buttons in threes and wear no plume.

The Irish Guards wear their buttons in groups of four and have blue plumes on the right of their bearskins. They were formed in 1902 in accordance with the wishes of the dead Queen Victoria who had been more than impressed by the gallantry of Irish soldiers fighting in the Boer War.

The Welsh Guards, formed in 1915, have their buttons in groups of five and wear white and green plumes on the left of their bearskins.

CHEVENING

The first time he saw Chevening, the seventeenth-century Palladian mansion which is now his country home, Prince Charles shook his head and said, "No, thank you." Perhaps understandably. It was hardly in first-class condition – the roof was sagging and one wall was so badly cracked that it had had to be shored up to keep it from possible collapse – and certainly not the average young man's idea of a bachelor pad. Tucked away in the folds of the North Downs some 25 miles south of London, the centre-piece of a 3,000-acre estate, Chevening, with its side pavilions and colonnaded walkways, was possibly designed by Inigo Jones. General George Stanhope (the 1st Earl Stanhope) bought it in the reign of George I for £28,000. Seven generations of Stanhopes lived there until the 7th Earl died in 1967 without leaving an heir.

Instead, he left a rather complicated will in which the house (complete with paintings, tapestries and furniture) and estate were left to the nation together with a trust fund of around £250,000 to provide for its upkeep on condition that it was offered first to the Prince of Wales (whom the late Earl had once met) and, if he did not want it, to other descendants of King George VI in order of seniority. If none of the Royals wanted it, then it was to be offered, in turn, to the prime minister, to other Government ministers, to the High Commissioner for Canada and the US Ambassador in London.

One by one, Charles and others of the Royal Family turned it down. So it passed down the line to Anthony Barber, Chancellor of the Exchequer at the time. He was willing enough to live there until he found out that he would be taxed on the estimated value of occupying the place. He promptly amended the 1963 Finance Act, but did not wish to benefit from his own amendment. So the Lord Chancellor of the day, Lord Hailsham, moved in instead. However, within months the Conservatives were out of office and he was obliged to move out again.

The change of Government gave Prince Charles, now twenty-five, a chance to change his mind. With his decision to live at Chevening, restoration work, paid for out of the trust fund, was hurriedly put in hand. Cracked walling was repaired, an extra floor tacked on by the 3rd Earl was removed and the original mansard roof restored. Wall tiles were similarly removed to expose the original brickwork. The house was re-wired, replumbed, redecorated, and the 27-acre garden brought to heel again. The work was completed in 1975, providing a house of some 36 rooms (apart from the side pavilions). On the ground floor is a reception room, morning room, dining-room and a magnificent drawing-room with a marble fire-place, a ceiling of Italian plasterwork and chandeliers of Waterford crystal. A curving staircase of Spanish oak climbs to the first floor as though somehow suspended in mid-air. There are four bedrooms and a similar number of bathrooms on the first floor and a further six bedrooms and four more bathrooms higher still. All in all, a bit large perhaps for a bachelor, but an ideal family home. All that was needed, as the late Earl's secretary remarked at the time, was for Prince Charles "to find a wife, settle down and have children".

CIVIL LIST

Behind the enthusiasm with which it welcomed Charles II back to the throne in 1660, Parliament was worried by the fact that monarchs of the day still had the army in one pocket and the navy in another. It could hardly be otherwise when it was the monarch who paid the armed forces, along with other expenses of government, from money raised by taxes and special levies as well as the revenues from the Crown Lands (now known as the Crown Estate). The brief reign of Charles' brother, James II, served to harden Parliamentary doubts (*see* Lineage). Fortunately for Parliament, the army switched sides and James was forced to flee the country. Counting itself fortunate, Parliament set out to ensure there should be no repetition by introducing the Civil List ("Civil" because while the husband-and-wife monarchy of William and Mary continued to pay the officers of state, judges, ambassadors and the civil service, it was now Parliament who paid the armed forces).

To enable Monarchy to meet its public expenses, Parliament made available an annual sum of £700,000, though this sometimes had to be increased by supplementary grants. George II argued that the amount allowed him was insufficient and it was increased to £830,000. George III, no fool in matters of finance prior to his illness, came up with a better idea. He suggested that Parliament should pay all the expenses of government, judges, ambassadors and the civil service included, as well as allowing him a sum sufficient for domestic and monarchical expenses, while, in return, he would hand over to Parliament his revenues from the Post Office, the Excise and the Crown Lands.

To Parliament, it seemed like a good idea at the time, but it was the King who had very much the better part of the bargain. Parliament voted him £800,000 a year, though supplementary grants increased this to something over £1 million some years. The revenues from the Crown Lands, which Parliament took in exchange, amounted to only £89,000 that first year. And that was gross. After administrative costs had been deducted, a mere £11,000 remained.

So when William IV came to the throne, Parliament seized the opportunity to reduce the Civil List to £510,000 a year, subsequently cutting it still further to £385,000 for the young Queen Victoria.

But the principle had been established and since then it has been the custom for monarchs to surrender the Crown Estates (though not the revenues of the Duchy of Lancaster or Duchy of Cornwall [*see* Duchy of Lancaster *and* Duchy of Cornwall]), as Elizabeth II did in her first year of monarchy in return for a Civil List annuity of £474,200 with supplementary allowances for Prince Philip, the Queen

Mother and Princess Margaret. For nearly twenty years the 1952 figures remained static. Inflation did not, and in 1969, interviewed in the United States, Philip came out with the surprising remark that "next year we (the Royal Family) will be in the red". Parliament set up a Select Committee to look into things. The Select Committee, with William Hamilton dissenting, recommended a considerable increase and, despite some vociferous and sometimes vituperative opposition in the House of Commons, Parliament agreed.

Since then, the Civil List has been increased year by year to combat inflation, with the Queen contributing, directly and indirectly, to the cost of maintaining monarchy at the standard to which it has become accustomed. Until the 1970s the Civil List also included a substantial sum known as the Queen's Privy Purse, in effect her personal salary as monarch. This has now been discontinued and what she receives from the Civil List is calculated on the basis of monarchical expenses only, the salaries and wages of those who work for her, the cost of feeding them, of entertaining, of maintaining cars, horses and suchlike. Not that one should cry poverty on the Queen's behalf. While she no longer receives any money for herself from the Civil List, she continues to receive the untaxed revenues of the Duchy of Lancaster (*see* Tax), running into something over £400,000 a year in recent years.

The Civil List approved by Parliament in 1978 totalled £1,950,000 plus annuities for Prince Philip, Princess Anne, Prince Andrew, Princess Margaret, the Queen Mother and Princess Alice, Duchess of Gloucester.

> Prince Philip: £93,500
> Princess Anne: £60,000
> Prince Andrew: £17,262
> (calculated on the basis of £20,000 a year from the age of eighteen)
> Queen Mother: £175,000
> Princess Margaret: £59,000
> Princess Alice, Duchess of Gloucester: £30,000

That list includes no annuity for Prince Charles because, just as his mother receives the revenues of the Duchy of Lancaster, so he has his own income from the Duchy of Cornwall. However, Parliament also approved payments to meet the expenses of royal duties performed by others of the Royal Family not in receipt of an annuity, though on a rather odd basis. These extra payments totalled a further £165,500 with the Queen agreeing to reimburse the Consolidated Fund, from which the payments were made, by exactly the same sum out of her revenues from the Duchy of

Lancaster and private sources. Individually, the payments were as follows:

> Duke of Gloucester: £39,000
> Duke of Kent: £60,000
> Princess Alexandra: £60,000
> Princess Alice, Countess of Athlone: £6,500

The 1978 increases produced a further outburst from parliamentary left-wingers. The Queen was criticized for paying "no taxes on her vast fortune" while the Queen Mother and Princess Margaret were castigated as "hangers-on".

Those critics in search of further ammunition could find it in the fact that the Queen's increased Civil List and the increased allowances to others of the Royal Family were not the end of the matter. The Queen paid her staff out of the Civil List, maintained her own cars and horses, met the cost of garden parties and other entertaining, and even paid British Rail for the use of the royal train. But she did not pay for the maintenance of the Queen's Flight or the royal yacht or the repair and maintenance of Buckingham Palace and Windsor Castle. These things are paid for out of public funds, though the Queen does pay for the upkeep of Balmoral and Sandringham, which are her private property.

Allowing for all this, the total cost of monarchy – Civil List, upkeep of palaces, maintenance of the Queen's Flight and royal yacht – was estimated (complete accuracy is impossible) at something like £7 million in 1976. With the increases in the Civil List announced since, with the cost of maintaining palaces, aircraft and yacht rising with inflation, it has clearly risen still further since then. However, so has the revenue from the Crown Estate which is handed over to Parliament.

The Crown Estate, which owes its origins to Edward the Confessor, extends these days to more than 320,000 acres, one of the largest and most valuable property holdings in Britain. In London it includes much of the area around Regent's Park, most of Regent Street, Lower Regent Street and Carlton House Terrace as well as properties in St James's Street, Pall Mall, Haymarket, Trafalgar Square, Whitehall, Kensington, Holborn and the City of London. It has estates at Eltham, Hainault, Hampton, Richmond and Oxshott and further property holdings at Ascot, Windsor, Bagshot, Evesham, Dover and Hastings. It includes agricultural land in twenty-five counties, land and shooting rights in Scotland, salmon fishing rights, sand and gravel pits, jetties and oyster beds as well as substantial holdings in government stocks. By 1976–7 the £89,000 gross income of George III's day had jumped to £12,650,000. Expenses had similarly increased, of course – to £7,650,000 – but there was still a surplus of £5 million for the Exchequer.

In 1979, further to allow for inflation, there was another increase in the Civil List, bringing it to £2,134,200. There were also increases in the allowances to Prince Philip, Princess Anne, the Queen Mother and Princess Margaret but not for Prince Andrew or Princess Alice, Duchess of Gloucester.

The 1979 figures were:

Prince Philip £98,000
Princess Anne £63,000
Prince Andrew £20,000
The Queen Mother £200,000
Princess Margaret £64,000
Princess Alice, Duchess of Gloucester £30,000

CLARENCE HOUSE

Clarence House, the London residence of the Queen Mother, stands immediately across from St James's Palace and from its windows it is possible to witness the traditional ceremony of proclamation in Friary Court when a new monarch succeeds to the throne. It is named after the Duke of Clarence who later became William IV and for whom it was designed by John Nash. Building took four years, 1825–9. It was later the home of the Duke of Connaught, seventh child of Queen Victoria, but fell into disuse when he went to Canada as Governor-General in 1911. The Red Cross used part of it as offices during World War II until bomb damage was added to the years of neglect.

All in all, it had little enough to commend it as a royal home when the newly-married Princess Elizabeth and Prince Philip first looked it over. It had no bathrooms, no electric light and even the old-fashioned gas lighting no longer worked. But they were eager for a home of their own and a year's work, together with an expenditure of £55,000, saw it completely renovated. They moved in on July 4, 1949 – "Independence Day", as Philip remarked with a quizzical grin.

They lived there for nearly three years, until Princess Elizabeth became Queen Elizabeth II on the death of her father. Their second child, Princess Anne, was born there. With the Queen's accession it became briefly the focal point of monarchy. It was to Clarence House that the High Commissioners of the Commonwealth went to offer their condolences; it was there that members of the Government went for their first audiences of the new, young Queen.

Neither the Queen nor Prince Philip had any desire to leave Clarence House. After all, it was their first real home and, while it was large enough to be royal, it was also small enough to be homely. But it was not, as Winston Churchill pointed out, a palace . . . and monarchy required a palace. So the new, young Queen, however reluctantly, moved into Buckingham Palace while her mother, now Queen Mother instead of Queen, moved out of the palace and into Clarence House, which has been her home ever since.

CLOTHES AND COSMETICS

The amount the Queen spends on clothes each year is a close-kept secret between her fashion designers and the Keeper of the Privy Purse (who pays the bills for her). In a year which involves a state visit to some foreign monarch or president, or a tour of some part of the Common-wealth – and there are few years which do not include one or the other – her dress bill clearly runs into several thousands of pounds. There can be little doubt that the Queen has probably the most extensive ward-robe of any woman in the world, from the weighty, pearl-encrusted gown made for her 1953 coronation to the new coats and dresses which, at almost any point in time, are being made for yet another provincial progress or overseas visit. Her clothes are stored in three wardrobe rooms on the floor above her private apartment at Buckingham Palace in the care of Margaret Macdonald, who was her nurse in childhood and is today known as her Dresser, and her two assistants.

Yet with so many clothes to pick from, Elizabeth, in the privacy of her palace home, prefers something simple and comfortable (though "simple" should not necessarily be equated with cheap), a plainish silk or cotton dress in summer, wool in winter. On holidays she goes around in comfortable, time-tested clothes, tweeds at Sandringham, tweeds or tartan at Balmoral, her feet shod in low, sturdy shoes instead of the higher-heeled ones she wears for public occasions. At Balmoral she has a choice of three tartans, Royal Stewart, Hunting Stewart and the Bal-moral tartan which her great-great-grandfather, the Prince Consort, designed. If the weather is wet or windy, she merely dons a raincoat and ties a head-scarf over her hair.

Unlike most girls, she was by no means enthused by clothes as a young princess or, indeed, even into her early years of monarchy. As a teenager in the immediate post-war years she continued to cut a rather juvenile figure in a succession of pleated skirts and woollen jumpers. The late Sir Norman Hartnell, who designed so many of her clothes over the years, is on record as saying, "One did not feel that she was really inter-ested in clothes." Comfort and serviceability were of more importance to her than fashion. Even as monarch, she jibbed the first time she saw her clothes – ball gown and tiara – laid out for an official banquet in all their jewelled glory. "I can't possibly wear all that," she protested, though in the end she did.

It worried her in those days that she might look a shade too exotic. "I am not a film star," she would say, and even the dipping, coquettish brim of a new hat for Ascot had to be straightened before she would agree to wear it. The result, in those early days, was frequently for the fashion critics to label her clothes "dowdy" or the equivalent. But such charges no longer stand up.

The first sign of a change came in 1957 with a state visit to France. Paris was at that time the fashion capital of the world and Hartnell, hoping to persuade his No. 1 client to wear something more glamorous than the traditional royal crinoline, included among his designs a figure-hugging dress of silver lace over silver tissue. "I was thrilled when she chose it and worried as to whether she would like it when she tried it on," he said.

The Queen did like it when she tried it on and planned to wear it for a floodlit trip along the Seine. But in Paris, at the last moment, caution again exerted itself and she announced that she would wear a crinoline instead. She was persuaded to revert back to the original choice only when someone said that perhaps she would have difficulty negotiating the narrow gang-plank of the river boat in a bulky crinoline. So she wore Hartnell's figure-hugging creation and stunned Paris. *Ravissant* was the word the French used to describe her.

So a breakthrough in royal fashion was achieved, though it was to be another decade or more before the Queen departed finally from the pastel shades which were for so long part of the royal dress tradition. Not until 1971, when she was due to visit Turkey, did she really go along with the often reiterated suggestion that she should wear brighter, more vivid colours.

Norman Hartnell had been designing clothes for Elizabeth II since she was a nine-year-old princess. The first dress he designed for her was the one she wore as a bridesmaid at the 1935 wedding of her uncle, the late Duke of Gloucester. He designed both her wedding dress and her coronation gown. To prevent any get-rich-quick mass production firm rushing out cheap copies of the wedding dress, he whitewashed his workroom windows, kept the designs in a safe and had his workroom manager sleep on the premises in a camp bed at night.

Copying royal fashions was big business in the early days of the Queen's monarchy, and one US firm even came out with what it claimed was a copy of the royal nightie. As far as ordinary outdoor clothes were concerned, the newspapers had only to picture the Queen in anything new for the photographs to be studied under magnifying glasses and the copyists to go to work. Within twenty-four hours the first cheap, ready-to-wear copies would be on their way to the London stores and what is probably an all-time record was set up when she was photographed in what was termed a "magpie" dress, white in front and black at the back. The first copies were turned out in six hours flat.

Two other leading designers – Hardy Amies and Ian Thomas, who once worked for Hartnell – also helped with the task of creating the bulk of the royal wardrobe. Very occasionally, the Queen will drive to the Hartnell showroom in Bruton Street to see the latest collection (*see* Shopping) – if she buys anything, it is, of course, immediately withdrawn from the collection so that no one else has the same coat or dress – but for the most part they go to her. First they submit suggested designs in the form of full-length miniatures of the Queen so that she can see exactly how she will look in the suggested outfit. Samples of the materials to be used are attached. Months of work go into preparing a new wardrobe for a state visit or Commonwealth tour. A single dress can involve several fittings in her private apartment at Buckingham Palace, with a single state visit requiring as many as thirty new dresses, coats and evening gowns.

A new state gown may require more than the average two or three fittings. Each state gown is designed with that one occasion in mind and the Queen's gowns, over the years, have echoed the country she is visiting, with an embroidered design of maple leaves for Canada, mimosa for Australia, poppies and marguerites for France, and cherry blossom for Japan.

And each outfit must have its matching accessories, hats, shoes and handbags. All these have to be selected, made, tried on. A series of unwritten rules have evolved over the years governing the Queen's clothes. She must be able to sit as well as stand with dignity, to climb in and out of cars without risk of embarrassment. There must be no bows or other frills which might perhaps catch on unexpected projections when she tours factories or building sites. Handbags must slip over the arm, leaving her hands free for handshakes or accepting posies from small children on her walkabouts. Colours must be clearly visible from a distance; gloves white so that her waving hand is clearly seen; hats – except occasionally for Ascot – small and head-hugging so that no shadow masks her face..

Her hairdresser visits the palace to do her hair – naturally wavy and light brown, though greying a little these days – and accompanies her when she goes on tour. For public appearances in Britain she usually wears her hair centre-parted and, to make-up, uses a peach-tinted powder foundation and a pinky-red lipstick with a shading of blue-grey mascara to emphasize her blue eyes and long lashes. For appearances under electric light she uses a deeper tone of powder and lipstick. Natural varnish suffices for her fingernails.

For overseas trips her make-up will vary according to the clothes she is wearing and the prevailing climate. For higher altitudes she uses a moisturizing foundation lotion; in humid climates a tinted lotion-powder. Visiting countries like Australia and India she wears a deeper tone of powder to enhance the tan she quickly acquires. She matches the colour of her lipstick to the dress she wears, perhaps tangerine on one occasion or robin red on another.

Perhaps her most difficult make-up problem was at the time of her coronation. For that, she required make-up which would clash with neither of her two robes, one crimson, the other purple, which would look equally well under the yellow lights of Westminster Abbey and the rose-tinted lighting of the state coach, which would photograph as well in colour as in black and white, which would show up well on television yet not look overdone when her face was seen, magnified in close-up, on the largest of cinema screens. Several different combinations were tried and discarded. Finally, after experiments on a girl model of similar complexion and facial bone structure, cosmetic experts came up with the answer, or at least a satisfactory compromise – a peach-tinted powder foundation, a touch of red-blue rouge, light brown mascara and a specially created lipstick, red with blue undertones, which they named Balmoral.

COACHES AND CARRIAGES

The Gold State Coach in which Queen Elizabeth II rode to her coronation in 1953 dates from the days of George III. He had it built to celebrate Britain's victories over the French and their allies in Canada, India, Germany. Designed under the supervision of Sir William Chambers, the four-ton coach is elaborately carved, gilded and painted. The tritons which festoon it symbolize – or did in George III's day – Britain's domination of the seas. On the roof three cherubs support the royal crown while the pole is carved to represent a bundle of lances. Its painted panels were the work of the Florentine artist Giovanni Battista Cipriani, one of the founders of the Royal Academy. It is 24 feet long, 8 feet 3 inches wide and 12 feet high. It was originally designed to be driven by a coachman, but the box seat was removed on the orders of Edward VII so that the royal occupants could be better seen. It has been used for the coronation of every monarch since George IV.

Several other coaches are also housed in the royal mews at the rear of Buckingham Palace. There is the Irish State Coach, so-called because it was bought by Queen Victoria after she had seen it at a Dublin exhibition in 1852. This is the coach in which the present Queen rode to her wedding in Westminster Abbey and which she regularly uses for the annual State Opening of Parliament (*see* Opening of Parliament). There is Queen Alexandra's State Coach which also plays a part in the

State Opening of Parliament – it conveys the crown from the Tower of London to Westminster – as well as sometimes being used to bring new ambassadors to the palace to present their credentials to the Queen. There is the Glass Coach, originally bought for George V's coronation, in which the Queen and Prince Philip returned to Buckingham Palace after their wedding ceremony. There is King Edward VII's Town Coach which is also used as an ambassadorial conveyance as well as for royal weddings, and there is the 1902 State Postillion Landau which was also built originally for Edward VII and which is today used by the Queen when she drives to welcome some visiting head of state and for the return procession through London. There are a number of other landaus, state and semi-state, most of them originally acquired by Queen Victoria, including a specially decorated one in which she rode to her Diamond Jubilee thanksgiving service in St Paul's Cathedral. They are still used from time to time for royal processions, while one or other of the two elegant barouches may sometimes be seen conveying the Queen Mother to an outdoor ceremony like Trooping the Colour. The Ascot landaus with their basket-work sides, used for the royal procession along the course at Ascot (*see* Ascot), are kept at Windsor.

The horses which draw the various coaches and carriages are also stabled in the royal mews, usually ten greys and twenty bays. The greys are traditionally known as the Windsor Greys. However, this is not a breed, but simply derived from the fact that in Queen Victoria's day, and for some years after, they were always kept at Windsor. It was not until after the death of George V that they were transferred to Buckingham Palace. Among the greys, Oldenburg horses from Germany predominate. The bays, from which Prince Philip selects a team for driving competitions, include both Oldenburgs and half-bred Cleveland Bays.

The horses and some of the coaches can be viewed by the public when the royal mews are open on two afternoons a week. The word "mews", incidentally, has really nothing to do with either horses or coaches. It was originally the place where the monarch kept his hawks and falcons. The word became associated with horses when Henry VIII moved his horses into the falconry, or mews, after the royal stables had been burned down.

CORONATION

The ceremony of coronation is long and tiring. Only those few who have undergone it – sixty or less over a thousand years of history, for not all Britain's monarchs have been crowned – have really understood the strain it imposes on nerves and emotions alike. "A terrible ordeal," the

Queen's grandfather, gruff King George V, termed it.

So it was understandable that those responsible for planning the 1953 coronation of Elizabeth II, anxious to ease the strain on her as much as possible, should have suggested curtailing this and that.

To each such suggestion the Queen's response was, "Did my father do it?"

Told that he had, she said, "Then I will too."

And in doing things the way her father did them, she was also, in essence, doing what her Saxon forebears had done a thousand years before. Saxon chieftains were anointed by "pouring oil on head from a horn"; this is still done today, except that the horn has been refined into a medieval spoon. The presentation of a sceptre and the setting of a crown on the head is the same today as it was then. So is the kissing of the monarch by representatives of the people. Even some of the phrasing of the prayers remains unaltered and the mass cry with which the people hail the new monarch – "May the King live for ever!" in Saxon times – is almost the same.

The $2\frac{1}{2}$ hours of Elizabeth II's coronation ceremony took twelve months of planning and preparation. The Queen's husband, Prince Philip, was chairman of the coronation committee, but he would be the last to deny that the bulk of the work was done by others, principally the 16th Duke of Norfolk. As hereditary Earl Marshals of England, successive Dukes of Norfolk have the traditional responsibility for arranging, at the beginning of a reign, the coronation and, at its end, the funeral of the monarch.

Among the problems confronting the 16th Duke was that of squeezing 7,600 people into a building designed to accommodate considerably fewer. He managed it by decreeing that seats should be only eighteen inches wide, though peers could have an extra inch because of the voluminousness of their robes. It was his task also to send out invitations to commoners. Peers were invited – "commanded" is perhaps a more apt word – by the Queen herself in the following terms:

"Right Trusty and Well-Beloved Cousin. We greet You well. Whereas We have appointed the Second Day of June 1953 for the Solemnity of our Coronation, these are therefore to will and command You, all Excuses set apart, that You make your personal attendance upon Us at the time above mentioned, furnished and appointed as to your Rank and Quality appertaineth, there to do and perform such Services as shall be required. . . ."

In many of the preparations the new, young Queen played an active part. She went along with her grandmother, the ageing Queen Mary, to look at the coronation gown which had been worn by her great-great-grandmother, Queen Victoria. Seeing that it was white, she observed, "Queen Victoria was unmarried at the time she was crowned." She was a married woman and her gown, she thought, should reflect the fact. Norman Hartnell, who designed it, suggested embroidering it with symbolic designs in pearl, crystal and *diamanté*: England's rose, Scotland's thistle, the Irish shamrock and the Welsh leek. The Queen picked up the idea and took it further so that in the end her gown not only shimmered with those symbols, but also with the Canadian maple leaf, the Australian wattle, the New Zealand fern, the lotus of India and Ceylon, the wheat and jute of Pakistan and the protea of South Africa, all members of the Commonwealth at the time.

Similarly, she intervened in the debate as to whether or not the ceremony should be televised. The coronation committee had decided against, but opted for a compromise when a storm of public protest resulted. The procession in Westminster Abbey could be televized, but not the actual ceremony of coronation. It was the Queen herself who decided on full television coverage. She wanted as many of her subjects as possible to share the occasion as fully as possible, she said.

Items not used since pre-war days, and some for longer than that, were brought out of storage at Buckingham Palace, the state coach (*see* Coaches and Carriages), gold plate, royal liveries. The coach was refurbished and equipped with an interior lighting system worked from batteries tucked away under the seats. The pink silk stockings forming part of the liveries had been holed by moths. Cotton ones were ordered in replacement. New gold aiglettes bearing the new Queen's EIIR cypher were also ordered for the liveries. Some in Scotland disapproved of the cypher, muttering that Elizabeth I had never been Queen of Scotland, and sent her a cup inscribed simply ER. She sent it back with a request that the inscription should be corrected.

In the run-up to the ceremony there were rehearsals at Westminster Abbey with the Duchess of Norfolk acting as stand-in for the Queen. However, the Queen herself took part in one rehearsal. Her husband, she thought, played his part with too much light-heartedness and she called him back to do it again. There were other rehearsals in the privacy of her palace home. With the chairs in the Picture Gallery set out to represent the seating in the state coach, with a long white sheet pinned to her shoulders in place of a robe and with a footman standing in for Prince Philip, the Queen, assisted by her six maids of honour – Lady Jane Vane-Tempest-Stewart, Lady Mary Baillie-Hamilton, Lady Jane Heathcote-Drummond-Willoughby, Lady Anne Coke, Lady Moyra Hamilton and Lady Rosemary Spencer-Churchill – practised getting in and out of the coach with grace and dignity.

Inevitably, there were a number of crises along the way, among them a shortage of carriages, horses and coachmen. A film company came up with some additional broughams and landaus, the War Office (as it was then called) provided horses and members of a coaching club came eagerly forward to don royal livery for the day.

A more important crisis concerned the holy oil which would be required for the anointing ceremony. There had been some left over from the coronation of the Queen's father, but this had vanished in a war-time air raid. Moreover, the firm of pharmacists which had been making the oil since Queen Victoria's day had gone out of business. Fortunately, for the sake of sentiment, an elderly kinswoman of the pharmacy family had kept a few ounces of the original base. She was tracked down and a Bond Street chemist, J. D. Jamieson, was thus enabled to make a fresh batch of oil, nobly giving up his smoking habit to improve his sense of smell.

The death of Queen Mary, some ten weeks before the coronation, could have caused an even more major crisis but for her dying wish that the ceremony should not be postponed on her account. Sadly, death robbed the ageing Queen of another wish – to see her granddaughter with the crown on her head. Or did it?

There is a legend among royal servants that, shortly before Queen Mary's death, the crown was taken secretly to Marlborough House and there, in her grandmother's bedroom, the new young Queen wore it briefly for the old Queen's benefit.

Be that as it may, it is a fact that both crowns involved, the massive Crown of St Edward and the lighter Imperial State Crown (*see* Crown Jewels), were both taken to Buckingham Palace in advance of the ceremony for the Queen to try them on. To accustom herself to the Imperial State Crown, which she would wear for her processional return from Westminster Abbey, the Queen wore it about the palace for the best part of a day, while working at her desk, having afternoon tea and even while feeding the corgis.

Coronation day dawned in a drizzle of rain which later turned to a downpour. For her journey to the Abbey the Queen wore her Parliamentary robe of crimson velvet and the diamond diadem made originally for George IV and worn before her by Queen Mary, Queen Alexandra and Queen Victoria. At one stage of her journey she was so overcome by the emotion of the moment that tears glistened briefly in her eyes. She was received at the Abbey by the Archbishops of Canterbury and York and the Officers of State. She was preceded into the Abbey by the secular lords bearing the Regalia which was surrendered to the Archbishop of Canterbury to be placed on the altar. The procession moved to the words of Psalm CXXII which has been sung at every coronation since that of Charles I: "I was glad when they said unto me, We will go into the house of the Lord." There was a cry of "*Vivat Regina Elizabetha*" from the scholars of Westminster School, accorded the honour of hailing each new monarch by James II because, it is said, they knelt publicly to pray for Charles I on the day of his execution.

Broadly speaking, the coronation ceremony can be divided into three main sections. There is the acceptance of the monarch by the people followed by the taking of the coronation oath. This is followed by the anointing. Then the anointed monarch is invested with the trappings of monarchy and crowned.

The first part of the ceremony began with the Archbishop of Canterbury advancing in turn to the east, south, west and north of the Abbey and saying, "Sirs, I here present unto you Queen Elizabeth, your undoubted Queen. Wherefore all you who are come this day to do your homage and service, are you willing to do the same?" The trumpets sounded and those in the Abbey responded with a shout of "God save Queen Elizabeth."

Then came the administering of the oath, with the Queen promising to govern the United Kingdom and the countries of the Commonwealth according to "their respective laws and customs", to uphold law and justice and to maintain the Protestant Reformed Religion. Kneeling at the altar, her right hand on the Bible, the Queen took the oath: "The things which I have here before promised, I will perform and keep. So help me God."

So the ceremony moved forward, by way of Communion, to the very heart of the coronation ritual. While the choir chanted the anthem "Zadok the priest and Nathan the prophet", which has been heard at every coronation since at least that of Edgar in 973, the maids of honour divested the Queen of her robe and jewellery. Seated in the Chair of King Edward (*see* Throne) with Scotland's Stone of Scone tucked beneath it, the Queen was partly screened by a cloth of gold held by four Knights of the Garter as the Archbishop of Canterbury poured the consecrated oil from the ampulla into the coronation spoon and anointed her hands, breast and head in turn "as Solomon was anointed king by Zadok the priest and Nathan the prophet".

Invested in the *Colobium Sindonis* (a surplice of white linen) and the *Supertunica* (a surcoat of cloth of gold), the Queen was then handed the jewel-encrusted Sword of State made for the coronation of George IV and charged, "With this sword do justice, stop the growth of iniquity, protect the holy Church of God, help and defend widows and orphans, restore the things that are gone to decay, maintain the things that are restored, punish and reform what is amiss, and confirm what is in good order."

The sword was then replaced on the altar before being drawn from its scabbard and borne before the Queen while her heels were touched with the Spurs of St George and the Bracelets of Sincerity fastened about her wrists. The spurs used to be buckled on, but this ceased with the coronation of Queen Anne because of her gout-swollen legs. The ceremony of the bracelets had lapsed even before that, since the coronation of Edward VI, but was restored in 1953 following the gift of a new pair of gold bracelets from the countries of the Commonwealth.

The Queen was invested in a robe of imperial purple and given the Orb with its jewelled cross which she handed in turn to the Dean of Westminster to be placed on the altar. The ruby and sapphire Ring of Kingly Dignity – also known as the Wedding Ring of England – was placed upon the fourth finger of her right hand. She was handed the Royal Sceptre, symbol of "kingly power and justice", and the Rod with the Dove, symbol of "equity and mercy". Then came the actual moment of crowning.

The massive Crown of St Edward was held briefly aloft, dedicated, then lowered on to the Queen's head, which seemed to bow momentarily under its great weight. Again the trumpets sounded, again the people cried "God save the Queen" while outside the Abbey, in Hyde Park and at the Tower of London, guns fired a royal salute.

Crowned, the Queen moved from the Coronation Chair to the Throne. On behalf of the spiritual peers, the Archbishop of Canterbury vowed to be "faithful and true" to the monarch. Prince Philip likewise paid homage, kneeling before his wife and saying: "I, Philip, Duke of Edinburgh, do become your liege man of life and limb and of earthly worship; and faith and truth will I bear unto you, to live and die, against all manner of folks. So help me God." Rising, he touched the crown and kissed the Queen on the left cheek. Similar homage was paid in turn, by the royal dukes, Gloucester and Kent, by the Duke of Norfolk, as senior duke, and by the premier marquess, earl, viscount and baron.

Kneeling on a faldstool at the altar, her crown removed, her husband beside her, the Queen received the final blessing before donning the Imperial State Crown and processing through the Abbey to the triumphant chords of the *Te Deum Laudamus*.

Not all the coronations in Britain's long history have been so moving and without incident as that of Elizabeth II. Some have been violent; others almost hilarious. The teenage Edwy, when he was crowned king back in 955, quickly disappeared from the feast which once formed part of the coronation ceremony. Archbishop Dunstan, going to seek him, was horrified to find him tumbling his wife on the floor in an adjacent room. The feast, incidentally, remained an integral part of the coronation until the time of George IV. But William IV was so disgusted by the guzzling that went on at his brother's coronation that he discontinued it.

William the Conqueror's coronation was violent and bloody. His Norman bodyguard mistook the cheering of the crowd for incipient rebellion. In the scrimmage which followed several Saxons were killed and the Abbey set on fire.

Elizabeth I's coronation lasted two days, one for the procession and the second for the actual crowning. The Queen, after consulting her astrologer, selected January 14 and 15, 1558, as propitious days, only to have the archbishop of the time declare that he would have no part in the consecration of "a bastard and a heretic". A solitary bishop was finally persuaded to officiate, anointing the Queen with oil which she complained "smelt ill".

Her half-sister Mary refused to sit in the Coronation Chair because Edward VI, who she regarded as a heretic, had sat in it before her. She also objected that the oil was "no longer holy".

Charles I had his oil specially made to a formula which included orange blossom, roses, jasmine, cinnamon, ambergris, musk and civet.

So stout and gout-ridden was Queen Anne that she found it difficult to stand during the ceremony.

Perhaps the most brilliant coronation of all time, even if his brother thought it vulgar, was that of George IV who surrounded himself with pages drawn from among the best-known prize-fighters of the day. Their presence was needed when the King's discarded wife, the fat and vulgar Caroline, tried to force her way into the ceremony from which her husband had barred her.

By contrast with George IV's spendthrift coronation, that of Queen Victoria was so economic it was nicknamed "the Penny Crowning". The young Queen refused any rehearsal and was full of complaints. The crown "hurt a great deal", the orb was too heavy and the ring too big. She had a smaller one made. But the Archbishop pushed it on the wrong finger, it became stuck and she had to go to bed with it still on. It was removed with soap the next morning.

King Edward VII's coronation had to be postponed because he developed appendicitis. Edward VIII's coronation did not take place at all and the manufacturers of coronation souvenirs were out a pretty penny (though some of those same souvenirs are now collectors' items). Even the coronation of George VI was not entirely without incident. The Archbishop, holding the oath for the King to read, obscured some of the words with his thumb; the Lord Chamberlain could not buckle on the royal sword-belt and the King had to do it himself; the crown was nearly put on back to front; and someone stood on the royal robe, causing the King to stumble and almost fall.

But the coronation of Elizabeth II passed off without a hitch. Despite pouring rain, dense crowds cheered her all along the roundabout processional route back to the palace. The orb which her great-great-grandmother had complained was too heavy, though Elizabeth II appeared to be holding it in her hand, actually rested on a specially constructed ledge in the coach while the sceptre, seemingly in her other hand, was actually held in concealed brackets. Even for coronations things are not always what they seem.

Not that the thousands who poured into London that day, the millions more who watched on television, cared a jot. British and foreign alike, they found themselves caught up in an emotional mood which was a compound of love, awe and pride. "As this day draws to its close," said the newly-crowned Queen, broadcasting to the nation that night, "I know that my abiding memory of it will be not only the solemnity and beauty of the ceremony, but the inspiration of your loyalty and affection."

COUNSELLORS OF STATE

Whenever the Queen is away from Britain she authorizes her Counsellors of State to act for her in her absence. She would do the same – "to prevent delay or difficulty in the despatch of public business" – if she was temporarily ill.

There are six Counsellors of State. They are the Queen's husband, the Queen Mother, and the four persons next in line of succession to the throne (*see* Succession) who are "not disqualified by age". The heir to the throne qualifies at the age of eighteen; others not until they are twenty-one. So, until Prince Andrew reaches the age of twenty-one, the other four Counsellors of State are Prince Charles, Princess Anne, Princess Margaret and the Duke of Gloucester. When Prince Andrew qualifies, he will take the place of the Duke of Gloucester.

While Prince Philip, as the Queen's husband, comes first on the list of Counsellors of State, he is usually out of the country at the same time as the Queen. However, that still leaves five others and only two are normally required at any one time.

In the Queen's absence (or if she were ill), it is the Counsellors of State who convene the Privy Council (*see* Privy Council), who give royal assent to Acts of Parliament, who would issue a proclamation should it be necessary, and generally act in place of the monarch. However, there is also much that they cannot do. They cannot (except on the Queen's express instructions) dissolve Parliament, they cannot grant any rank, dignity or title and they cannot disband units of the army. And their writ, unlike the Queen's, extends only to the United Kingdom and Britain's few remaining colonies, and not to the countries of the Commonwealth.

CROWN JEWELS

Determined that nothing should survive of the monarchy in the after-

math of the Civil War, Oliver Cromwell ordered the Crown Jewels – or
"The Regalia", as they are also styled – to be melted down and sold off.
It was royal bargain day at knock-down prices and not a few Members
of Parliament took advantage of the fact. What is known as the Black
Prince's Ruby, which once glinted in the helmet of Henry V at Agincourt and is today in the Imperial State Crown, went for £4. In fact, the
entire collection realized only £2,647, of which the melted-down gold
fetched only £238.

As a result, when Charles II was restored to the throne there was not
even a crown with which to crown him and his coronation had to be put
off until a new one could be made. In fact, a whole new set of regalia –
crown, sceptres, orb and swords – was made by the royal goldsmith, Sir
Robert Vyner, at a cost of £31,978.

Most of the Regalia now on view at the Tower of London dates from
that time, though there are one or two items of apparent earlier workmanship which would seem to have survived Cromwell's bargain basement. For instance, while the handle of the Coronation Spoon, used for
anointing the Sovereign (*see* Coronation), was made by Vyner, the bowl
appears to date from the twelfth century. Similarly, the Ampulla
(golden eagle) from which the holy oil is poured into the spoon,
although it appears to have been somewhat reworked in Vyner's day,
is of a basic workmanship which suggests that it may be the same one
which was used for the coronation of Henry IV in 1399 and even for that
of King John in 1200.

There are several crowns in the collection. Principal among them is
the great Crown of St Edward, as it is styled, even though it was actually made for Charles II along with most of the other items. Made of
gold studded with diamonds, rubies, emeralds, sapphires and pearls, it
is so big (remember that it was originally made to fit over a seventeenth-century periwig) and so heavy (nearly five pounds) that each
monarch wears it only once in a lifetime, and then for only the few
moments of actual crowning.

Following the coronation ceremony the monarch changes it for the
Imperial Crown, also known as the Crown of State or the Imperial State
Crown. This was made for the coronation of the youthful Queen
Victoria who feared that the massive Crown of St Edward would slip
right over her head. Its frame, patterned in the form of oak leaves, is
of gold and it is adorned with a mass of precious stones; 5 rubies, 11
emeralds, 18 sapphires, 277 pearls and a staggering 2,783 diamonds.
Among all this winking, shimmering mass is the Black Prince's Ruby,
a sapphire said to have come from the ring of Edward the Confessor,
and four drop pearls which legend has it were once the ear-rings of
Elizabeth I though there is no actual documentary evidence to that
effect.

It was this crown (which is regularly worn for the annual State Opening of Parliament [*see* Opening of Parliament]) which rested on the coffin of King George V as it was hauled to Westminster Abbey on a gun carriage. A jolt of the gun carriage caused the Maltese cross which tops the crown to fall off. It was quickly retrieved by Lieutenant Huntington, in charge of the bearer party, but not before the new King, Edward VIII who was later to become Duke of Windsor, had seen what happened. He took it as an ill omen and subsequent events were to prove him right.

Among the diamonds in the Imperial Crown, set just below the Black Prince's Ruby, is the Second Star of Africa, a stone of 309 carats cut from the famous Cullinan diamond, a diamond so large that Frederick Wells, superintendent of the Premier Mine, 300 miles north-east of Kimberley, thought that it was a chunk of glass which had been "salted" as a joke when he first prodded it out of the rock face with his walking stick in 1905. But it was a diamond all right, 3,025 carats in its rough state. It was named after Sir Thomas Cullinan, chairman of the mining company, bought by the Transvaal Government for £150,000 (though insured for ten times as much) and given to King Edward VII in 1907 for his sixty-sixth birthday. The cleaving of the stone was entrusted to Amsterdam cutter J. Asscher. At the first attempt, it was the cleaving blade – not the diamond – which fragmented. The second attempt proved successful, but by then Asscher was under so much strain that he fainted clean away. The two pieces into which he had split the Cullinan were subsequently cleaved again and again until there were nine major gems, ninety-six small brilliants and several carats of fragments. The largest of the gems, the Great Star of Africa ($516\frac{1}{2}$ carats) was set in the Sceptre with the Cross and the second largest in the Imperial Crown. Two more of the major gems, the Third (92 carats) and Fourth (62 carats) Stars of Africa are in the Queen Consort's Crown made for Queen Mary in 1911. The remainder went to the cutter as his fee for cleaving the stone, but later found their way back into the possession of the Royal Family, though as private property and not Crown Jewels (*see* Jewellery).

In the crown made in 1937 for the Queen Consort, who is now the Queen Mother, is the famous Koh-i-Noor diamond from India which legend says will bring good luck to any woman who wears it but bad luck to a man. The Koh-i-Noor, at one time insured for £2 million, is originally said to have weighed 793 carats, though cutting has reduced it to its present 106 carats. It was given to Queen Victoria by the East India Company. But she nearly didn't get it. Given the stone to look after, Sir John Lawrence popped it into one of his waistcoat pockets and promptly forgot all about it. Six weeks later, when it was decided to present it to the Queen, he could not find it. He sent for his servant and asked, as casually as possible, if he had come across "a piece of glass" in a waistcoat pocket. The servant had, and, liking the look of it, had kept it in a box filled with pins, buttons and beads.

The Imperial Crown of India was the one worn by George V when he visited his Indian Empire following his coronation in 1911. He had planned a second coronation out there, as Emperor of India, but Parliament did not approve. At least he could wear his crown to receive the homage of the Indian princes, he suggested. Parliament did not approve of that either. Neither St Edward's Crown nor the Imperial Crown could be taken out of the country. So the King had a new crown made, studded with 6,170 diamonds, at a cost of £70,000.

Altogether there are fifty-eight items in the collection of Crown Jewels, the most recent being the pair of gold bracelets given by the countries of the Commonwealth for the coronation of Queen Elizabeth II. The Sceptre with the Cross, though altered since by the insertion of the Great Star of Africa, was originally made for the coronation of Charles II, as was the second sceptre – known as the Rod with the Dove – which also features in the coronation ceremony, the Sovereign's Orb, 42 ounces of gold encrusted with rubies, emeralds and sapphires bordered with rows of pearls, and the golden spurs.

There are three coronation rings, the one used for the coronation of Elizabeth II consisting of a large sapphire set with four rubies in the form of a cross. This was made originally for William IV. There are five swords. The main one, the massive two-handed Sword of State is borne before the monarch at the State Opening of Parliament. It is also carried in procession at coronations, though for the actual coronation ceremony it is replaced by the jewelled Sword of Mercy, with its pattern of England's rose, Scotland's thistle and the Irish shamrock worked in diamonds, rubies, sapphires and emeralds, which George IV had made for his coronation at a cost of £6,000.

Not long after the restoration of Charles II there was a daring attempt to steal the newly-made Regalia. An Irish adventurer named Colonel Blood masterminded the attempt. Posing as a clergyman he struck up a friendship with Talbot Edwards, custodian of the Jewel House. On May 9, 1671, he turned up at the Martin Tower, where the jewels were then housed, along with his "nephew" – it was actually his son-in-law, Tom Hunt – and two "friends". He asked if they could view the Regalia. The custodian duly obliged. He was promptly hit over the head with a mallet and the conspirators made a grab for the jewels. Blood used the mallet to flatten the crown so that he could conceal it under his cloak. Hunt tried to hack the sceptre in two to hide it in a travelling bag and a man named Parrott seized the orb.

They were disturbed in their efforts by Edwards' son, Harry, returning unexpectedly from soldiering in the Low Countries. He promptly raised the alarm. Even so, the quick-witted Blood was equal to the occasion, shouting "Stop, thief!" at the top of his voice as he made off with the crown. He was already across the drawbridge and racing along the wharf to where the getaway horses were tethered before the ruse was spotted. In the skirmish with the guards which followed, Blood drew a pistol and wounded an officer, Captain Beckman. One of the four thieves did manage to get away, but the other three – Blood, Hunt and Parrott – were taken and the stolen Regalia recovered.

The story has a curious sequel. Blood was pardoned by the King, released, had his Irish estates restored to him and was even given a pension of £500 a year. Perhaps Charles II, who loved a good joke, was taken with the man's audacity. And perhaps – for Charles was also constantly in need of money – he was in on the plot.

Following the robbery attempt, the Regalia was transferred to the Round Tower, and was nearly destroyed in 1841 because of the very precautions taken to safeguard it. Fire broke out at the Tower of London and flames threatened the Jewel House. An attempt to save the Regalia was thwarted by the fact that the Jewel House was locked and the keys in the safe keeping of the Lord Chamberlain. Only the prompt action of a police officer named Pierse finally salvaged the Crown Jewels. He prised the bars of the Jewel House apart with a crowbar, wriggled through and, choking with smoke, stood his ground long enough to pass the Regalia to safety.

DOGS

Among royal pets, the corgis have tended to hog the public spotlight over the years. But there is another breed of dog the Royal Family also favours, the labrador. In the days of the Queen's childhood labradors had the run of Royal Lodge along with the corgis. But they are a shade too big and boisterous to be let loose among the priceless knick-knacks at Buckingham Palace. So, today, the labradors, yellow and black, are kept at Sandringham, where they are also bred and trained. One of them, Sandringham Samba, was given by the Queen to President Giscard d'Estaing of France when he paid a four-day state visit to Britain in 1976. The Queen, Prince Philip, Prince Charles and Prince Andrew each have their particular pet among the Sandringham labradors, which are also taken to Balmoral when the Royals go there for their long summer vacation.

As for the corgis, they first came by their royal pedigree in the 1930s when the present Queen, then a small princess, was bought one by her parents. Later, another was acquired for Princess Margaret. They were Pembroke corgis with tongue-twisting official names, Rosavel Golden Eagle (shortened to "Dookie" in the family circle) and Rosavel Lady Jane. Members of the public who saw the princesses out with them were at first mystified by the breed, but over the next twenty years the corgi became the fourth most popular dog in Britain as everyone rushed to imitate the Royals.

Dookie and Jane were followed by Carol and Crackers, so named because they were born at Christmas. But it was Susan, a gift on her eighteenth birthday, which was to become the Queen's special pet. She was so attached to her that she even took her on honeymoon with her. Susan survived well into the Queen's years of monarchy and, when she died, was buried at Sandringham where a small white headstone pays tribute to her as the "beloved companion of the Queen".

Long before that, however, she had produced two offspring, Sugar and Honey. Honey went to live with the Queen Mother at Clarence House, where in due course she became the mother of Bee, while Sugar stayed on at the palace where her puppies were the childhood pets of Charles and Anne. Charles named his corgi Whisky while Anne's was called Sherry. Anne, in particular, taught her corgi all manner of tricks, including a hoop-jumping act.

Later came Heather who produced Foxy, Tiny and Busy. The subsequent generation of Brush, Shadow and Smokey are the Queen's pets today, along with Chipper, Piper and May who are the offspring of dalliance between the Queen's corgi, Tiny, and Princess Margaret's dachshund, Pipkin.

The Queen is a true dog-lover, preferring to mix their food and feed them herself whenever she is at home and not above dumping them in a sink and washing them down personally if they become muddy when dashing about at Sandringham or Balmoral.

The kennels at Sandringham date back to the days of the Queen's great-grandfather, Edward VII. He favoured the Clumber breed of spaniels because of their rough shooting ability. It was not until after his death that Queen Alexandra, during her years of widowhood at Sandringham, introduced the royal strain of black labrador. Their Kennel Club prefix in those days was *Wolferton*. It was the Queen's grandfather, George V, who changed it to *Sandringham*.

The kennels were closed and the dogs dispersed during the brief reign of Edward VIII (Duke of Windsor), but the Queen's father reopened them on a small scale for the six or eight yellow labradors he used for his personal shooting. Then in 1949 he decided to build up the Sandringham strain again and the famous Windsor Bob was taken there for breeding.

The Queen takes a keen interest in the Sandringham kennels. As a result, the breeding programme has gone from strength to strength. Four Field Trial champions have been bred there, Sandringham Ranger, Sandringham Slipper, Sherry of Biteabout and, the most famous to date, Sherry's son, Sandringham Sydney.

In 1968 the Queen had the old brick-and-stone kennels of Edward VII demolished and replaced by smaller wooden ones with chain-link runs able to accommodate about forty dogs. Usually there are about twenty-five dogs in the Sandringham kennels; the older and more experienced dogs are used by the Royal Family during the shooting season, and the younger ones are trained as gundogs. However, at certain times, usually in the spring and early summer, the number will rise as puppies are born to the four or five best bitches used for breeding. All the puppies are named by the Queen and are registered at the Kennel Club with the *Sandringham* prefix. One or two from each litter are kept for training, thus ensuring estate gamekeepers of a steady supply of working dogs, labradors and spaniels, while the remainder are sold at eight weeks old to be trained as working dogs by other people.

A word of warning to dog-lovers. While the grounds at Sandringham and part of the house are open to the public in summer, the kennels are not.

DUCHY OF CORNWALL

Unlike others of the Royal Family, Prince Charles has no official allowance from the state. Instead, he derives his income from the Duchy of Cornwall, a royal estate created by Edward III to ensure that his son should live in a style befitting the Black Prince. Charles inherited the estate when, as the monarch's eldest son, he became Duke of Cornwall on his mother's accession to the throne. He was only three at the time and the Queen arranged with Parliament that eight-ninths of the Duchy's revenues should go to the Exchequer until Charles reached the age of eighteen.

Whatever may once have been the case, the bulk of the estate is no longer in Cornwall. There are holdings – farms, villages, woodland, quarries, mines and oyster beds to a total of some 12,000 acres – in five other English counties as well as in the Isles of Scilly and the Kennington area of London. And it is this Kennington area, some 45 acres of office and apartment blocks, including the famous Oval cricket ground, which is today the most valuable.

When Charles first inherited the estate in 1952 the revenues were around £90,000 a year. But careful management, the modernization and conversion of much of the London property, to say nothing of the effects of inflation, resulted in a considerable rise in revenue by the time he came into his full inheritance at the age of twenty-one. Because of this, he arranged to surrender fifty per cent of his income from the Duchy to the Exchequer in lieu of income tax (*see* Tax). In 1977 the Duchy had an accumulated income of £290,605, including a credit balance of £190,605 brought forward from the previous year. As arranged, half of this was handed over to the Treasury, leaving the Prince, in the words of a Duchy spokesman, with an income of "a little over £145,000".

DUCHY OF LANCASTER

As well as being Queen of the United Kingdom, Elizabeth II is also Duke – not Duchess – of Lancaster. This seemingly curious state of affairs has its origins in 1267 when Henry III created his second son, Edmund Crouchback, Duke of Lancaster and Leicester. Over the course of the next century or so, Crouchback and his heirs – Henry

Wryneck, Henry Grismond and John of Gaunt, who became Duke of Lancaster by marrying Crouchback's great-granddaughter – built up a chain of holdings which stretched right across England from the Wash to the Mersey. These holdings formed the immensely valuable Duchy of Lancaster.

When John of Gaunt's son, Henry Bolingbroke, ousted Richard II and proclaimed himself Henry IV, he also seized the Duchy of Lancaster and bestowed it on his eldest son, Henry of Monmouth. From then on the Duchy passed to whoever was strong enough to seize and hold the crown and, even after the crown ceased to be a bright bone of contention, the Duchy continued to be regarded as the personal prerogative of the reigning monarch. And today's reigning monarch is Elizabeth II.

In 1952, the first year of her reign, when she surrendered most of her other royal holdings (the Crown Estate) to Parliament, as monarchs customarily do, in exchange for an annual allowance known as the Civil List (see Civil List), the Duchy of Lancaster was not included. While she has this, the Queen will never be poverty-stricken. The Duchy extends today to some 52,000 acres of agricultural land and moorland scattered across a dozen counties, mainly Yorkshire, Lancashire, Staffordshire, Cheshire and Glamorgan. More important perhaps, it also includes that area of London known as the Manor of the Savoy (on which the Savoy Hotel stands), other property in the City of London, commercial property in eight provincial centres and housing developments in three more. Because it is regarded as the personal prerogative of the monarch, the financial accounts of the Duchy are never made public, but some idea of the income stemming from it can be gauged from recent adjustments made to the Civil List (to make allowance for what the Queen receives from the Duchy). From these, it would seem that her Duchy income in recent years has been something in excess of £400,000 a year.

DUKE AND DUCHESS OF GLOUCESTER

The Queen's cousin, Prince Richard (Alexander Walter George), never expected that he would become Duke of Gloucester. That title was the birthright of his elder brother, Prince William.

The two brothers were the sons of Prince Henry of Gloucester, himself the third son of the prince destined to become King George V. The title of Duke of Gloucester was created for him in 1928 and in 1935 he married Lady Alice Montagu-Douglas-Scott (now Princess Alice, Duchess of Gloucester), daughter of the 7th Duke of Buccleuch. Born on Christmas Day 1901, she was only a few days short of her fortieth birthday when their first son, William, was born on December, 18, 1941. Richard was born nearly three years later, on August, 26, 1944, and was only a few months old when the family set off for Australia where his father, following a long career in the army – he was slightly wounded while serving in France on the staff of Lord Gort in the early days of World War II – was to be Governor-General from 1945–7.

By the constrained standards of royal life, the late Duke gave both sons a broad education. William, after going to Eton, went to Stanford University in California where he obtained a diploma in economics. He worked for a time with a merchant bank in the City of London before entering the diplomatic service.

Richard, after going similarly to Eton, went to Magdalene College, Cambridge, and qualified as an architect (RIBA). It was while at Cambridge that he first met Birgitte Eva Van Deurs, the Danish girl he was to marry. They are said to have met at a tea party, over a traditionally English meal of hot buttered muffins. Born on June, 20, 1946, the daughter of an Odense lawyer, Asger Henriksen, she had taken her maternal grandparents' name of Van Deurs when her parents parted and was in Cambridge to improve her English. That accomplished, she returned to Denmark where she worked for a silversmith in Copenhagen and took a three-year commercial course before returning to London as a secretary at the Danish embassy.

The couple were married on July 8, 1972. By royal standards, it was a quiet and perhaps unusual wedding, celebrated not in Westminster Abbey, but in the thirteenth-century Norman church at Barnwell, Northamptonshire, where the Gloucesters have their country estate. There were no pages, no bridesmaids even, and the phrase "to obey" was omitted from the bride's wedding vows. Richard's elder brother, William, who had given up his diplomatic career to run the family estate after their father suffered a stroke in 1968, was best man.

Six weeks later, at the youthful age of thirty, William was dead.

For him, life had always been something of an adventure. Early on there had been a photographic safari to Ethiopia. Later, when he was posted as a diplomat to the British embassy in Tokyo, he flew his own aeroplane all the way to Japan. The year before his death he finished seventh in the King's Cup air race. He was taking part in another air race and had just taken off from Halfpenny Green, near Wolverhampton, when he was killed. His Piper Cherokee banked sharply, struck a tree, plunged into the ground and exploded in flames.

With the death of his father two years later, on June 10, 1974, Richard became Duke of Gloucester. His widowed mother, who among her several royal roles is Air Chief Commandant of the Women's Royal Air Force, took the title of Princess Alice, Duchess of Gloucester. Four months later, on October 24, 1974, Richard's wife, the new Duchess of

Gloucester, gave birth to their first child in St Mary's Hospital, Paddington, a prematurely born son weighing 4 lbs 2 ozs. They named him Alexander Patrick George Richard. As the son of a duke, he also has the title Earl of Ulster. Another child, a daughter, Lady Davina Elizabeth Alice Benedikte Windsor, was born, also at St Mary's, on November 20, 1977.

DUKE AND DUCHESS OF KENT

The faces of the Duke and Duchess of Kent are perhaps best-known through their annual appearances in the royal box at Wimbledon. The Duke, among his other offices, is president of the All-England Lawn Tennis and Croquet Club, to give Wimbledon its full title. He has been Duke of Kent since the tender age of six when his father was killed in a war-time air crash.

His father, born in 1902, was the youngest but one child of the Prince and Princess of Wales who later became King George V and Queen Mary (the youngest was Prince John who died from epilepsy at the age of thirteen). He was created Duke of Kent at the time of his marriage in 1934 to Princess Marina, the strikingly beautiful daughter of Prince Nicholas of Greece. The present Duke was born the following year, on October 9, 1935, and christened Edward George Nicholas Paul Patrick. Shortly after his birth the family moved to Coppins, a country home near Iver in Buckinghamshire which had been left to them by Marina's godmother, Princess Victoria, daughter of Queen Alexandra.

In 1939 the late Duke was due to have taken up an appointment as Governor-General of Australia, but the outbreak of World War II caused the appointment to be indefinitely postponed. Instead, he undertook shore-based duties with the Navy and later transferred to the Royal Air Force. He became the first of the Royal Family ever to fly the Atlantic when he flew to Canada in a Liberator in 1941 to visit air crews training there as well as take a look at aircraft factories in the United States. He stayed at the White House with President Roosevelt and the two men, prince and president, made such an impression upon each other that Roosevelt was to stand as godparent to the Kents' third child (*see* Prince and Princess Michael of Kent).

Only seven weeks after the birth of that child, the Duke was off again, this time to visit British forces in Iceland. He took off in a Sunderland flying boat from the Cromarty Firth near Invergordon. The flying boat had a crew of ten and there were three others in the Duke's entourage. Also on board was Wing Commander Moseley, commander of No. 228 Squadron. Of all these, only one, the tail-gunner, Andrew Jack, was to survive the crash twenty-five minutes after take-off when the aircraft, flying through thick cloud, ploughed into a Scottish hillside. It was August 25, 1942.

The years which followed were not easy ones for the widowed Princess Marina. While she may not have been poor by ordinary standards, she found herself obliged to cut down on staff and run Coppins on a shoestring. At times when things were particularly difficult items from her dead husband's collection of pictures, silver and china would pop up for sale in public auction rooms. In this way, she managed to put her son, the new young Duke, through Eton and send him to boarding school in Switzerland. From there he went on to the Royal Military Academy at Sandhurst and an army career with the Royal Scots Greys.

It was while he was in the Scots Greys, a lieutenant stationed at Catterick, that the Duke met Katharine Lucy Mary Worsley, born on February 22, 1933, the only daughter of the late Sir William Worsley of Hovingham Hall. They were married at York Minster on June 8, 1961. Their first child, George Philip Nicholas, Earl of St Andrews, was born on June 26 of the following year. A daughter, Lady Helen Marina Lucy Windsor, followed on April 28, 1964, and another son, Lord Nicholas Charles Edward Jonathan Windsor, was born on July 25, 1970.

By then the Duke's mother was dead. She died on August 27, 1968. On her death, the Duke took over the presidency of the All-England Club which she, in turn, had taken over from her dead father.

In 1972, because Coppins was too vulnerable from a security viewpoint, the Duke and his family moved into York House, St James's Palace, with Anmer Hall, on the Queen's private estate at Sandringham in Norfolk, as a holiday retreat. In June, 1976, after twenty-one years in the army during which he had risen to the rank of lieutenant-colonel, the Duke resigned to take up a post as vice-chairman of the British Overseas Trade Board. By way of explanation he said, "It's beyond question that junior members of the Royal Family – outside Buckingham Palace, that is – are going to have to earn their daily bread some way or other."

DUKE AND DUCHESS OF WINDSOR

Almost the first act of Edward VIII, when his father died and he found himself king, was to hurry downstairs at Sandringham and order the "damn clocks" to be set to the correct time. Through two generations, clocks there – including even the clock on the parish church – had been set half an hour ahead of the rest of Britain, a royal eccentricity designed to get guests out of bed early and ensure a full day in the open banging away at pheasants and partridges. But to the king who later became Duke of Windsor, those clocks, set half an hour ahead of

Greenwich, represented the sole remaining vestige of his disciplinarian father's stern authority (*see* King George V and Queen Mary).

That son and father never understood each other was not necessarily the fault of either. As a toddler the son was unwittingly placed in the care of a sadistic nurse who would pinch him or twist his arm whenever she took him to see his parents so that he was tearful and frightened in their presence. He was, in any event, frightened of his father and, as a boy, lived in dread of a summons to his father's study. If he himself wished to see his father, he had to make an appointment through a page.

He was born on June 23, 1894, at White Lodge, Richmond, the home of his maternal grandparents, the Tecks, first child of Prince George and Princess May (later Queen Mary), grandson of the Prince of Wales who was not yet Edward VII, great-grandson of Queen Victoria. With so illustrious a background, he was christened Edward Albert Christian George Andrew Patrick David, the last four names being those of the patron saints of England, Scotland, Ireland and Wales. In the family circle he was simply David.

As a child, he was shy and highly strung, not only frightened of his father, but in awe even of his mother, who he saw as someone cold and remote. Throughout his childhood he had no friends except his sister and brothers. Like them, he was brought up mainly at Sandringham with occasional shifts to London, Windsor and Balmoral. His early education was a sketchy one supervised first by a governess and later by a tutor. At the age of thirteen, following the royal tradition established by George II when he sent his grandson to sea as a midshipman in 1758, he was packed off to Osborne as a naval cadet. From there he went on to the Royal Naval College at Dartmouth before serving three months as a midshipman aboard the battleship *Hindustan*.

On his sixteenth birthday, shortly after his father's accession to the throne in 1910, he was created Prince of Wales (*see* Princes of Wales). Two years later he was sent to Magdalen College, Oxford. As heir to the throne, he was spared the necessity for taking the customary entrance examination and his personal tutor, Henry Hansell, went with him to supervise his studies. Between terms at Oxford he was sent to France to improve his French and to Germany to brush up his German. At his own request, on the outbreak of World War I he was granted a commission in the Grenadier Guards. He pestered the authorities to let him go to France and in 1915 he was appointed to the staff of Major-General Lord Cavan, who had charge of the Guards Division. Determined to "do his bit", he was frequently to be found in the actual trenches and emerged from one visit to the front line to find his car riddled with bullet holes and the driver dead. In 1916 he went to Egypt and the Sudan and in 1917 served briefly with the XIV Army Corps in Italy.

He was back in London in 1918 when an air raid alert caused him to take shelter in a cellar in Belgrave Square. Also taking shelter in the same cellar that night was Freda Dudley Ward, the young wife of a Liberal Member of Parliament from whom she was later to be separated and divorced. The meeting of the Prince of Wales and the MP's wife marked the beginning of a relationship which was to last thirteen years. The Prince was to have other affairs from time to time, notably with Thelma Lady Furness, but until Mrs Simpson came on the scene in 1931 he always went back to Freda. Initially, he was mad about her. When he was in London he saw her every day and, wherever he was, would telephone her each morning. They went dancing, racing and golfing together, on holiday together, and when he moved into his own bachelor establishment at York House in 1919 it was naturally Freda who helped him with the décor and furniture arranging.

Inevitably, there were long and frequent separations, one at least of which had him in tears at the moment of parting from Freda. He was Britain's blue-eyed, straw-haired boy, the prince who symbolized all the hopes and aspirations of post-war Britain. As such, he was despatched aboard *HMS Renown* and *HMS Repulse* in turn to show the flag round the world . . . to Newfoundland, Canada, and the United States in 1919, Australia and New Zealand in 1920, India and Japan in 1921 (that trip lasted eight months), Canada again in 1923, yet again plus the United States again in 1924, South Africa and South America in 1925. Day after day he was kept busy shaking hundreds of hands until his right hand was so sore he had to use his left to sign autographs. His habit of signing autographs was one of which his mother, Queen Mary, did not approve. But others loved him for it; loved everything about him. And this was true not only of the countries of the Empire. The United States, having rid itself of George III, welcomed his great-great-great-grandson back with scenes of wild enthusiasm. Everywhere he went he was fêted, lorded, hero-worshipped, constantly surrounded by delectable females only too eager to catch his eye and attract his attention. It is hardly to be wondered at that it went to his head more than a little.

While all this was going on, a girl named Bessie Wallis Warfield was growing up in the United States. She was born at Blue Ridge Summit, Pennsylvania on June 19, 1896, the posthumous daughter of Teakle Wallis Warfield. He was from Maryland. Her mother, the former Alice Montague, hailed from Virginia. With her father dead, mother and child alike were dependent upon the generosity of relatives until her mother re-married. In 1916, when she was twenty, Bessie herself was married. The wedding ceremony took place at Pensacola, Florida, and the bridegroom was Earl Winfield Spencer, a lieutenant in the US navy's aviation corps. As a result, among those briefly presented to the

Prince of Wales at a dance given in his honour when *HMS Renown* called at San Diego was a young matron named Wallis Spencer.

That first marriage was not a happy one. Spencer was neurotic and possessively jealous, and he drank heavily. When he was posted to the Far East his wife did not initially accompany him. However, she did join him in China in 1924, but soon left him again and in 1927 was granted a divorce at Warrenton, Virginia.

Eight months later, in July, 1928, in London, she married Ernest Simpson whom she had first met some time previously in New York. Born in New York and Harvard educated, Simpson was the son of an English father and an American mother. At the time of their marriage – his second, incidentally – he had taken out British citizenship and was working in the London office of his father's business.

The couple lived in a flat in Bryanston Court. It was late in 1930 when Wallis Simpson, who had been Wallis Spencer when she first met the Prince of Wales, met him again. This time it was at a house party given by Lady Furness, one of the two ladies Mrs Simpson was subsequently to supplant in the Prince's affections. In June, 1931, wearing a train and ostrich feathers borrowed from Lady Furness, she was presented at court, the Prince later running her and her husband back to their Bryanston Court home in his car.

He was now in his thirties, as blue-eyed as ever but no longer a boy, preferring golf, dancing and cocktails to such traditional royal pastimes as shooting and stalking, finding Biarritz more fun than Balmoral and, as though determined to break away from the stereotyped royal image, affecting such novelties as suede shoes and loud checks for leisure wear. The Simpsons quickly became part of the small, private circle with which he surrounded himself and in 1932 they were invited to Fort Belvedere, a royal hideaway built in the reign of George II. Having restored its mock battlements and rusted guns after years of neglect, the Prince used it as a weekend retreat, where he could entertain his friends on the bagpipes and ukelele and indulge in his "secret vice" of needlework. The Simpsons' 1932 visit to the Fort was the first of several.

Then, in 1934, the Prince suddenly found himself without either of his customary lady friends. His long-time favourite, Freda Dudley Ward, was preoccupied with the serious illness of her elder daughter and Lady Furness was off to the United States on a three-month visit. "Look after the Prince of Wales for me," she said, jokingly, to Mrs Simpson before her departure. By the time she returned she no longer held first or even second place in the Prince's affections. As for Freda, she telephoned St James's Palace to tell him that her daughter was now better – only to find he had given instructions that no further calls from her were to be put through.

That was the year Mrs Simpson, chaperoned by her aunt, Mrs Bessie

Merryman, went on holiday to Biarritz with the Prince, just as another lady, Alice Keppel, had once gone there with his grandfather but without a chaperon (*see* King Edward VII and Queen Alexandra). The following February they visited Kitzbühel, Vienna and Budapest together. That summer they were together in Cannes, cruising to Corsica as well as revisiting Vienna and Budapest. When stories of their relationship reached his ears, the Prince's father, George V, commented gloomily, "After I am dead, the boy will ruin himself in twelve months." It was to prove a remarkably accurate forecast.

With his father's death at Sandringham in January, 1936, the Prince of Wales was now King Edward VIII. He flew to London by air to take the oath of accession. He saw it as his mission, he said, "to modernize the monarchy within its traditional glory and strength". It seemed a point of bright promise.

But the brightness, sadly, was soon to fade. Coming events were already casting their shadow as Mrs Simpson and her husband stood with him at a window of St James's Palace to watch the ceremony of proclamation. Their names appeared in the court circular as having dined with the new King. Later, Mrs Simpson's name appeared again, but this time without that of her husband. Having ordered economies to be carried out at Sandringham and Balmoral, both of which he regarded as expensive white elephants, and having performed a bare minimum of public engagements, the King chartered the yacht *Nahlin* from Lady Yule and, with Mrs Simpson as his companion, set off to cruise the Dalmatian coast. Initially, for visits ashore, he adopted the easily-seen-through pretext of styling himself "Duke of Lancaster", but this was quickly abandoned. So was concealment of his feelings for Mrs Simpson in photographs constantly taken together.

Little by little, he endeavoured to coerce others of the Royal Family into accepting Mrs Simpson. Driving a glossy American station-wagon, he took her to Royal Lodge one day to visit his brother and sister-in-law, the Duke and Duchess of York. All four, together with the Yorks' small daughters, Princess Elizabeth and Princess Margaret, had tea together, but it was not an easy meal.

That autumn Mrs Simpson was the King's guest at Balmoral. While the British Press published little or nothing of all this, American newspapers were far less inhibited. More and more details of the "royal romance" were published there, with the European Press quick to follow suit. On October 26 the *New York Journal* said openly that Britain's new king intended to marry Mrs Simpson once she was divorced from her second husband.

But if the Press in Britain was still silent, the "royal romance" was certainly the subject of discussion in top Government circles. Even before the *New York Journal* came out with its story of intended marriage, Prime Minister Stanley Baldwin had been to Fort Belvedere to see the King in an endeavour to have Mrs Simpson's divorce petition withdrawn.

"That is the lady's private business," the King told him, icily. "I have no right to interfere."

So on October 27, in the quiet East Anglian town of Ipswich, Mrs Simpson was granted a *decree nisi* on the grounds of her husband's adultery at an hotel in Bray with a lady answering to the unusual name of Buttercup Kennedy.

That accomplished, things moved quickly towards the inevitable climax. On November 3 the King performed the state opening of Parliament. On Armistice Day, November 11, he attended the traditional ceremony of remembrance at the Cenotaph in Whitehall. Following that he spent three days with the Home Fleet at Portland. He returned to Fort Belvedere to find a letter from his private secretary, Major Alexander Hardinge, awaiting his attention. Couched in the most respectful terms, it warned him that the British Press could not be expected to maintain its silence much longer; that when the facts were published it could provoke such a political storm that the Government might have no other course but to resign. The letter concluded:

"If Your Majesty will permit me to say so, there is only one step which holds out any prospect of avoiding this dangerous situation, and that is for Mrs Simpson to go abroad without further delay – and I would beg Your Majesty to give this proposal your earnest consideration before the situation becomes irretrievable."

The King, for so long accustomed to getting his own way in things, was both shocked and angered by Hardinge's letter. So shocked that he did not reply to it; so angry that he never saw Hardinge again.

Over the course of the next two days he told his mother (Queen Mary), his sister (the Princess Royal) and his brothers that it was his firm intention to marry Mrs Simpson once her *decree nisi* was made *absolute*. On November 16 he summoned Prime Minister Baldwin and told him too.

"Sir, this is most grievous news," Baldwin replied.

There was frantic discussion in high places in the hope of finding a way out of what was fast becoming an impossible situation. A morganatic marriage was suggested. This meant that Mrs Simpson would become the King's wife, but not the Queen of England, and that any children of the marriage would be excluded from succeeding to the throne. The King himself even proposed that he should marry as Duke of Lancaster, not King of England, to which Baldwin replied that the people would never accept such a thing. There was, in fact, no way in which "the people" could actually be consulted or their wishes ascertained. Indeed, not even Parliament was consulted, though the heads of some Commonwealth countries were. On the question of a possible morganatic marriage, Baldwin told Parliament on December 4, "His Majesty's Government are not prepared to introduce such legislation."

By then, the whole situation had already gone beyond the point of no return. That point was reached on December 1 when the Bishop of Bradford, Dr Alfred Blunt, addressing his annual diocesan conference, commended the King to God's grace – "For the King is a man like any other" – if he were to do his duty properly.

"We hope he is aware of this need," said Dr Blunt. "Some of us wish he gave more positive signs of such awareness."

The Bishop was to say later that his words were actually directed at the new King's irregular church attendances. But the British Press, led by the *Yorkshire Post*, was quick to give them a very different meaning and seize upon this heaven-sent opportunity to break its long silence and print the story of the King and Mrs Simpson.

Arriving back at Euston Station from a visit to Edinburgh on December 3, the King's brother and heir presumptive, the Duke of York, found himself greeted with glaring headlines. Driven by the King's chauffeur, Mrs Simpson left the country the same day, taking refuge from the constitutional storm in the Cannes villa of her old friends, Mr and Mrs Herman Rogers. From there on December 7, through Lord Brownlow, she issued a statement in the third person in which she said: "Mrs Simpson, throughout the last few weeks, has invariably wished to avoid any action or proposal which would hurt or damage His Majesty or the throne. Today her attitude is unchanged and she is willing, if such an action would solve the problem, to withdraw forthwith from a situation which has been rendered both unhappy and untenable."

But if Mrs Simpson was prepared to withdraw from an "unhappy and untenable" situation, the King was not. On December 10 the Speaker of the House of Commons received the following message from him:

"After long and anxious consideration I have determined to renounce the Throne to which I succeeded on the death of my father, and I am now communicating this my final and irrevocable decision. Realizing as I do the gravity of this step, I can only hope that I shall have the understanding of my people in the decision I have taken and the reasons which have led me to take it.

"I will not enter now into my private feelings, but I would beg that it should be remembered that the burden which constantly rests upon the shoulders of a Sovereign is so heavy that it can only be borne in circumstances different from those in which I now find myself.

"I conceive that I am not overlooking the duty which rests on me to place in the forefront the public interest when I declare that I am conscious that I can no longer discharge this heavy task with efficiency or satisfaction to myself. I have accordingly this morning executed an Instrument of Abdication in the terms following:

"I, Edward VIII of Great Britain, Ireland and the British Dominions beyond the seas, King, Emperor of India, do hereby declare my irrevocable determination to renounce the Throne for myself and for my descendants and my desire that effect should be given to this Instrument of Abdication immediately."

The Instrument of Abdication had been witnessed by the Dukes of York, Gloucester and Kent, the three brothers of the King (for such he still was until Parliament ratified the step he had taken). The statement continued:

"I deeply appreciate the spirit which has actuated the appeals which have been made to me to take a different decision, and I have, before reaching my final determination, most fully pondered over them. But my mind is made up. Moreover, further delay cannot but be most injurious to the peoples whom I have tried to serve as Prince of Wales and as King, and whose future happiness and prosperity are the constant wish of my heart.

"I take my leave of them in the confident hope that the course which I have thought it right to follow is that which is best for the stability of the Throne and Empire and the happiness of my peoples. I am deeply sensible of the consideration which they have always extended to me, both before and after my accession to the Throne, and which I know they will extend in full measure to my successor."

The King's message concluded by urging that his brother, the Duke of York, (*see* King George VI) should take over the throne immediately.

The Instrument of Abdication was ratified by Parliament the following day – December 11, 1936 – and the 325 days' reign of Edward VIII was at an end. Later that day, the ex-King, as he now was, dined with others of the family at his brother's home, Royal Lodge, Windsor. The meal over, he bowed to the brother who was now King in his place and drove to Windsor Castle to make his farewell broadcast. Broadcasting as His Royal Highness Prince Edward, he said in part:

"But you must believe me when I tell you that I have found it impossible to carry the heavy burden of responsibility, and to discharge my duties as King as I would wish to do, without the help and support of the woman I love.

"And I want you to know that the decision I have made has been mine, and mine alone. This was a thing I had to judge entirely for myself. The other person most nearly concerned has tried up to the last to persuade me to take a different course.

"I have made this, the most serious decision of my life, only upon the single thought of what would in the end be best for all.

"This decision has been made less difficult for me by the sure knowledge that my brother with his long training in the public affairs of this country and with his fine qualities, will be able to take my place forthwith, without interruption or injury to the life and progress of the Empire.

"And he has one matchless blessing, enjoyed by so many of you and not bestowed on me, a happy home with his wife and children."

He concluded his broadcast with the words: "God bless you all. God save the King." That done, he drove through the night to Portsmouth, where, at two o'clock in the morning, he boarded the destroyer *Fury* and sailed into what was to develop into a largely self-imposed exile.

The Simpson divorce decree became *absolute* on April 27, 1937, and on June 3 the ex-King and the one-time Bessie Wallis Warfield were married at the Château de Candé, the home of Charles Bedaux, a French-born naturalized American. The ceremony was performed by the Revd R. A. Jardine, vicar of St Paul's, Darlington.

Almost the first act of the brother who succeeded to the throne was to announce to his Accession Council that he proposed to create the ex-King Duke of Windsor, though this decision was not given legal form until after the new King had been safely crowned. This was on May 12, 1937. On May 28 it was announced that: "The King has been pleased by Letters Patent under the Great Seal of the Realm bearing date the 27 May 1937 to declare that the Duke of Windsor shall . . . be entitled to hold and enjoy for himself only the title style or attribute of Royal Highness so however that his wife and descendants if any shall not hold the said title style or attribute."

To the ex-King it was a bitter blow to learn that his wife was not to enjoy the same rank as the wives of his brothers, Gloucester and Kent. And in his bitterness lay some of the seeds of the long split in the Royal Family. But others were also partly to blame. Queen Mary, the mother he had found so cold and remote in childhood, never forgave him for what she regarded as his failure to carry out his royal duty and would never consent to meet the woman he married. His sister-in-law too, the Duchess of York who became Queen Elizabeth and is now the Queen Mother, was unforgiving until it was too late to matter any more.

Despite his brother's decree, the Duke of Windsor, as he now was, always insisted that his wife was "Her Royal Highness". He referred to her as such himself and, outside Britain, insisted on others doing the same. He based his argument on the fact that he himself was born His Royal Highness and that his wife therefore acquired a similar title by simply marrying him. Others of the Royal Family did not see things the same way.

Following their marriage, the Windsors lived for a time in Austria before settling in France, where they leased a villa at Antibes and a house near the Bois de Boulogne in Paris. There was at this time a controversial visit to Nazi Germany and an unwise meeting with Adolf Hitler. On the outbreak of World War II, the destroyer *Kelly*, commanded by Louis Mountbatten, (*see* Earl Mountbatten of Burma) was assigned to bring them back to Britain. They stayed with Lady Alexandra Metcalfe at Hartfield and the Duke was offered a choice of jobs. He could be either Deputy Regional Commissioner for Wales or a liaison officer with the British Military Mission in France. He picked Wales, but found himself in Vincennes just the same with the rank of major-general.

With the fall of France, the Windsors retreated to Biarritz, joined the queue of refugees waiting at Perpignan and were finally allowed into Spain. From there they moved on to Portugal. Winston Churchill, now prime minister, offered to send a flying boat to bring them back to Britain, but the Duke dug his heels in, refusing to return if his wife was not accorded equality with the wives of his brothers. A way out was found by offering him the governorship of the Bahamas. He regarded this as a continuation of exile and the post as a petty one, but accepted just the same. In March, 1945, five months before his term of office expired, he resigned. The following September the Windsors returned to France.

The Duke journeyed to London with a proposal that he should become a sort of roving royal ambassador, but nothing came of the idea. In fact, he visited London several times in the immediate post-war years to see his mother and his brother, the King, but both continued to refuse to meet his wife though she was sometimes in London with him. Nor was the family situation eased by the fact that the Queen (*see* Queen Elizabeth, the Queen Mother) excused herself from meeting even her brother-in-law. Whenever he visited Buckingham Palace, there was always, it seemed, some prior engagement which took her out just before his arrival.

In France, the Windsors lived for a time in the Bois de Boulogne, later moving to a converted mill some forty-five miles from Paris. They made frequent trips to the United States and the Duke was again in Britain in 1952 for his brother's funeral and in 1953 at the bedside of his dying mother. It was at his brother's funeral that he met his sister-in-law, the Queen who was now Queen Mother, for the first time since the family dinner following his abdication. Once so fond of each other, they met almost as strangers.

The Windsors are often referred to as having been "exiled" from Britain. In fact, they were not; nor could they have been. They were free to come and go as they pleased. That they came so infrequently was due to the family split over the abdication and the Duke's resentment of the fact that his wife was not given the title of Her Royal Highness. It was for these reasons that he did not accept several invitations given to him at varying times, among them one to the 1960 wedding of Princess Margaret.

It was not until 1965 that there was any sign of a *rapprochement*. When the Duke, now aged and ailing, entered the London Clinic for eye surgery, the niece he had once known as Lilibet – now Queen Elizabeth II – went there to visit him. She met his wife there too, the first time the two women, Queen and Duchess, had seen each other for more than thirty years. Among the Duke's other visitors at the London Clinic were his sister-in-law, Princess Marina, widow of the Duke of Kent, and his sister, the Princess Royal, who was to die unexpectedly only thirteen days later.

In 1966 the Queen invited the Windsors to attend the unveiling ceremony at Marlborough House of a plaque to the Duke's mother, Queen Mary. This time the Duke accepted. The ceremony was delayed somewhat so that they could travel from New York by sea, a royal car was placed at their disposal and they returned to France afterwards in an aircraft of the Queen's Flight. The Queen Mother unbent sufficiently to accept a kiss on the cheek from the Duke and to shake hands with the Duchess. After the ceremony the Windsors lunched with the Duke's brother and sister-in-law, the Gloucesters. In a television interview which punctuated the brief visit it was made abundantly clear that, whatever title the Duke might insist on his wife being accorded in Paris or New York, in Britain at least she was not Her Royal Highness. Throughout the interview, while the Duke was carefully addressed as "Your Royal Highness", the Duchess was equally carefully addressed only as "Your Grace".

The last time Queen Elizabeth II was to see the uncle who had once, briefly, been King Edward VIII was in 1972. She was paying an official visit to Paris and took time out to visit his home in the Bois de Boulogne, climbing the stairs, along with her husband and son, to the bedroom where the Duke lay dying from cancer. He died on May 28, 1972. The body was taken back to Britain for burial and his widow followed. For the funeral service at St George's Chapel, Windsor, she sat between the Queen and Prince Philip. She stayed overnight at Buckingham Palace, her first visit there since those far-off days of 1936 when her name appeared in the court circular as a dinner guest of King Edward VIII.

EARL MOUNTBATTEN OF BURMA

While there can be few people who have never heard of Mountbatten of Burma, many find it hard to pinpoint exactly who he is. "Most people think Dickie's my father," Prince Philip told his biographer, Basil Boothroyd.

Mountbatten is not Philip's father, but his uncle, his mother's brother. As war-time "Supremo" for South-East Asia and the last Viceroy of Britain's Indian empire, he is one of the more colourful figures to have strutted the stage of recent history, a man who takes particular pride in the fact that he can trace his family lineage even further back than his nephew's royal wife can trace hers . . . through forty-four generations to someone named Duke Ydulf, a mid-European chieftain who lived around A.D. 600.

Let us pick up the family history in 1851. That year, while Queen Victoria was visiting and revisiting the Great Exhibition in Hyde Park, Prince Alexander, younger brother of the Grand Duke of Hesse-Darmstadt as well as being brother-in-law to the Russian Tsarevich, was eloping in a droshky with an orphan named Julia von Haucke. The resulting marriage was ruled to be morganatic, Julia was denied the title of princess and Alexander was dismissed from his post as a major-general in the army of Imperial Russia. He promptly joined the Austrian army instead. However, by 1858 his brother had relented sufficiently for Julia to call herself a princess and for their first son, born at Graz in 1854 (there had been a daughter born in Geneva before that), to have the title Prince Louis of Battenberg.

From an early age Prince Louis had an overwhelming ambition to go to sea. There was at that time no German navy. But Austria had one and his father offered to get him into it. Not good enough, said young Louis. He wanted to join the British navy. His father pointed out that he could do so only by changing his nationality. So Louis changed his nationality, joined Britain's royal navy, and became a close friend of the Prince of Wales who was later to be King Edward VII – so close that the two of them had at least one mistress in common, Lillie Langtry. He also married one of Queen Victoria's granddaughters, Princess Victoria of Hesse, and fathered four children – Alice (born 1885), the mother of Prince Philip; Louise (1889), who married King Gustav VI of Sweden; George (1892); and Louis, the youngest, who was born on June 25, 1900.

Prince Louis had entered the navy as a youthful cadet. By the time World War I broke out in 1914 he had worked his way up to the high position of First Sea Lord. Both sons had followed him into the navy. George was serving in the battle cruiser *New Zealand* while Louis – or "Dickie" as everyone called him – was a cadet at Osborne. It was largely due to Prince Louis, in collaboration with Winston Churchill, then First Lord of the Admiralty, that Britain's navy was in a sufficient state of readiness to meet the German threat when war came. Despite this, the British remembered that he had been born a German and the anti-German hysteria which swept the country – even innocent dachshunds were booted in the streets – saw him hounded from office when the war was little more than a year old.

Technically, he resigned, writing Churchill a letter in which he said: "I have lately been driven to the painful conclusion that at this juncture my birth and parentage have the effect of impairing in some respects my usefulness to the Board of Admiralty. In these circumstances I feel it to be my duty, as a loyal subject of His Majesty, to resign the office of First Sea Lord, hoping thereby to facilitate the task of the administration of the great Service to which I have devoted my life."

News of his father's downfall reached Dickie at Osborne, where he had been a cadet for just over a year. From Osborne he went on to the Royal Naval College at Dartmouth where he passed out eighteenth of a class of eighty. As a midshipman he saw the war out aboard the battle cruiser *Lion* and the dreadnought *Queen Elizabeth*, though he saw no actual fighting. By that time his name was no longer Battenberg. In 1917, at the same time that King George V was adopting the name of Windsor for the Royal Family (*see* Name), Prince Louis of Battenberg had become Louis Mountbatten (the name of an island fort in Plymouth Sound as well as being the anglicized version of Battenberg) with the titles of Marquess of Milford Haven, Earl of Medina and Viscount Alderney.

As a young man caught up in the social whirl which followed the war, Dickie Mountbatten found himself from time to time in the company of his royal family relatives, the sons of George V. Just as his father had been close to an earlier Prince of Wales, so Dickie now became a close friend of the Prince of Wales who was to wind up as Duke of Windsor. In 1920 when the Prince sailed aboard the battle cruiser *Renown* for a tour of Australia and New Zealand (*see* Duke and Duchess of Windsor), Dickie, now a lieutenant, went along as one of his naval aides. It was following his return from this trip, at a ball in London given by the American hostess, Mrs Cornelius Vanderbilt, in 1921, that he first met the beautiful Edwina Ashley.

Her family history was almost as romantic as that of his own. If Dickie could claim that his grandfather had eloped with an orphan maid-of-honour, Edwina could equally say that hers had arrived in Britain from Cologne at the age of sixteen with nothing more to his name than a bag of clothes and a violin. He went on to become Sir Ernest Cassel, a man with a vast fortune made from railroads, mines, canals, irrigation schemes. Sadly, his wife had died from tuberculosis after only three years of marriage. His daughter, Maud, who married Major Wilfred Ashley (later Lord Mount Temple) similarly died young from tuberculosis after giving birth to Edwina and her sister, Mary.

Following her mother's death, Edwina went to live with her grandfather at Brook House in Park Lane, arguably the finest mansion in London, its walls – even those in the kitchens – lined with 800 tons of marble imported specially from Tuscany. At the time Mountbatten met her she was acting as her grandfather's hostess, entertaining such celebrated guests as the Churchills and the Asquiths.

Mountbatten's father and Edwina's grandfather both died that same year, within four days of each other. Mountbatten himself had already been picked to accompany the Prince of Wales on another of his tours, this time to India. "Why don't you come to India too?" he suggested to Edwina. She seized eagerly upon the idea, but there was a slight snag. Wealthy though she now was – her grandfather had left her a fortune – she had no ready cash until all the complicated legalities had been carried out. So she borrowed £100 from a cousin to pay for a second-class round trip to India.

They met up again in Delhi and had only six days together. Much of that time found Mountbatten busy about his official duties – until the Prince of Wales heard how things stood between them. "Perhaps this will help," he said, and gave Mountbatten the key to his bungalow in the grounds of Viceregal Lodge. Years later, as Viceroy and Vicereine of India, Edwina and Dickie were to pay a sentimental return visit to that bungalow.

They became engaged in Delhi and were married at St Margaret's, Westminster, the following year, July 18, 1922. The King and Queen were among the guests, the Prince of Wales was best man, Prince Philip's four sisters were bridesmaids, the bridal car was hauled from the church to the reception at Brook House by a naval gun crew, and their honeymoon lasted six months. It included a tour of Europe and another of the United States, where they visited President Harding at the White House, as well as Los Angeles, Chicago, the Grand Canyon,

New York and Niagara Falls. They were young and Edwina was rich.

Their first daughter, Patricia, was born in London in 1924; their second, Pamela, in Barcelona in 1929. By that time Mountbatten was a lieutenant-commander. Edwina's fortune enabled them to live in luxury. In Malta, when Mountbatten was posted there for a long tour of duty, she bought them their own villa. In Britain their main base continued to be Brook House, where their flamboyant life-style did not always make them popular. They were famous for their parties, always uninhibited, sometimes almost wild.

Virtually inseparable at the beginning of their married life, they were apart a lot in the 1930s. With a cousin, Edwina travelled to America, visiting both Hollywood and Harlem. With a sister-in-law, she went on an archaeological tour of Persia. She visited the West Indies, Mexico, South America, toured the length of Africa by car and travelled across Russia on the Trans-Siberian railway.

In 1932 Mountbatten was promoted to commander and in 1934 he was given his first command, the destroyer *Daring*. In 1935 Edwina sold Brook House. An apartment block was built on the site and, as part of the deal, the Mountbattens had the entire top two floors as a magnificent penthouse of some thirty rooms. When the Prince of Wales became King Edward VIII in 1936 Mountbatten was appointed as his naval aide-de-camp. But he was close too to the brother who was still Duke of York and the Duke sought his advice at the time of the abdication crisis.

"You'll make a splendid king. A naval officer's training is the best possible preparation," (*see* King George VI) Mountbatten told him.

When the fog of abdication cleared, he found himself appointed naval aide-de-camp to King George VI in turn, and two years later, with the death of his brother George in 1938, he also had responsibility for the care and education of the nephew who, in effect, had been his brother's ward, Prince Philip of Greece (*see* Prince Philip). These two facets of his life came together that day in 1939 when he accompanied the King and his daughters to Dartmouth and his nephew, Philip, was detailed to show Princess Elizabeth around.

If Mountbatten, that day, played an important part in the future of the Royal Family, he also played an important part, like his father before him, in ensuring that Britain's navy was ready when war with Germany erupted for a second time in 1939. It was largely due to his persuasion and persistence that virtually every British ship, and indeed most US ships, were equipped with the fast-firing Swiss Oerlikon anti-aircraft gun after it had originally been rejected by the US Naval Ordnance Department and Britain's Admiralty had stalled for two years more. Despite his flamboyant life-style, Mountbatten was nothing if not a keen and hard-working naval officer with the advantage of his own social contacts and his wife's money to enable him to get things done.

Inventive too. He invented a new signalling shutter, a radio wave-length indicator and a new-style torpedo sight, among other things. On a navel, though not "naval", level he is also credited with ousting fly buttons in favour of the zip-fastener.

With the outbreak of World War II, he assumed command of the 5th Destroyer Flotilla and almost his first task was to fetch the Duke and Duchess of Windsor back from France to Britain. His destroyer, *HMS Kelly*, was to see a considerable amount of action, being damaged by a mine, helping with the evacuation of Norway, being torpedoed in the North Sea, bombarding Germany shipping at Benghazi. It was finally sunk on May 23, 1941, by enemy 'planes during the German invasion of Crete. Mountbatten and other survivors – only 110 out of a complement of 240 – were fished out of the Mediterranean by a sister destroyer.

Edwina was similarly busy in her own right. She sent their two daughters to America, gave up the penthouse and moved into a small rented house in Chester Street (where Prince Philip sometimes stayed when on leave) and turned the other house she had inherited, Broad-lands in Hampshire, into a hospital annexe. She herself joined the St John Ambulance Brigade as an auxiliary nurse and was quickly divisional deputy superintendent-in-chief.

In 1941, Mountbatten, after briefly commanding the aircraft carrier *Illustrious*, was promoted from captain to acting commodore and appointed head of Combined Operations. His brief Churchill told him, was to turn Britain "from a bastion of defence into a springboard for attack". It was a role in which Mountbatten's inventive mind revelled. He was responsible for backing such projects as the amphibious tank and the Mulberry floating harbours, so vital when it came to D-Day, as well as dreaming up Pluto, the pipeline used to pump oil from Britain to France in the aftermath of invasion. Promoted yet again to the triple rank of vice-admiral in the navy, lieutenant-general in the army and air marshal in the air force, he helped plan the commando raids on St Nazaire, Vaagse in Norway, Bruneval and Dieppe where so many Canadians died so gallantly. He was involved also in planning the landings in North Africa and the invasion of Sicily as well as in Overlord, code name for D-Day. With characteristic flamboyance he demonstrated his idea for a floating airfield to the combined British and American high command by having a block of ice brought into the Quebec ballroom where the meeting was being held. He drew his revolver, fired and the ice shattered. A block of Pykrete, a mixture of frozen water and sawdust from which it was proposed to construct the landing strip, was then placed in position. Mountbatten fired again. As he had predicted, the Pykrete did not shatter. Instead, the bullet ricocheted off, narrowly missing Admiral Ernest J. King in the course of its passage.

The subsequent success of D-Day owed not a little to his planning and ingenuity, but by the time things came to fruition in Europe he had already moved on to become Supreme Commander in South-East Asia. His first task was the psychological one of putting the heart back into a beaten polyglot army of British, Indians, Gurkhas, South Africans, Chinese, Burmese, Australians, French and Dutch. The extent to which he succeeded is shown in the fact that, though he had to return most of his landing craft and munitions for the invasion of Europe and never did get the battle fleet he was promised, from the time of his arrival there were no more disastrous defeats. Indeed, at Arakan, in February, 1944, British and Indian divisions of the XV Corps finally destroyed the myth of Japanese invincibility.

Characteristically, Mountbatten's headquarters, first in a Maharajah's palace in Delhi and later in the botanical gardens at Kandy, were on the same lavish style as the old Brook Street mansion. Edwina travelled out from Britain to join him, playing her part in the turning tide by visiting dressing stations and medical centres, hospitals and convalescent homes. Their daughter, Patricia, now serving with the Women's Royal Naval Service, was also assigned to his headquarters. Following the recapture of Mandalay and Rangoon by the 14th Army, Mountbatten planned an amphibious attack on Singapore, but before this plan could be put into effect the war ended with an atom bomb on Hiroshima.

With the Japanese surrender aboard *USS Missouri*, Mountbatten transferred his headquarters to Singapore, almost a monarch in his own right with the responsibility for "ruling" 128 million people spread over $1\frac{1}{2}$ million square miles of South-East Asia. Edwina too played her part, helping with the repatriation of internees and prisoners-of-war, visiting internment camps and prison hospitals so energetically that she arrived in Sumatra even before the allied armies. On the suggestion of Clement Attlee, who had taken over from Churchill as Britain's prime minister, King George VI created Mountbatten a viscount – the following year he was made an earl – with the unusual provision that, since he had no son, the title could descend through the female line. He was also appointed to the Order of the Garter.

In 1946 the Mountbatten's elder daughter, Patricia, married Sir John Knatchbull, 7th Baron Brabourne, who she had first met when he was serving as one of her father's aides in South-East Asia, and later that year Attlee asked Mountbatten to go to India as that country's last Viceroy. It seemed an almost impossible task to wind up the Raj so that the British could pull out of India, a powder-keg mixture of 400 million people, Hindus and Moslems, Sikhs, Buddhists and Christians, without leaving a blood bath in their wake. Mountbatten looked upon it as "an insoluble problem" and was reluctant to go. But just as he had once encouraged George VI towards kingship, so the King now encouraged him. "You're the only man who can hope to pull it off," he told Mount-batten.

So Mountbatten went, accompanied by Edwina and their younger daughter, Pamela. Before going he also helped to smooth things in another direction, inviting editors of some of the leading national news-papers to have drinks with him in Chester Street. Almost casually, it seemed, he introduced his nephew who was handing round the drinks, thus helping to ensure a benevolent Press reception for the subsequent announcement of the nephew's betrothal to Princess Elizabeth.

With independence and partition, Nehru's Government invited him to become first Governor-General of the new India. He had hopes that Pakistan might extend a similar offer and that the twin role would enable him to exert a conciliatory influence. But Ali Jinnah took the role of Governor-General of Pakistan for himself. Nevertheless, Mount-batten accepted the Indian offer.

As he had foreseen, things did not go off peacefully. Sikhs slaught-ered Moslems and Moslems slaughtered Hindus. There were mass-acres, refugees, cholera. Mountbatten chaired the emergency committee set up to cope with all this while the seemingly indefatigable Edwina again flew thousands of miles to visit refugee camps and hospi-tals.

They returned to Britain in 1948 and Mountbatten resumed naval life as commander of the light cruiser *Newcastle*. With Edwina, he spent five of the next eight years in Malta. In 1952 he was appointed Mediter-ranean commander-in-chief and in 1953 he was promoted to admiral, made naval aide-de-camp to Queen Elizabeth II and appointed com-mander-in-chief of NATO forces in the Mediterranean. Back in Eng-land in 1955, Winston Churchill, in one of his last acts as prime minister, appointed him First Sea Lord – that self-same role his father, Prince Louis, had been forced to relinquish some forty years previously.

With the reorganization of Britain's Ministry of Defence in 1963–4, the post of First Sea Lord ceased to exist. But Mountbatten of Burma sailored on as Chief of Staff to the Minister (later Secretary of State) for Defence and chairman of the Chiefs of Staff Committee, a post he relin-quished in 1965.

But long before this tragedy had struck. In January, 1960, the Mountbattens' younger daughter, Pamela, was married to interior decorator David Hicks. Four days later Edwina, in a triple capacity which included being superintendent-in-chief of the St John Ambu-lance Brigade, set out on her annual tour of the Far East. She visited Cyprus, India, Malaya and Singapore on her way out and on February 18, 1960, arrived at Jesselton in North Borneo. She stayed at Govern-ment House, saw the sights and attended an official dinner. That was Friday. On the Saturday morning, feeling slightly unwell, she stayed in bed, but was up and about again to keep three official appointments in the afternoon and appear briefly at an evening reception.

In London, in the early hours of the morning, Mountbatten received the tragic, almost unbelievable, news that his energetic vivacious, seemingly indefatigable wife was dead.

EARL OF HAREWOOD

As small boys, the 7th Earl of Harewood and his brother, the Hon. Gerald Lascelles, would sometimes be taken along by their mother to 145 Piccadilly, home of the then Duke and Duchess of York, to have afternoon tea with the small cousins who grew up to be Queen Elizabeth II and Princess Margaret. Their mother, christened Victoria Alexandra Alice Mary, was the Princess Royal who died in 1965. Only daughter of the royal couple who were later to become King George V and Queen Mary, she was born on April 25 1897, some sixteen months after the brother destined to be George VI and nearly three years ahead of the late Duke of Gloucester.

In February, 1922, when she was twenty-four, she married Viscount Lascelles, heir to the Harewood earldom, a man fifteen years her senior. The present earl, christened George Henry Hubert Lascelles, was born on February 7, 1923, and his brother, Gerald David Lascelles, on August 21, 1924. Unlike their cousins born later, the children of the then Dukes of York, Gloucester and Kent, they were not born Royal Highnesses, their grandfather, George V, having ordained that the title of prince or princess should be borne only by the children of the Sovereign (himself) or the Sovereign's sons, not his daughters (*see* Succession). Nevertheless, at the time of their births, because their mother was the first of her generation to marry and have children, they were respectively sixth and seventh in the line of succession to the throne. The birth of Princess Elizabeth in 1926 was to change that, of course, and in the years which followed, as their uncles married and had children, as those children in turn had yet more children, they were to find themselves pushed further and further down the ladder of succession.

Their mother was created Princess Royal in 1932. During World War II she served as head of the Auxiliary Territorial Service as well as being president of both the Red Cross and the RAF Nursing Service. It was in her ATS capacity that she one day carried out an inspection visit to the centre where her niece, Princess Elizabeth, was training as a driver. "Now I know what happens when you and Papa go anywhere," Elizabeth told her mother when she got home that evening. "Spit and polish all day long."

The present (7th) earl served in the army during the war, was captured by the Germans in Italy in 1944 and held prisoner until the war ended. He succeeded to the earldom on the death of his father in 1947 and on September 29, 1949, married Maria Donata (Marion) Stein, daughter of the late Erwin Stein. A son David (Viscount Lascelles) was born on October 21, 1950, followed by James on October 5, 1953, and Robert on February 14, 1955. His brother had meantime married the actress Angela Dowding in 1952. They had a son, Henry Ulick, on May 19, 1953, and were divorced in 1978.

The earl himself was divorced in 1967. The divorce of neither brother directly involved the Queen. George III, in pushing the Royal Marriage Act through Parliament (*see* Marriage), had not felt it necessary to insist that his heirs and successors should also require royal consent to their divorces. But when, following his divorce, the earl, now down to eighteenth in the line of succession, wanted to marry Mrs Patricia Tuckwell, the former secretary and divorced Australian by whom he had had a son in 1964, then the Queen found herself having to negotiate a delicately poised royal tightrope. As head of the Church of England, she could hardly condone her cousin's divorce by consenting to his re-marriage. If she withheld consent on the other hand, Harewood, being over the age of twenty-five, could appeal to the Privy Council with all the publicity that that would involve. The dilemma was resolved by Prime Minister Harold Wilson who, after bringing the matter up in Cabinet, was able to "advise" the Queen to consent to the marriage, thus making her decision "political" rather than religious. Consent given, the earl married Mrs Tuckwell on July 31, 1967, while his ex-wife subsequently (March 14, 1973) married Jeremy Thorpe, former leader of the Liberal Party.

FAMILY TREE

For the family tree of the Royal Family from Queen Victoria to the present see pages 70–71

FLYING

During her 1977 Silver Jubilee tour of Australia, New Zealand and Papua, New Guinea, Queen Elizabeth II flew a total not far short of 31,000 miles. In the course of that tour she made forty-six separate flights in eight different types of aircraft operated by ten airlines. It has become commonplace these days for her to fly anywhere and everywhere without Government ministers turning a hair, which is very different from what happened in 1951 when, as a princess, she was due to visit Canada as deputy for her sick father. She had planned to go by sea, but at the last moment her father's health took a turn for the worse and departure had to be postponed. It was Prince Philip who suggested that they could still make Canada on time if they flew the Atlantic. The idea almost caused heart failure in Government circles, but Philip pushed it and, finally and reluctantly, Prime Minister Clement Attlee agreed. The trip, in those pre-jet days, took seventeen hours.

These days, for flights out of Britain, the Queen usually travels in a specially adapted British Airways jet-liner, the first thirty rows of seats being removed to provide a small dining-room seating eight and a cosy sitting-room with divans which turn into beds at night. Her royal cypher is on the cutlery, decanters and silver salvers. There are also two pint-sized dressing-rooms, one for her, the other for her husband, each with its own six-foot wardrobe. Members of her entourage, perhaps as many as forty (*see* Travels), are accommodated further back.

For internal trips she has her own Queen's Flight which consists these days of three Andovers, a *de luxe* version of the Hawker Siddeley

748 twin turbo-prop airliner, each normally able to accommodate 12–16 people (though the layout can be varied to take up to 32 people at a push) in addition to the crew, as well as two Westland helicopters. However, the Queen does not normally fly by helicopter, although an exception was made in the case of her Silver Jubilee visit to Northern Ireland, the risk involved in a helicopter flight being considered less than that of an IRA bomb or bullet on the ground.

The Queen's Flight is based at RAF Benson in Oxfordshire, where it has its own hangar, stores, workshops and offices. Its cost, including paying the officers and men (who number approximately twenty-four) who operate it, is a charge on the Defence Budget. In 1978 this was £1,800,000, a figure justified, said the Defence Under-Secretary, by the Flight's potential role in communications. It should also be borne in mind that the Queen and her family are not the only ones who use the Flight. Aircraft are frequently loaned to Government ministers and something like forty per cent of the cost can be attributed to ministerial and other non-royal flights.

The foundation of what is now the Queen's Flight was one of the few achievements of the Duke of Windsor during his brief reign as Edward VIII. In his day it consisted of only two aircraft and was known, of course, as the King's Flight. He himself was keen on flying from an early age. He learned to fly in the 1920s and made his first solo flight in 1929. By that time, as Prince of Wales, he already had a dual-control Bristol Fighter maintained for his personal use by the RAF's No. 24 (Communications) Squadron at Northolt. He was soon flying here, there and everywhere, much as the Queen does today. In 1930 he flew from Malakal to Khartoum and on – by short hops in those days – to Cairo; from Marseilles to Lyons to Le Bourget, then across the Channel to a touch-down in Windsor Great Park. The following year, in company with his brother, the Duke of Kent, he did a large part of his South American tour by air, flying from Lima to Arequipa (approximately 500 miles), from Antofagasta to Santiago (700 miles), from Santiago to Valparaiso.

He owned, in turn, two De Havilland Moths, four Puss Moths, a Vickers Viastra, a De Havilland Dragon and two Dragon Rapides. He took his own Puss Moth with him on that 1931 South American tour and in 1934 arrived at the Hendon RAF display in the Vickers Viastra. On the death of his father in 1936, as King Edward VIII, he became the first British monarch to fly when he flew from Norfolk to London to attend his Accession Council.

Shortly after, for the sake of personal economy, he prevailed upon the Air Ministry to take over the upkeep of his two Rapides and to pay his pilot and mechanics. So the King's Flight came into being on July 20, 1936, with the King's personal pilot, Flight Lieutenant Fielden (later

FAMILY TREE

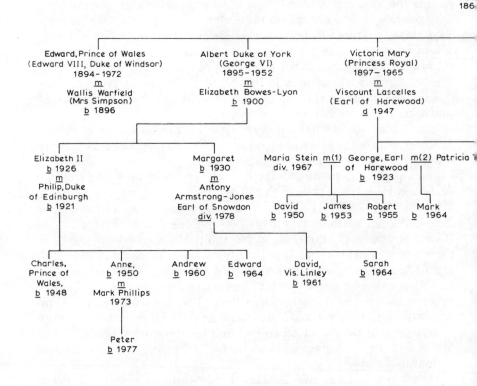

Albert (Edwc
1841-191

Ge
186

Edward, Prince of Wales
(Edward VIII, Duke of Windsor)
1894-1972
m
Wallis Warfield
(Mrs Simpson)
b 1896

Albert Duke of York
(George VI)
1895-1952
m
Elizabeth Bowes-Lyon
b 1900

Victoria Mary
(Princess Royal)
1897-1965
m
Viscount Lascelles
(Earl of Harewood)
d 1947

Elizabeth II
b 1926
m
Philip, Duke
of Edinburgh
b 1921

Margaret
b 1930
m
Antony
Armstrong-Jones
Earl of Snowdon
div. 1978

Maria Stein m(1) George, Earl m(2) Patricia
div. 1967   of Harewood
                 b 1923

David   James   Robert   Mark
b 1950   b 1953   b 1955   b 1964

Charles,
Prince of
Wales,
b 1948

Anne,
b 1950
m
Mark Phillips
1973

Andrew
b 1960

Edward
b 1964

David,
Vis. Linley
b 1961

Sarah
b 1964

Peter
b 1977

Air Vice Marshal Sir Edward Fielden) as captain.

With World War II, the Flight became the nucleus of No. 161 Squadron, based at Tempsford and engaged in flying agents and supplies to resistance groups in various European countries. The war and its after-

e Albert of Saxe-Coburg & Gotha
1819-1861

cess Alexandra of Denmark
1844-1925

ess Victoria Mary of Teck (Queen Mary)
1867-1953

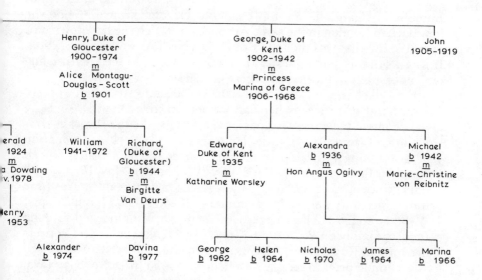

math saw flying become more and more an integral part of royal life. King George VI, the Queen's father, who had also learned to fly in the 1920s at what was then known as the Government Aerodrome, Waddon, flew to Tunisia to visit British troops in North Africa. His brother, the Duke of Kent, flew the Atlantic to visit air crews training in Canada and factories in the United States, and was later killed in an air crash when setting off to visit troops in Iceland. In Australia, as Governor-General immediately after the war, the late Duke of Glouces-ter found flying a necessity in order to cover the vast distances involved.

With the end of the war, George VI decided to reconstitute the King's Flight and ordered four Vickers Vikings, one fitted out as a flying work-shop. These were extensively used during the 1947 tour of South Africa. The Flight, in those days, also included a Hoverfly helicopter and a fifth Viking was added later.

Elizabeth II began her reign with a flight from Nanyuki in Kenya to Entebbe in Uganda in an unpressurized Dakota. From Entebbe she flew back to London in the same Argonaut in which she had flown out, operated by what was then the British Overseas Airways Corporation. It was a suitably symbolic start to a reign which has seen her use air-craft as casually as the first Elizabeth once used coach and horses.

If the Queen is, almost certainly, the world's most travelled woman, her husband still exceeds her handsomely in miles flown. Nor is he always content to be merely a passenger, but likes to take over the con-trols himself from time to time. He learned to fly back in coronation year, graduating from Chipmunks to Harvards and then to an Airspeed Oxford. He first went solo at RAF White Waltham in May, 1953.

The Prince of Wales learned to fly at RAF Oakington during his time at university and went solo in January, 1969. From March–August 1971 he attended RAF College, Cranwell, where he trained to wing standard, mainly on Provost jets. In 1974 he took a helicopter conver-sion course at Royal Naval Air Station Yeovilton followed by advanced flying training prior to serving as a helicopter pilot with No. 845 Naval Air Squadron aboard the commando ship *Hermes*. The biggest danger, he joked, was that he might end up with haemorrhoids.

FURNITURE AND *OBJETS D'ART*

The Queen has what is, almost certainly, the finest collection of Geor-gian furniture anywhere in the world. That she does so is due in no small measure to the good taste of the much-misunderstood George III and the magpie instincts of the son who succeeded him as George IV. To a very large extent, both Buckingham Palace and Windsor Castle are furnished with items made for or bought by the two Georges.

George III, when he first bought Buckingham Palace – then less splendidly known as Buckingham House – in 1861, had furniture made for it by those two outstanding cabinet-makers of the day, Thomas Chippendale and William Vile. As a result, there are still today over one hundred Chippendale chairs in Buckingham Palace alone. George III was also as enthusiastic a collector of clocks as George V was later to be of stamps (*see* Stamps), and many of the clocks which still keep time in the various royal homes date from his day, among them an astronomical clock, amazing even by present-day standards, which not only tells the time at various longitudinal points on the earth's surface, but gives the phases of the moon, the position of sun and stars, the movement of the planets and the tide at no fewer than forty-three different places.

But it was the extravagantly high-living George IV who really started collecting things on a truly royal scale. He was like a magpie, snapping up anything and everything . . . furniture, paintings (*see* Picture Collection), armour, bronzes, statuary, Sèvres porcelain, Gobelin tapestries, Aubusson carpets. His collection of swords and fire-arms, kept at Windsor, is the finest in existence. He even collected theatrical prints – he had 116 prints of David Garrick alone – while his collection of wild animals, kept in those days at Windsor, was to form the foundation of London's Zoological Gardens.

He was particularly enamoured of anything French and had dreams of turning Windsor into an English-style Versailles. He collected Napoleonic relics; swords, medals, batons. He amassed a corresponding collection of busts and bronzes of Louis XIV and his marshals. When the French Revolution caused the aristocrats of France to sell off their treasured possessions, he was quick to nip in. He bought voraciously, spending sometimes at the rate of £1,000 a week on furniture alone. As a result, he was at one time something like £640,000 in debt, but his collection of French art was by then the finest outside France itself while the collection of eighteenth-century French furniture which he brought together is acknowledged as the finest in the world.

William IV, when he succeeded his brother on the throne, added yet more porcelain, Rockingham, Worcester and Davenport, to the royal collection. Or, more probably, his wife, Queen Adelaide, did. William himself was hardly a man with that much good taste. Certainly it was another Queen – Alexandra, wife of Edward VII – who brought together the royal collection of Fabergé, objets d'art in gold, silver and precious stones delicately worked by Peter Carl Fabergé, the famous goldsmith and jeweller of St Petersburg (now Leningrad).

It was through her sister, by turn Crown Princess, Tsarina and Dowager Tsarina of Imperial Russia, that Alexandra first came to know of Fabergé's work. His miniature animals especially delighted her, and friends and relatives began giving them to her as birthday gifts, a tiny dormouse with gold whiskers and diamond eyes, elephants in rock crystal and jade, a mouse, a bear, even an ant-eater, toucans and parrots, cockatoos and flamingos, dogs of different breeds, poodle and bulldog, collie and dachshund. The King caught something of his wife's enthusiasm and in 1907 he had Fabergé model his farm animals at Sandringham, pigs, hens, ducks, shire horses and his prize shorthorn bull. He also commissioned models of his great Derby winner Persimmon, his favourite dog, Caesar, and his wife's pet pekinese. By the time all was done there were some three hundred pieces in the collection.

It is kept today in the main drawing-room at Sandringham and includes vases of flowers and fruit, photograph frames, paper knives and cigarette boxes as well as miniature animals. Particularly poignant are two of the famous Easter Eggs which Fabergé used to make for the Russian royal family. One is the egg which the Tsar gave to the Tsarina in 1905; the other he gave to her at Easter, 1914. Inside it is a cameo on which are carved miniatures of their five children who were to die so brutally in the cellar at Ekaterinburg only four short years later.

Queen Mary, like George IV, was another magpie collector, if on a much less extravagant scale. She collected snuff-boxes, tea-caddies, jade, Battersea enamel, porcelain, furniture. She was a particular admirer of William Vile who she considered every bit as good as Chippendale. If she could be said to have specialized in anything, it was items of personal or historical interest to the Royal Family such as a cedar-wood tea-caddy bearing portrait medallions of George III and Queen Charlotte, or a Georgian snuff-box bearing a medallion of the Prince Regent. She patronized the elegant dealers in Bond Street, but was even happier when she could rummage around small back-street antique shops elsewhere in London or near Sandringham. On the odd occasion that she came across a real "find" – like an old print of William IV's niece, Princess Charlotte, which she found in the store cellars of a shop in Pont Street – she was highly delighted.

More than anyone since the days of George IV, it was she who brought back a sense of order to the royal collection of furniture and *objets d'art* at Buckingham Palace. She scoured antique shops in search of items which had been pilfered and sold over the years, hunted through lumber rooms and old chests at the palace, nearby St James's Palace, Windsor Castle and elsewhere in search of discarded treasures. She tracked down one of a pair of throne-like gilt chairs made originally for George IV to Kensington Palace and reunited it with its companion piece. Both chairs are now in the Throne Room at Buckingham Palace.

On another occasion, a painting by Zoffany of George III and his family aroused her detective instinct. There was a pedestal clock in the painting which she had never seen. Again she began to search through lumber rooms and cellars. Finally, in one of the cellars at Windsor, she found the long-lost clock and, along with it, a load of other discarded, forgotten, immensely valuable furniture. That pedestal clock, restored to working order, now ticks away the hours in the corridor outside the Queen's private apartment.

GARDEN PARTIES

Each summer the Queen gives a number of garden parties, on average three at Buckingham Palace in London and one at Holyroodhouse in Edinburgh. Now firmly part of the royal tradition, garden parties were first introduced by Queen Victoria. As a new young Queen, very different from the black-clad matriarch she became later, Victoria was delighted with the idea of entertaining her subjects *al fresco*, though she did not actually call such gatherings "garden parties". She called them "breakfasts".

The idea lapsed somewhat in the reign of her son, Edward VII. He preferred to entertain of an evening rather than during the day. The idea of daytime gatherings was revived by King George V and Queen Mary and turned, gradually, into the sort of garden party the palace lawns know today. The Queen's parents continued the idea, entertaining between six and seven thousand people at a time. The present Queen has widened the invitation list still further, inviting as many as nine thousand guests to each garden party.

In theory, anyone can apply to the Lord Chamberlain's office at St James's Palace for an invitation to a royal garden party. In practice, the bulk of such invitations usually go to people prominent in their locality, mayors and councillors, those engaged voluntarily in charitable or social work, doctors and nurses, scientists, professors and clergymen, including people in the Commonwealth if it is known that they will be in London at the time and even to the occasional foreigner, either resident in or visiting Britain. For instance, in 1978 a block of twelve tickets was issued to the South Yorkshire Council. However, a number of them went unused because Socialist councillors to whom they were offered said they would go only if their travel expenses were reimbursed and attendance at the garden party was regarded as a council duty for which they would be "paid".

Most people regard an invitation to a royal garden party, in the words of another councillor, as "an honour and a privilege". They cheerfully pay their own expenses for the thrill of entering Buckingham Palace by way of the Grand Hall and passing through the elegant Bow Room into the 39-acre gardens at the rear. By the time they are all gathered together the palace lawns are almost hidden from view by a mass of morning suits and military uniforms, gaily coloured dresses and the occasional sari or national costume of overseas guests. Two bands from the Guards Division play alternately and around four o'clock in the afternoon one of them will strike up the National Anthem as a signal that the Queen and others of the Royal Family are about to appear on the scene. Guests who are not out of the Bow Room by that time will find themselves temporarily locked in until this small ceremonial part of the proceedings is over. The playing of the National Anthem, incidentally, is also a signal to the caterers that they can start serving tea – Indian, served in thin china cups together with a selection of cucumber sandwiches, bridge rolls, chocolate cake and ice-cream.

The Queen herself has usually scanned the invitation lists in advance and indicated to her aides those guests she would like picked out and presented to her. While she heads in one direction through a more or less spontaneously-formed lane in the crowd, pausing here and there to chat briefly, others of the Royal Family carve their own lanes and do their own chatting. It was at a royal garden party, incidentally, the day following the announcement of his betrothal to the then Princess Elizabeth, that Philip underwent his baptism of fire in public life, looking far from relaxed as he squired his bride-to-be among the crowds of guests.

Eventually all members of the family meet up again under the scarlet and gold canopy of the royal pavilion (a hangover from the colourful Delhi Durbar staged in India by the Queen's grandfather) where they too sip tea and perhaps nibble a cucumber sandwich. More guests are presented to them from time to time until, over the course of some two hours, the Queen will have met, however briefly, between one and two hundred of her nine thousand guests. Around six o'clock the National Anthem is played again, this time as a signal that the Royals are withdrawing to the palace and also as a gentle hint to those invited that it is time they were thinking of going home.

GATCOMBE PARK

Exactly how much the Queen paid for Gatcombe Park, the 730-acre estate and country mansion near Minchinhampton in Gloucestershire which she bought as a *pied-à-terre* for her daughter and son-in-law, Princess Anne and Captain Mark Phillips, in the summer of 1976, is a royal family secret. Newpaper estimates at the time ranged from £300,000 to £750,000, with further guesses of between £250,000 and £500,000 for the adjoining 500-acre farm which was added to the estate a year later. Whatever it was, it was too much, according to anti-royalist parliamentary left-wingers. "An appalling, almost obscene, flaunting of wealth," one shrilled, indignantly.

An eighteenth-century country mansion built in Bath stone, with five main bedrooms, four reception rooms as well as a library, billiards room and magnificent conservatory, staff accommodation, a stable block, farm buildings and cottages, Gatcombe Park was formerly owned by Lord Butler, Master of Trinity College, Cambridge, and a former Home Secretary, who inherited it from his father-in-law, Samuel Courtauld. In addition to a farm of some 530 acres, the original estate also includes 200 acres of woodland and a trout lake. For the Princess and her husband, it is conveniently located . . . not far from where Mark's parents live at Great Somerford, in the middle of the Beaufort Hunt country, and within easy reach of the horse trials at Badminton and Amberley. Predictably, with their love of horses, a planning application to enable them to build further loose boxes was among the couple's first moves when they took possession of their new home.

GOVERNORS-GENERAL

Even a jet-age monarch like Elizabeth II cannot be in two places at the same time and, though she pays frequent visits to Commonwealth countries, custom still requires the bulk of her time to be spent in Britain. So she has Governors-General to deputize for her in countries such as Australia and Canada, New Zealand and the Bahamas of which she is also head of state (*see* Monarchy).

The Governor-General of a country is the Queen's personal representative in that country. He does not represent whatever government happens to be in power in Britain. This was made clear by the 1926 Imperial Conference which laid down that a Governor-General was the "representative of the Crown, holding in all essential respects the same position in relation to the administration of public affairs in the dominion as is held by His Majesty the King (the Queen's grandfather was on the throne at the time) in Great Britain" and "not the representative or agent of His Majesty's Government in Great Britain or of any department of that government."

Until comparatively recent times it was the custom to despatch junior members of the Royal Family and other eminent Britons to Commonwealth countries to serve the monarch in this capacity. But these days the Governor-General is appointed by the Queen on the recommendation of the prime minister of the country concerned and is usually a national of that country, as Sir John Kerr was appointed

Governor-General of Australia in 1974 on the recommendation of Gough Whitlam.

It was a recommendation Whitlam was bitterly to regret some sixteen months later. Intervening to break the political deadlock which had arisen between the Labour-controlled Lower House of the Australian Parliament and the Senate, Kerr resorted to the use of the royal prerogative. In his capacity as the monarch's personal representative in Australia, he issued a "royal" proclamation dismissing Whitlam from his post of prime minister. The Queen herself, it should be stressed, was not involved in this, nor indeed even consulted. Kerr acted on his own initiative as the monarch's personal representative, as he was entitled to do. And when the Lower House of Australia's Parliament refused to accept a Liberal substitute, Malcolm Fraser, as caretaker prime minister in Whitlam's place, Kerr went the whole hog and dissolved Parliament, thus precipitating the general election which vindicated his actions by returning Fraser to power.

FURNITURE AND *OBJETS D'ART*. *Above left*: George IV, from the picture by Sir Thomas Lawrence in the Waterloo Gallery, Windsor Castle. Known as "the first Gentleman of Europe", he was one of the most extravagant collectors of furniture and paintings. GARDEN PARTIES. *Above right*: The Queen chats to her guests at one of her garden parties in 1962. GATCOMBE PARK. *Below*: Gatcombe Park, the eighteenth-century mansion bought for Princess Anne and Captain Mark Phillips by the Queen in 1976.

HAEMOPHILIA. *Above left*: The youngest of Queen Victoria's four sons, Leopold, Duke of Albany, was a haemophilic. He died, a victim of this 'bleeding disease', in 1884 at the age of thirty-one. HOLYROODHOUSE. *Above right*: The Palace of Holyroodhouse, Edinburgh, is the Queen's official residence in Scotland.
HONOURS AND INVESTITURES. *Below*: The Queen confers a knighthood on Mr Henry Kelliher of Auckland, New Zealand, at a public investiture in Wellington, 1963.

KING EDWARD VII AND QUEEN ALEXANDRA. *Above left*: Queen Alexandra with her children. (*Left to right*) Princess Louise, Princess Maud (later Queen of Norway), the Duke of Clarence and the future King George V. Seated is Princess Victoria. *Above right*: King Edward VII.

KING GEORGE V AND QUEEN MARY. Leaving St Margaret's Church with Queen Alexandra (*centre*) after the wedding of Lord Louis Mountbatten to Miss Edwina Ashley, July 1922.

KING GEORGE VI. Pictured here
with his consort Queen Elizabeth and
his daughters, Princess Elizabeth
(tallest) and Princess Margaret, after
his Coronation in 1937.

KING GEORGE VI. With Queen
Elizabeth and Princess Margaret at
London Airport to say farewell to
Princess Elizabeth and Prince Philip at
the start of their Commonwealth Tour
in 1952.

LINEAGE. *Above left*: Ethelred II
(The Unready) born *c.* 968. (Coin
enlarged x 2.) *Right*: The effigy of
Henry IV in Canterbury Cathedral.
Below left: Henry V – the warrior king
who won the great victory over the
French at Agincourt. *Below right*:
Edward VI, from the picture by
Holbein. The only son of Henry VIII,
he succeeded his father on the throne at
the age of nine, but died aged 16 and
was buried at Westminster.

MAUNDY. The distribution of His Majesty's Maundy, by the sub-almoner in the Chapel Royal at Whitehall, as represented in this drawing by S. H. Grimm, dated 1773.

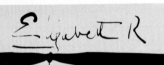

I solemnly promise and swear to govern the Peoples of the United Kingdom of Great Britain and Northern Ireland, Canada, Australia, New Zealand and the Union of South Africa, Pakistan and Ceylon, and of my Possessions and the other Territories to any of them belonging or pertaining, according to their respective laws and customs.

I will to my power cause Law and Justice, in Mercy, to be executed in all my judgements.

I will to the utmost of my power maintain the Laws of God and the true profession of the Gospel. I will to the utmost of my power maintain in the United Kingdom the Protestant Reformed Religion established by law. And I will maintain and preserve inviolably the settlement of the Church of England, and the doctrine, worship, discipline, and government thereof, as by law established in England. And I will preserve unto the Bishops and Clergy of England, and to the Churches there committed to their charge, all such rights and privileges as by law do or shall appertain to them or any of them.

The things which I have here before promised, I will perform and keep.

So help me God.

MONARCHY. The Oath signed by H.M. Queen Elizabeth II at Her Coronation on 2nd June, 1953.

OPENING OF PARLIAMENT. The Queen opens the new session of Parliament, November 1976. ORDER OF THE GARTER. The Queen Mother and Prince Charles on their way to St George's Chapel for the service of The Most Noble Order of the Garter, June 1978.

ORDER OF THE GARTER. The choir and chancel of St George's Chapel, Windsor Castle, in the centre of which Henry VIII, Jane Seymour, Charles I and a child of Queen Anne are buried. It was during Edward IV's reign that work began on the Chapel, a magnificent building that is steeped in royal history. The annual ceremony of dedication of The Most Noble Order of the Garter, founded by King Edward III in 1348, is held here; the banners of the Knights of the Garter can be seen hanging above their intricately carved stalls.

H

HAEMOPHILIA

"This disease is not in our family," a horrified Queen Victoria protested when she was told that the youngest of her four sons, Leopold, Duke of Albany, born in 1853, had haemophilia.

Wherever it came from, subsequent history leaves no doubt that Victoria herself was a carrier of this rather rare disease which results in excessive bleeding from quite trivial injuries and a prolonged coagulation period. Not only do slight cuts bleed profusely, but bumps and bruises can cause internal haemorrhaging into the joints and cavities of the body, as was the case with Leopold in boyhood. At the wedding of his elder brother, the Prince of Wales, when he was ten, he was nipped on the leg by the four-year-old visiting relative from Germany who grew up to become the Kaiser. His mother was immediately frantic with worry in case that playful nip should have set off "the bleeding disease".

A later boyhood mishap, which would have been trivial to any normal youngster, left Leopold lame in one knee. Another resulted in the loss of so much blood that he was reduced to a state of "extreme and dangerous exhaustion".

In all other respects Leopold grew up an extremely normal young man, as witness his subsequent infatuation for Lillie Langtry. He bought a drawing of her by the artist Frank Miles and hung it over his bed. That was before his brother, the Prince of Wales, made her his mistress.

Nevertheless, as a haemophilic, it seemed very unlikely that Leopold would ever find a girl willing to marry him. But he did. In 1882, when he was twenty-nine, he married Princess Helen of Waldeck Pyrmont and they had a daughter (*see* Princess Alice, Countess of Athlone). Then in March 1884, after only two years of marriage, Leopold sustained yet another relatively minor injury. In twenty-four hours he was dead from haemorrhage of the brain.

Though Leopold was the only one of Queen Victoria's sons to suffer from haemophilia, her daughters transmitted it to the royal houses of Europe. Even before Leopold's death, the three-year-old son of his sister Alice (she married Louis IV, Grand Duke of Hesse) had died from it following a fall from a window. It was a severe enough fall, but no bones were broken and a normal child would have survived. But three-year-old Frederick, like his uncle Leopold, died within hours from haemorrhage of the brain.

From Alice, through her daughter Irene, the disease was passed to two of the four sons of Prince Henry of Prussia. One of them, named Henry after his father, died of it at the age of four, though the other son, Waldemar, survived to the age of fifty-six. Through another daughter, Alexandra, who married the Emperor Nicholas II of Russia, it was transmitted to their only son, the Tsarevich Alexis, who suffered many sometimes agonizing haemorrhages before he was murdered, along with the rest of the family, at Ekaterinburg in 1918.

Alice's eldest sister, Princess Victoria, married the German prince who became Emperor Frederick III. Their eldest son, the Kaiser who nipped Leopold's leg in childhood, escaped the disease (though he was born with a malformed arm), but a young son, also named Waldemar, may have suffered from it. It is impossible to be certain because of the secrecy which surrounded his illness, but he died in 1879 at the age of eleven.

However, the youngest of Queen Victoria's daughters, Beatrice, like her sister Alice, certainly passed on the disease to those who came after, transmitting it through her daughter, Victoria Eugénie, to the Spanish royal family. As a result, two of the three sons of Alfonso XIII died from haemorrhage, coincidentally after both were involved in road accidents, Prince Gonzalo in 1934 and Crown Prince Alfonso in 1938.

Alfonso and Gonzalo, like Alexis of Russia and Henry of Prussia, were all in the third generation of Queen Victoria's descendants. In the generations since there has been no sign of the disease, which would seem to have disappeared as mysteriously as it erupted.

HEIGHTS

Prince Andrew is the tallest of the Royal Family, though Prince Charles and their father, Prince Philip, run him close. Andrew is 6 feet, Philip 5 feet 11½ inches and Charles 5 feet 11 inches.

Princess Anne, at 5 feet 6½ inches, is somewhat taller than her mother, the Queen. The Queen is 5 feet 4 inches, though high heels usually afford her some slight additional height on public occasions. Both the Queen Mother and Princess Margaret are 5 feet 2 inches.

HEIR APPARENT/HEIR PRESUMPTIVE

In the matter of succession to the throne(*see* Succession), there is no question of equal opportunity for women. The old law of primogeniture still applies and males of the same parentage take precedence. So Prince Charles, as the first-born son, became Heir Apparent to the throne on his mother's accession as Queen Elizabeth II.

By the same token, his mother was never Heir Apparent; always Heir Presumptive. "Presumptive" because, as the eldest daughter of King George VI, she could – in theory, at least – have been ousted at any time from her place in the line of succession by the birth of a son to her parents, as Princess Anne dropped from her original second place to third and then fourth following the birth of her two younger brothers, Prince Andrew and Prince Edward.

The same thing applies where the next in line is the monarch's brother, as was the case during the brief reign of Edward VIII. The Duke of York, who was to ascend the throne as George VI following the abdication, was never more than Heir Presumptive because of the possibility that Edward VIII, while he was still King, might yet marry and have children.

In the absence of a male heir, however, daughters do not have an equal claim to succeed to the throne, though there were some who thought they did when George VI, a man with two young daughters, became King. But the matter was put beyond doubt by a question and answer session in Parliament.

Replying to a question on the point, the Home Secretary said, "His Majesty's Government is advised that there is no doubt that in present circumstances Her Royal Highness The Princess Elizabeth would succeed to the throne as sole heir." And, of course, she did.

HOLYROODHOUSE

The Palace of Holyroodhouse in Edinburgh – the Queen's official residence in Scotland (Balmoral is her private property) – stands on the site of an abbey guest-house once used as lodgings by the kings of Scotland. It was James IV of Scotland, when he married Henry VII's daughter, Margaret, who first began building a palace on the site, around the end of the fifteenth century. James V carried on the work, but it was with his daughter, the ill-fated Mary Queen of Scots, that Holyroodhouse first came into its own as a royal palace. And it is with her tragic name that it will always be associated.

It was in Holyroodhouse that Mary argued religion with the dogmatic John Knox. It was there that her Italian favourite, David Rizzio, was dragged from her pregnant presence, flung down the steps and hacked to death.

Mary's son, James VI, continued to hold court there until he rode south in 1603 to become James I of England as well. Except for King James IV's Tower, which contains the historic rooms in which much of the drama of Mary Queen of Scots ran its grim course, the original palace was largely destroyed by fire during its Civil War occupation by Cromwellian troops.

The present palace was begun in 1671 by Charles II, but money ran out and for two and a half centuries it remained unfinished. Nevertheless, the Young Pretender, Bonnie Prince Charlie, danced the night away in the long picture gallery during his 1745 attempt to seize the crown, and George IV became the first English monarch (if you ignore his Hanoverian descent) to wear the kilt, his legs modestly hidden in flesh-coloured tights, when he held court there in 1822.

It was King George V, with the enthusiastic support of Queen Mary, who completed the building of the palace, though even before that Queen Victoria had begun the present custom of staying at Holyrood-house for a few days each year on her way to or from Balmoral. Elizabeth II has continued the custom, making her visits the occasion of an investiture for her Scottish subjects, a garden party (with tubs of outsize thistles to greet the arriving guests) and perhaps a banquet with pipers marching and skirling round the banquet table in the Long Gallery.

HONOURS AND INVESTITURES

Queen Elizabeth II, it is said, has occasionally raised an enquiring and mildly surprised eyebrow at some of the names tendered to her for knighthoods in the recent past. Nevertheless, because the royal prerogative is no longer what it once was, the honours have been bestowed.

The award of honours was once the exclusive prerogative of the monarch. It was William the Conqueror who introduced the system to Britain. In his day, a knight was someone whose holding of land was conditional on performing military service for the king, and for centuries after him the honours system remained a way of bribing people to support the monarch and rewarding those who did. Charles I even sold honours outright for cash as a way of raising money without turning to Parliament, while James I conceived the idea of hereditary baronetcies as a means of raising both money and men for the defence of Ireland as well as to establish a series of plantations on the confiscated Irish lands of the earls of Tyrone and Tyrconnel. But the delightful story that the word "sirloin" derives from the fact that James was so delighted with a loin of beef set before him that he drew his sword and knighted it on the spot is, we fear, untrue. The same act is also credited to both Henry

VIII and Charles II, but the word in fact comes from *sur-loin* simply meaning "the part above the loin".

As power passed more and more into the hands of Parliament, so the award of honours, instead of being vested solely in the monarch of the day, became more and more the prerogative of the prime minister. Instead of being used to raise money or men for the monarch, they were – and are – used as a reward for political services or a way of securing extra votes in the House of Lords. David Lloyd George, in particular, brought the whole business into extremely bad odour during his 1916–22 premiership by ladling out a staggering 25,000 Orders of the British Empire following the institution of that award in 1917.

Some of these King George V approved only with considerable reluctance, and it was because of the King's protests at being obliged to confer honours on people he thought did not deserve them that names put forward to be honoured for political services are today vetted by the Political Honours Scrutiny Committee. This committee consists of members of the Privy Council (*see* Privy Council) who are not also members of the Government. Despite such scrutiny, the occasional undeserved award still seems to slip through the net.

Of the many Orders of Chivalry instituted over the centuries of British history, several – among them the Most Exalted Order of the Star of India, the Most Eminent Order of the Indian Empire and the Imperial Order of the Crown of India, all founded by Queen Victoria – are today virtually obsolete, no awards having been made since 1947. Of the rest, far and away the most important – indeed, the oldest and most illustrious honour in Europe – is the Most Noble Order of the Garter (*see* Order of the Garter). The others are:

The Most Ancient Order of the Thistle. This Scottish order was founded in 1687, fell into disuse with the abdication of James II, and was later revived by Queen Anne. By a statute of 1827 it consists today of the Sovereign and sixteen knights.

The Most Honourable Order of the Bath. Traditionally thought to have been founded by Henry IV in 1399 and revived by George I in 1725.

The Most Distinguished Order of St Michael and St George. Founded by William IV in 1818.

The Order of Merit. Strictly speaking, not a knighthood. It was instituted in 1902 as a way of rewarding those who had distinguished themselves in art, literature, science or the public service without actually conferring a knighthood upon them. Membership is limited to twenty-four with the addition of foreigners who can be made honorary members.

The Royal Victorian Order. Founded by Queen Victoria in 1896 and conferred today as "a reward for personal services" to the monarch.

The Most Excellent Order of the British Empire. Instituted in 1917, it is awarded to men and women who have rendered service to the Empire and includes both military and civil divisions. It is divided into five classes: Knight or Dame Grand Cross (GBE), Knight or Dame Commander (KBE or DBE), Commander (CBE), Officer (OBE) and Member (MBE).

Of all these, four – the Garter, the Thistle, the Order of Merit and the Royal Victorian Order – are in the personal prerogative of the monarch. The remainder, including the Order of the British Empire, are in the hands of the prime minister. They may be his (or her) own nominees or channelled through from the armed services or other Government departments such as the Foreign Office. Honours conferred upon citizens of Commonwealth countries are similarly the prerogative of the country concerned.

Usually, two lists of honours are published each year. One is the New Year's Honours List; the other is the Birthday Honours List, which is put out in June to mark the monarch's official – as distinct from actual – birthday. In addition, the dissolution of Parliament usually results in a small extra list of awards to those who have found favour with the retiring prime minister.

The actual knighthoods or decorations are usually conferred by the Queen at a series of investitures held at Buckingham Palace in February and March for those named in the New Year's list and in July and November for those in the Birthday list. But not always. The Queen, if she is so minded, can knight someone in private audience or anywhere else for that matter, as she knighted Sir Francis Chichester at Greenwich in 1967 following his round-the-world voyage, with his ketch *Gipsy Moth* in the background.

On average, the Queen usually holds fourteen investitures a year at Buckingham Palace (or at the Palace of Holyroodhouse in Edinburgh for Scottish awards) during the course of which she confers about 2,000 knighthoods and decorations. Investitures at Buckingham Palace are usually held in the ballroom because it is the largest of the state rooms, sufficiently large to permit each recipient to bring two guests in accordance with a custom introduced by George V during World War I.

Gilt chairs are set out for the benefit of these guests, and a string orchestra from the Guards Division dispenses soothing music from the balcony. Up to 200 proud recipients will be honoured at an investiture, which lasts usually around 75 minutes. Each person being honoured files past the Queen in turn, either standing while she fastens the appropriate decoration to a small hook attached previously to the recipient's clothing or, if a knighthood is being conferred, kneeling on a small stool while the Queen applies a light touch to each shoulder with a Scots Guard sword inherited from her late father.

HOUSEHOLD

What is known as the Queen's Household has comparatively little to do with the domestic management of royal homes. Indeed, with the exception of the palace steward and the chief housekeeper, the names of royal servants figure hardly at all in the list. Pages, footmen, maids and chauffeurs are conspicuous only by their absence. They are members of "the staff" – which is not at all the same as the Household.

So what is the Queen's Household? Like many other departments of royal life, it is a hand-me-down from the days when monarchs ruled instead of merely reigning. To this end they surrounded themselves with their own trusty cohorts. And because it is a hand-me-down, much of today's Household no longer serves any useful function and is maintained merely out of tradition, while other functions have changed with the times. The result of all this is a curious amalgam of ancient tradition and modern efficiency plus a dash of parliamentary watchfulness – though that too is now merely traditional, a hangover from the days when Parliament thought it wise to keep a wary eye on the monarch.

On paper, the names of those who comprise the Queen's Household runs to a total of some 300–400 names (the number varies from time to time). In practice, the majority of those whose names figure in the list perform only occasional and largely ceremonial duties. To name but a few, there is the Poet Laureate, who pens the occasional ode to commemorate historic landmarks in royal life; the Master of the Horse, who once commanded royal troops in battle and today rides at the wheel of the royal carriage on ceremonial occasions; the Treasurer of the Household (not to be confused with the Keeper of the Privy Purse and Treasurer to the Queen); the Comptroller of the Household (not to be confused with either the Master of the Household or the Comptroller of the Lord Chamberlain's department); and the Vice Chamberlain.

The Keeper of the Privy Purse, the Master of the Household and the Comptroller in the Lord Chamberlain's office, despite the quaintness of their titles, fulfil present-day functions. The Treasurer of the Household, the Comptroller of the Household and the Vice Chamberlain, on the other hand, are hangovers from the long struggle for power between monarch and parliament (*see* Monarchy).

Having won the right to rule, Parliament thought it wise to have its own men planted inside the monarch's household. However, this required constant changes as first one political party, then another, came to power. This sort of thing was not at all to the liking of the strong-minded Queen Victoria and, with the Tories coming to power, she brought matters to a head by flatly refusing to change her ladies-in-

waiting, mainly Whigs. Then there was the little matter of lighting a
fire for the Queen. She instructed the Master of the Household to have
it done, only to be informed that it was not his concern. Whose was it
then? the Queen wanted to know. Ah, well, that was a little complicated, it seemed. The laying of the fire was a matter for the Lord Steward, but the actual lighting of it was the responsibility of the Lord
Chamberlain.

This was nonsense, of course, and Queen Victoria was not slow to say
so. As a result, the right to appoint people to the Royal Household
reverted again to the monarch with the exception of the three posts
already mentioned, Treasurer, Comptroller and Vice Chamberlain.
These continued to be, and still are, appointed by Parliament, though
their duties are now little more than symbolic. The Vice Chamberlain,
for instance, each year when the Queen opens Parliament, hies himself
to Buckingham Palace and remains there as "hostage" in guarantee of
her safe return.

Of the several hundred names listed today as forming the Queen's
Household, only about sixty (that number too varies from time to time)
can be said to work for her on a regular day-to-day-basis. Very roughly
(because the various areas of responsibility are undefined and sometimes overlap), the Queen's Household can be split into five sections.
They are: Ceremonial; Modern Monarchy; Finance; the Royal Mews;
and actual Housekeeping. Each has a key man at its head, respectively
the Lord Chamberlain, the Private Secretary, the Keeper of the Privy
Purse, the Crown Equerry and the Master of the Household.

Top of the list comes the Lord Chamberlain, a title not to be confused
with that of the Lord Great Chamberlain. The Lord Great
Chamberlain's role of watching over the Palace of Westminster is,
like that of the Earl Marshal of England, a traditional and hereditary one. The Lord Chamberlain, on the other hand, is appointed
by the Queen to mastermind a large and varied selection of ceremonial functions. With the exception of the coronation and funeral
of the monarch and the annual state opening of Parliament (which
remain the traditional responsibility of the Earl Marshal, a title
vested in successive Dukes of Norfolk), the Lord Chamberlain is responsible for running the ceremonial side of royal life, from royal
weddings and funerals (other than the monarch's own funeral) to
garden parties and visits by foreign heads of state. It is the Lord
Chamberlain's job to know who should be invited to this or that
function, send out the invitations, decide the seating and rule on the
question of what constitutes correct or incorrect attire (though his
rulings on attire are not always strictly observed in this socialistic
age). Working from St James's Palace with the aid of a comptroller
and assistant comptroller, secretary and assistant secretary,

registrar, state invitation assistant, ceremonial assistant and assorted clerks, he also appoints royal physicians and chaplains, issues royal warrants, (*see* Shopping) oversees the royal chapels, the royal library and the royal collections of art and antiques (*see* Picture Collection *and* Furniture and *Objets d'Art*). He makes such ceremonial appointments as the Gentlemen at Arms, who actually defended the Palace of Westminster during the Wyatt rebellion of 1533 but today do no more than parade with their halberds (long-handled battle-axes) on state occasions; the Yeomen of the Guard, more historic hangovers of the fighting men they once were; Gentlemen Ushers; and, in Scotland, the Royal Company of Archers. Under him come the Keeper of the Jewel House, the Surveyors of the Queen's Pictures and the Queen's Works of Art, the Librarian and the Curator of the Print Room, the Poet Laureate and the Master of the Queen's Music, the royal Bargemaster and the Keeper of the Swans, a post dating from the days when swans were bred for food. Traditionally, the Queen still owns all mute swans which are not pinioned or marked as the property of someone else. To make sure the monarch does not get their birds, the Dyers and Vintners Companies mark them in the course of an annual ceremony known as "swan-upping".

But perhaps the most influential of all the senior posts in the Queen's Household is that of Private Secretary. In addition to heading the royal secretariat, the Private Secretary arranges the Queen's public appearances in Britain and her visits overseas, handles her correspondence (with the exception of personal correspondence), drafts her speeches and oversees the royal archives. More importantly perhaps, the Private Secretary serves also as a pipeline between monarch and government and acts as a sounding board for public opinion. Just as the monarch retains the right to "encourage or warn" the government of the day, so the Private Secretary has a duty to encourage or warn the monarch as circumstances may require.

It was Edward VIII's Private Secretary, Sir Alexander Hardinge (late Baron Hardinge of Penshurst) who took upon himself the unhappy task of warning the King of the probable consequences if he persisted with the idea of marrying Mrs Simpson (*see* Duke and Duchess of Windsor). It fell to another Private Secretary, Sir Alan Lascelles, to dissuade King George VI from sailing with the invasion fleet on D-Day.

In the long history of monarchy, the influential role of Private Secretary comes fairly late on the scene. Earlier monarchs had their scribes and messengers, but they were no more than that. It was not until Prince Albert, finding the role of merely being Prince Consort irksome and trivial, also became Private Secretary to his wife, Queen Victoria, that the role began to acquire the influence and importance it has today. Following her husband's death, Queen Victoria appointed Lord Stamfordham to the post. Carrying on where Albert had left off, he made the position largely what it now is, so effectively, indeed, that George V, to whom he was also Private Secretary, was to say of him, "He taught me to be a King."

If the power of the monarch has lessened since Queen Victoria's day, the paperwork has not. As a result, the Private Secretary now has both a deputy and an assistant as well as a secretary of his own and several clerks. As Keeper of the Queen's Archives, he has the assistance of an assistant keeper, a registrar and two assistant registrars. To deal with the Press he also has a Press Secretary who, in turn, has two assistants and more clerks, though the entire team is hardly more informative than Queen Victoria was herself. Queen Victoria issued her own court circular in which she meticulously recorded the day to day lives of herself and her growing family, even mentioning when this or that child had been out for an "airing". The palace Press office today, though informative enough concerning public functions – royal visits, investitures and so forth – would not dream of revealing any such "personal" information.

The Keeper of the Privy Purse oversees the royal accounts, including those of the Duchy of Lancaster as well as the financial administration of the Queen's private estates at Sandringham and Balmoral and the royal stud. The accounts he deals with are more those of a small business than of a private household – food bills in excess of £73,000 a year at the last count, laundry bills of over £12,000, household replacements running around £50,000 a year, and the wages of some 450 officials and servants, full and part-time.

The Crown Equerry oversees the garages and stables, is responsible for cars, carriages and the horses which are harnessed to them, for hiring and sometimes firing chauffeurs, coachmen and grooms.

The Master of the Household is responsible for the domestic organization of Buckingham Palace. Just as royal accounts are more in line with those of a small business than a private household, so running the palace (*see* Buckingham Palace) is more like supervising a major – and first-class – hotel than looking after a private house. Under the Master of the Household, in addition to the palace steward and the chief housekeeper, come the scores of servants who make up "the staff", pages and footmen, chefs and porters, maids and cleaning women, electricians, plumbers, upholsterers, carpenters and french polishers. With so many servants, there are, inevitably, servants who do nothing else but attend to the needs of other servants.

The palace steward acts in the nature of a lieutenant to the Master of the Household, supervising the pages and footmen, including the quaintly-named Pages of the Back Stairs who attend personally upon the Queen and Prince Philip, as well as the equally quaintly-named Yeomen of the Glass, Silver and Gold Pantries and the Yeoman of the Cellars. The chief housekeeper is another lieutenant, supervising the maids and cleaning women as well as overseeing the vast linen room in the basement with its huge store of sheets and pillow-cases, tablecloths and napkins, towels and dusters. The royal chef oversees the kitchens (*see* Meals).

From time to time, and especially if some foreign head of state is expected, the Queen will send for the housekeeper to discuss household arrangements. That apart, she sees the Master of the Household perhaps once a week to discuss any problems which may have arisen. She sees the Keeper of the Privy Purse slightly less frequently, perhaps once a month.

There are two other categories of Household aides who should be mentioned and perhaps require explanation. They are equerries and ladies-in-waiting. The Queen has a permanent equerry and usually one or perhaps two temporary equerries seconded from the army, navy or air force under a system introduced by her father during World War II. Peter Townsend, incidentally, was among the first of these temporary equerries (*see* Princess Margaret and Lord Snowdon) and is listed still as an extra equerry though it is years since he was seen at Buckingham Palace.

Working in close conjunction with the Private Secretary, the equerry on duty – or "in waiting", as it is styled – looks after a number of miscellaneous matters, including the Queen's travel arrangements and seeing to it that any guests she has to stay are comfortably accommodated. Prince Philip and Prince Charles similarly each have their own small team of equerries who take it in turns to perform similar duties for them. They do not, of course, have ladies-in-waiting.

The Queen's ladies-in-waiting fall into two groups, both of which are supervised by a duchess who bears the archaic title of Mistress of the Robes. Like so many of those who serve the Queen, her duties are not what the title would seem to imply. She is no longer responsible for the Queen's clothes, though she was once (and received the pick of royal discards as her reward). Today, however, the care of the Queen's clothes is the responsibility of a three-strong team known as "Dressers", the senior of whom is Margaret Macdonald, the one-time nurserymaid who has been in royal service since the Queen was a baby princess only a few weeks old and has been known to her ever since by the affectionate diminutive of "Bobo".

In addition to supervising the ladies-in-waiting, the Mistress of the Robes also accompanies the Queen on state occasions. Next in line come the Ladies of the Bedchamber, two at the last count, both titled, who similarly attend the Queen on topflight occasions and accompany her on overseas visits. They do not, however, attend upon her from day to day. This is the task of the Women of the Bedchamber – four at the last count plus two Extra Women of the Bedchamber – who are on duty for two weeks at a time. Their duties are relatively light but varied, accompanying the Queen on occasions which warrant neither the Mistress of the Robes or a Lady of the Bedchamber, making telephone calls for her and answering those letters from loyal subjects which require something more than a merely formal or stereotyped reply. They receive no salary for all this, counting their appointment as an honour, but do get an honorarium towards the cost of their clothes and other expenses.

The following are among the principal members of the Queen's Household as this book goes to press;

Lord Chamberlain: Lord Maclean
Mistress of the Robes: The Duchess of Grafton
Private Secretary: Sir Philip Moore
Press Secretary: Michael Shea
Keeper of the Privy Purse: Major Sir Rennie Maudsley
Master of the Household: Vice Admiral Sir Peter Ashmore
Crown Equerry: Lieutenant-Colonel Sir John Miller

JEWELLERY

Not counting the Crown Jewels, (*see* Crown Jewels) which are the property of the state rather than the monarch (as King George V found out when he wanted to take the crown out of the country and was told that he could not), Queen Elizabeth II has a collection of jewellery, part inherited, part given to her over her years of monarchy, which must surely be unrivalled in the western world. Yet, somewhat surprisingly, she had very little jewellery at the time of her marriage to Prince Philip, and not a single tiara. Her grandmother, Queen Mary, gave her one as a wedding gift, though the tiara she actually wore for the ceremony was borrowed from her mother.

The vast jewel collection of today started with a triple string of pearls she was given in childhood by her grandfather, George V. Queen Mary later gave her a pair of matching ear-studs. Other gifts followed as she grew to womanhood, among them a diamond and sapphire leaf-shaped brooch and a pair of gold flower brooches with diamond and sapphire centres, all given to her by her parents. For her eighteenth birthday her father also gave her a sapphire bracelet with diamond links.

Public duties as a princess resulted in further brooches, a diamond flower brooch from John Brown's shipyard when she launched *HMS Vanguard*, a brooch with diamond petals and a sapphire centre for launching *British Princess*, and a diamond brooch from what was then the British Overseas Airways Corporation for ensuring that the airliner *Elizabeth of England* was safely airborne.

In South Africa, on the occasion of her twenty-first birthday, she was almost inundated with diamonds. The South African Government gave her a collection of twenty-one large diamonds which, together with another large diamond given to her by De Beers, she wears today as a necklace of fifteen stones with a matching bracelet made from the remaining seven. Another birthday gift was a diamond and platinum brooch in the shape of a flame lily from the children of what was then Southern Rhodesia, while her parents gave her twin diamond brooches designed like ivy leaves.

Her return from South Africa was followed by betrothal to Prince Philip. Her engagement ring was a solitaire diamond with diamond shoulders. The stones had been given to Prince Philip by his mother and came from a ring his father had given her years before. However, the ring Philip had made up for his bride-to-be proved fractionally too large and was later returned to be altered.

The wedding produced another shower of jewellery for the future Elizabeth II. The Sheik of Bahrain gave her a pair of pearl and diamond drop ear-rings and the Nizam of Hyderabad sent her a bandeau tiara with a matching necklace and pendant. The diamond centre clip and the two side roses of the tiara can be detached and worn separately. Dr John T. Williamson, the Canadian geologist who discovered his own diamond mine in Tanganyika, gave her the world's most perfect rose-pink diamond. Weighing 56½ carats when mined and 23.6 after cutting, it now forms the centre-piece of a jonquil-shaped brooch with five petals of white diamonds and a stem and leaves of baguette diamonds. From tip to tip it measures 4½ inches. Philip gave her a diamond bracelet. Her parents gave her a diamond and ruby neckace as well as a pair of diamond chandelier ear-rings which necessitated having her ears pierced before she could wear them. Her father also passed over to her two strings of pearls, one of which dated from the days of Queen Anne while the other is believed to have once belonged to George II's wife, Queen Caroline.

Her grandmother, Queen Mary, in addition to the tiara already mentioned – which the Queen, incidentally, still refers to as "Granny's tiara" – also marked the wedding by passing over to her granddaughter a pair of pearl ear-rings which had been one of her own wedding gifts, a diamond bow brooch, a diamond and ruby bracelet, a pair of Indian diamond bracelets and a diamond Victorian stomacher.

Generous though Queen Mary was at the time of her granddaughter's wedding, she was to leave her much more when she died in 1953, the bulk of her own jewel collection, including three more tiaras, pearls of all shapes and sizes – a double string of pearls, pearl ear-rings, pearl bracelets – along with diamond ear-rings, a diamond bracelet and diamond brooches galore. There was a bow brooch, a scroll brooch, a lovers' knot brooch, a pearl brooch surrounded by circles of diamonds and a brooch with diamond and pearl drops which had been another of Queen Mary's own wedding gifts.

There was much more; and much of it had an historic value far outweighing its intrinsic worth. There was a necklace of pearls and diamonds which once belonged to Queen Alexandra who was given it by her father, Frederick VII of Denmark. There was a sapphire and diamond brooch also handed down from Queen Alexandra, to whom it had been given by her sister, the Empress Marie Feodorovna of Russia.

One of the tiaras, a graduated circle of diamond bars which doubles as a tiara and a collar for the throat, dates from the days of George II, while another belonged once to the Grand Duchess Vladimir of Russia. It consists of intertwined diamond scrolls in which can be suspended either drop pearls or the pear-shaped diamond drops which Queen Mary's mother won in a German state lottery.

Also in that 1953 inheritance were what the Queen calls "Granny's chips". These were the chippings of the Cullinan diamond which the cutter received as his fee for cleaving the stone (*see* Crown Jewels). Some chips! They include a pear-shaped diamond of 92 carats and a square diamond of 62 carats which combine to form a brooch, another diamond brooch of $18\frac{3}{8}$ carats, a marquise diamond of $11\frac{3}{4}$ carats which forms part of an emerald and diamond necklace, another marquise diamond ($9\frac{3}{16}$ carats) which forms the pendant of a brooch of which the centre is a diamond of $6\frac{3}{8}$ carats, and a pear-shaped diamond of $4\frac{9}{32}$ carats set as a ring. One of the marquise diamonds was bought from the cutter by King Edward VII as a gift for Queen Alexandra while the remaining "chips" were bought by the South African Government who later gave them to Queen Mary.

For the Queen's coronation Brazil sent her a necklace and matching ear-rings of aquamarines and diamonds which delighted her so much that she had a tiara made to go with them. Later, to complete the ensemble, Brazil also gave her a matching bracelet containing seven giant aquamarines. During the course of the world tour which followed her coronation she collected, among other things, a wattle-shaped brooch of rare yellow diamonds measuring four inches from tip to tip (from Australia). Other jewelled gifts have included a fern-shaped diamond brooch from New Zealand and a necklace of 96 rubies from Burma. The French gave her what is said to be the smallest watch in the world. Made of gold and platinum, it has a face only $\frac{5}{16}$ of an inch in diameter.

The watch, in fact, was the second of its kind. The original was given to her parents to give to her when they paid a state visit to France. She was twelve at the time. She wore the watch almost daily for seventeen years, then lost it while out walking her dogs at Sandringham. She was on her way back when, going to glance at the time, she was horrified to find that the watch was no longer on her wrist. Hurriedly, she retraced her steps, scanning the ground as she went. In the days which followed farm workers, police, Boy Scouts and troops with mine detectors all combed the area. Without result. But shortly after, when she herself paid a state visit to France, she was thrilled and delighted to be presented with an exact replica of the missing watch.

The jewelled miniatures which the Queen wears so often are more than a matter of personal adornment. They are Family Orders, the most personal of royal honours, an idea which originated with George I. Those which George bestowed consisted of his own cameo set in brilliants. Today's miniatures are painted on ivory and set in diamonds. They are given only to ladies of the Royal Family. The two the Queen wears were given to her by her father and grandfather. Since coming to the throne, she has, in turn, bestowed her own Family Orders on her mother, her sister Margaret and others among the royal ladies.

K

KING EDWARD VII AND QUEEN ALEXANDRA

Edward VII was only a few months short of his sixtieth birthday, a portly prince addicted to food, drink, attractive women and outsize cigars, not necessarily in that order, when he succeded to the throne on the death of his mother, Queen Victoria. There had been a long and frustrating wait in the wings of monarchy, during which he was neither taken into his mother's regal confidence nor given a proper job of royal work, before succeeding finally to the star role. No wonder that, boarding the royal yacht in the immediate aftermath of his mother's death at Osborne on the Isle of Wight, he demanded to know why the vessel's royal standard flew at half-mast.

It was because the Queen was dead, he was told. "But the King lives," he snapped back.

Whatever he had expected the rewards to be, his nine brief years of monarchy were not what he had expected. Combined with deteriorating health, the problems of kingship were such as to reduce him at times to a state of depression in which he sometimes spoke of possible abdication.

While he reigned as Edward VII, he was in fact christened Albert Edward after his father, Prince Albert, and known as Bertie in the family circle. He was born at Buckingham Palace on November 9, 1841, the second child of Queen Victoria. Her first, born the previous year, had been a girl. So Bertie, as eldest son, was heir to the throne. As such, he was created Prince of Wales on December 4 even before he was christened on January 25.

His parents had the idealistic concept of raising him as a perfect prince who would one day succeed to the throne as a perfect king. Or perhaps it is more accurate to say that Baron Christian von Stockmar, adviser to the Coburgs and subsequently to the young Victoria and her Coburg husband, first conceived the idea. Albert hailed it with delight and Queen Victoria, of course, felt that Albert could do no wrong.

So, at the age of seven, the heir to the throne was handed over to a team of tutors for an intensive training programme which occupied him six hours a day, six days a week. He was taught English, German, French and Latin, for a monarch must be multi-lingual; calculation, algebra and geometry; chemistry and military science; handwriting, music, drawing and religion. He was examined at regular intervals. If the results were not deemed satisfactory, he was put on a diet, not to reduce his weight, but because it was a theory of the time that this would improve his intellect and temper. He was taught to ride, hunt, shoot, stalk and fish, all of which were considered essential attributes in a royal male. He had to keep a daily journal which was subject to frequent inspections. Partly because it was all too much for him and partly because it was in his nature, he rebelled often, screaming at his tutors, even throwing things at them, stamping his feet in frustrated fury. Still his parents pressed on with the experiment, comparing him unfavourably with his much cleverer elder sister, Princess Victoria. Apart from his weak-natured younger brother, Prince Alfred (born 1844), he had no companions of his own sex and age as he journeyed through boyhood. Instead, he was surrounded constantly by adults, obliged to tag along with his parents when they attended such public functions as the opening of the Great Exhibition and the funeral of the Duke of Wellington.

As a teenager, he expressed a wish to join the army. But he was heir to the throne and his parents would not hear of it. Instead, he was consigned to the gloomy Palace of Holyroodhouse in Edinburgh for a three-month cram course before being sent, in turn, to Oxford and Cambridge Universities. At Oxford six other undergraduates were hand-picked to share his lectures, but he had to lodge at a house in the town and had little opportunity of mixing with them outside the lecture hall. At Cambridge, too, he had to live away from the university, at Madingley Hall, riding the four miles to and from his lectures each day on horseback. Parental instructions were strict. He must on no account lounge around or go about with his hands in his pockets. He was not to play football, cricket, billiards and certainly not cards. The occasional game of real tennis – lawn tennis had not yet been invented – was permitted.

He continued to pester his parents to let him join the army. They gave way only to the extent of letting him undertake a ten-week course with the Guards in Ireland. Even that was ruined for him by his father's insistence that he must learn the duties of every officer rank from ensign upwards with sufficient promptitude to earn promotion every two weeks and command a battalion at the end of ten. Not surprisingly he did not succeed. However, he did learn something else his parents had not counted on, the facts of life from an actress, Nellie Clifden.

Just as they arranged everything else for him, so his parents arranged his marriage to Princess Alexandra Caroline Marie Charlotte Louise

Julia of Denmark. Princess Alexandra was born in the Yellow Palace in Copenhagen on December 1, 1844, second of the six children of the former Princess Louise of Hesse-Cassel and Prince Christian of Schleswig-Holstein-Sonderburg-Glücksburg (the line from which Prince Philip is also descended), heir to the throne of Denmark. In an age when royalty married royalty, this Danish family, with its dominant mother, was to prove itself as remarkable as that of Queen Victoria. Not only did Alexandra become Princess of Wales on marriage, and later Queen of England, but two of her brothers became Frederick VIII of Denmark and George I of the Hellenes, while a sister, Princess Marie Sophia Frederika Dagmar, became Empress of Russia.

On March 10, 1863, some sixteen months after his father had died from typhoid (*see* Queen Victoria and Prince Albert), the Prince of Wales and Princess Alexandra were married in St George's Chapel, Windsor. He was twenty-one, she was eighteen. They set up home at Marlborough House in London, renovated for them at a cost of £60,000, and at Sandringham in Norfolk, then a 7,000-acre country estate bought for £220,000. The Prince was voted another £40,000 a year by Parliament with a further £10,000 for his bride. This was in addition to his revenues from the Duchy of Cornwall (then around £50,000 a year), a further £6,000 from the Sandringham rents and a small income from invested capital. Yet it all insufficient for the way of life the newly-weds adopted. From the outset, expenditure exceeded income by something like £20,000 a year. The deficit was made good out of capital until that was gone. Gambling losses and inordinate expenditure on his Sandringham estate – one batch of improvements and alterations alone cost him over £80,000 – were to find the heir to the throne in increasingly heavy financial water as time went by.

Partly through her grief over Albert and partly because she mistrusted her eldest son, Queen Victoria quickly abandoned all idea of moulding him into the perfect successor. Going to the other extreme, she now took active steps to prevent him from succeeding his father as head of various societies and commissions. Lacking a proper job of work, the young Prince of Wales threw himself more and more into a non-stop round of pleasure. His mother labelled him "Frivolous". His young wife was just as pleasure-seeking until ill-health forced her to call a halt. Their married relationship was marred not only by a succession of pregnancies – five in the first six years of marriage – but by a succession of illnesses, including a hip affliction which left her with a limp and increasing deafness inherited from her mother. All this while she was still only in her twenties.

Altogether the couple had six children: Albert Victor, Duke of Clarence (who died of pneumonia at the age of twenty-eight), was born in 1864; George (who became King George V [*see* King George V and

Queen Mary]), in 1865; Louise Victoria in 1867; Victoria in 1868; and Maud in 1869. Their last child, Alexander, born at Sandringham in 1871, lived only a few hours.

Given the responsibility of a real job of royal work, the young Prince of Wales might have settled down. The point is debatable. What is certain is that, without it, he cultivated pleasure to the point of excess. Hunting, shooting, yachting, gambling, parties and women became a way of life for him. He ate prodigiously, drank heartily, smoked excessively, getting through a dozen large cigars and twenty cigarettes a day. He ate five meals a day, some of them running to ten courses, and sometimes with snacks in-between. As a result, he was soon to lose his youthful handsomeness and by middle age he was so fat – forty-eight inches round the waist – that his friends nicknamed him "Tum-tum".

Whatever he had lacked in childhood, as a married man, because he was who he was and because he spent money like water, there was no shortage of friends. All too often they were friends of the wrong type, all too willing to forgive the quirks of his personality; he was amiable and arrogant, impulsive and shrewdly cautious, over-hearty or unduly sensitive by turns. They even forgave his fondness for schoolboyish practical jokes, like popping a dead seagull into bed with a drunken friend. And there was no shortage of attractive women willing to take the place of a sick or pregnant wife. He had a succession of mistresses, Lillie Langtry, Lady Brooke (later Countess of Warwick) and the Hon. Mrs Keppel, and passing affairs with many more.

It was a way of life which, almost inevitably, brought him more than once to the verge of scandal. His mother, Queen Victoria, was shocked when he was compelled to give evidence in a divorce action, denying in court that he had committed adultery with twenty-one-year-old Lady Mordaunt. He was equally compelled, later, to give evidence in a slander action and, on another occasion to avoid possible court action, obliged to write a grudging letter of apology to Lord and Lady Beresford. He once challenged Lord Randolph Churchill to a duel (which did not take place) and for the next eight years refused to speak to him. Finding themselves socially ostracized because of this, Churchill and his American-born wife, Jennie Jerome, took refuge in Ireland for a time. Later, however, the two men, prince and politician, became close friends.

Through all this, the Prince's wife, Princess Alexandra, continued to love him adoringly, forgiving his infidelities and even seeking to make friends of his mistresses. But though she never ceased to love her husband, her health would no longer let her share his pleasure-seeking way of life. More and more she devoted herself to the children, developing a possessiveness which saw her continuing to treat them as children long after they were grown up.

For her part, Queen Victoria did all she could to persuade her son to a more serious and sober way of life while at the same time ensuring that he was given neither authority nor responsibility. Despite her opposition, he managed to accumulate a number of honorary presidencies and chairmanships. He spoke occasionally in the House of Lords, and each year he carried out a small number of public functions, laying foundation stones, opening new buildings or inspecting old ones. He also tried hard to persuade his mother to abandon her widowed seclusion and appear more in public. When she would not, he hosted visiting foreign royalties on her behalf.

In November, 1871, at the age of thirty, he was taken ill at Sandringham. It was typhoid, contracted while staying at Lady Londesborough's house near Scarborough. His life was despaired of and his mother was summoned to his bedside. But while others who had also been at Scarborough died – Lord Chesterfield and the Prince's groom, Charles Blegge – the Prince himself pulled through. Filled with remorse, as he had equally been in the aftermath of his father's death, he decided that he wished to be of service to the nation. William Gladstone, the prime minister, promptly revived an earlier idea that the Prince should spend his winters as a sort of overlord in Ireland and his summers carrying out "the social and visible functions of monarchy" as his mother's deputy in London. Queen Victoria would not countenance any such scheme. Her son, she told Gladstone, would not willingly go to Ireland (and she may well have been right in this) while any question of deputizing for her in London was none of the Government's concern.

Throughout all this time the Prince travelled extensively, to Canada and the United States, Ireland and Europe, Russia and India, sometimes with his wife, sometimes without her. She was not with him on the extensive tour of India he made in 1875 at a cost in excess of £200,000 met jointly by the British and Indian governments. The tour lasted six months and seems to have been noted principally for the amount of big game shot and the fact that the Prince and his entourage sat down to dinner each evening in short jackets of dark blue cloth, black bow ties and black trousers. The tuxedo had been invented.

When Britain sent an expeditionary force to Egypt in 1882, he pleaded to go with it. But, again, his mother did not like the idea and the Government refused to countenance it over her head. Instead, he had to be content with subsequently hosting a series of victory banquets in London. He had no more success when he sought permission to go along with the relief force Britain sent to Khartoum in 1884.

However, he did manage to become a member of the Royal Commission on the Housing of the Working Classes that year and it was in keeping with his character that he insisted on exploring some of the worst slums in London in person. Horrified by what he saw, he made an impassioned speech in the House of Lords. Later he was also a member of the Royal Commission on the Aged Poor, attending thirty-five out of forty-eight meetings over a course of two years and insisting on maintaining a line of strict political neutrality.

Officially, because of his mother's opposition, he was not permitted to see confidential Government papers. Unofficially, because some members of various governments sympathized with his position, he did sometimes glimpse reports of Cabinet meetings and the like. Through his numerous relatives and friends in Europe he also tried at times to supplement the usual channels of international diplomacy, though his efforts in this direction were not helped by a quarrel with his German nephew Prince William (later Kaiser William II).

The two men, English uncle and German nephew, disliked each other intensely. William jeered at his uncle as "the old peacock". The Prince of Wales sniped back at "William the Great". Their personal enmity did nothing to help the political relationship between Britain and Germany.

During his long apprenticeship as Prince of Wales, Queen Victoria's eldest son was often unpopular with the British public. But the British will forgive a man anything if he is a good sportsman and so it was when the Prince's horse, Persimmon, won the 1896 Derby, a success he was to repeat in 1900 with Diamond Jubilee after also winning the Grand National with Ambush II.

Contrary to his dead mother's wishes, he did not perpetuate his father's name by ascending the throne as King Albert Edward. Instead, he dropped the Albert and became Edward VII. Against his wife's wishes, they moved from Marlborough House into Buckingham Palace with ascendence to monarchy. The alterations he ordered there and at Windsor cost a small fortune. But whatever he had been like as prince in waiting, as king he was conscientious in the extreme, especially in matters of public life. Among other things, he revived the annual state opening of Parliament, which his mother had permitted to lapse. Indeed, almost as though determined to make up for lost time, he wanted to do everything. Too much work, too much weight and the fact that he continued to lead a whirlwind social life brought him quickly to a state of near exhaustion. Appendicitis was diagnosed and peritonitis set in. As a result, his coronation, originally scheduled for June, 1902, had to be postponed to enable him to recover from an appendectomy performed at Buckingham Palace. But illness had one beneficial result. He had lost nearly thirty pounds in weight and that, coupled with a convalescent cruise aboard the royal yacht, saw him in fine fettle for a postponed and curtailed coronation on August 9.

Throughout his short reign Edward VII worked hard towards the preservation of peace in Europe and the avoidance of social disorder at home. By birth or marriage he was related to many other of the crowned heads of Europe in addition to his far-from-favourite German nephew, William. Another nephew was the Tsar of Russia, the King of Denmark was his brother-in-law and the Queen of Spain was his cousin. Because of all this he was able to play a large part in the field of foreign public relations though he in no way controlled Britain's foreign policy. The last vestiges of those days had died during Queen Victoria's long reign. So he was not truly responsible, whatever legend says to the contrary, for the *entente cordiale* between Britain and France, though he did much towards creating the atmosphere which led to it. He worked equally hard towards maintaining friendly relations with Russia. But enmity between him and his German nephew continued, with William more and more convinced that his uncle's European travels were designed to ring Germany with enemies. This was not the case, though one of the King's state tours of Europe, taking in Lisbon, Gibraltar, Malta, Naples, Rome and Paris, was mounted with the ulterior motive of outshining "William the Great".

Edward VII was frequently an absentee monarch, conducting business with the Government by letter or telegram from wherever he happened to be staying. Alice Keppel was his most frequent companion. As his health failed more and more, he became increasingly difficult and depressed. But always he remained as restless as ever. In 1909 he won the Derby for the third time, this time with Minoru. He was in Biarritz with Alice Keppel the following March when he collapsed.

Queen Alexandra, when she heard the news, was desperate to go to him. But her royal pride, for once, was greater than her love for the husband who had led her such a matrimonial dance. She was not prepared to play second fiddle to his mistress.

However, by April 27 the King had recovered sufficiently to return to Britain. He spent a weekend at Sandringham, where he contracted a further chill. Back in London again, he saw his doctors. Against their advice, he insisted on carrying on with the work of monarchy. By May 6 it was clear that he was dying. It was then that his wife, Queen Alexandra, did what seems an extraordinary thing by normal standards. She sent for his mistress, Alice Keppel, to come and see him for the last time. That night, at the age of sixty-eight, he died.

His widow survived him for fifteen years. In 1913, to mark the fiftieth anniversary of her arrival in Britain as a young princess and bride-to-be of the Prince of Wales, she founded Alexandra Rose Day. Her later years were spent, deaf, crippled and bronchial, at Sandringham, where she continued to occupy the main house while her son, King George V, made shift with the very much smaller York Cottage. And it was at Sandringham that she died on November 25, 1925, a few days short of her eighty-first birthday.

KING GEORGE V AND QUEEN MARY

As only the second son of the prince who, after a long wait, finally succeeded Queen Victoria on the throne, George V of the loud voice and
brilliantly blue eyes, was not born to be the bearded father-monarch he
eventually became. Kingship was the birthright of his elder brother,
born some eighteen months previously. But as so often in history, fate
took a hand in the game.

Georgie, as he was known in the family, was born on June 3, 1865, at
Marlborough House, London home of the Prince and Princess of Wales
(the former Princess Alexandra of Denmark) (*see* King Edward VII and
Queen Alexandra). He was christened in St George's Chapel, Windsor,
and given the names George Frederick Ernest Albert. His early upbringing, largely at Sandringham, his parents' country home in Norfolk, was tied to that of his elder brother, christened Albert Victor but
known as Eddy in the family circle. When Eddy was seven and Georgie
six, they started lessons together under a tutor. They were taught
English, French and Latin, history and geography, algebra and geometry, drawing and music, with games of cricket for exercise and
relaxation.

As an educational programme, it was not all that different from
that of their father before them. But there was one major difference. Whereas their father's young nose had been kept hard pressed
to the educational grindstone, theirs were not. Indeed, their
tutor was frequently moved to protest at the way their parents,
especially their mother, distracted and spoiled them. As for their
grandmother, Queen Victoria, she thought they were allowed to run
rather wild.

It was soon apparent that the two brothers possessed very different
levels of intelligence and quite different personalities. The younger
Georgie was "the bright one" (though not brilliant), quick to learn, a
vivacious and warmly affectionate youngster. Eddy, by contrast, was
dull and lethargic, even – as his parents were eventually to realize
– "backward".

In an ordinary family, apart from natural parental disappointment,
it might not have mattered that the elder brother was so much more
backward than the younger. In the Royal Family it did. For Eddy, as
the elder, was destined in due course to follow his grandmother and
father on the throne. As future King it had been planned that he should
continue his education at boarding school while his brother, the second
son, went into the navy. But Eddy, it was clear when the time came,
lacked the ability to succeed at school. Moreover, if the two brothers
were kept together, their parents reasoned, perhaps a little of Georgie's
brightness might yet rub off on Eddy. So in 1877 both were sent to the

training ship *Britannia* as naval cadets. Georgie continued to shine, revelling in shipboard life, making rapid and pronounced progress as a cadet. But unfortunately for parental hopes, not a spark of his brightness rubbed off on Eddy.

As a result, all thought of sending Eddy to school had to be abandoned, and the brothers remained together. Accompanied by their tutor and a brace of naval instructors for French and mathematics, they were dispatched as midshipmen aboard the corvette *Bacchante* on two cruises which, with a short break between, lasted the next two and a half years. Not until Eddy was nineteen and Georgie approaching his eighteenth birthday were they at last separated. While the backward elder brother remained at Sandringham with his three sisters, Louise, Victoria and Maud, the bright younger one joined *HMS Canada* in pursuit of a naval career which was to last the next fifteen years. It was during his years in the navy that he first grew the beard by which most people remember him, and developed the interest in postage stamps which was largely responsible for today's extremely valuable royal collection (*see* Stamps). By 1890 he had risen to the rank of lieutenant and was given command of the gunboat *Thrush*. Further promotion to commander and captain was to come later and he ended his career, though he was then no longer on the active list, as a rear-admiral.

It was early in 1892 that fate took a hand in the game. The elder brother, Eddy, now Duke of Clarence and Avondale, now also considerably self-indulgent as well as backward, a young man of numerous amorous adventures, had recently become betrothed to a girl it was hoped would serve as a steadying influence on him. Princess May of Teck, as she was known, was a tall, slim girl with a tightly-corseted figure and a ready laugh, a great-granddaughter of George III, a great-niece of George IV and William IV. Born at Kensington Palace on May 26, 1867, coincidentally in the same room in which Queen Victoria had been born, she was the daughter of Duke Franz of Teck and Princess Mary of Cambridge. Her full name was a considerable mouthful: Victoria Mary Augusta Louise Olga Pauline Claudine Agnes.

The wedding had been fixed for February 27, and in early January May and her parents joined their future in-laws at Sandringham for Eddy's twenty-eighth birthday celebrations. George was there too, home on leave from the navy.

The birthday went off miserably. Eddy spent most of it in bed, nursing a cold. May had a cold, too. So did Eddy's mother. His sister, Victoria, was down with influenza. Over the next few days, while Victoria's condition improved rapidly, Eddy became steadily worse. Pneumonia developed and on January 14, with the rest of the family crowded round him in the small, bay-windowed bedroom, he died.

George was devastated by the death of the brother from whom he had been inseparable for so many years. With Eddy's death, he was now next in line of succession to the throne and in May of that year he was accordingly gazetted Duke of York. But his naval career, though interrupted, was not yet at an end and he assumed command of *HMS Melampus.*

It seems to have been Queen Victoria, eager to maintain the web of royal marriages, who first suggested that it would be nice if her grandson married the princess who had earlier been betrothed to his dead brother. Perhaps she got the idea from the fact that her Danish daughter-in-law's sister, Princess Marie, had similarly married Alexander, the new Tsarevich of Russia, after his elder brother, to whom she had originally been betrothed, died from tuberculosis.

The idea took root and on July 6, 1893, George and May were married in the Chapel Royal, St James's Palace. For the future King George V, that day marked the beginning of more than forty years of happy marriage. The newly-weds made their home at Sandringham, though not in the main house. That remained the country residence of George's parents. George and May made do with a villa in the grounds which had been built originally to house any overflow of guests from the main house. It was known as The Bachelors' Cottage, but they renamed it York Cottage when George's father gave it to them as a wedding present. As a royal residence, it was decidedly cramped and inconvenient – so small that the smell of cooking permeated everywhere – but George loved it, as indeed he loved everything about "dear old Sandringham", as he called it. It was, he said, "the place I love better than anywhere in the world."

They lived in York Cottage for thirty-three years, continuing to live there whenever they could escape from London long after they had become King and Queen. They moved out finally only when the death of George's mother, the widowed Queen Alexandra, freed the main house for their occupation. All their children except the first were born at York Cottage.

After the fashion of the day, children were born at almost regular intervals. Their first-born, who later became Prince of Wales, King Edward VIII and Duke of Windsor in that order (*see* Duke and Duchess of Windsor), was born at White Lodge in Richmond Park, the home of Princess May's parents, in 1894. The others all born at York Cottage, were Albert (later King George VI [*see* King George VI]) who was born in 1895, Mary (later Princess Royal) in 1897, Henry (Duke of Gloucester) in 1900, George (Duke of Kent) in 1902, and John in 1905.

It must have seemed at the time as if each new royal generation must have its heartbreak child. With Queen Victoria it had been the haemophilic Leopold. With the Prince and Princess of Wales who were to become Edward VII and Queen Alexandra, it had been both Alexander, who died within a few hours of being born, and the backward Eddy, dying at twenty-eight. Now it was John, born an epileptic in an era before the illness could be controlled by drugs. Because of his attacks he was segregated from the rest of the family, living at an outlying farm on the Sandringham estate in the care of a kindly nurse, Mrs Bill. He died there in 1919 at the age of thirteen.

Soon after the birth of their third child in 1897 it became increasingly clear to George that, as Duke of York, royal duties would sooner or later have to take precedence over his naval career, and the following year, after briefly assuming command of *HMS Crescent*, he said goodbye to the sea. With the death of his grandmother, Queen Victoria, in 1901, and the accession of his father as King Edward VII, he became heir apparent and that November, in celebration of his own sixtieth birthday, his father created him Prince of Wales.

For the nine years of Edward VII's reign, the son divided his time between the relatively inconsequential royal duties of Prince of Wales, with Marlborough House as his London residence, and the way of life he enjoyed so much more, as the sporting "squire" of Sandringham. Among his early duties as Prince of Wales were tours of Australia and New Zealand, South Africa and Canada. Later came similar princely tours of India and Burma. In other directions he was given very little grounding in royal affairs by a father who guarded his royal prerogative almost as jealously as Queen Victoria had done in her day.

With the death on May 6, 1910, of the father he thought of in death as "my best friend and the best of fathers", a stunned Georgie found himself King. Princess May was now Queen. Her first name was really Victoria, but they agreed that there could be only one Queen Victoria. So she became Queen Mary.

As stiffly handsome as she had once been slenderly beautiful, shy, dutiful and cultured, believing as firmly in the responsibilities of monarchy as she did in the royal prerogative, she was to support him loyally throughout his twenty-six-year reign. George V reigned during an era when Britain and the world were alike subject to tremendous change. Elsewhere, during his years of monarchy, eight other kings, five emperors and eighteen minor dynasties, were to fade into oblivion. The land masses coloured red on the maps hanging on school walls were to begin the long progress of transformation from the old empire of Victorian and Edwardian times to the present Commonwealth. Yet despite all this, in Britain the monarchy was to be more popular and more firmly rooted when he died than when he first succeeded to the throne.

It was by no means easy going. At the outset he found himself reigning over a nation torn by industrial unrest. With Queen Mary, he tried to ease the situation by embarking on a series of tours of the mining and industrial areas, pioneering the way for the royal provincial progresses of today. Together, King and Queen rode in colliery trains, patted pit ponies, inspected their stables and took tea in the cottage homes of Welsh miners.

In setting out to identify himself in this way with his subjects, George V was not being in the least hypocritical. He saw himself always as an ordinary man (though one which an accident of birth and a twist of fate had elevated to an extraordinary position). His education had been relatively homespun and his years in the navy had given him an essentially practical outlook on life. Fond though he had been of his father, he was, both as man and monarch, totally different from Edward VII. He was neither playboy nor spendthrift and certainly had no desire to indulge in the sort of amateur diplomacy on which his father had thrived as king. His main interests were his stamp collection, shooting, yachting and Sandringham, which he infinitely preferred to London just as he preferred musical comedy to opera and poker to bridge. Unlike his father, he was a completely moral and highly religious man who advocated reading a chapter of the Bible every day. His own son, the Duke of Windsor, who never got on with him, was to sum him up later as a man who believed firmly "in God, the invincibility of the Royal Navy and the essential rightness of whatever was British."

Oddly, for a man who did not particularly care for pomp and ceremony, he conceived the idea, following his coronation on June 22, 1911, of travelling to India where he would be crowned a second time as Emperor. It would be the first time an Indian empress or emperor had actually visited India and the King visualized great advantages following upon such a spectacular visit. The Government was not so sure. They thought a second coronation – as Emperor – might set a precedent for his successors. As a compromise, it was agreed that he could visit India and wear his crown there, though not actually be crowned, as Emperor. The result was the dazzlingly spectacular Delhi Durbar at which the princes of India paid homage to him. However, the crown he wore was not the one with which he had been crowned in Westminster Abbey. That was not permitted to leave the country. So he had a new one made at a cost of £60,000.

George V was largely unknown to the vast majority of the British people when he first succeeded to the throne. World War I was to change all that, bringing him both respect and popularity.

As tension between Britain and Germany mounted, the King tried hard to defuse the situation. He invited his cousin, the Kaiser, to London for the unveiling of the monument to Queen Victoria which fronts Buckingham Palace. While his father had riled William by referring to him as "William the Great", George V referred to him flatteringly as Queen Victoria's "eldest grandson". In 1913, still hoping that the situation could be contained, the King and Queen Mary travelled to Berlin for the marriage of the Kaiser's only daughter. It was all to no avail and on August 4, 1914, following the powder-train of events which began with the assassination of the Austrian Archduke Ferdinand and exploded with Germany's invasion of Belgium, George V held a Privy Council for the purpose of declaring war on Germany.

If he could no longer lead his troops into battle as an earlier King George had done, George V could and did work indefatigably behind the lines. His attitude was typified by the orders he gave concerning visits to the front line by his son, the Prince of Wales. Those responsible for the prince's safety were to ensure that he ran "no unnecessary risks", the King wrote, adding, "But of course risks there must be."

During the course of the war the King himself visited the fleet five times and the army in France the same number. During one visit to France, his horse took fright, reared and rolled over on him, fracturing his pelvis. It was an accident from which he never completely recovered and during the remaining nineteen years of his life he was often in pain.

He held 450 inspections, visited 300 hospitals and personally bestowed a staggering 50,000 medals for bravery. He was constantly writing to the Commander in Chief, the Minister of Munitions or the Home Secretary, asking about this or suggesting the other. On a lesser plane, he gave up drinking as an example to his subjects. It was one which few of them saw fit to follow. In Britain, he again toured industrial areas with the emphasis on visits to munitions factories and shipyards. Sometimes Queen Mary was with him; sometimes he was on his own while she was busy elsewhere visiting hospitals and convalescent homes. Always she supported him tirelessly, deputizing for him during the weeks of his own convalescence which followed his accident in France.

His last visit to the Western Front was on August 7, 1918. The following morning the tanks of the British Fourth Army broke through the German lines and the end was finally in sight after four long and bloody years.

But the years which followed the war were as restless and depressed as those which had gone before. His frock-coat and striped trousers seeming to echo all that was most dutiful and determined in the British character, George V reigned like a bearded and benevolent father figure, often more in tune with his subjects than many of the politicians who represented them in Parliament. Queen Mary's toque hats and long-handled umbrellas, reinforcing her upright bearing, echoed the same theme of durability and resilience.

As a small girl, the granddaughter who is now Elizabeth II, spoke of him as "Grandpa England". Others thought of him in much the same way even if, in that very different era, they would have considered it *lèse-majesté* to have spoken of him so familiarly. Time and again he conveyed to the government of the day his mounting concern over both unemployment and the repressive actions of the Black and Tans in Ireland. Though it offended his sensibilities that the Labour Party should sing the *Red Flag*, he did much to encourage the short-lived minority first Labour Government of 1924. He resorted to the monarch's right "to warn" in cautioning against the introduction of provocative legislation when the 1926 General Strike first erupted. Time and again he protested at being compelled to bestow knighthoods and other honours on what he considered to be undeserving recipients and his repeated protests did much to remove the abuse to which the honours system was subject at that time.

He was sixty-four in 1928 when he went down with toxaemia. It proved to be a long and serious illness. Twice he was operated on and twice he had a relapse. It was the following year before he was up and about again, and he had still not fully recovered in 1931 – indeed, he was never to recover completely – when he found himself facing the biggest political crisis of his reign. For neither the first nor the last time, the nation was living beyond its means and the national economy was on the verge of collapse. Again the King exercised his royal prerogative when he asked Ramsay MacDonald to form a coalition government to steer Britain out of the crisis. Argument has raged since as to whether, in doing that, he was acting on MacDonald's own advice to him. As King, he was certainly doing what he thought was needed.

He was consistently a conscientious and hard-working monarch. Daily he plugged away at the contents of his boxes – Cabinet minutes, Foreign Office reports and dispatches, letters from governors-general and ambassadors. He read everything diligently; saw his ministers regularly. He held regular levees, formal receptions known as "drawing-rooms", investitures and garden parties, both at Buckingham Palace and, for a week each year, at the Palace of Holyroodhouse in Edinburgh. He was no absentee monarch, as his father had so often been. When not in London, he could invariably be found at his beloved Sandringham. "I have a house in London and a home at Sandringham," he would tell his friends. It was from Sandringham in 1932 that he made the first royal Christmas Day broadcast, the forerunner of today's royal telecasts.

On May 6, 1935, to mark their Silver Jubilee, he and Queen Mary attended a thanksgiving service at St Paul's Cathedral. Together they drove also through the poorer parts of London, bedecked with flags, loud with loyal cheers. The King was extremely moved.

Like his granddaughter, Queen Elizabeth II, he was a much more emotional person than most people realized. But he was also a man who shied away from displaying emotion. His wife understood that. His small granddaughter, whom he called Lilibet, may have sensed it in the way children sometimes do. But his own children neither sensed nor understood it. As a result, their reaction to him in childhood was a combination of awe and fear. Not until they were grown up was there any degree of closeness between them and their father and even that did not apply to the eldest son who was to succeed briefly to the throne as Edward VIII (*see* Duke and Duchess of Windsor).

But the King was close to his grandchildren, especially Lilibet and her sister, Margaret, and it was perhaps thoughts of his grandchildren which caused him to say in his Silver Jubilee broadcast, "I am speaking to the children above all. Remember, children, the King is speaking to you." For George V, it was a rare moment of public emotion.

By that time he was already suffering from a further bout of the bronchial trouble which plagued him on and off. It cleared up briefly, then came back again. That Christmas he broadcast from Sandringham as usual, but by January 17 he was noting in his diary, "Feel rotten." By January 20 he was very ill, but, conscientious as always, insisted upon holding a Privy Council meeting in his bedroom. By evening it became clear that his life, in the words of the official bulletin, was "moving peacefully towards its close."

The rest of the story is told in the last of a succession of diaries which he started in 1880 as a boy of fifteen and continued to keep all his life. But the last entry is written by Queen Mary: "My dearest husband . . . passed away on January 20 at five minutes to midnight."

Characteristically, Queen Mary's first action, when her husband died, was to stoop and kiss the hand of her eldest son, now King Edward VIII.

She was both hurt and angered by that son's subsequent abdication and, for the rest of her life, consistently refused to meet the woman for whom he gave up the throne. Throughout the reign of her second son, who succeeded to the throne as George VI, she played a considerable part in training her granddaughter, Princess Elizabeth, along the path of future monarchy (*see* Queen Elizabeth II). And when that granddaughter finally became Queen Elizabeth II, Queen Mary was among the first to welcome her on her return from Kenya.

"I wanted your old Granny to be the first to greet you," she said, curtseying.

Straightening up, still the epitome of regal dignity at eighty-four, she eyed the new monarch's skirt with slight, but evident, disapproval. It was, she observed, "much too short for mourning".

She died on March 24, 1953, a few weeks before her eighty-sixth birthday, a few weeks before her granddaughter's coronation. Conscientiously dutiful to the end, she made it plain as she lay dying that neither her illness nor death if it came must be permitted to interfere with the planned coronation.

KING GEORGE VI

When George VI, still Duke of York for a few more hours yet, saw his mother on the eve of his elder brother's abdication, the emotion of the moment proved too much for him. On his own admission, he "broke down and sobbed like a child." He still could not believe what was happening. To him, as to his mother, Queen Mary – and, indeed, to his other two brothers and his sister – it was unthinkable that a member of their family should place private desire ahead of public duty.

Like his father before him, George VI was not born to be king. But just as a twist of fate (the death of his elder brother) brought George V to the throne, so another twist of fate forty years later (the abdication of another elder brother) was to make George VI king.

Unlike the younger brothers of some other monarchs far back in the royal lineage, George VI had not the slightest craving for kingship. He had never been trained for the job, he said, and felt quite unfitted to perform it. Despite these feelings, despite the emotional sobbing on the eve of his brother's abdication, he did not shirk what he saw as his royal duty. "I will do my best to clear up the inevitable mess," he wrote, "if the whole fabric does not crumble under the shock and strain of it all."

That the fabric of monarchy did not crumble in the aftermath of the abdication was due in no small measure to the strength of character the Queen's father brought to bear on the kingship he never wanted.

George VI was born in York Cottage, Sandringham, the second son of a second son. He was born on December 14, 1895, a fact which distressed Queen Victoria, his grandmother, because it was the anniversary of the deaths of her husband and a daughter, Princess Alice. Indeed, his parents wrote to "Gan Gan", as the Queen was known in the family, virtually apologizing for the fact that they had been so inconsiderate.

He was christened Albert Frederick Arthur George, but known in the family circle, as his grandfather, King Edward VII was also known, as Bertie. His childhood was no happier than that of his elder brother, nor indeed of the other brothers and sister to be born later. The same nurse who physically tormented the elder brother, (*see* Duke and Duchess of Windsor) ignored the younger one almost to the point of neglect. Frightened of his father, in awe of his mother, he grew into a withdrawn and insecure child who would sit in a darkened room rather than ask anyone to light the gas. Naturally left-handed, he was compelled by his parents to use his right. He also suffered from knock-knees for which he had to wear splints which were often painful. The result of all this, starting around the age of seven, was the stammer from which he was to suffer whenever he became unduly nervous or excited.

His education, under a governess and then a tutor, was a sketchy one. Among other things he learned the princely arts of riding, shooting and fishing. As a small boy, he played football and cricket, though football games with the village lads from nearby West Newton were genteel in the extreme, with his tutor, who acted also as a referee, quick to bring a halt to the proceedings if there seemed any likelihood of his royal charges being on the receiving end of a boisterous tackle. Later came golf and tennis. Tennis he played left-handed, which may have had something to do with the fact that, in partnership with his equerry and friend, Louis Greig, he was later to make a brief appearance in the 1926 men's doubles at Wimbledon. His shooting was even better than his tennis and in time he was to become one of the top guns in the country.

But this was in the future; at the age of thirteen, like his elder brother before him, he was packed off to the Royal Naval College at Osborne where he passed out bottom of his term. At Dartmouth he fared slightly better, coming 61st out of an entry of sixty-seven. Nevertheless, he enjoyed naval life, though his career was marred by seasickness, gastric upsets, influenza, pneumonia and appendicitis. He was seasick when *HMS Collingwood* put to sea in World War I, but still performed his duties as sub-lieutenant in charge of one of the twelve-inch guns with sufficient "coolness and courage" during the Battle of Jutland to warrant a mention in dispatches.

In November, 1917, he was invalided out of the navy with duodenal ulcers, but switched instead to the recently-formed Royal Naval Air Service. With the formation of the Royal Air Force in 1918 he became a flight-lieutenant. Characteristically, he wanted to learn to fly, but that ambition had to wait some eleven years (*see* Flying).

In 1920, while undergoing a year's cramming in history, geography and physics at Trinity College, Cambridge, in company with his younger brother, Henry, he was created Duke of York. He accepted the presidency of the new Industrial Welfare Society and promptly added economics to the subjects he studied at Cambridge. Thus began the sustained interest in industrial affairs which was to cause the rest of the Royal Family to refer to him jokingly as "The Foreman".

The following year he held the first of the Duke of York camps with which his name was to be associated for so long. These camps were designed to bring together boys of very different classes, the poor and the affluent. Up to the outbreak of World War II, both as Duke of York and King George VI, he himself joined regularly in this annual get-together of rich and poor (except one year when he was suffering from blood poisoning), eagerly singing the words and performing the gestures of such action songs as "Under The Spreading Chestnut Tree", the camp's signature tune.

Years later, when she was Queen Elizabeth II, his eldest daughter was to surprise those with her on a visit to Canada by joining as whole-heartedly and quite spontaneously in the same words and gestures. Asked how she knew them, she explained, "My father taught me."

By the time of that first camp he had already met the girl he was des-tined to marry, Elizabeth Bowes-Lyon (*see* Queen Elizabeth, the Queen Mother). Over a period of two-three years he courted her assiduously. As the King's son, of course, he had to have his father's per-mission before he could ask for her hand in marriage (*see* Marriage). George V gave permission, but added gruffly, "You'll be lucky if she'll have you." It seemed at first that the father was right. Twice the Duke asked her to marry him and twice, politely, she said No. But the third time, in January, 1923, while they strolled among the trees at St Paul's, Walden Bury, one of her family homes, she surprised him by accepting. "I'm not sure my reply wasn't more of a surprise to me than it was to him," she confided later.

They were married at Westminster Abbey on April 26, 1923. In due course two daughters were born to them, Elizabeth in 1926 and Marga-ret in 1930.

Inevitably, as the King's son, as president of this or patron of that, on official visits to countries like Ireland, Kenya and Uganda, he was faced with the necessity for making public speeches. The stammer which afflicted him at times of tension or excitement made this an extremely painful ordeal for him. But duty-conscious as he was, he never sought to avoid making a speech any more than, a few years in the future, he was to duck the burden of monarchy.

He did everything he could to find a cure for his stammer or, failing a complete cure, at least some way in which he might control it. He saw specialist after specialist, nine in all; experimented with every system of speech training and voice production he could find. As specialist after specialist and experiment after experiment failed, he became steadily more convinced that he was beyond cure. The depression of the chronic stammerer set its mark upon him and there was danger of a decline into aphasia (partial or complete loss of speech) when someone told him of Lionel Logue.

Logue was an Australian who was reported to have worked wonders in Perth with a system of rhythmical diaphragmatic breathing. Re-cently he had moved to London and opened a consulting room in Harley Street. The Duke, when he first heard of Logue, was almost too depressed to make the effort. It could end only in another failure, he said. His wife persuaded him otherwise . . . "Just one more try, dar-ling."

"I can cure you," Logue told him when he saw him in October, 1926, "but it will need a tremendous effort on your part."

Indeed it did. In addition to spending an hour a day with Logue, several more hours daily had to be devoted to the necessary exercises. Depression would sometimes flood back and, with it, the thought that he was heading only towards another failure. When he despaired, it was his wife's encouragement which sustained him and kept him working on his exercises.

He was not yet cured, and extremely apprehensive in consequence, when he boarded the battleship *Renown* in 1927. He was heading for Australia where he was due to open that country's first Parliament, a considerable ordeal for a long-time stammerer. Throughout the voyage, for two hours every day, with his wife keeping him company and affording encouragement, he continued his exercises. She was with him too, smiling encouragement, when he made his speech in Canberra with hardly a trace of the old stammer. Impulsively she seized his hand in hers. "Darling," she said, "you were splendid. I'm so proud of you."

Back in Britain again, the Duke continued his work as president or patron of numerous worthy causes, among them the Miners' Welfare Commission, the Dockyard Settlements and the National Playing Fields Association. Royal chores apart, he lived quietly with his wife and daughters at 145 Piccadilly. He had no desire for the bright lights and high living favoured by his elder brother, the Prince of Wales. Weekends were later spent at Royal Lodge (*see* Royal Lodge) in Windsor Great Park which the Yorks took over, restored and enlarged.

The Prince of Wales was at one time a frequent visitor to 145 Piccadilly, joining happily in family games with parents and children. "He has one matchless blessing not bestowed upon me," the elder brother was to say later of the younger. "A happy home with his wife and children." But long before he said that his visits had become increasingly rarer following his involvement with Mrs Simpson and his succession to the throne. Indeed, as events moved inexorably towards the crisis of abdication, the younger brother found it almost impossible to see the elder at all.

It was on November 17, 1936, that the Duke of York first learned of his brother's desire to marry Mrs Simpson. In vain he tried to persuade him to change his mind. Horrified by the newspaper headlines which greeted him when he returned to London from Scotland on December 3, frightened by the prospect that he might find himself king, he tried again. But the brother who had so recently become King Edward VIII was still determined on marriage.

The two brothers arranged to meet again the following day at the King's Windsor home, Fort Belvedere, but at the last moment the meeting was put off by the elder brother. The next day too, Saturday, he again shied away from meeting his brother. The King would see him on

Sunday, the Duke of York was told. But on Sunday the elder brother yet again postponed the meeting.

They met finally on the Monday evening. The King was still determined to marry Mrs Simpson, prepared to abdicate rather than give her up. If so, the younger brother would be king. The prospect appalled him.

"This is absolutely terrible," he told his wife. "I never wanted this to happen. David has been trained for this all his life. I have never even seen a state paper."

"We must take what is coming to us and make the best of it," she replied, philosophically.

That was their private view. In public the new King showed more resolution. "I am new to the job," he told Prime Minister Stanley Baldwin, "but hope that time will be allowed me to make amends for what has happened."

He became King the day Parliament ratified his brother's Instrument of Abdication – December 11, 1936. For him, the problems of accession were greater than they had been for his brother or father. To make a speech, picking words he could pronounce without too much difficulty, was one thing. The archaic and unalterable phrasing of the ancient accession declaration was quite another. In the short time available, with the help of Lionel Logue, he practised assiduously until he could repeat it without faltering.

At the time of his accession his wife was ill in bed with influenza. It was left to Queen Mary to take charge of her granddaughters, the two small princesses, while they watched the ceremony of their father's proclamation from a window of Marlborough House. But they were back home at 145 Piccadilly when their father returned, waiting to bob him a curtsey as he entered the house. For a moment he was taken completely aback. Then he swept them into his arms and kissed them both.

In an attempt to paper over any cracks caused by the abdication and to emphasize the unbroken continuity of monarchy, he took his father's name as king and stuck to the coronation date already arranged for his elder brother. More exercises, more help from Logue, enabled him to utter the responses required of him during the long ordeal of the coronation ceremony on May 12, 1937, and even to broadcast that night. It was Logue, sitting beside him, who whispered the words, "Now take it quietly, sir," overheard at the beginning of that broadcast. For a time, however, the new King preferred to discontinue his father's habit of broadcasting to the Commonwealth and Empire on Christmas Day.

As king, he had to learn things virtually from scratch. He had never been trained for the role and, as he had said himself, had scarcely, if ever, seen a state paper. As diligently as he had earlier set out to conquer his long-time stammer, so he now set about learning to be a king. In

June, 1939, following a tour of Canada, he became the first reigning monarch of Britain ever to visit the United States, where he was welcomed with a degree of enthusiasm one would scarcely have expected to be displayed towards any descendant of George III. A few months later, for the second time in many people's lifetimes, Britain was at war with Germany.

If a king could no longer lead his men into battle, George VI could, and did, provide the inspiration which wins battles. That first Christmas of the war he again broadcast to the nation and Commonwealth, concluding with a quotation from a collection of poems entitled *The Desert* by Marie Louise Haskins.

"I said to the man who stood at the Gate of the Year, 'Give me a light that I may tread safely into the unknown.' And he replied, 'Go out into the darkness and put your hand in the Hand of God. That shall be better than a light and safer than a known way.'"

Despite the German air raids, he declined to send his daughters to safety in Canada. Even at the height of the blitz he continued to use Buckingham Palace as his headquarters with the royal standard flying defiantly at the masthead. He and his wife were together in their small sitting-room at the palace on September 13, 1940, when two bombs exploded near the palace railings, two more in the courtyard, one scored a direct hit on the chapel while a sixth buried itself in the garden where, for all anyone knows, it may be buried still.

"I'm glad we've been bombed," the Queen reportedly said. "It makes me feel we can look the East End in the face."

With her at his side, the King toured London's bomb-shattered East End. As he picked his way among the ruins of houses, shops and factories, a voice in the crowd called out, "Thank God for a good King."

"Thank God for a good people," the King called back.

He visited many other bombed cities, Birmingham and Swansea, Bristol and Bath, Hull, Portsmouth and Southampton. The ruins of Coventry were still smouldering as he picked his way among unexploded parachute bombs. He never appeared in public other than in military uniform. He learned to use both pistol and Sten-gun and took them with him everywhere against the possibility of German invasion.

Hitherto it had been the custom that only officers received decorations from the King himself. George VI extended this initially to NCOs and subsequently to all ranks of the armed forces as well as to those meriting civilian awards for bravery. The next of kin of those killed on active service also found themselves invited to Buckingham Palace to receive posthumous awards. All in all, over the course of the war years, the King personally decorated no fewer than 37,000 men and women.

The creation of the George Cross and George Medal for civilian gallantry was his own idea and the design was based on a rough sketch he had done. It was his own imaginative idea too, in April, 1942, to award the George Cross to what he referred to as "the Island Fortress of Malta".

He approved and signed thousands of Orders in Council by which Britain was largely governed in those years of war. A direct telephone line linked him to the Prime Minister, Winston Churchill. He visited the Home Fleet, British and Allied troops, RAF stations and the bases of the US 8th and 9th Air Forces. He visited shipyards and factories, and even had lathes installed at Windsor Castle so that he and his aides could add their bit to the production effort. He paid five visits to the various battle fronts, inspecting France's unfortunate Maginot Line in 1939, visiting North Africa and Malta in 1943, going to Normandy shortly after D-Day, and later visiting Italy, Belgium, Holland and the Ardennes.

Had he had his way, he would even have sailed with the invasion fleet on D-Day, admittedly in the capacity of a spectator rather than a combatant. Churchill had the same idea. That neither of them went in the end was due to a last-minute intervention by Sir Alan Lascelles, the King's Private Secretary.

Horrified when he heard what was proposed, he confronted the King with a shrewd and telling question. What advice, he wanted to know, was he to give Princess Elizabeth concerning the choice of a new prime minister in the event that both her father and Churchill were killed virtually simultaneously.

The danger was a very real one if the two men went ahead with their separate plans to watch the D-Day landings, as the King was quick to realize. But if he could not go, he did not see why Churchill should do so. He wrote to him accordingly: "You said yesterday that it would be a fine thing for a king to lead his troops into battle as in the old days. If a King cannot do this, it does not seem right to me that his Prime Minister should take his place."

The letter reached Churchill just as he was about to leave for General Eisenhower's headquarters. If Nelson, at the Battle of Copenhagen, could turn a blind eye to the signal flags ordering him with withdraw, Churchill, on the eve of D-Day, felt that he could hardly do the same with regard to the King's letter. He decided instead, as he informed the King, "to defer to Your Majesty's wishes and indeed commands."

George VI's very real interest in the problems of working people, so well demonstrated in his pre-war years as Duke of York, continued during his post-war years as King. His attitude enabled him to get along well with the post-war Labour Government, though he thought that Herbert Morrison treated meetings of the Privy Council too lightly and that Aneurin Bevan showed disrespect to the monarchy by talking to the King with his hands in his pockets. Both as monarch and "squire" of Sandringham, he continued to work industriously and conscientiously, paying considerable attention to detail. Indeed, as far as Sandringham (which he loved as much as his father had) was concerned, he insisted that everything – down to hirings, firings and alterations to workers' cottages – was submitted to him before being carried out. As monarch, he used his influence to persuade Earl Mountbatten of Burma (*see* Earl Mountbatten of Burma) to undertake the difficult and thankless task of helping India to independence by accepting the post of the last viceroy. Force of circumstances prevented the King himself from ever actually setting foot in India and in 1948, by proclamation, he abandoned the title of Emperor which his great-grandmother, Queen Victoria, had assumed seventy-one years before.

Prior to that, in 1947, he toured South Africa with his family, the last monarch to do so, hoping that his visit might do something towards reconciling the racial and nationalistic differences of the country. In the course of a round trip of 19,000 miles, which included visits to all four provinces and three High Commission territories as well as Rhodesia, he lost seventeen pounds in weight.

That South African tour, following so closely on the heels of the strain and worry of the war years, undermined his health. In 1948 he and the Queen celebrated their silver wedding. A few months later he was complaining of increasing pain in his legs. Ten days before his daughter, Princess Elizabeth, gave birth to her first child, royal physicians found that the King was suffering from arteriosclerosis – obstruction of the circulation – of both legs. A royal tour of Australia and New Zealand, planned for 1949, had to be postponed. Rest and electrical stimulation were prescribed, but his condition did not respond. His right leg was particularly affected and in March, 1949, to forestall possible amputation, a lumbar sympathectomy was successfully carried out by Professor (later Sir) James Learmouth assisted by Professor Patterson Ross.

When Learmouth visited Buckingham Palace to make his final postoperative examination the King suddenly produced a sword. "You used a knife on me. Now I'm going to use one on you," he joked and knighted him on the spot.

For a short time it seemed as though the King's health had been completely restored. Unfortunately, it had not – and he would not agree to ease up. Doggedly, he continued to work a ten-hour day. In May, 1951, he opened the Exhibition of Britain, a pale shadow of the Prince Consort's splendid Great Exhibition of a hundred years earlier. By June 1 he was again confined to his room with what the initial medical bulletin insisted was simply "an attack of influenza". The tone of subsequent bulletins became more sombre. Influenza became "a small area of catarrhal inflammation". In fact, the King was suffering from cancer of the left lung and by September it was clear that further surgery was imperative. On September 23 the lung was removed by a team headed by Clement (later Sir) Price Thomas, one of Britain's foremost chest surgeons.

It was the shooting season, and the King was a first-class shot. All through his convalescence he talked of going out shooting; of getting back to work. In October, he did in fact effect the dissolution of Parliament (at the request of Clement Attlee) from his bed. But for other functions Counsellors of State (*see* Counsellors of State) took over. By November a general election had brought the Conservatives back to political power and Churchill was again prime minister. But there was no state opening of Parliament. The King was not yet sufficiently recovered.

On December 10, coincidentally the fifteenth anniversary of his brother's abdication, he resumed the reins of office, tackling the contents of his boxes again. With Christmas approaching, he insisted that he must make his annual Christmas Day broadcast as usual. And make it he did, though not quite as usual. It took him two days to pre-record it phrase by painstaking phrase.

At Christmas he journeyed as usual to his beloved Sandringham. He could not climb the stairs there and a bedroom was made up for him downstairs. Yet he seemed to be on the mend and never more so than the day he put a walking stick to his shoulder and said, "I believe I could shoot again now."

It had been arranged that Princess Elizabeth and her husband should carry out the postponed tour of Australia which the King was still not well enough to make. In poor health though he still was, he journeyed to London to see them off. There was a family visit to the Theatre Royal in Drury Lane to see the American musical *South Pacific*, and on January 31 the King, his face haggard, his hair whipped by a biting wind, stood on the tarmac at London Airport to wave farewell as his daughter's Argonaut took off on the first leg of a tour she was destined not to complete.

Then it was back to his beloved Sandringham. There, on February 5, 1952, while his wife and Princess Margaret were visiting the artist Edward Seago in his Broadland home, the King went shooting again. It was a day of what is known as "rough shooting" during which the King, wearing heated gloves and boots to aid his circulation, bagged eight hares and a high-flying wood pigeon. Then it was back to the house to rest, to say prayers with his grandchildren, Charles and Anne, before they went to bed, to dine with his wife and daughter, take a turn round the grounds and listen to the radio news before going to bed himself just after ten o'clock.

At half-past seven the following morning, when his valet James Macdonald brought him his early-morning pot of tea, he was unable to rouse him. A local physician, Dr James Ansell, was hastily summoned from his home in nearby Wolferton, but there was nothing he could do. The "People's King", as George VI became known during those grim and bitter years of World War II, had died in his sleep.

There can be no more fitting epitaph to him than the words of his daughter, Queen Elizabeth II, when she unveiled a memorial to him in the Mall on October 21, 1955:

"Much was asked of my father in personal sacrifice and endeavour, often in the face of illness; his courage in overcoming it endeared him to everyone. He shirked no task, however difficult, and to the end he never faltered in his duties to his peoples. Throughout all the strains of his public life he remained a man of warm and friendly sympathies – a man who by the simple qualities of loyalty, resolution and service won for himself such a place in the affection of us all that when he died millions mourned for him as for a true and trusted friend."

KINGS AND QUEENS OF ENGLAND

Name	Born	Right of Succession	Married	Access.	Died
Saxon:					
Egbert	c.770	Conquest and alliance	Redburga	829	839
Ethelwulf	c.795	Son of Egbert	(1) Osburh (2) Judith	839	858
Ethelbald	unknown	Son of Ethelwulf	Judith (his stepmother)	858	860
Ethelbert	unknown	Son of Ethelwulf		860	866
Ethelred	unknown	Son of Ethelwulf		866	871
Alfred	c.849	Son of Ethelwulf	Elswith	871	899
Edward (Elder)	c.871	Son of Alfred	(1) Egwina (2) Elfled (3) Edgiva	899	924
Athelstan	c.895	Son of Edward/Egwina		924	939
Edmund	c.921	Son of Edward/Edgiva	(1) Elgiva (2) Ethelfled	939	946
Edred	c.923	Son of Edward/Edgiva		946	955
Edwy	c.941	Son of Edmund/Elgiva	Elgiva	955	959
Edgar	c.943	Son of Edmund/Elgiva	(1) Ethelfled (2) Elfrida	959	975
Edward (Martyr)	c.962	Son of Edgar/Ethelfled		975	979
Ethelred (Unready)	c.968	Son of Edgar/Elfrida	(1) Elgiva (2) Emma of Normandy	979	1016
Edmund (Ironside)	c.993	Son of Ethelred/Elgiva	Eldgyth	1016	1016
Dane:					
Canute	c.995	Conquest	(1) Elgiva (2) Emma (Ethelred's widow)	1016	1035
Harold (Harefoot)	c.1016	Son of Canute/Elgiva		1035	1040
Hardicanute	c.1018	Son of Canute/Emma		1040	1042
Saxon:					
Edward (Confessor)	c.1004	Son of Ethelred/Emma	Edith, daughter of Earl Godwin	1042	1066
Harold II	c.1022	Son of Earl Godwin, brother-in-law of Edward (Confessor)		1066	1066

Monarch	Born	Relationship	Queen(s)	Accession	Death
Norman:					
William the Conqueror	1027	Conquest	Matilda of Flanders	1066	1087
William Rufus	c.1056	Son of William the Conqueror		1087	1100
Henry I	1068	Son of William the Conqueror	(1) Matilda, daughter of Malcolm III of Scotland (2) Adelicia of Louvaine	1100	1135
Stephen	c.1097	Son of William's daughter, Adela	Matilda of Boulogne	1135	1154
Plantagenet:					
Henry II	1133	Son of Henry I's daughter Matilda	Eleanor of Aquitaine, divorced Queen of Louis VII of France	1154	1189
Richard Lionheart	1157	Son of Henry II	Berengaria of Navarre	1189	1199
John	c.1167	Son of Henry II	(1) Avisa (2) Isabella of Angoulême	1199	1216
Henry III	1207	Son of John	Eleanor of Provence	1216	1272
Edward I	1239	Son of Henry III	(1) Eleanor of Castile (2) Margaret of France	1272	1307
Edward II	1284	Son of Edward I	Isabella of France	1307	1327
Edward III	1312	Son of Edward II	Philippa of Hainault	1327	1377
Richard II	1367	Grandson of Edward III	(1) Anne of Bohemia (2) Isabella of France	1377	1400 dep. 1399
Lancaster:					
Henry IV	1367	Grandson of Edward III	(1) Mary de Bohun (2) Joanna of Navarre	1399	1413
Henry V	1387	Son of Henry IV	Catherine of Valois	1413	1422
Henry VI	1422	Son of Henry V	Margaret of Anjou	1422	1471 dep. 1461
York:					
Edward IV	1442	Great-great-grandson of Edward III	Elizabeth, widow of Sir John Grey	1461	1483
Edward V	1470	Son of Edward IV		1483	1483
Richard III	1452	Brother of Edward IV	Anne of Warwick	1483	1485

Name	Born	Right of Succession	Married	Acces.	Died
Tudor:					
Henry VII	1457	Great-great-great-grandson of Edward III	Elizabeth, daughter of Edward IV	1485	1509
Henry VIII	1491	Son of Henry VII	(1) Catherine of Aragon (2) Anne Boleyn (3) Jane Seymour (4) Anne of Cleves (5) Catherine Howard (6) Catherine Parr	1509	1547
Edward VI	1537	Son of Henry VIII/Jane Seymour		1547	1553
Jane (Lady Jane Grey)	1537	Great-granddaughter of Henry VII	Lord Guilford Dudley	1553 dep. 1553	1554
Mary I	1516	Daughter of Henry VIII/Catherine of Aragon	Philip II of Spain	1553	1558
Elizabeth I	1533	Daughter of Henry VIII/Anne Boleyn		1558	1603

KINGS AND QUEENS OF SCOTLAND

The history of the early Scottish kings is obscure in the extreme. Kenneth MacAlpine, king of the Scots of Dalriada, began the unification of the country when he defeated the Picts, took over Lothian and formed an alliance with Strathclyde. That was around 844. For the next two centuries, with succession to kingship seemingly based on tanistry – the election of the strongest of the family or clan – rather than on primogeniture, successive Kenneths and Malcolms either murdered or were murdered. Duncan I, though he succeeded his grandfather, Malcolm II, was apparently regarded as a usurper. This led to his murder by Macbeth, sub-king of Moray, who was in turn overthrown by Duncan's son, Malcolm Canmore, who became Malcolm III in 1057. Thereafter we are on increasingly safer historical ground.

Name	Born	Right of Succession	Married	Acces.	Died
Malcolm III	*	Son of Duncan I	(1) Ingibiorg (2) Margaret Atheling	1057	1093
Duncan II	*	Son of Malcolm/Ingibiorg		1093	1094
Donald Bane	*	Brother of Malcolm III		1094	1097
Edgar	*	Son of Malcolm/Margaret		1097	1107
Alexander	*	Son of Malcolm III	Sybilla, daughter of England's Henry I	1107	1124
David I	1084	Son of Malcolm/Margaret	Maude of Northumbria	1124	1153
Malcolm IV	1141	Grandson of David I		1153	1165
William the Lion		Brother of Malcolm IV	Ermengarde	1165	1214
Alexander II	*	Son of William	(1) Joanna, daughter of King John (2) Mary of Picardy	1214	1249
Alexander III	*	Son of Alexander II/Mary	(1) Margaret, daughter of Henry III (2) Joleta	1249	1286
Margaret, Maid of Norway	1283	Granddaughter of Alexander III		1286	1290
John de Baliol	1249	Great-grandson of brother of William the Lion		1292	1296
Robert Bruce	1274	Great-great-grandson of brother of William the Lion	(1) Isabella (2) Elizabeth de Burgh	1306	1329
David II	1324	Son of Robert Bruce/Elizabeth		1329	1371
Robert II	1316	Grandson of Robert Bruce/Isabella	(1) Elizabeth Mure (2) Euphemia	1371	1390
Robert III	1340	Son of Robert II	Annabella Drummond	1390	1406

Name	Born	Right of Succession	Married	Access.	Died
James I	1394	Son of Robert III	Jane Beaufort	1406	1437
James II	1430	Son of James I	Mary of Gueldres	1437	1460
James III	1451	Son of James II	Margaret, daughter of King of Denmark	1460	1488
James IV	1475	Son of James III	Margaret, daughter of Henry VII	1488	1513
James V	1513	Son of James IV	(1) Madeleine of France (2) Mary of Guise	1513	1542
Mary	1542	Daughter of James V/Mary of Guise	(1) Dauphin of France (2) Lord Darnley (3) Earl of Bothwell	1542 dep. 1567	1587

* Historically unknown or uncertain

KINGS AND QUEENS OF THE UNITED KINGDOM

Name	Born	Right of Succession	Married	Access.	Died
Stuart:					
James I (VI of Scotland, 1567)	1566	Son of Mary Queen of Scots and great-great-grandson of Henry VII	Anne of Denmark	1603	1625
Charles I	1600	Son of James I	Henrietta Maria	1625	1649
		(A Commonwealth was declared from 1649 to 1660)			
Charles II	1630	Son of Charles I (proclaimed King of Scotland 1649)	Catherine of Portugal	1660	1685
James II (VII of Scotland)	1633	Son of Charles I	(1) Anne Hyde (2) Mary of Modena	1685 dep. 1688	1701
William III and Mary II	1650 1662	Grandson of Charles I Daughter of James II/Anne Hyde		1689 1689	1702 1694
Anne	1665	Daughter of James II/Anne Hyde	George of Denmark	1702	1714
Hanover:					
George I	1660	Great-grandson of James I	Sophia Dorothea of Celle	1714	1727
George II	1683	Son of George I	Caroline of Brandenburg-Anspach	1727	1760
George III	1738	Grandson of George II	Charlotte of Mecklenburg-Strelitz	1760	1820
George IV	1762	Son of George III (Regent from 1811)	Caroline of Brunswick	1820	1830
William IV	1765	Son of George III	Adelaide of Saxe-Meiningen	1830	1837
Victoria	1819	Granddaughter of George III	Albert of Saxe-Coburg	1837	1901
Saxe-Coburg:					
Edward VII	1841	Son of Victoria	Alexandra of Denmark	1901	1910
Windsor:					
George V	1865	Son of Edward VII	Victoria Mary of Teck	1910	1936
Edward VIII	1894	Son of George V	Mrs Wallis Simpson (*née* Warfield)	1936 abdic.	1972
George VI	1895	Son of George V	Elizabeth Bowes-Lyon	1936	1952
Elizabeth II	1926	Daughter of George VI	Philip, Duke of Edinburgh	1952	

II.

LINEAGE

If you include the brief reign of poor little Jane Grey and the duality of William III and Mary II, Elizabeth II is the sixty-second monarch, and the seventh queen in her own right, to occupy the throne of England since the ninth-century days of Egbert the Great. In her flows the blood of both Saxons and Normans, of the sturdy Tudors and the Scottish Stuarts, of the Princes of Orange and the Electors of Hanover.

She is related, through her descent from the Princes of Orange, to most of the other surviving royal houses of Europe, to Queen Margrethe II of Denmark and Queen Juliana of the Netherlands, to King Carl Gustaf of Sweden and King Olav V of Norway, to Juan Carlos of Spain, Badouin of the Belgians and the Grand Duke of Luxembourg.

Intermarriage among Europe's royal houses over the generations has created a spider's-web of relationships so complex that she and her husband, Prince Philip, are at one and the same time third cousins (through their descent from Queen Victoria), second cousins once removed (from King Christian IX of Denmark) and fourth cousins once removed (through collateral descendants of George III).

Through her maternal grandfather, the 14th Earl of Strathmore and Kinghorne, she is also descended from Colonel Augustine Warner, who emigrated from England to the new-found colony of Virginia early in the seventeenth century, and whose other descendants were to include George Washington and General Robert E. Lee.

Not all England's monarchs since Egbert – the eleventh-century invading Danes, for instance – are to be found in the mainstream of Elizabeth II's descent, but most are, as the accompanying charts show (actual monarchs are given in capitals).

Inevitably, a blood line which reaches back more than a thousand years will include the weak as well as the strong, bad as well as good, simpletons as well as the wise, saints and sinners, heroes and cowards, murderers and their victims.

Little is known about Elizabeth II's ninth-century Saxon ancestor, Egbert the Great. We know when he died, but not when he was born. We know that he was the son of Ethelmund, who was driven into exile in the "land of the Franks", which is now part of France, by Offa of Mercia. We know that he returned when the Witan (or Council) offered him the kingship of Wessex.

In those far-off times, England was divided into a number of small, more or less independent tribal kingdoms. Kent, Essex, East Anglia and Sussex were all small separate kingdoms, their geographic areas corresponding roughly with those which bear the same names today. Wessex was bigger. Mercia and Northumbria were bigger still. Northumbria stretched roughly from the Humber to the Firth of Forth, with the Scottish border, a far from fixed demarcation line, running south from the Firth of Forth to the mouth of the Mersey. Wales was situated more or less where it is now, but there was also West Wales – a kingdom made up of Cornwall and much of Devon.

Each little kingdom had its separate king – until the return of Egbert as king of Wessex. He conquered Mercia, absorbed Sussex and Essex, formed an alliance with East Anglia, was accepted as *bretwalda* – a Saxon word which seems to have meant "overlord" – by Kent and was somewhat grudgingly conceded the same title by Northumbria. By 829, though he did not really rule Northumbria and East Anglia, and certainly not Wales, he was close to being England's first real king.

On Egbert's death in 839, his freshly and loosely united kingdom began to fall apart again. His son Ethelwulf siphoned off part of it to his own son, Ethelbald, while another son, Ethelbert, took over his father's share when Ethelwulf died. With the death of his brother Ethelbald, Ethelbert again amalgamated the whole territory. On his death it passed to another brother, Ethelred and then to yet another. The fourth brother was Alfred the Great who, as every schoolchild knows, burnt the cakes between attacking and being attacked by the marauding Danes.

More is known about Alfred than about any of his three brothers. He was born about 849 and took as his wife Elswith or Aelhswith (the spelling varies) of Gaini. In those days, in England as in Scotland (*see* Kings and Queens of Scotland), a system of tanistry rather than primogeniture applied to kingship and Alfred was elected king by the Witan in preference to the youthful son of the dead Ethelred. He ruled for twenty-eight years until 899 and most of that time was spent battling against the Danes. At one point he was forced to cede to them half of his kingdom,

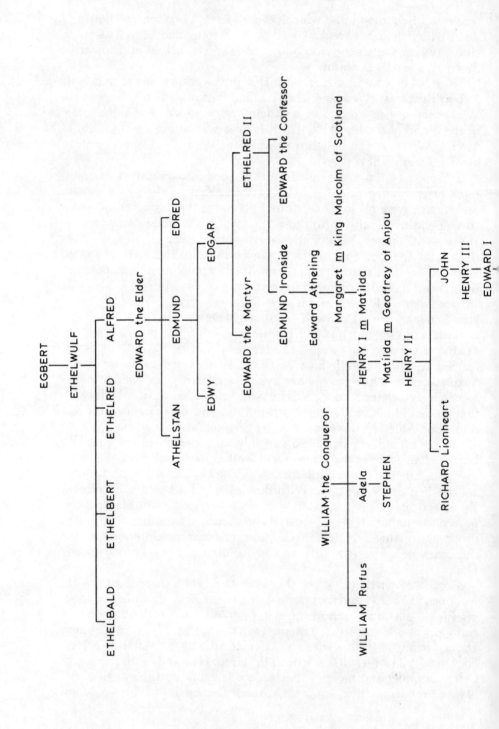

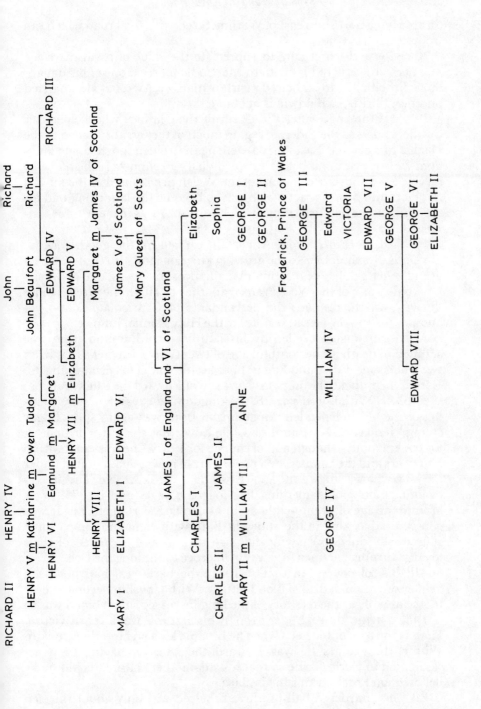

an area lying north and east of Watling Street, the great road which ran from London to Chester.

Alfred was the first king to appreciate the value of royal marriage alliances. To cement his claim to Mercia he married one of his daughters, Ethelfleda, to Ethelred, earldorman of Mercia. He married another, Elfrida, to Baldwin II of Flanders.

It was Ethelfleda, after the death of their father, who helped her brother, Edward the Elder, to regain much of the territory ceded to the Danes. Mercia and East Anglia were again welded into a single kingdom with Wessex and before Edward died – around 924 – he had also received the allegiance of some of the Welsh princes and of the king of the Picts and Scots, a fact which was to become the launching pad for the claim to the Scottish throne which Edward I was to make three centuries later.

Edward the Elder's son, Athelstan, carried on the good work by annexing Northumbria to the growing kingdom and also continued his grandfather's policy of matrimonial alliances, marrying one of his sisters to the king of the West Franks, another to Hugh the Great whose dynasty was to displace the descendants of Charlemagne, and yet another to Otto the Great, restorer of the Holy Roman Empire.

Athelstan was succeeded by his half-brother, Edmund, who was stabbed to death at the youthful age of twenty-five, leaving as his heirs two small sons, Edwy and Edgar, both far too young to become king. So Edred, their uncle, the only surviving son of Edward the Elder, ruled in their place. With Edred's death, the kingdom, always a tenuous grouping of the old independent kingdoms at best, was again split, Edgar ruling Mercia and Northumbria while Edwy took the rest. Fortunately for the kingdom – though not, of course, for Edwy – he was dead within four years and the country, or a major part of it, was again united under the king who was to become known as Edgar the Peaceable. The process of unification took something like fourteen years and in 973, at or around the age of twenty-eight as far as can be ascertained, Edgar was consecrated as king in the abbey at Bath with eight sub-kings (some sources say only six) paying homage to him and, in token of their loyalty, turning oarsmen to row him in procession along the Dee.

All this, of course, in that still semi-barbaric era, had not been achieved without a deal of blood-letting. With kingship becoming ever more valuable as the territory of the king increased, more blood was to be spilled in the future. Edgar's son by his first wife was an early victim. He was thirteen or fourteen when he became king on his father's death. Within three years he was Edward the Martyr, having been assassinated in Corfe Castle so that his stepmother, Elfrida, could make her own son Ethelred king in his place.

Like his murdered half-brother, Ethelred was only about thirteen when he was thrust into kingship by his ambitious mother. He lived to be over fifty, a ripe old age for those turbulent times, but never acquired a great deal of "rede" (the Saxon word for "wisdom"). As a result, he was known as Ethelred the Unready and his thirty-eight-year rule was something of a nightmare as he vacillated between extorting taxes – Danegeld – to buy off the invading Danes and massacring those Danes who settled and sought to colonize England. Then, in 1013, the Danish king, Sweyn Forkbeard, sailed up the Humber with an army and Ethelred, as unready as ever, was forced to flee the country.

He died in 1016 and was succeeded theoretically by his son, Edmund Ironside. In practice, the kingdom was split yet again, Edmund ruling the south and Forkbeard's son, Canute, taking the north. But within a year Ironside was dead and Canute, at the age of twenty-one, had the lot. He was to rule England for the next eighteen years.

With Ironside's death, the royal line from which Elizabeth II is descended was temporarily at an end. But in time it was to stage a comeback.

Canute's death in 1035 left a tangled web of possible claimants to the kingship of England. There were the two sons of Ethelred the Unready's second marriage to Emma of Normandy, Alfred and Edward. But Emma, after Ethelred's death, had married Canute and there was also their son, Hardicanute. Then there were Canute's two bastard sons, Sweyn and Harold, making a total of five claimants in all.

Hardicanute and Sweyn, however, were quickly preoccupied in disputing the kingships of Denmark and Norway. Alfred and Edward had gone to Normandy with their father, the dead Ethelred. Alfred returned to England only to find himself seized, blinded and murdered, and Edward, seeing what had happened to his brother, wisely decided to remain where he was.

In the midst of all this confusion, Canute's other bastard, Harold – not being nicknamed Harefoot for nothing – decided the time was ripe for him to nip in and seize both the crown and the treasury. His half-brother, Hardicanute, was not going to stand for that. He promptly mounted an invasion, but before he could put his plans into practice Harold was already dead.

Hardicanute himself did not survive much longer. Roistering at the wedding feast of one of his retainers two years later brought on a fit from which he died. About the only good thing he did during his brief, oppressive rule was to bring Edward back from exile in Normandy. With Hardicanute's death in 1042 Edward was elected king – he was crowned at Winchester on Easter Sunday the following year – and the old Saxon line, now with more than a dash of Norman blood in its veins, was again back in the royal saddle.

An intensely devout man who has come down in history as "the

Confessor", Edward promptly began building himself an abbey just west of London – West Minster – with a palace nearby from which he could keep an eye on the building programme. Had he been less preoccupied with all this, or perhaps less devout, he might have got round to consummating his marriage to Edith, daughter of Earl Godwin of the West Saxons, and the royal line might have been spared a further hiccup. But non-consummation effectively ensured that there was no son to succeed him and his death in 1066 found his brother-in-law, Harold Godwin, laying claim to the crown. Edward had granted it unto him, he said.

Whatever the truth of that, two others thought they had a better claim or certainly not a worse one, Harold Hardrada of Norway and William, Duke of Normandy. Hardrada was the first to swoop, sailing up the Humber to land at York. Harold Godwin marched his troops north, surprised Hardrada at Stamford Bridge and defeated him. Hardrada was killed in the battle and Harold was still celebrating his victory three days later when word reached him that William had arrived on the scene and was busy landing troops at Pevensey Bay at the far end of the kingdom. Harold did a smart about-turn and marched south. On October 14, 1066, on the hill of Senlac near Hastings, the two armies, Saxon and Norman, confronted each other.

Harold's army, the bulk of it consisting of peasants armed with nothing more lethal than spears and pitchforks, was hardly a match for William's better equipped and more disciplined force, which included two thousand armoured horsemen, the battle tanks of the day. The Saxons fought gallantly enough, but by evening only Harold and his bodyguard of house-carls, trained fighting men, were still in business. Then Harold himself was wounded by an arrow and the Norman horse-tanks finally penetrated the protective wall of Saxon shields to hack him to pieces. On Christmas Day that year, in Edward the Confessor's West Minster, the conquering William was crowned king of England.

William's eldest son, Robert, being otherwise occupied in Normandy at the time of the Conqueror's death in 1087, his second son, William Rufus of the ruddy complexion, took the English crown. Like so many of the country's monarchs in those violent days, he came to a bloody end. Accidentally or otherwise, he was shot with an arrow while hunting in the New Forest on a day when, coincidentally or otherwise, his younger brother, Henry, was also hunting in the same forest.

Henry became King Henry I, though his elder brother, Robert, Duke of Normandy, disputed his claim. Robert would have done better to have held his peace. He ended up losing Normandy as well as England to Henry and spent the last twenty-eight years of his life as his brother's prisoner.

Elsewhere a few drops of royal Saxon blood still lingered on, Malcolm III of Scotland having married Margaret, a descendant of Edmund Ironside, Ethelred and Edgar. To bolster his claim to the throne, Henry married their daughter, Matilda.

When Henry died in 1135, supposedly after guzzling a surfeit of lampreys, he left a positive regiment of illegitimate children – nine sons and eleven daughters at least – but only one legitimate child, a daughter, Matilda. There had been a son, William, but he had died when the *White Ship* was wrecked. The Great Council, however, thought a woman too weak a vessel to rule the country and offered the crown instead to Stephen, a grandson of the Conqueror.

Matilda, who had married the Count of Anjou, Geoffrey Plantagenet, so-called because of the sprig of broom (*plantagenesta*) he wore in his helmet, wasn't about to put up with that. She demonstrated that she was anything but weak by invading England. For years the power struggle ding-donged back and forth. Matilda captured Stephen, but freed him in exchange for her half-brother, Robert of Gloucester. Stephen, in turn, came close to capturing her at Oxford, but she escaped by being lowered from the castle battlements on a rope and making her way across the frozen river camouflaged in a white cloak. Peace was finally restored by the Treaty of Wallingford in 1153 under which Stephen agreed that Matilda's son, Henry, should succeed him as king.

So the great-great-great-grandson of Edmund Ironside was crowned at Winchester in 1154 as King Henry II. Married to Eleanor of Aquitaine, the richest princess in Western Europe, he was lord of an empire which stretched from the borders of Scotland to the Pyrenees, not only King of England, but Duke of Normandy, Count of Anjou, Count of Touraine and Duke of Aquitaine. He ruled more of France than the French king did. It kept him busy. Of the thirty-five years he ruled England, he spent twenty-one of them outside the country, riding ceaselessly from one part of his huge empire to another. A quite unscrupulous monarch of boundless energy, he nevertheless found time to restore his English inheritance, until then a lawless kingdom in which conflict raged constantly between the conquering Normans and the resident Saxons, to some sort of order.

For all that, he died a lonely and embittered man, at Chinon in 1189, three weeks after being defeated by a French army which included two of his own sons, Richard and John. So much for family loyalty in those bad old days. Richard, who succeeded him, was King of England for ten years, but spent only a few months actually in the country. And his wife, Berengaria of Navarre, never set foot in England at all. While Richard, nicknamed "the Lionheart", was busy about his crusades, his brother, John, was making a rare old mess of running his brother's

Monarchy and the Royal Family

kingdom. When Richard finally died of the wounds he received while besieging the castle at Châlus, John appropriated the crown for himself, though Arthur, the son of his elder brother Geoffrey, in fact had a prior claim. But Arthur, like many another claimant to the throne in medieval times, died suddenly in curious circumstances, quite possibly murdered on John's orders.

John continued to make a mess of things, losing much of his father's old empire – Normandy, Anjou, Touraine. In England he behaved so badly that the barons finally brought him to heel at Runnymede. But having signed the Magna Carta in 1215, he promptly decided to ignore it, whereupon the barons appealed to France for help. In May, 1216, the French king invaded England. However, John died a few months later and his nine-year-old son was crowned as Henry III.

For the next 160 years, from the succession of Henry III in 1216 to the death of Edward III in 1377, son was to succeed father on the throne in unbroken line, though not all ruled with equal success. John's son proved to be a weak, pious king, as indecisive and incompetent as his father. Again the barons rebelled. In a pitched battle at Lewes Henry was defeated by his brother-in-law, Simon de Montfort, but later rescued and reinstated by the son who became Edward I.

Nicknamed "Longshanks" because he was so tall and lean, Edward was everything his father was not. And certainly war-like. Away on a crusade when his father died in 1272, he returned to subdue Wales, building castles that were like great walled cities to keep the Welsh in check. He swore he would not sleep two nights in the same place until he had done the same with the Scots. Conquer Scotland he did, in a lightning twenty-one-week campaign, but failed to hold it. More than merely a warrior king, he was also largely responsible for the real beginnings of Parliament (*see* Monarchy). He was an exceedingly complex man for his day and age whose tomb in Westminster Abbey was to be inscribed: *Edwardus Primus Malleus Scotorum hic est.* Yet when his first wife, Eleanor of Castile, died in Nottinghamshire in 1290, he wrote, "In life I loved her dearly; nor can I cease to love her in death." He ordered an elaborate stone cross to be built at each place where her body rested on its way to burial at Westminster, three of which still survive.

He himself was on his way north again in 1307, for another attempt to subdue Scotland, when he died at Burgh-on-Sands. As so often in the history of monarchy, a strong king was to be followed by a weak one. The homosexual Edward II, who succeeded his father, lost what the father had gained in Scotland to Robert Bruce, was deserted by his French wife, Isabella, and ended up being brutally murdered in Berkeley Castle. While the great barons again jostled for power around the throne, Isabella and her lover, Roger Mortimer, ruled the country in her son's name. But their triumph was to be short-lived. At the age of eighteen, that same son was to imprison his mother, execute Mortimer, reimpose the power of monarchy and introduce the great age of knighthood and chivalry. Edward III was still only twenty when he trounced the Scots at Halidon Hill in 1333. Similarly, reviving the old claim to the kingdom of France, he trounced the French at Crécy. The French had thought the English trapped and encircled, but reckoned without the formidable power of the longbow, wielded with deadly effect by the archers from Sherwood and Macclesfield whom Edward recruited into his army. Seven feet tall, the longbow was the most lethal weapon of the age. An expert bowman could lose arrows at the rate of six a minute with a velocity powerful enough to pierce chain-mail at up to three hundred yards. At Crécy on that night of August 26–27, 1346, they are said to have slain 1,500 French knights and a staggering 10,000 foot soldiers.

At Poitiers, under the command of Edward's son, the Black Prince, the English had another striking and bloody victory over the French, but the Black Prince died before he could succeed his father and it was Edward's grandson, Richard II, a boy of ten, who followed him as king when he died in 1377. His rule began with high promise. Barely a teenager when the Peasants' Revolt erupted in 1381, he nevertheless rode out to confront the rebels. When the peasants' leader, Wat Tyler, was slain by the Lord Mayor of London, it looked as though the whole of the royal party would be massacred in revenge. It was the coolness and audacity of the young Richard which saved the day.

"Will you kill your King?" he cried as the rebels strung their longbows around him. "You have lost your leader. Now I will lead you. Let him who loves me, follow me."

The youthful appeal and courage of the boy-king turned the trick. But like many another popular idol, Richard let success go to his head. He grew into a fickle, vindictive, despotic monarch, quick to execute or exile all who opposed him, among them his cousin, Henry Bolingbroke, Duke of Lancaster, the son of John of Gaunt. Bolingbroke he exiled, but in 1399, while Richard was in Ireland, the exiled cousin launched an invasion from France. In three weeks, with an army of only three hundred men, he made himself master of England. Richard was ambushed, captured and imprisoned in Pontefract Castle where he died, almost certainly murdered, in 1400 while cousin Bolingbroke proclaimed himself Henry IV.

Bolingbroke based his claim to the crown not only on the fact that he was a grandson of Edward III – though the old king's great-grandson, Edward Mortimer, ranked ahead of him in that particular line of succession – but that he was also, through his mother, a great-great-grandson of Edmund Crouchback, brother of Edward I. It was something of an outrageous claim, but even more remarkable was the fact that Parliament accepted it. Not everyone else did and there was rebellion after rebellion, as well as fighting in Wales, Scotland and France to occupy his attention. Henry ruled as a ruthless tyrant, putting down the first rebellion against him with utter ferocity, executing and dismembering the bodies of thirty rebel leaders. Fearing intrigue at every turn, he became suspicious of even his own heir, the prince who was to become Henry V when his father died, face and body disfigured, apparently from leprosy, at Westminster Palace in 1413.

Dubious though his father's claim to the crown had been, the son was determined not only to keep his royal inheritance but to add to it. Lean and hatchet-faced, he had learned the trade of war as a boy of fifteen, fighting against Owen Glendower in Wales and the rebellious Percys in Northumberland. Now, as king, he was to prove himself a military genius, pawning both his crown and the crown jewels of the day to meet the cost of mounting an invasion of France with 2,000 knights and 6,000 bowmen. At Harfleur and again at Agincourt, he scored resounding victories. Surrounded and outnumbered three to one at Agincourt, his men starving, he achieved victory, as Edward III had done before him, through the deadly accuracy of the longbow. At the end of a day of bloody battle some six thousand French lay dead while the English had lost only four hundred men.

Two years later Henry returned to France with a yet larger army, laying siege to every Norman city in turn, Caen, Verneuil, Falaise. He starved the capital, Rouen, into surrender, allied himself with the Burgundians against the French and ended up marrying the French king's daughter, Catherine of Valois, and seeing himself accepted as heir to the throne of France. But though only in his early thirties, his body was already worn out by a lifetime of battles. And the fighting was not yet over. His health failing, he insisted on being carried to the siege of Cosne on a litter and died soon afterwards, from dysentery. He was thirty-four and had ruled for nine years which rank among the most outstanding in English military history.

His son by Catherine of Valois was barely nine months old when he succeeded to the throne as Henry VI. He grew into a pious and weak-minded nincompoop who wore a hair shirt next to his body at the same time that he wore the crown on his head and crept around spying on his servants to ensure that they had no women in their beds. Under him, England lost all her French conquests except Calais and at home the country was torn by civil war as the rival houses of York and Lancaster vied for the crown. Henry himself had little stomach for the fight, but his wife, Margaret of Anjou, was made of sterner stuff. She defeated the Yorkists at Wakefield and not only beheaded Richard of York, who claimed the throne as great-grandson of Edward III, but crowned his severed head with a paper crown and displayed it on the battlements.

For years the fortunes of war swayed back and forth. At Towton, Margaret and Henry were defeated in turn and forced to flee to Scotland while the tall, lusty son of the dead Richard crowned himself Edward IV.

Henry was taken prisoner and confined to the Tower of London. But Edward's marriage to Lady Elizabeth Grey, and the way he favoured her relatives, enraged the "Kingmaker" Earl of Warwick who had helped him gain the throne. As a result, Warwick switched sides and in 1469 it was Edward's turn to flee the country while poor feeble-minded Henry was brought tottering from the Tower and reinstalled on the throne. However, Edward was not yet beaten. In a come-back campaign he defeated the Lancastrians at Barnet (where Warwick was slain) and again at Tewkesbury (where Henry's young son was killed). Henry himself was returned to the Tower where he died – murdered or executed, according to which side you were on – the night Edward rode back into London as king.

For the next twelve years Edward ruled as a cruel, ruthless and lusty monarch, quick to bed any attractive woman who chanced to catch the royal eye. The slightest flicker of opposition to his rule was quickly extinguished. Even his own brother, the Duke of Clarence, was despatched to the Tower when he was suspected of disloyalty and died there, drowned, it is said, in a butt of malmsey wine.

But the power struggle for that rich prize, the crown, was still far from over. Edward IV died in 1483 at the age of forty, leaving as his successor a thirteen-year-old son. It was an opportune moment for the boy's uncle, Edward's only surviving brother, Richard, Duke of Gloucester, to make his own bid for the crown. Aided by the Duke of Buckingham, he kidnapped the boy-king, marched on London and proclaimed himself Guardian of the King's Person. Guardianship took the form, nine days before the date set for the youngster's coronation, of confining both him and his younger brother, the Duke of York, to the Tower. The following month Richard crowned himself king instead. For a short time after, his two small nephews were occasionally seen playing in the gardens of the Tower. Then they disappeared. It was not for nearly two centuries that their remains were discovered, buried ten feet down in a wooden chest. Charles II, who was on the throne when the gruesome discovery was made, had them reinterred in Westminster Abbey.

But the crown he had seized was to remain on Richard's head for only two years. He was soon in conflict not only with his Lancastrian rival claimants to the crown but with his own Yorkist supporters. The Duke of Buckingham, who some think was actually responsible for the murder of Richard's two small nephews, suddenly deserted Richard and came out in support of an almost unknown Welshman living in exile in Brittany, Henry Tudor, Earl of Richmond, descendant of a secret marriage between Henry V's widow, Catherine of Valois, and her Clerk of Wardrobe, Owen Tudor. Richard moved swiftly. He captured Buckingham and executed him in the market square at Salisbury. But not swiftly enough to prevent the exiled Tudor landing in Wales at the head of an army. The two forces clashed head on at Bosworth. Richard had the bigger army and might have won the day had not many of his men deserted to the enemy. By nightfall Richard was dead, slain at the head of a cavalry charge. The crown he had been wearing was found under a gorse bush and set upon the head of Henry Tudor. The year was 1485.

Neither Henry V's widow nor the Clerk of Wardrobe she subsequently married came of the royal blood-line. So once again England had a king who was not of the blood royal, as Henry Tudor – now Henry VII – was quick to recognize. To cement his claim to the throne he lost no time in marrying Elizabeth of York, daughter of Edward IV and sister of the murdered princes. Through her the old royal blood continued to flow unchecked.

In other ways too, Henry VII cemented and augmented the power of the crown. Starting his reign in debt, he subjugated the great nobles by a system of fines and confiscations, taxed his other subjects unremittingly and was thus able to leave his son, Henry VIII, both a vast fortune and a system of government rigidly controlled by the monarch. With an eye to the future unification of England and Scotland, he also married his daughter, Margaret, to King James IV of Scotland.

The Tudors, father, son and three grandchildren – Henry VII, Henry VIII, Edward VI, Mary and Elizabeth – ruled England for the next 120 years. Henry VIII was a handsome, beardless youth when he succeeded his father in 1509, brilliant and gifted, athletic and intellectual, open-handed and merry. In a few short years he had degenerated into a bloated despot and, by the time his rule ended in 1547, he had squandered the fortune his father had bequeathed him and left the kingdom almost as torn as it was at the time of the Wars of the Roses.

His first marriage was to Catherine of Aragon, widow of his dead brother. Obsessed by the need to sire a son as well as eager to possess the vivacious, raven-haired Anne Boleyn (who declined to become his mistress, as her sister had done), he broke with Rome in order to divorce Catherine, dissolved the monasteries and took over their wealth. Tiring of Anne, he beheaded her on the grounds of infidelity and married the gentle Jane Seymour who died giving birth to the sickly future Edward VI. As a measure of diplomacy, he then married Anne of Cleves, found her not at all to his liking and quickly divorced her in favour of the young and beautiful Catherine Howard. But he was no longer the sexual athlete he had once been and, tiring of his fumbling passion, Catherine took herself a lover, was caught in the act and followed Anne Boleyn to the executioner's block. As his final act of matrimony Henry wedded the intellectual Catherine Parr, who outlived him.

Before dying, Henry laid down his own order of succession to the throne. First came his son by Jane Seymour, Edward VI. Then, if Edward died without heir, Henry's daughter Mary by Catherine of Aragon and her heirs; then Elizabeth, his daughter by Anne Boleyn, and her heirs; then the Grey family as heirs of Henry's youngest sister, Mary. Under the influence of the unscrupulous Duke of Northumberland, the sickly young Edward VI was to alter all this, setting Mary and Elizabeth aside as being only "of the half-blood". As a result, on his death in 1553 at the age of sixteen, the crown passed to Lady Jane Grey, fifteen-year-old great-granddaughter of Henry VII, to whom Northumberland had cunningly contrived to marry one of his sons, Lord Guilford Dudley.

Jane was proclaimed queen on July 10, 1553. On July 19 Mary "of the half-blood" proclaimed herself queen, rallied East Anglians to her banner and marched on London. Northumberland was executed. The youthful Jane and her equally youthful husband were sent to the Tower. Their lives might have been spared had Mary's plan to marry Philip of Spain not become the flashpoint for a rebellion aimed at restoring Jane to the throne. The rebellion was put down, though only just, and Jane and her husband, a constant threat to Mary while they lived, went to the block.

Mary was desperate to make England a Catholic nation again (and hundreds were to be burned at the stake as she pursued that end) and equally desperate to have a child to succeed her. On one occasion she joyfully announced that she was pregnant with child, but it proved to be only an attack of dropsy, the disease from which she subsequently died, still childless.

Her death in 1558 brought Anne Boleyn's daughter, Elizabeth, to the throne of a bankrupt and divided country. Declared a bastard by her own father, her first suitor executed for wooing her, imprisoned by her half-sister, Elizabeth was to rule for the next forty-four years as a semi-divine virgin queen. The Archduke Charles, the French Duke of Alençon, Lord Robert Dudley (who she made Earl of Leicester), her Lord Chancellor, Christopher Hatton, and Sir Walter Raleigh, who named Virginia after her virginity, all had hopes of marrying her at varying times. She married none of them. But under her, England became great again. "I know I have the body of a weak and feeble woman, but I have the heart and stomach of a king," she told her troops at Tilbury in the face of possible Spanish invasion. Under her, the Spanish Armada was defeated, Drake sailed round the world (Elizabeth was a shareholder in the enterprise) and Shakespeare wrote his immortal plays.

With her death in 1603, unmarried and childless, the long years of the Tudor dynasty were finally at an end. But not the royal line. Henry VII's foresight in marrying one of his daughters to James IV of Scotland, though it had earlier resulted in the execution of Mary, Queen of Scots, because of the threat she posed to Elizabeth's throne, now brought his Scots-born great-great-grandson to the throne. James I, as he was to be in England, was the son of Mary, Queen of Scots and her second husband, the murdered Darnley, incidentally also a descendant of Henry VII. He became James VI of Scotland the year following his birth (though his effective rule did not actually begin for another sixteen years), when his mother was forced to flee the country after marrying the Earl of Bothwell who almost certainly plotted, and may even have had a hand in carrying out, Darnley's murder.

Scots Jamie proved to be a spendthrift homosexual lording it over a raffish and corrupt court, interpreting the divine right of kings as licence to do as he pleased. "Kings . . . sit upon God's throne on earth," he wrote while cheerfully dissolving Parliament if it did not do what he wanted. He was crafty too, sufficiently astute to give way on those odd occasions when the going became too tough, a policy his Scots-born son, Charles I, would have done well to copy. But Charles inherited only his father's belief in the divine right of kings, not his cunning. As a result, he blundered and stammered his way into civil war rather than yield an inch of what he considered to be his royal prerogative. He remained obstinate to the end, refusing to recognize the parliamentarian court before which he was tried in the Palace of Whitehall. "I do stand more for the liberty of my people than any that come to be my pretended judges," he said. He was brave as well as obstinate. The weather was bitterly cold that January morning in 1649 when he walked to the hastily-erected scaffold outside the palace banquet hall. So he wore two shirts, one on top of the other. He did not want to shiver in case people thought it was due to fear rather than the cold, he said.

The eleven years of Cromwellian republic which followed his execution proved to be as onerous as the rule of any Stuart monarch and the restoration of the monarchy in 1660 came as a welcome relief. Charles II, who had fought in the Civil War as a boy of twelve, had been proclaimed king in Scotland immediately on his father's death. Having been crowned at Scone in 1651, he invaded England, fighting his way as far south as Worcester before suffering defeat at the hands of Cromwell and narrowly escaping capture by hiding in the oak tree at Boscobel and elsewhere before finally taking refuge in France. Now he returned in triumph to reign as the "Merry Monarch", restoring the quaint old custom of permitting anyone who was suitably dressed to stroll into his palace at mealtimes and watch him eat. Tall and lusty, he was a man of many mistresses, among them Catherine Peg (later Lady Green), a singer named Mary Davies, the wife of Viscount Shannon, Barbara Villiers and Louise de Kéroualle (who he made Duchess of Cleveland and Duchess of Portsmouth respectively), Lucy Walters and, of course, Nell Gwyn. "Do not let poor Nelly starve," are said to have been his dying words.

Though he left numerous bastard offspring by his many mistresses, there was no legitimate heir when he died. Accordingly, he was followed on the throne by his brother, James II, who proved to be anything but a merry monarch. Another believer in the divine right of kings, as well as an avowed Catholic, James maintained his own army, ruled without the aid of a parliament and even suspended the law. The birth of a son to his second wife, Mary of Modena, meant an end to any hope of Protestant succession if that particular blood-line was permitted to continue on the throne. Parliament turned for help to William of Orange, who had married James's daughter by his first wife, Anne Hyde, and was himself a grandson of Charles I. William landed at Torbay with a Dutch army, the English army went over to him, and James was caught boarding a ship in which he proposed to flee the country. However, William saw all sorts of complications ensuing if James was brought to trial as Charles I had been. Accordingly, he turned a blind eye to a second attempt at escape, enabling James to get clear of the country and die in exile at St Germain.

James's daughter, Mary, journeyed to England to share the throne with her Dutch husband. She died of smallpox in 1694. William survived until 1702 and on his death the crown passed to his sister-in-law Anne, James's other daughter by Anne Hyde. Stout and fretful Anne may have been, but under her England was again, however briefly, the decisive power in Europe due to Marlborough's victories at Blenheim, Ramillies, Oudenaarde, Malplaquet and Admiral Rooke's capture of Gibraltar.

Married at eighteen to Prince George of Denmark, Anne was pregnant no fewer than seventeen times. But only one of her children survived infancy and he died at the age of eleven. So with her death in 1714, another royal victim of dropsy, the crown reverted to the Hanoverian descendants of James I's daughter, Elizabeth (*see* Succession). This brought the boorish and bulbous-eyed Elector of Hanover to England as George I. He was fifty-four at the time and made the trip in the company of two mistresses, one fat, the other thin, whom his English subjects promptly nicknamed "The Elephant and Castle" and "The Maypole" respectively. His wife, Sophia Dorothea of Celle, remained behind in Hanover, imprisoned there by her husband because of her supposed infidelity with Count Königsmark. When she died in 1726 her husband celebrated the fact by going to the theatre, and it was a further six months before he finally decided to bury her. He was on his way by coach to do this in 1727 when he suffered a cerebral haemorrhage and died at Osnabrück Castle. He was succeeded by the son he had always disliked and distrusted, the peppery, punctilious George II who has come down in history as the last British monarch to lead his troops in battle. Sword in hand, shouting "Now, boys, for the honour of England", he led a charge against the French and their allies at Dettingen.

At home, the second of the Georges played a much larger part in public life than his father had ever done, often disastrously. Only in the last three years of his reign, thanks largely to William Pitt, was Britain's flagging reputation redeemed by Clive's victory at Plassey (which resulted in the control of India) and Wolfe's capture of Quebec (which paved the way for the conquest of Canada). George II died of a heart attack in a lavatory in 1760. His eldest son, Frederick, Prince of Wales – whom George had labelled "the greatest ass, liar and beast in the world" to which Frederick retorted that his father was "a miserly martinet with an insatiable sexual appetite" – had died nine years earlier and it was Frederick's son who succeeded his grandfather. He was twenty-two at the time and the first of the Georges to be born in Britain, good, decent, dull and perhaps more than a shade priggish. But a devoted and faithful husband for all that he had been prevented from marrying the girl he really loved, Sarah Lennox, daughter of the Duke of Richmond, that "sweet lass of Richmond Hill". The wife he did marry, Charlotte of Mecklenburg-Strelitz, rewarded his faithfulness and devotion with fifteen children. But between George III and his eldest son, as between previous fathers and sons of the Hanoverian dynasty, there was to be nothing but trouble.

History largely blames George III for the loss of Britain's American colonies. So, for that matter, does America's Declaration of Independence. In fact, though the king was undoubtedly immature and obstinate in his dealings with his American subjects, the blame really lay with Lord Frederick North and the Parliament of the day. History has also tagged George III with the label "insane". Today's more advanced medical knowledge suggests that he suffered from porphyria, a metabolic disorder. Whatever the cause, by the time he was fifty he was becoming more and more irrational. Curiously, his illness at first, coupled with the domesticity of his home life, made him increasingly popular. During the Napoleonic Wars he was a focal point for national unity, as his descendants, George V and George VI, were to be in World Wars I and II, and his final disintegration in 1811, six years after Nelson's victory at Trafalgar, was looked upon as a national tragedy. Theoretically he remained king for nine more years, a blind and white-bearded figure stumbling pathetically about his isolated apartment at Windsor in a purple dressing-gown while, beyond the castle walls, his spendthrift, self-indulgent son, the Prince Regent, mimicked his sick father's ravings.

Despite the fact that George III had sired fifteen children, nine sons and six daughters, the royal line at this time came perilously close to extinction. To understand how this anomalous state of affairs came about, it is necessary to look at the royal offspring one by one. Of the nine sons, two had died in infancy. That left seven:

1. The Prince Regent (later George IV). Early in his life he had contracted a morganatic marriage with Maria Fitzherbert, a twice-widowed Catholic. Later, in the interests of the official royal line, he contracted a second marriage with the fat and vulgar Princess Caroline of Brunswick. He liked her so little that he was drunk at his own wedding and soon discarded her to return to Mrs Fitzherbert. But not before he had sired a daughter, Charlotte. She married Prince Leopold of Saxe-Coburg. But in 1817, while still in her early twenties, she died in childbirth while producing a stillborn son. So no heir to the throne in that direction.
2. Frederick, Duke of York. At the time of Princess Charlotte's death he had been married for something like a quarter of a century. But in all that time he had had no children.
3. William, Duke of Clarence (William IV). He had had a lot of children, ten in fact, but had never gone through the formality of getting married. The children had all been born to his long-time mistress, an actress named Mrs Jordan. Consequently, they were all illegitimate and could not succeed to the throne.
4. Edward, Duke of Kent. He too was unmarried and happy enough to dally with a mistress, Julie de St Laurent.
5. Ernest, Duke of Cumberland. He had been married for nearly three years at the time of Princess Charlotte's death, but so far no children had resulted.
6. Augustus, Duke of Sussex. He had married Lady Augusta Murray in defiance of his father's Royal Marriage Act (*see* Marriage). As a result, the marriage was declared null and void and his children barred from succeeding to the throne.
7. Adolphus, Duke of Cambridge. He was unmarried.

So much for George III's sons. Of his daughters, one had died, two were unmarried and hardly like to marry, and three, while married, were childless.

So while there were still sons aplenty to succeed the King, there was no legitimate successor in the next generation. Such grandchildren as there were were either illegitimate or barred from the succession. In this worrying situation, William, Edward and Adolphus were quickly told that they must marry and start producing legitimate heirs. Threatened with the loss of their royal emoluments if they did not, they hastened to obey, even though, for William and Edward, it meant discarding their beloved mistresses. All three were married within two months of each other, Adolphus to Princess Augusta of Hesse, Edward to the widow of the Prince of Leinengen, and William to Princess Adelaide of Saxe-Meiningen.

The outcome was that William sired two daughters, but both died in infancy. Adolphus had a son and Edward a daughter. The King's fifth son, Ernest, also surprised everyone by unexpectedly siring a son. Of the three living legitimate grandchildren, it was Edward's daughter who was next in line after the brothers themselves. The succession was safe.

The Prince Regent was fifty-seven when his unfortunate father died and he became King George IV. Like Henry VIII before him, he had been handsome and gifted in youth. But years of dissipation, over-eating and over-drinking, now forced him to resort to both corsets and cosmetics if he was to cut any sort of figure in public. But his love of a good show continued and his coronation was perhaps the most lavish spectacle of its kind ever staged (*see* Coronation). The discarded Queen Caroline was barred from the ceremony. She tried to force her way in, but did not succeed. In striking contrast to his earlier roistering years as Prince Regent, however, as King George IV he spent almost the entire ten years of his reign in seclusion with his mistresses. An extravagantly generous patron of the arts, he left a vast collection of paintings, furniture and bric-à-brac on his death in 1830 (*see* Furniture and *Objets d'Art and* Picture Collection).

The next brother in line, Frederick, Duke of York, having died in 1827, George IV was succeeded by the sailor of the family, William IV, third son of George III, a hearty and eccentric monarch given to expressing himself in salty language and not above spitting in public if he felt so inclined. He was nearly sixty-five when he came to the throne after some twenty-one years in the navy. Next in line after him was brother Edward, Duke of Kent. But he died before William.

The daughter Edward had sired as a result of that hastily-contracted marriage to the widow of the Prince of Leiningen was eighteen that night in 1837 when Uncle William IV died and horsemen set off through the darkness to salute her as the new Queen. Her name was Victoria.

(The remainder of the royal lineage will be found in the following sections: Queen Victoria and Prince Albert; King Edward VII and Queen Alexandra; King George V and Queen Mary; King George VI; Queen Elizabeth, the Queen Mother; and Queen Elizabeth II.)

MARRIAGE

Horrified when two of his brothers contracted what he considered to be scandalous marriages with commoners, that highly moral, even strait-laced monarch George III decided that there should be no repetition of such "scandal" in the Royal Family. One brother, the Duke of Gloucester, had married the once-widowed illegitimate daughter of Sir Edward Walpole. Five years later, the other brother, the Duke of Cumberland, was secretly married to another widow, Mrs Anne Horton. When the secret leaked out George III promptly announced that anyone who "waited upon" the couple would no longer be received at court. He also directed the prime minister, Lord North, to bring in legislation which would prevent any such thing happening again. The outcome was the Royal Marriage Act of 1772, the provisions of which still hold good today.

It was passed in Parliament by only a small majority. Many opposed it and their feelings were perhaps best summed up by the Member of Parliament who labelled it a law giving royal princes "leave to lie with our wives while forbidding them to marry our daughters."

Under the Royal Marriage Act, it is illegal for any descendant of King George II (other than the issue of princesses who have married into foreign families) to contract a marriage without the consent of the reigning Sovereign. The penalties for doing so – on paper, at least – are severe. They include loss of civil rights, loss of land and goods, and im-prisonment. The marriage becomes null and void and any children are regarded as illegitimate.

There is no such thing in British law, as the Duke of Windsor dis-covered in the days when he was King Edward VIII, as a morganatic marriage (*see* Duke and Duchess of Windsor). In his desire to marry Mrs Simpson, the Duke suggested, in fact, that Parliament should pass an Act permitting him to do so morganatically, but Prime Minister Stanley Baldwin declined to introduce any such legislation.

For others, however, there is a slight get-out clause which Parliament insisted on inserting before passing George III's prohibitory Bill. This clause permits any descendant of George II who is over the age of twenty-five and is refused the Sovereign's permission to marry, to give twelve months' notice to the Privy Council and to marry at the end of that time provided Parliament raises no objection. There was speculation that Princess Margaret (*see* Princess Margaret and Lord Snowdon), having just reached the age of twenty-five, might have invoked this clause when Peter Townsend returned to Britain in 1955. It is history now that she did not.

The marriage of anyone in line of succession to the throne is also restricted by the Act of Settlement of 1701, at least if they wish to remain in the line of succession (*see* Succession). This Act bars anyone who marries "a papist" from succeeding to the throne, and it was because of this that Prince Michael of Kent (*see* Prince and Princess Michael of Kent) renounced his right of succession in 1978 to clear the way for his marriage to the Baroness Marie-Christine von Reibnitz, a Catholic.

MAUNDY

Like so many of Britain's traditions, the origins of the Royal Maundy, a charity distributed annually on the Thursday of Holy Week, are lost in the mists of time. Even the origins of the word "maundy" are obscure. Some think it comes from the French *maunde* which comes in turn from the Latin *mandatum*, meaning a commandment. Others think it stems from *maund*, an old Saxon word for the basket from which the lady of the manor once distributed bread to the poor.

No one knows for sure when the ceremony first started, though it was possibly in the reign of the pious Edward the Confessor. Certainly it was being observed in his day, though in very different form from today. Edward sought to demonstrate his humility and compassion by washing the feet of the poor in emulation of Christ. The ceremony continued in this form for some centuries after Edward, though Elizabeth I, displaying regal fastidiousness rather than humility, ensured that her court officials washed the feet of the poor in scented water before she herself set to work on them. James II discontinued the whole business, but the Queen's grandfather, King George V, resurrected it, though in a very different form.

The Queen's father continued the new form of ceremony, as the Queen does herself. In its new form, the ceremony consists of distributing alms to as many old men and old women as the years of the monarch's age. The alms, contained in a thonged Tudor-style purse, consist of specially-minted silver coins to the value of one, two, three and four sterlings, a sterling being the ancient penny of Norman times, from which, incidentally, the present pound sterling is derived. The original pound sterling was a weight – the weight of 240 silver sterlings – which is why there were 240 pennies in a £ until decimalization took over in Britain.

In 1957 the Queen decided to distribute the Royal Maundy that year at St Albans Abbey, the first time the ceremony had taken place outside London since the days of Charles II. She has since distributed the Royal Maundy at various other out-of-London centres. While the coins she distributes are specially minted, they remain legal tender, though few, if any, of them ever find their way over the counters of shops or banks in the normal course of business. They are far too highly prized for that by those who qualify to receive them, with coin collectors and dealers constantly hovering on the outskirts and ready to bid far above the face value of the coins in the event that a recipient should be tempted or forced by circumstances to dispose of them. One man who received Royal Maundy from Queen Elizabeth II in the first year of her reign has since received frequent offers of £100 upwards for his set of four small silver coins.

MEALS

Unlike the Queen's great-grandfather, Edward VII, who ate so much he almost doubled his girth, today's Royal Family are extremely modest eaters. And conscious of the dangers which lie in store for those who eat too much of the wrong things. For this reason, fattening pies and stodgy puddings, ice-cream and gooey cakes, seldom, if ever, make an appearance in the private dining-room at Buckingham Palace. Neither is porridge or cereal seen at breakfast time. Instead, there are sometimes eggs, boiled or scrambled, sometimes bacon or sausages, sometimes kippers, followed by toast and marmalade. The Royals know in advance what they will be getting from the suggested menu for the following day's meals which the head chef sends up from the kitchens around tea-time each day. The Queen ticks those items she prefers.

No servants wait on the royal couple at breakfast time. Instead, they serve themselves from a range of dishes kept warm on hotplates. The Queen also prefers to make her own breakfast pot of China tea, using water from an electric kettle mounted in a swivel stand to make pouring easier, an idea which originated in the inventive brain of Prince Philip. She takes her tea with milk but no sugar. Philip prefers coffee for breakfast.

Just as there is no porridge or cereal for breakfast, so – unless there are guests to be entertained – there is no soup or other starter for lunch and no sweet with which to finish. Sometimes the royal couple lunch together or, if Prince Philip is out or away, the Queen lunches alone. Lunch consists usually of a main course of fish or meat – lamb is a particular favourite – with small helpings of appropriate vegetables and a side plate of salad, followed by biscuits and cheese. Except when there are guests, no rare wines from the palace cellars grace the luncheon table. Instead, the Queen usually sips a glass of orange squash. There is coffee on the sideboard if she should happen to want it.

By royal standards, dinner at Buckingham Palace is an almost equally informal affair these days. Unless they are entertaining guests, neither the Queen nor her husband change into evening dress for dinner, though the Queen Mother, just down the road at Clarence House, still does so even when dining alone. Nor, unless they have guests, do the Queen and Prince Philip have servants to wait on them for dinner (though there is at least one hovering just outside the dining-room in case he is wanted). And as at lunch, if they are on their own, there is no first course. Dinner, in fact, is almost a repetition of lunch, a main course – perhaps lamb cutlets, perhaps fillet steak, perhaps chicken – with appropriate vegetables and a side plate of salad. Philip may have a glass of wine, usually white, with the meal, though he prefers beer at lunch-times. The Queen will sometimes join him in having wine, will sometimes stick to orange squash and occasionally opts simply for water. Usually, there is no sweet course to follow. Instead, royal husband and wife prefer another light savoury dish – perhaps kidneys rolled in bacon or scrambled egg topped with anchovies – with fruit, perhaps an apple or a few grapes, to conclude. Coffee – white without sugar for the Queen, black with sugar for Prince Philip – winds up the meal.

MONARCHY

To most of her subjects she is simply "The Queen", though one banner which greeted her as she drove through London on the occasion of her 1977 Silver Jubilee down graded her to the more plebeian, if also more affectionate, "Liz". To those who are not her subjects she is, usually, Elizabeth the Second. Her full title is a somewhat convoluted mouthful: *Elizabeth the Second, by the Grace of God of the United Kingdom of Great Britain and Northern Ireland and her other Realms and Territories Queen, Head of the Commonwealth, Defender of the Faith.*

Such a convolution would appear to have originated from the quill pen of an over-enthusiastic clerical draughtsman entrusted with the task of framing the royal title a generation or so back. The actual wording may have changed since then – Britain's monarchs ceased to be Emperors/Empresses of India in 1947, for instance – but the inverted phrasing remains.

The other "Realms and Territories" over which she reigns (as at July, 1979) are Australia, the Bahamas, Barbados, Canada, Dominica, Fiji, Grenada, Jamaica, Mauritius, New Zealand, Papua New Guinea, St Lucia, Tuvalu (formerly the Ellice Islands) and the Solomon Islands, of all of which she is also Queen, represented in her absence by a Governor-General (*see* Governors-General). In addition, she is recognized as Head of the Commonwealth by some twenty-six other states, four of which – Lesotho, Malaysia, Swaziland and Tonga – have their own monarchs. The other twenty-two are republics. They are: Bangladesh, Botswana, Cyprus, Gambia, Ghana, Kenya, Malawi, Naura, Nigeria, the Seychelles, Sierra Leone, Sri Lanka, Tanzania, Uganda, Zambia, Guyana, India, Kiribati, Malta, Singapore, Trinidad and Tobago, and Western Samoa.

Add them all together and you have an estimated population of over 900 million people occupying a total area in excess of ten million square miles.

In Britain she is also Sovereign of the British Orders of Knighthood (*see* Honours and Investitures), Sovereign Head of the Order of St John and Lord High Admiral. In theory, she is all-powerful, the source of justice and the fountain of honour. Judges, ambassadors and archbishops are alike appointed in her name. British passports are likewise issued in her name and it is to her, with a considerable degree of pomp and ceremony still, that foreign ambassadors appointed to London present their credentials. One of the state landaus is despatched from the royal mews to fetch them to Buckingham Palace. They dress up for the occasion either in diplomatic uniform or evening dress, and are flanked on one side by the Marshal of the Diplomatic Corps and on the other by the Master of the Household as they are ushered into the Queen's presence to hand her their Letters of Credence. The Letters of Credence which Britain's own ambassadors similarly present to foreign heads of state are written in the Queen's name: "We therefore request that you will give entire Credence to all that he (the British ambassador) will communicate to you in Our name." But despite the fact that it is to the Queen in person that foreign ambassadors present their credentials, it is these days the Foreign Secretary, hovering close at hand on such occasions, who is the true power behind the throne when it comes to foreign affairs.

The rest of the Monarch's traditional awesome powers are similarly nearly all – though not quite all – little more than a polite fiction these days. By the exercise of her Royal Prerogative, it is said, the Queen could disband Britain's army, auction off the ships of the navy, dismiss the civil service, cede territory to a foreign power or declare war. In practice, of course, she can no longer do anything of the sort.

Embodied also in the Royal Prerogative is the right to dismiss a government or dissolve Parliament. The government of the day, whatever its political persuasion, is always "Her Majesty's Government" and no parliamentary bill can become law until it has received her royal assent in the traditional Norman French . . . *La Reyne le veult* (roughly speaking, The Queen consents). In practice, a modern monarch like Elizabeth cannot refuse to approve anything Parliament has decided. Queen Anne was the last to do so, exercising her Royal Veto again in the traditional Norman French . . . *La Reyne s'avisera* (The Queen will think it over). That was back in 1707.

Even the Speech from the Throne with which the Queen opens each fresh Parliament (*see* Opening of Parliament) is written for her by the prime minister and his/her aides. By accepted custom, she must read it word for word exactly as written, whether or not she agrees with the policies put forward by it. Indeed, in some ways, a modern monarch like Elizabeth II would seem to have less real power than her subjects. They can always combine to vote a new government into office at election times. The Queen has no vote. Neither, for that matter, do royal dukes.

Yet, as we shall see presently, one fragment of real power still remains in the monarch's hands as the surviving remnant of the days when monarchs were supreme beings whose lightest word was law. In those days, they levied their own taxes, raised their own armies, rewarded friends and supporters, beheaded their enemies, led their troops into battle. All this was a long time ago, of course. George II was the last monarch to ride into battle at the head of an army. And even in his day most of the power of monarchy had already drifted into the hands of Parliament.

The changeover had its first small beginnings back in 1076 when William the Conqueror, in an attempt to appease the Saxons he had conquered, summoned their wise men to form his Great Council. History records that the Great Council met at Gloucester on Christmas Day, at Winchester at Easter and at Westminster at Pentecost. It can hardly have met that often for the simple reason that William was hardly ever in the country. Nor does he appear to have taken much notice of the advice the wise men gave him. Or perhaps it was that, being truly wise, they tendered only the advice they felt he wanted to hear.

The next twist in the chain of change came with Henry II, first of the Plantagenet kings. With much of Europe to rule as well as England – he spent twenty-one years of his thirty-four-year reign riding restlessly from one end of his Anglo-Norman-Anjou-Aquitaine empire to the other – Henry did not want more trouble than was absolutely necessary from either the Church, wealthy and powerful in those days, or the great barons. In an attempt to curb the power of both, and maintain his own regal rights in his absence, he instituted a system of Common Law with regular courts, more or less trained judges and juries of twelve good and true men.

The barons, of course, were not happy about all this. Nor, indeed, were Henry's own sons. The misdeeds of one of these sons, John, when he became king in turn, led to the signing of the Magna Carta, so often hailed as the basis of English liberty. In fact, the Magna Carta had comparatively little to do with the preservation of liberty, as we understand the word today. It was much more concerned with restoring the earlier privileges of the barons. In any event, neither John nor his sucessor, Henry III, always bothered to observe the provisions of Magna Carta and it was this fact which led to Simon de Montfort's rebellion and the subsequent Great Council of 1265.

While that Great Council of 1265, with its representatives from the shires, the cities and the boroughs, was perhaps England's first real Parliament, it remained for Edward I to institute a system of convening Parliament at more frequent, if still irregular, intervals. "That which touches all must be approved by all," he murmured piously while taking good care that it was only his own laws and taxes which Parliament approved.

Yet at the same time, perhaps without realizing, he was also conceding the principle that a monarch could no longer act without the approval of Parliament. The Parliament of Edward I's day consisted at first only of the more powerful barons and knights. Such lesser lights as the younger sons of noble houses were still rigidly excluded from the rank of hereditary legislators. Determined to have their say, they allied themselves with the burgesses from the boroughs, who also felt that they were accorded too small a voice in things. So the House of Commons, as it was in fact if not in name, came into existence alongside the hereditary House of Lords.

Decade by decade, monarchy by monarchy, Parliament acquired more power. But the overall voice was still that of the king and the Tudor dynasty was virtually a succession of regal dictatorships. Henry VII seldom bothered to convene Parliament at all. Henry VIII, perhaps the most powerful and certainly the most terrifying monarch in English history, did summon Parliament at intervals but only to use it for his own ends. His daughter, Elizabeth I, is generally thought of as a democratic monarch. In fact, Parliament was in session for a total of only twenty-two months during the entire forty-five years she was on the throne. It was only towards the end of her long reign that Parliament at last began to feel its feet sufficiently to voice an occasional, and usually timid, opinion on those things, such as foreign policy, religion and the possibility of royal marriage, which the Virgin Queen insisted were her own prerogative.

But if Parliament was growing steadily stronger, monarchs were not yet prepared to yield entirely. A clash was sooner or later inevitable and it came with Charles I. Inheriting his father's firm belief in the divine right of kings, but not the old man's pragmatism in handling a changing situation, he sought to rule without Parliament and paid for it eventually with his head.

The eleven years of Cromwellian republicanism which followed proved as tyrannical as the rule of any Stuart monarch and Parliament was more than ready to welcome back Charles II. But another clash came with the succession of his brother, James II. Like his father before him, James tried to rule without Parliament – and ended up in exile following the arrival of William of Orange.

Parliament, now very much in the driving seat, attached conditions to the husband-and-wife monarchy of William and Mary in the form of a Bill of Rights. The Bill of Rights prohibited the monarch from suspending the law, levying taxes or raising an army without parliamentary consent. It also introduced a rough and ready system which marked the start of free elections.

In addition, the advent of William and Mary resulted in the beginning of today's system of Cabinet government. William, in 1693, was the first monarch to select his principal officers of state from the party which had a majority in the Commons. These were the Whigs to whom he and Mary largely owed their occupancy of the throne. That first-ever Cabinet of the leading Whigs was known as "the Junto" and regarded by other members of Parliament with a considerable degree of suspicion.

The newly-formed Junto (or Cabinet) quickly assumed more and more power, largely through the 1701 Act of Settlement. The Act of Settlement, in addition to ordering the future line of succession to the throne (*see* Succession), also laid down the dictum that ministers in future would be responsible for the acts of the Sovereign. If this meant that a king, or queen, could do no wrong, it also meant that a monarch could no longer do anything worthwhile except on the advice of the Junto.

In those days the King still presided over meetings of the Junto or Cabinet. Even that ceased with the arrival from Hanover of George I, who was more enthused by the doubtful charms of the two mistresses he brought with him than he was by the politics of his new kingdom. George was more than willing for others to run the country provided he was generously compensated for reigning over it. In any event, he spoke little or no English. So his place at the head of the Cabinet table was taken by a senior minister – who in time was to become known as the prime minister.

By the time the youthful Queen Victoria succeeded to the throne, political power – aided by the illness of George III and the indolence of the son who succeeded him – had passed almost completely from Monarch to Parliament. But Victoria was not about to cede what little power still remained to her without a struggle. For a start, she insisted that all dispatches to foreign governments must be submitted to her for approval before being sent. And not infrequently she – or, more probably, Prince Albert, the husband who acted also as her private secretary – altered them.

It was certainly Albert who altered a Foreign Office dispatch which, left unaltered, might have led to war between Britain and the United States. It was at the time of the American Civil War. The *USS San Jacinto* intercepted a British vessel, *Trent*, boarded it and arrested two Confederate commissioners who were on board at the time. Britain's Lord Palmerston promptly fired off an indignant demand for restitution and compensation. Fortunately, he had to submit it to the Queen before sending it off. Albert, when he saw it, thought it left the Americans no way of extricating themselves without unacceptable loss of face. Accordingly, he toned down the dispatch somewhat. The result of his changes was that the North released its two Confederate prisoners and the whole business was smoothed over.

Perhaps the nearest Queen Elizabeth II has come to doing anything similar was in 1965 when Rhodesia staged its unilateral Declaration of Independence. At that time she wrote the Rhodesian leader, Ian Smith, a personal letter reminding him of his duty to the Crown. Unlike Prince Albert's altered dispatch to the Americans, however, her letter to Smith had no effect.

Despite Queen Victoria's rearguard action in defence of monarchical rights, the constitutional expert of her reign, Walter Bagehot, was extremely close to the mark when he wrote, in *The English Constitution* published in 1867, "The Sovereign has, under a constitutional monarchy such as ours, three rights – the right to be consulted, the right to encourage, the right to warn." More recent monarchs have sometimes added a fourth right . . . the right to influence (as the present Queen's grandfather, George V, with Britain on the verge of bankruptcy in 1931, influenced Ramsay MacDonald and others of the Labour Party into joining with the Conservatives to form a coalition government).

Queen Victoria, of course, had a fourth right of her own which Bagehot would seem to have overlooked – the right to be heeded. She interfered in the appointment of government ministers; curtly informed Gladstone, when he became Prime Minister, that foreign policy was not to be changed; and severely castigated Lord Palmerston, when he was Foreign Secretary, on an occasion when he took action first and advised her afterwards instead of consulting her in advance.

It is impossible to visualize the dominating Queen Victoria proffering a timid "I'm sorry – I wasn't criticizing" to one of her ministers as her great-great-granddaughter was to do when a member of her socialist Government took an innocuous royal remark concerning Parliamentary procedure the wrong way. And the fearsome Henry VIII would have had the man's head off.

To some foreign observers it might seem that the Monarch of today, endlessly progressing around Britain, tirelessly flying to all parts of the world, has become little more than a booster of morale at home and an exports promoter abroad. Yet royal trips to foreign parts can sometimes have a deeper and more important significance. If Queen Elizabeth II can no longer indulge in foreign diplomacy to the extent that her great-great-grandmother did, she can at least prepare the ground and pave the way for successful diplomacy. And the same is true of Prince Philip, Prince Charles and others of the family.

Elizabeth II, as she progresses around Britain and jets off to the far corners of the world, is more than merely a symbol, though she is that too of course, a focal point for national emotions at times of tragedy or triumph . . . an ordinary woman raised by a few twists of fate to extraordinary status, venerated even in this permissive age by the vast majority of her subjects and even by a great number of people who owe her no allegiance. An hereditary monarch reflects the deep craving in people for an archetypal ideal, a leader who can do no wrong. Elizabeth II, queen, mother and grandmother, at one and the same time mystically remote from and on the same plane as everyone else, answers that need extremely well.

And even in its present emasculated form a constitutional monarchy performs a real, as distinct from a traditional, function. So long as Bagehot's three rights remain, an hereditary monarch like Elizabeth II can offer her ministers encouragement and warnings based on longer, and perhaps wider, experience than their own.

Prime ministers, like elected presidents, come and go at the whim of the electorate. An hereditary monarch does not. Elizabeth II, in more than twenty-seven years of monarchy as this book goes to press, has already seen eight prime ministers – Churchill, Eden, Macmillan, Douglas-Home, Wilson, Heath, Callaghan and Margaret Thatcher – come, and all but one of them go.

Of course, prime ministers in Britain – like presidents in the United States – today have far more real power than the Sovereign. But prime ministerial and presidential decisions alike are not always taken for the best of motives. They are subject to many influences, including the desire to be re-elected.

An hereditary monarch like Queen Elizabeth II is not concerned about re-election. Politically, he or she should be – and there is no reason to think that Elizabeth II is not – completely neutral, above the hurly-burly of national politics, concerned solely with the well-being of the nation as a whole.

Circumstances have never yet required Elizabeth II to exercise her royal position to the extent that her grandfather did in the formation of that 1931 national government. Even that part of the Royal Prerogative which allows her to appoint or dismiss prime ministers has been only lightly exercised. She did exercise it, to a degree, in 1957 when Anthony Eden (later Lord Avon) resigned for medical reasons in the aftermath of the Suez crisis. There were at the time two main contenders for the title, Harold Macmillan and R. A. Butler. Butler had already deputized for Eden, but the Queen picked Macmillan. But she did so only after Churchill and Lord Salisbury had assured her that it was he who would have the majority support in the Cabinet.

Again in 1963, when Macmillan in turn was compelled to resign through ill-health, she selected Sir Alec Douglas-Home to succeed him, but only after receiving Macmillan's own assurance that Douglas-Home was "the preponderant first choice".

Since then, Britain's political parties having taken to electing their own leaders, the exercise of the Royal Prerogative has been automatic. It would, after all, be pointless to nominate as prime minister anyone other than the elected leader of the party commanding a majority, however slim, in the House of Commons.

As for dismissing a government (as distinct from merely accepting the resignation of a prime minister), it is a long time since any monarch did that. The last was William IV in 1834. But the right to do so is embodied in the Royal Prerogative. And though most of the powers of Britain's monarchy may today be no more than a polite fiction, the power actually to dismiss a government (given a monarch with courage enough to use it) remains a last bastion against the possibility of a totalitarian régime.

R

NAME

So great was the anti-German hysteria which swept Britain during World War I that no one dared play a note of Wagner and even inoffensive dachshunds were hissed – and sometimes booted – in the streets. There was even a rumour that King George V must be pro-German since he had German relatives and a German name.

The Queen's grandfather, one of the most stolidly British of all British monarchs, was horrified when the rumours about himself reached his own ears. That he had German relatives was undeniable – the Kaiser was his cousin – and he could do nothing about that. But he could certainly change his name. Was it really German?

No one knew for sure. No king had had any occasion to use a name since the Stuarts rode south from Edinburgh to occupy England's throne as well as that of Scotland. George V was not a Stuart, of course. He was descended, through George III, from the Electors of Hanover, with the additional complication that his grandmother, Queen Victoria, had married Prince Albert of Saxe-Coburg and Gotha. In all the two and a half centuries since the Hanoverians took over the throne, only one member of the family had ever had occasion to use a name. Not wishing to use his title when he went to sea as a young midshipman, the prince who later became William IV had asked for his name to be entered in the ship's books as Guelph.

So was Guelph the King's name? George V consulted the College of Heralds, who rather doubted it. More likely it was Wettin, they said. Or perhaps Wiper.

Well, whatever it was, the King wanted it changed. Various suggestions, from the cumbersome Tudor-Stuart to the dubious Fitzroy were forthcoming. The King shook his head. He wanted something stolidly British, he said. Plantagenet was also suggested, but that was hardly British, having originated with the Counts of Anjou. York, Lancaster and even England were likewise suggested, all stolidly British, but none of them to the King's liking.

156

It was the King's Private Secretary, Lord Stamfordham, who finally came up with an acceptable solution. Harking back to that most chivalrous of all monarchs, Edward III, he recalled that he had been styled Edward of Windsor. So why not Windsor as the King's family name.

George V was delighted. On July 17, 1917, he held a Privy Council for the purpose of approving an Order in Council by which he formally renounced all titles and honours of Saxony, Saxe-Coburg and Gotha, together with all other German honours and titles, and decreed that "our house and family shall henceforth be known as the House and Family of Windsor." The Order further ordained that "all descendants in the male line of our said grandmother Queen Victoria, other than female descendants who may marry or may have married, shall bear the said name of Windsor."

Almost simultaneously, on the King's invitation – which was tantamount to a royal command – other leading families with German names and titles swapped them for something more British. The Duke of Teck became the Marquess of Cambridge, Prince Alexander of Teck became the Earl of Athlone, while the Princes Louis and Alexander of Battenberg became the Marquess of Milford Haven and the Marquess of Carisbrooke respectively with the family name of Mountbatten (*see* Earl Mountbatten of Burma).

Like so many things conceived in haste with the best of intentions, that 1917 Order in Council overlooked something. While it appears to have visualized that the House of Windsor would occupy Britain's throne for evermore, it ignored the possibility that the throne's occupant might one day be female and that females marry.

Thirty years later, in 1947, the then Princess Elizabeth, first in the line of succession to the throne, married the former Greek prince who had taken the name Mountbatten on British naturalization and who her father had made Duke of Edinburgh a few days before the marriage. Her grandfather's 1917 Order in Council having expressly exempt "female descendants who may marry" from its provisions, there seems little doubt, despite some theories to the contrary, that she became a Mountbatten on marriage and that her heir, Prince Charles, was likewise, under the British custom that a child take the father's name, born a Mountbatten.

On the other hand, it had clearly been her grandfather's wish that the "House and Family of Windsor" should continue on the throne. To resolve any ambiguity, the Queen, on April 9, 1952, two months after her accession, issued her own Order in Council by which she decreed "that I and my children shall be known as the House and Family of Windsor and that my descendants, other than female descendants who marry and their children, shall bear the name of Windsor."

That seemed straightforward enough. There were only two descendants at the time, Prince Charles and Princess Anne. Under this new Order, both became Windsors instead of Mountbattens, though Anne, in due course, would take the name of the man she married.

Then in 1959 the Queen again found herself pregnant. And by then she would seem to have had second thoughts. The result was yet another Order in Council issued on February 8, 1960, eleven days before the birth of Prince Andrew. This decreed that "while I and my children shall continue to be styled and known as the House and Family of Windsor, my descendants other than descendants enjoying the style, title or attribute of Royal Highness and the titular dignity of Prince or Princess and female descendants who marry and their descendants, shall bear the name of Mountbatten-Windsor."

What on earth did all this mean? The constitutional legal eagles who had drawn it up on the Queen's behalf may have known what was intended, but no one else did for certain. An explanatory statement issued at the same time did little to explain things.

The statement said: "The Queen has always wanted, without changing the name of the royal house established by her grandfather, to associate the name of her husband with her own and his descendants."

Confronted with all this, constitutional experts took widely different views as to what was meant. One worked out that it was intended that the name Mountbatten-Windsor should be borne only by the Queen's great-grandchildren and their descendants, which seemed rather a long way in the future. The late Edward Iwi, on the other hand, deduced that "Reading the words of the declaration and message together . . . we may feel that the Queen intended the name of Mountbatten-Windsor to be in the lineage of her children, not merely to be given to her great-grandchildren and their descendants."

His view has proved to be the correct one. In 1973 when Princess Anne married Captain Mark Phillips, she did so in the name of "Anne Mountbatten-Windsor", thus making clear at long last what her mother had intended all along, the linkage of her grandfather's adopted name of Windsor with her husband's equally adopted name of Mountbatten.

But while the children of the Queen's marriage may have become Mountbatten-Windsors, it is still "the House and Family of Windsor", in the person of the Queen herself, who wears the crown.

PALACES. *Above left*: The White Tower of The Tower of London, a palace notorious for its history of torture and execution. *Above right*: The entrance gateway to Hampton Court Palace. *Below left*: Friary Court, St James's Palace: it is in this courtyard that each new monarch is first proclaimed. *Below right*: The Palace of Westminster – historically the oldest of London's royal palaces, although no monarch has lived there for four centuries.

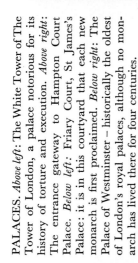

PICTURE COLLECTION. *Above*: The famous triple portrait of Charles I by Van Dyck. *Below: William Anderson with Two Saddle-Horses* by George Stubbs, dated 1793. This painting belongs to the series of thirteen pictures of uniform size painted by Stubbs for the Prince of Wales (later George IV).

Right: *The Duchess of Richmond* by Sir Peter Lely. This is thought to be one of the earlier paintings in Lely's series of *Windsor Beauties*, probably not later than *c.* 1662.

Below: *The Interior of a Tavern* by Jan Steen, *c.* 1660. This painting was purchased by George IV in 1814.

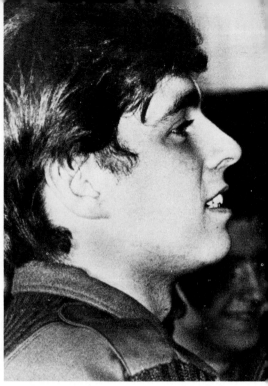

PRINCE EDWARD. *Above left*: Prince Edward at the Farnborough Air Show in 1978. PRINCE ANDREW. *Above right*: the tallest of the three princes, Prince Andrew.

PRINCE CHARLES. Prince Charles, heir to the throne.

PRINCE AND PRINCESS
MICHAEL OF KENT.
Prince and Princess Michael of
Kent with their new baby,
Lord Frederick Windsor, born
April 6th, 1979.

PRINCE PHILIP. Looking
determined, Prince Philip
competes in the National
Carriage Driving
Championships in Windsor
Great Park, September, 1978.

PRINCES OF WALES. *Above*: King George V and Queen Mary with their eldest son (later Edward VIII and Duke of Windsor), at his investiture at Caernarvon Castle in 1911. *Below*: Queen Elizabeth II and Prince Philip with Charles, the 21st Prince of Wales, after his investiture at Caernarvon Castle in 1969.

Above left: PRINCESS ALEXANDRA AND THE HON. ANGUS OGILVY. *Above right*: PRINCESS ALICE, COUNTESS OF ATHLONE. *Below*: PRINCESS ANNE AND MARK PHILLIPS. Proud parents with their newly-christened son, Peter, in the White Drawing-Room of Buckingham Palace.

PRINCESS MARGARET AND LORD SNOWDON. *Above left*: Princess Margaret and Group Captain Peter Townsend at Badminton, 1953. *Above right*: Lord Snowdon and his new wife, formerly Mrs Lucy Lindsay-Hogg, leaving the Kensington Register Office, December 1978. *Below*: An informal picture of Princess Margaret and the Earl of Snowdon taken during their tour of Uganda in 1965.

OPENING OF PARLIAMENT

Once a year age-old ceremony and what little remains of the executive power of Britain's once all-powerful monarchy are brought together. For this one day only Westminster reverts to its true role as the monarch's palace (*see* Palaces), with the House of Lords again serving as the royal parlour to which the Queen's advisers are summoned to "parley" with her, though there is in fact no actual parleying. Everything that is said – and everything that is done – is cut and dried in advance.

The occasion is known these days as the State Opening of Parliament. It starts with the Queen, accompanied usually by Prince Philip and sometimes by one or more of the children, driving in state from Buckingham Palace to Westminster. However, she does not use the elaborately carved and gilded state coach in which she rode to her coronation. Instead, she continues her father's preference for the Irish state coach, a relic of Queen Victoria's day, drawn by a team of Windsor greys (*see* Coaches and Carriages). It is a splendid occasion of traditional pomp and ceremony. She is accompanied by a Sovereign's escort of the Household Cavalry, the Master of the Horse rides at the carriage wheel in full regalia and the streets between Buckingham Palace and Westminster are lined by men from the Guards Division.

While the Queen is on her way to Westminster, another smaller procession is heading, almost unnoticed, in the same direction from the Tower of London. Central to this secondary procession is not a person, but a symbol of monarchy, the Crown of State. It rests in its carriage on a velvet cushion and is escorted, as the Queen herself is, by a detachment of the Household Cavalry. At the Palace of Westminster Monarch and Crown meet.

Ahead of the Queen's arrival, the cellars, galleries and corridors of Westminster are searched as they have been every year since Guy Fawkes and his fellow-conspirators tried to blow the place up in 1605. At one time the search was merely ceremonial, a tradition carried out by the Yeomen of the Guard (not to be confused with the "Beefeaters"

159

of the Tower of London from whom they can be distinguished by their crossbelts, originally intended to support their arquebuses, despite the similarity of their scarlet tunics, white ruffs and black Tudor hats). The Yeomen of the Guard are the oldest royal bodyguards in the world, having been formed by Henry VII after the Battle of Bosworth in 1485. Even so, their ancient pikes and lanterns are hardly suited to coping with present-day terrorism. So in recent years the traditional search has again become the real thing it originally was. Since 1971, when there was a threat (purporting to have come from the IRA) to as- sassinate the Queen when she opened Parliament, the traditional Yeomen have been reinforced in their search with bomb experts and sniffer dogs.

Arriving at Westminster, the Queen is greeted by the Lord Great Chamberlain, traditional Keeper of the Palace of Westminster. She goes first to the robing room set aside for her. There she puts on her crimson Robe of State with its ermine lining and eighteen-foot train, and changes her diamond and pearl diadem for the Crown of State. Two pages of honour take the weight of her train as, escorted by her husband, she makes her formal and ceremonial entry into her "par- lour" – the House of Lords. She is preceded by the Lord Great Cham- berlain and the Earl Marshal of England, both walking backwards; by Heralds and Kings of Arms. Her ladies-in-waiting bring up the rear. A fanfare of trumpets heralds her entry while outside, in St James's Park, the guns of the Royal Horse Artillery boom a royal salute.

Peers bow and peeresses curtsey to her. Everyone present is dressed as befits such a great state occasion, the peers in their parliamentary robes of scarlet cloth and white ermine, the judges in their robes and wigs, diplomats in diplomatic uniform, their wives in long gowns and glittering tiaras. The Queen settles herself on a gilded throne under a Gothic oak canopy (*see* Throne). "My lords, pray be seated," she says.

No monarch has been formally permitted to enter the House of Com- mons since Charles I swooped on it in 1642 and arrested five leading members. Instead, a messenger in a frock-coat and gaiters known as the Gentleman Usher of the Black Rod is sent to summons the members of the Commons to the royal presence. The Queen's father liked this to be done while he was still in the robing room, but his daughter has reverted to the earlier tradition of sending for them only when she herself is seated.

The Commons enter into the spirit of the occasion with almost schoolboyish glee, uttering mock cries of alarm – "Black Rod! Black Rod!" – as the Queen's messenger approaches, and, in a mock gesture of defiance, slamming the door of the chamber almost in the poor man's face. Having knocked three times on the oaken door with his staff, he is finally admitted to deliver his summons to the Queen's presence. Led

by theSpeaker of the Commons, as many members as can be accommodated crowd through to the bar of the House of Lords and remain there
standing – another mock gesture of defiance – while the Queen reads
the Speech from the Throne.

The Lord Chancellor kneels, takes the speech from an embroidered
purse and hands it to her. Though technically the Queen's speech, it is
in fact always written by the prime minister of the day and outlines the
Government's policy for the coming session of Parliament. And the
Queen must read it word for word as written, a fact which necessitates
her wearing glasses these days. Not since the days of Queen Victoria,
who once, at a time of crisis between Germany and Denmark over
Schleswig-Holstein, insisted on re-phrasing certain anti-German remarks,
has any monarch ventured to change the prime minister's wording.

ORDER OF THE GARTER

The Most Noble Order of the Garter is the most exclusive, though not
necessarily the most ancient, order of chivalry in the world. Exactly
how the Order originated is in doubt, but that it originated with
Edward III in 1348 seems certain. Popular legend has it that both the
name of the Order and its motto, *Honi soit qui mal y pense* (Shame on him
who thinks evil of it), had their origins in a ball at which the King's
favourite, Joan, Countess of Salisbury, the "Fair Maid of Kent", had
the misfortune to shed a blue garter while dancing a stately gig. Those
around her tittered. But not Edward III. He picked up the garter and
fastened it round his own leg, at the same time rebuking the titterers
with the words which were to become the motto of the Order.

Another version of the legend has it that it was not the Fair Maid of
Kent, but the King's wife, Queen Philippa, who dropped her garter in
the state apartments and that the words of the motto are those with
which she rebuked her husband when he found it and was suspicious as
to how it had been lost.

Unfortunately, some historians with no sense of the dramatic insist
upon a more mundane origin for the Order of the Garter, though they
do not agree as to exactly how it happened. One school of thought has it
that the Order was originally styled the Knights of the Blue Garter,
founded by Edward after the fashion of King Arthur and the Knights of
the Round Table, with an annual ceremony of dedication held on St
George's Day. Others, however, think that the Order originated at the
Battle of Crécy with the King removing his garter so that it could be
waved aloft as a signal to attack.

Whatever its origins, a blue and gold garter remains the symbol of
the Order, the motto is still the same, and a ceremony of dedication is

still held annually in St George's Chapel, Windsor. Since 1805 its constitution has been fixed at 24 knights in addition to the Sovereign and such lineal descendants of George III as it has been thought fit to appoint. Prime Ministers of the eighteenth and nineteenth centuries were not above dangling the Garter ribbon in front of those they wished to bribe politically, but since 1947 membership of the Order has again become the prerogative of the Monarch.

For a long time too it was customary to award the Order of the Garter to Europe's monarchs and their heirs. But, as Garter knights, this required them to swear an oath never to bear arms against their British Sovereign – an oath they obviously broke in times of war, as the German Kaiser and Crown Prince did in World War I. The fact that they did so incensed patriotic Britons to such an extent that there was talk of a raid on St George's Chapel with the intention of tearing down and destroying the banners of these enemy knights. To avoid such possible outrage, George V, in 1915, had the names of eight enemy knights struck from the rolls of the Order and their banners removed from the chapel. However, he insisted that their name-plates should remain fixed to their stalls in the chapel as a matter of historical record.

George VI, in 1940, similarly had the names of all German and Italian holders struck from the roll-call of British knighthoods. In 1941 the name of the Emperor of Japan was likewise deleted from the roll of the Order of the Garter and his banner removed from the chapel. It was thirty years later before he was reinstated. Other foreigners today numbered among the Knights of the Garter include the King of Norway, the King of the Belgians and the Grand Duke of Luxembourg.

These days there are Ladies of the Garter too. The Queen Mother was appointed to the Order in the days when she was Queen Elizabeth. The present Queen, as a princess, was similarly appointed by her father – a few days ahead of Prince Philip. To give her seniority over him, said her father, to whom such things were important. Since ascending the throne, the Queen, in turn, has appointed Prince Charles a Royal Knight of the Order.

Appointments to the Order of the Garter are traditionally announced on St George's Day (April 23), though the actual ceremony of investiture comes later, coinciding with the Order's annual service of dedication. This is held at Windsor each year on the Monday of Ascot week, usually the second or third Monday of June. Investiture is a private ceremony in the throne room of the castle. Wearing her mantle of blue velvet lined with white taffeta, the Queen, as Sovereign of the Order, fastens a garter round the left leg of the newly-appointed knight, places the riband of the Order over his left shoulder and fixes the star of the Order to his left breast. With Ladies of the Order, the garter is fastened around the left arm, just above the elbow, instead of the leg. Following lunch with her knights in the Waterloo Chamber, the Queen then leads them in procession to St George's Chapel for their annual service of dedication, each knight colourfully resplendent in a mantle of blue velvet emblazoned with the red cross of St George, a surcoat of crimson velvet and a black velvet hat decked with black heron's feathers and white ostrich feathers.

PALACES

Elizabeth II has many palaces. In addition to Buckingham Palace (*see* Buckingham Palace) where she lives and works during the week, Windsor Castle (*see* Windsor Castle) where she spends her weekends and the Palace of Holyroodhouse in Edinburgh (*see* Holyroodhouse) which she dutifully visits about once a year, there are several more in or close to London. Her more remote sanctuaries at Balmoral (*see* Balmoral) and Sandringham (*see* Sandringham) are not royal palaces, but private residences.

Historically the oldest of London's royal palaces, though no monarch has actually lived in it for four centuries, is the Palace of Westminster. It was Edward the Confessor, keen to keep a kingly eye on the church and monastery of West Minster which he was raising nearby, who first built himself a residence on the spot. It was hardly a palace in those days. The mighty structure of Westminster Hall, 240 feet long, where dead monarchs traditionally lie in state, was built by the Conqueror's son, William Rufus, in 1097. Richard II added the massive hammer-beam roof. Little good it did him. He was later deposed under that self-same roof.

In medieval times, with its crowds of servants, men at arms and hangers-on, it was more like a miniature city than a mere palace. It is said that a staggering 20,000 people, including a royal bodyguard of 4,000 archers, lived there in Richard's day.

Apart from the crypt of St Stephen's, Westminster Hall – in which William Wallace, Sir Thomas More, Guy Fawkes, Charles I and Warren Hastings stood trial at varying times – is the only part of the original palace to have survived the disastrous fire of 1834 when tax gatherers, disposing of the wooden tallies on which they kept their notched records, shovelled so many of them into a stove that they ended up setting fire to the building. It was rebuilt in the early part of Queen Victoria's reign to the Gothic design of Charles (later Sir) Barry. Prince Albert, as chairman of the Royal Commission for Redecoration, was largely responsible for the fine frescoes. Though it is wholly given over these days to the proceedings of Parliament, the Palace of Westminster is still in theory the monarch's principal residence and the one in which Elizabeth II, like her predecessors before her, invites her advisers to "parley" with her. Hence "Parliament". In fact, she visits it only once a year, for the annual State Opening of Parliament (*see* Opening of Parliament), and even then must confine herself to the House of Lords. Not since 1642, when Charles I made an uninvited entry to arrest and impeach its leading members, has a monarch been allowed to enter the House of Commons.

However, Elizabeth II was able to see it once. The chamber of the House of Commons was destroyed by German bombs during World War II and rebuilt afterwards. The Queen's father, George VI, expressed a wish to see what the inside of the new building looked like. With the new chamber technically not yet in use, the traditional ban was temporarily lifted so that the King's wish could be granted. He took his daughter, then Princess Elizabeth, along with him.

The Tower of London is equally a royal palace and has been since the days of the Normans, though here again it is a long time since any monarch lived there. The last was James I – Scotland's James VI – though even after that it was still the custom for successive monarchs to lodge there for the night preceding their coronation.

It was William the Conqueror who first built a fort on the site immediately following his Christmas Day coronation in 1066, setting it into a corner of the city walls of old Roman London. William Rufus and William de Longchamps, who for a time acted as regent for Richard the Lionheart while the king was away crusading, carried on the good work, extending the precincts beyond the walls and digging a defensive ditch. Successive monarchs extended, improved and fortified it still further until there was an outer wall flanked by towers and bastions and an inner wall with thirteen more towers, with no fewer than three drawbridges to be negotiated before it was possible even to penetrate the outer ward.

The Tower, in its time, has played many historic parts. It has been not only fortress and palace, but observatory and arsenal, mint and menagerie, prison (Rudolf Hess was briefly imprisoned there during World War II), torture chamber and place of execution. Kings and queens alike have been both executed and murdered within its grim walls, among them Anne Boleyn, the promiscuous Catherine Howard, poor, misused little Jane Grey, the boy-king Edward V and many more. Today it still serves as a national security vault for the Crown Jewels (*see* Crown Jewels), and each night the ancient Ceremony of the Keys still takes place as it has done for something like seven centuries, with the Chief Yeoman Warder ceremonially locking the gates of the Tower. His return journey with his escort takes him through the archway of the

Bloody Tower. The duty sentry challenges him.

"Halt. Who goes there?"

"The keys," replies the Chief Yeoman Warder.

"Whose keys?"

"Queen Elizabeth's keys."

"Advance Queen Elizabeth's keys. All's well."

The keys are then paraded to the guard room where the *Last Post* is sounded as the clock strikes ten.

King Henry VIII, in the days when monarchs still lived at the Palace of Westminster, found the place so crowded with courtiers and hangers-on that he moved to Whitehall. When that too became crowded in turn, Henry looked round for somewhere else where he and Anne Boleyn might have some privacy. His eyes lighted on an old leper colony. With leprosy dying out in England, he moved the four remaining inmates elsewhere and started to build himself a hunting lodge on the site. The result was the red and blue brick building of St James's Palace the gateway of which – all that remains of Henry's original building – still bears the entwined cyphers of the lusty Hal and his lady-love. Charles I was later to spend his last night on earth at St James's Palace before being executed at Whitehall. Charles II found it a handy love-nest in which to lodge successive mistresses. But it was not until the Palace of Whitehall, all except the banquet hall, was gutted by fire in 1698 that St James's Palace was elevated to the role of metropolitan palace of Britain's monarchs.

Queen Victoria was married there and continued to use it for public functions, drawing-rooms and levees, until a new wing could be tacked on to Buckingham Palace for this purpose. Today it continues to serve a multiplicity of royal functions. The Accession Council meets there and each new monarch is first proclaimed there, in Friary Court. It is from St James's Palace that the Lord Chamberlain masterminds royal ceremonial. The Duke and Duchess of Kent have an apartment there along with their working offices.

Just as Henry VIII was responsible for building St James's Palace, so he was responsible for acquiring another royal palace, Hampton Court, though at less expense. A frightened Cardinal Wolsey gave it to him in a forlorn attempt to regain royal favour. Henry, never one to look a gift-horse in the mouth, not only moved in, but proceeded to add the Great Hall, the chapel, the amazing astronomical clock and a court where he and Anne Boleyn could play tennis (what is known as real or royal tennis, not lawn tennis). For five reigns it was a favourite royal residence. Henry's daughter, Mary, honeymooned there with Philip of Spain. Charles II was later to spend his honeymoon there too. Then it fell out of favour until William III commissioned Wren to rebuild it. But William died before the work was completed and George III discarded it as a royal residence, preferring Windsor Castle. As a result, Hampton Court, though still adorned – as the gateway of St James's Palace is – with the entwined initials of Henry VIII and Anne Boleyn, is today relegated to providing grace-and-favour apartments in the gift of the monarch.

Kensington Palace is similarly split into a number of grace-and-favour residences. Princess Margaret lives there with her children. The Duke and Duchess of Gloucester have a house there. Originally known as Nottingham House, it became a royal residence when William III bought it from Heneage Finch, a former Lord Chancellor, for 18,000 guineas and set the indefatigable Wren to work rebuilding it. Queen Anne added the Orangery and George I was responsible for the state apartments, designed by William Kent, and for the king's staircase with its *trompe-l'oeil* balconies seemingly crowded with courtiers and guards. It was the childhood home of both Queen Victoria and Queen Mary.

PICTURE COLLECTION

It is difficult to think of a great painter whose work is not represented in the royal picture collection. Despite extensive depredations from time to time – many pictures were sold off in the aftermath of the Civil War, others vanished when James II absconded and William III transferred yet more, quite irregularly, to his Dutch palace of Het Loo – what remains is still staggering in both numbers and quality. It includes works by Rembrandt, Rubens, Vermeer, Raphael and Michelangelo. Portraits from Holbein to Winterhalter present a gallery of royalty down the years from Henry VIII. There are no fewer than twenty-six Van Dycks in the collection and literally hundreds of drawings by Leonardo da Vinci, while the collection of royal miniatures, which includes portraits of Henry VII, Henry VIII and Elizabeth I by Nicholas Hilliard, is the largest and oldest in existence.

Since 1962 some indication of the scope and richness of the collection has been given by public exhibitions staged in the Queen's Gallery, the entrance to which is in Buckingham Palace Road, and which should not be confused with the Picture Gallery, which is one of the state rooms of Buckingham Palace. In particular, the exhibition mounted in 1977 to mark the Queen's Silver Jubilee successfully reproduced the entire collection in miniature, with portraits of Plantagenet monarchs by unknown artists hanging in close conjunction to a Felix Topolski drawing of the coronation of Elizabeth II.

Henry V is the oldest monarch of whom a portrait of any significance survives. Painted in oils on a panel, as are similar portraits of Henry VI and Richard III, it hangs in Windsor Castle. The name of the artist is not known. The inventories of those days did not consider the artist to be of any importance. The probability is that all three portraits were actually painted in the reign of Henry VIII, who, in his younger days at least, was intensely interested in the arts. He was the patron of Hans Holbein the younger who he despatched to paint the portrait of Anne of Cleves which now hangs in the Louvre. Holbein's portrait apparently did the sitter rather more than justice, judging from the fact that Henry married and divorced Anne all in the space of six months.

Those early royal portraits by unknown artists, along with portraits of such foreign monarchs as Ferdinand II of Aragon, Queen Isabella of Castile and Louis XII of France, mark the start of the royal collection : That they do so is doubtless due to the time-honoured custom among monarchs of exchanging portraits as a gesture of friendship and also of handing out portraits of their offspring in the hope of arranging useful marriage alliances. Remember that Ferdinand II and Queen Isabella were Henry VIII's in-laws, while Louis XII sued successfully for the hand of Henry's sister, Mary.

It is thanks to Henry's daughter, Elizabeth I, that the earliest miniatures in the collection are rather better catalogued than the larger portraits. She kept them in a cabinet in her bedroom with their names "written in her own hand upon the papers". Among the earliest are Hilliard's miniatures of Henry VII, Henry VIII, Jane Seymour, Edward VI, Mary, Queen of Scots and Elizabeth herself.

Due to the influence of his mother, the cultured Anne of Denmark, and his brilliant elder brother, Henry, Prince of Wales, whose picture collection he inherited when Henry died in 1612, Charles I was an enthusiastic collector from an early age. Until the outbreak of the Civil War brought a halt to things, he bought and commissioned paintings with almost no regard for cost. Agents scoured France, Spain, Italy and the Low Countries on his behalf. He brought Dutch, Flemish and Italian painters to Britain, among them Van Dyck whom he both knighted and provided with a house. The result was many fine portraits of Charles himself, his family and courtiers, among them the famous *Charles I in Three Positions*, a triple portrait, full face, half face and profile, though this in fact was not actually commissioned by the king himself. It was commissioned by Cardinal Barberini so that Bernini could produce a bust from it. The original bust, sadly, was destroyed when the Palace of Whitehall was gutted by fire in 1698, but there is a copy at Windsor, where the portrait also hangs.

In 1627 Charles bought the collection of paintings and marbles owned by the Duke of Mantua, among which were works by Titian, Raphael, Correggio, Caravaggio and Andrea del Sarto. Together with paintings by Dutch and Flemish masters, some inherited, some bought, some given to him, by 1635 he had a collection of 1,570 pictures, including works by Rembrandt and Rubens, Van Eyck and Dürer. This fine collection – the finest assembled by a British monarch to that date – was split up, as the Crown Jewels were split up, in the aftermath of the Civil War. And like the Crown Jewels, many of the ex-monarch's paintings went for knock-down prices. A Rembrandt self-portrait was disposed of for £5 and Van Dyck's portrait of Queen Henrietta Maria went for only £30. Works by Holbein, Correggio, Raphael's *La Perla*, Titian's *Venus of Pardo*, a gift from the King of Spain as a sort of compensation prize for not winning the hand of the Spanish Infanta, and many more were sold off equally cheaply. As a result, paintings which once formed part of Britain's royal collection are now in the Louvre and the Prado as well as in art galleries and museums in New York, Washington, Leningrad and Vienna.

But while much was lost from the collection in this way, other paintings, fortunately, were returned in haste at the time of the restoration of the monarchy. In the scramble among self-seekers to ingratiate themselves with the new monarch, something like a thousand paintings were returned to the collection in a few years, among them Van Dyck's portrait of Henrietta Maria. In consequence, pictures which once belonged to the executed Charles and are still in the royal collection today include Van Dyck's formal portrait of the king, Albrecht Dürer's *Portrait of a Man*, Tintoretto's *The Nine Muses*, Correggio's *The Holy Family*, Rembrandt's *The Artist's Mother*, Angelo Bronzino's *A Lady in Green*, and Rubens' *Portrait of the Artist*. To celebrate his restoration, the States of Holland also gave Charles II a collection of twenty-seven paintings, among them Tintoretto's *Dominican*, Titian's *Portrait of a Man* and Lorenzo Lotto's *Head of a Man*.

Between indulging himself with his many mistresses, the "Merry Monarch" added further to the collection, paying out £2,686 for a collection of seventy-two pictures which included *Gentleman in Red* (described as a Holbein portrait of the young Henry VIII), Pieter Brueghel the elder's *Massacre of the Innocents* and Bloemaert's *Marriage of Cupid and Psyche*. He commissioned Robert Streeter to paint two pictures, *Boscabel House* and *The Royal Escape*, of his escape after the battle of Worcester, while Sir Peter Lely painted the series of *Windsor Beauties* which included some of the king's mistresses.

Charles II was wont to say that his picture collection "was not half of what my father owned". Be that as it may, by the time William and Mary were invited to take over the throne the royal collection was back to something like 1,200 paintings. It was also swollen by the addition of 779 drawings by Leonardo da Vinci which are known to have been in the royal library at Windsor since at least 1690. James II may have been responsible for their acquisition, though it seems unlikely. More probably they were either given to Charles II or acquired for him by Lely.

The collection would appear to have diminished somewhat rather than grown under the husband and wife stewardship of William and Mary. At the same time that they were adding more paintings, among them the works of the prolific Sir Godfrey Kneller, William was equally busy transferring others from the collection to his other palace in Holland. It was not until the years of the Georges that the collection really began to grow again.

Frederick, Prince of Wales, eldest son of George II and father of George III, was so keen on collecting he even attended auction rooms in person as well as commissioning works from contemporary artists. The result of his efforts was a further outstanding collection of Italian, French, Flemish and Spanish paintings, among them Guido Reni's *Cleopatra with the Asp* and Jan Brueghel's *Flemish Fair*.

George III is perhaps better remembered for the loss of the American colonies and the ravings of his later ill-health than as a collector of pictures. Nevertheless, he made some substantial and worthwhile additions to the collections he inherited as monarch and from his father, even if he was perhaps motivated more by the need to furnish the newly-acquired Buckingham House (*see* Buckingham Palace) and his kingly role as patron of the arts than by personal enthusiasm. It was during his reign that some of the finest drawings were added to the royal collection. He bought – a bargain at £20,000 – the outstanding collection built up by Joseph Smith, the English consul in Venice. This included the most spectacular collection of Canaletto's work ever assembled, fifty paintings and 142 drawings, as well as a further fifty paintings by Marco and Sebastiano Ricci and Vermeer's *A Lady at the Virginals*. He bought a further collection from Cardinal Albini which included works by Filippino Lippi and Michelangelo. He commissioned paintings by Johann Zoffany, including a portrait of himself with Queen Charlotte and their six eldest children, by Gainsborough and by Benjamin West, the American artist who was the second president of the Royal Academy. He bought back for the collection Van Dyck's *Five Children of Charles I*, but turned down in 1765 an opportunity to acquire the same artist's *Roi à la chasse*. "I have, at least for the present, given up collecting pictures," he wrote to his ambassador in Paris.

His son, Prince of Wales, Prince Regent and King George IV in turn, began collecting as quite a young man and was still doing so in the last year of his life when he bought Claude's *The Rape of Europe*. He spent as extravagantly on pictures as he did on everything else (*see* Furniture and *Objets d'Art*). As a result, he was almost permanently in debt. Little he cared. Aided by the French revolution and the Napoleonic Wars, which resulted in a vast flow of pictures from Europe to Britain, he bought freely at first, later more selectively, and within twenty years of the start of his own collection he owned one of the finest assortments of Dutch and Flemish paintings in existence. Among the pictures he bought were Rembrandt's *Christ at the Tomb,* Van Dyck's *Christ Healing the Paralytic,* Jan Steen's *The Morning Toilet, Interior of a Kitchen* by David Teniers the younger, and *The Card Players* and *Courtyard in Delft* by Pieter de Hooch. He bought paintings by such native-born artists as Sir David Wilkie, B. R. Haydon and Gainsborough, but, somewhat curiously, nothing by Constable. He commissioned as generously as he bought, military portraits, battle scenes, sporting subjects and endless portraits of Mrs Fitzherbert, with whom he was so infatuated. She was painted for him time and again, by Gainsborough, Romney, Reynolds, John Russell and Richard Cosway. He commissioned works by George Stubbs, Ben Marshall, and George Garrard; scenes of Scottish peasant life – *Blind Man's Buff* and *The Penny Wedding* – by Sir David Wilkie. Garrard did seven large paintings of the prince's horses, of which only one survives today in the royal collection, while Sir Thomas Lawrence alone received commissions totalling over £24,000, among them the portrait which hangs at Windsor of Sir Walter Scott, whose novels the fourth George so much admired. It was Lawrence, too, who executed the thirty paintings of Britain's generals and allies, among them Wellington, Blücher, the Tsar of Russia, Prince Metternich and Pope Pius VII, which adorn the walls of the Waterloo Chamber at Windsor, created by George IV in celebration of the Battle of Waterloo.

Queen Victoria viewed her uncle's extravagance with horror. Determined not to emulate it when she succeeded to the throne, she decided that she would spend only £2,000 a year on pictures. At first she mainly collected paintings by Landseer, but marriage to Albert was to steer her taste in other directions. He collected German, Italian and Flemish paintings for which his wife often supplied the money as well as buying others for him as birthday gifts. Among her gifts to Albert were Benozzo Gozzoli's *Death of Simon Magnus,* Gentile de Fabriano's *Madonna and Child with Angels* and Bernado Daddi's *Marriage of the Virgin.* The couple spent many of their evenings together sorting and cataloguing the vast collection of drawings which had accumulated at Windsor over the years, and Albert also compiled a photographic catalogue of the works of Raphael, one of the first in the history of art.

The couple commissioned extensively among a small selection of favourite artists. The results were not always good, though a few were outstanding. Many, however, were merely the oil and canvas forerunners of the family photographs Victoria was later to collect so assiduously. Among the earliest of these commissioned works was Sir Francis Grant's *Queen Victoria with Lord Melbourne and Others,* and C. R. Leslie's *Christening of the Princess Royal.* Later the Queen commissioned

William Frith and John Philip to paint the weddings of her children, G. H. Thomas and E. M. Ward to capture royal ceremonies on canvas, and David Roberts to paint *The Inauguration of the Great Exhibition*. She commissioned yet other artists, among them J. F. Herring and Thomas Sidney Cooper, to paint her dogs, horses and farm animals. She commissioned paintings of the Crimean War, the Zulu War and the Sudan; paintings of various aspects of her vast empire, Australia, Canada, India. *The Cove of Sidney* by the Australian artist, Marshall Claxton, reached her as a gift, but she acquired for herself two works – *Pioneer Mill* and *Last Day of the Drought* – by the Canadian painter, Homer Watson. From Landseer she commissioned *Windsor Castle in Modern Times*, a conversation piece which her descendants down to Elizabeth II were to follow with similar commissions.

The work of Franz Winterhalter was first brought to her attention by her Belgian relatives. Thereafter he painted for her for nearly twenty years as the last of the great court painters, turning out a seemingly endless succession of portraits of the Queen herself, Albert, their children, relatives, friends, members of her Household, her favourite statesmen and churchmen. There are still over a hundred Winterhalters in the royal collection today. That Queen Victoria was not necessarily the tight-lipped prude as which she is usually depicted on television is shown by the Winterhalter painting *Florinda*, with its abandoned semi-nudes, which she bought as one of her birthday gifts for Albert.

Following Albert's death in 1861, the Queen, though she continued to commission family portraits and pictures of family events, largely lost interest in the collection. Her son, Edward VII, was more interested in real live women than pictures of them, and his son, George V, was more enthused by postage stamps (*see* Stamps). Nor were their wives especially interested in paintings. Queen Alexandra collected *objets d'art* by Fabergé, while Queen Mary, though responsible for renovating the picture gallery at Buckingham Palace, was more concerned with furniture and antiques (*see* Furniture and *Objets d'Art*).

George VI added a few historical works to the collection along with some pictures by J. F. Herring and a series of views of Windsor painted for him by John Piper and his daughter, Elizabeth II, has since made a number of historical additions, among them the miniature of her Elizabethan namesake which had been missing from the collection since the days of Charles I. In conjunction with the Holyrood Amenity Trust, she has also bought for the Palace of Holyroodhouse the twin portraits of Prince Charles Stuart and his brother Henry which were painted by Louis-Gabriel Blanchet. But her main addition to the royal collection, in conjunction with Prince Philip, has been a series of pictures in oils, water colours, ink and chalk by contemporary British and Commonwealth artists, including Sydney Nolan's *Australian Landscape* and *Herd at the Waterhole*, L. S. Lowry's *The Carriage* and Sir Russell Drysdale's *Man in a Landscape* (which was given to her on her 1963 visit to Australia), along with works by Roger de Grey, Ivon Hitchens, Kenneth Rowntree, Alan Davie, Dame Barbara Hepworth, Graham Sutherland, Rex Batterbee and his Australian aboriginal protégé, Albert Namatjira.

PRINCE ANDREW

Arguably the most handsome, and certainly the tallest of the Royal Family – he is fractionally taller than his elder brother and their father, both of whom are nudging six feet (*see* Heights) – Prince Andrew, the Queen's third child and second son, has grown up to give the lie to rumour. Rumours about royal offspring are nothing new, of course. During the childhood of Andrew's aunt, Princess Margaret, it was rumoured that she was deaf and dumb, and she is clearly neither. With Andrew, rumour was less specific. There had to be "something wrong", people whispered. Otherwise why keep him hidden away, as it seemed he was being hidden for the first eighteen months of his life.

The real reason the Queen kept Andrew to herself was much simpler. It was just that she wished to savour the delights of motherhood afresh in reasonable privacy. After all, she had waited a long time. Her first-born, Prince Charles, was nudging eleven and she herself was already a month or so past her thirty-third birthday when she first realized that she was pregnant with Andrew. It was 1959 and pregnancy could hardly have come at a more inconvenient time, almost on the eve of her departure from London for a nine-week tour of Canada to include the official royal opening of the St Lawrence Seaway.

The Canadian prime minister, John Diefenbaker, made privy to the royal secret, suggested that the tour should be abridged. The Queen did not agree, though subsequent events were to prove her wrong. However, it was clear that she would not be able to follow the Canadian tour with a planned visit to Ghana and that was cancelled. An extra seamstress (to let out the royal dresses as the tour progressed) was also discreetly added to the Queen's entourage for the Canadian trip.

Weather conditions – the temperature at times was in the mid-nineties – turned the Canadian tour, plus a side-trip to Chicago, into an unusually strenuous one and the strain showed. Shrewd newspaper reporters were quick to put two and two together and it fell to the unhappy lot of Esmond Butler, acting royal Press secretary at the time – and not privy to the Queen's secret – to commit himself to an official denial. But denials could hardly be sustained when the Queen reached Whitehorse so exhausted that her physician advised bed. Reluctantly she cancelled a visit to Dawson City and Philip went there alone. Looking wan and tired, she managed to carry out further engagements in Edmonton before flying back to Britain.

The baby was born at Buckingham Palace on February 17, 1960, the first child to be born to a reigning monarch for 103 years. He was named Andrew Albert Christian Edward, Andrew having been the name of Philip's dead father while Albert was the real name of the Queen's father, the late King George VI. As a son, under the British system of primogeniture, he ranked ahead of Princess Anne as second in line of succession to the throne (*see* Succession).

Resolved that Andrew should not suffer the harassment to which Charles and, to a lesser degree, Anne had been subject in childhood, the Queen adopted a policy of family privacy for the new baby. No photographs of the christening were released for publication and not for sixteen months was Andrew seen in public. Hence the rumours. Not until June, 1961, when the Queen had him with her on the palace balcony following the Trooping the Colour ceremony, were mother and child seen in public together.

To a large extent, privacy continued throughout boyhood. Prior to going to boarding school – Heatherdown in Berkshire – Andrew was smuggled backwards and forwards to a private gymnasium in London for physical exercises and to an army sports ground to learn the rudiments of football and cricket. From Heatherdown he followed Prince Charles to Gordonstoun, from where, one year, there was an exchange visit to a school in Toulouse, France, which was carried out with all the secrecy of a top-level intelligence mission. Andrew made the trip in the name of 'Andrew Edwards''. There were also hush-hush holidays to Europe to learn to ski.

In 1975, with Andrew nearing his sixteenth birthday, his mother decided that it was time to ease him into public life. She had him with her at Dyce in Scotland when she pressed the symbolic button which set North Sea oil flowing south to British Petroleum's Grangemouth refinery. The following year he was with her in Montreal for the 1976 Olympic Games and, despite bomb threats from the IRA, he was also with her when she visited the new University of Ulster as part of her 1977 Silver Jubilee "progresses" around the United Kingdom.

Just as Charles had a scholastic break in Australia during his years at Gordonstoun, so Andrew had one in Canada. Prior to accompanying his mother to Northern Ireland he had spent six months at Lakefield College School, near Peterborough, Ontario. Then it was back to Gordonstoun to tackle his 'A' levels.

While Prince Charles may not really have enjoyed his schooldays,

Andrew did. Academically, he did reasonably well, passing his O-levels in English literature and English language, French, history, science and mathematics. He proved himself adept with his hands at things like carpentry, mechanics and pottery. An oil painting entitled *Canadian Landscape* which he did during his time at Lakefield was included in a Silver Jubilee exhibition of royal art held at Windsor Castle. During his years at school he also developed into an all-round sportsman, proficient at swimming, skiing and riding as well as cricket and rugby football, tennis and squash. As a member of the Gordonstoun Air Cadets, he took lessons in gliding at RAF Lossiemouth and qualified for his glider proficiency wings.

In December, 1978, some two months ahead of his nineteenth birthday, Andrew successfully passed the selection test necessary to train as a naval pilot. By opting for a naval career, he was not only following in the footsteps of his father and eldest brother, but also maintaining the 'second son' tradition of the Royal Family. Since Queen Victoria's day, the second sons of Britain's monarchs have all served with the Royal Navy.

PRINCE CHARLES

Like an understudy waiting in the wings in preparation to take over from the star of the show, Prince Charles, first-born son of Elizabeth II and heir to Britain's throne, waits upon future monarchy. Unless his mother opts for a quiet life and decides to abdicate (which seems unlikely to those who know her), the wait could be a long one. Females of the royal line tend to live long even if the males do not. The Queen Mother, still reasonably spritely, was born in 1900. Queen Mary, Queen Alexandra and Queen Victoria were all in their eighties when they died. The Queen could live as long, perhaps longer. If so, Charles, like Edward VII before him, could be close to pensionable age before he succeeds to the throne. Not that he is in any hurry. He does not believe that monarchs should retire and sees himself as having a sufficiently worthwhile royal role to play as Prince of Wales.

Wales is only one of several titles. The full mouthful is His Royal Highness The Prince of Wales and Earl of Chester, Duke of Cornwall and Duke of Rothesay, Earl of Carrick and Baron Renfrew, Lord of the Isles and Great Steward of Scotland. He is also a Knight of the Garter.

He was born at Buckingham Palace on November 14, 1948, almost exactly twelve months after his parents' marriage. King George VI was on the throne. He was the king's first grandchild, second in the line of succession after his mother, then Princess Elizabeth, and born a Prince of the Realm. But only just. Had he arrived a week earlier, he would have been born a commoner.

This narrow-squeak state of affairs was due to his great-grandfather. George V, when he adopted the name of Windsor for his family during World War I (*see* Name), also decreed that children born to the Sovereign or the Sovereign's *sons* should be princes or princesses. But in those days, before women's liberation and sexual equality, the royal Order in Council made no mention of children of the Sovereign's daughters. So while the children of George V's sons, the Dukes of York (later George VI), Gloucester and Kent were all born princes and princesses, those of his daughter Mary were not (*see* Earl of Harewood). Similarly, Charles, as the child of a *daughter* of the Sovereign, would not have been born a prince had his grandfather, George VI, not rectified the situation in the nick of time. Only five days before the birth the king issued a further Order in Council extending the title of prince or princess to the children of his elder daughter. But only those of his elder daughter, not the younger daughter. So while Charles and the sister and brothers who came later were all born princes and princess, the children of Princess Margaret were not.

Swaddled in the silk and lace robe which Prince Albert designed for the christening of Queen Victoria's first child, George VI's first grandchild was baptized in the Music Room at Buckingham Palace by the Archbishop of Canterbury. He was given the names Charles Philip Arthur George.

Though born at Buckingham Palace, Charles spent his early years largely at Clarence House into which his parents moved shortly after his birth. He had a nurse, Helen Lightbody, an Edinburgh Scot. There was also an under-nurse, Mabel Anderson, who was later to supervise the upbringing of Princess Anne and is today nurse to Anne's son, Peter. At this early stage of his life his upbringing was the rather rarefied one of most royal children. So rarefied indeed that he was to be almost grown-up before he realized that not all other children have nannies to look after them in childhood. "Are you their nanny?" he asked an astounded woman with two small children during a teenage visit to Wales.

Rarefaction persisted, perhaps even intensified, when his mother became Queen and the family moved into Buckingham Palace. He was now, as the monarch's eldest son, not only a prince but also Duke of Cornwall (*see* Duchy of Cornwall). But not yet Prince of Wales. A teacher, Betty Vacani, was brought in to teach him dancing and deportment. Another, Hilda Bor, gave him piano lessons. He had a governess, Katherine Peebles, who thought him a "rather nervous child". She taught him reading, writing and arithmetic, history and scripture, drawing and painting. French came later.

With so many females clustered so closely around him, it tended also to be a rather feather-bedded upbringing. Not at all the sort of upbringing Prince Philip thought suitable for a son of his. As a result, dancing lessons were suddenly discontinued and music lessons cut down. Instead, Charles was sent along to stretch his young limbs in a private gymnasium and learn to play football with other boys. There was also a temporary male tutor and visits to places like Westminster Abbey, the Tower of London and the Science Museum. More radical changes were soon to follow. Mrs Lightbody (Mrs was a courtesy title) was retired and settled in a Duchy of Cornwall grace-and-favour apartment at Kennington, and Charles was packed off to Hill House, a private day school in London. This somewhat bold experiment in royal education, like the educational visits which preceded it, aroused such a degree of public interest that the boy was surrounded everywhere he went by a crowd of reporters, photographers and rubber-necking sightseers. His mother appealed more than once to the Press and public to leave him alone, but her appeals had little effect.

Harassment continued even after he was sent at the age of nine to his father's old boarding school, Cheam, which had transferred from Surrey to Hampshire during the war years. During his first eighty-eight days at Cheam there were stories about him in the newspapers on sixty-eight days. The result, at the request of the school's joint headmasters, Mark Wheeler and F. B. Beck, was another royal appeal to Press and public to leave the boy alone.

Charles was never really happy at Cheam and certainly did not emulate his father's youthful athletic prowess, though he was good at swimming and, in his final year, captained the school football team. It was not one of Cheam's more successful football seasons. The school team not only lost every game, but had eighty-two goals scored against them, notching only four in reply.

One reason he never really settled down at Cheam was that most of the other boys regarded him as "different" and treated him accordingly. And, of course, he was different, a fact which was underlined that day in 1958 when he was summoned to the headmasters' study to watch the television transmission of his mother's announcement that he was being created Prince of Wales (*see* Princes of Wales).

He was not quite fourteen in 1962, when, still following in his father's scholastic footsteps, he transferred from Cheam to Gordonstoun, that highly individualistic school on the shore of the Moray Firth of Scotland, at that time under the headmastership of F. R. G. Chew. Apart from two terms which he later spent at school in Australia, Charles was at Gordonstoun for five years, ending as Guardian (head boy) which his father had been before him.

While there he gained his O-levels in English language, English literature, history, French, Latin and, with some slight difficulty, mathematics; his A-levels in French and history; won bronze and silver awards in his father's Duke of Edinburgh Award Scheme trained with the school's sea cadets; and played the title role in a school production of *Macbeth*. There was also the incident of the cherry brandy.

It was around the time of his fifteenth birthday. In the course of a schoolboy cruise aboard one of the school's two ketches, he arrived in Stornaway in the Isle of Lewis, where he found himself waiting in a local hotel while his detective, Donald Green, popped along to book some cinema seats. Unnerved by the stares of those around him, he retreated from the hotel lounge to the cocktail bar, where, in a youthful attempt to cover his embarrassment, he ordered himself a cherry brandy, a drink he had tasted occasionally while out shooting with his father. At his age, this was a breach of the licensing laws. He was seen by a woman journalist and the story, enhanced by an unfortunate denial from Buckingham Palace which was subsequently retracted, made big headlines around the world.

In 1966, as a break from Gordonstoun, he spent two terms at Timbertop, an outpost of the Geelong Church of England Grammar School in Victoria, Australia. Charles himself has said that it was at Timbertop that he first overcame the inherited shyness which is a family trait (though certainly not on Prince Philip's side). Lord Butler, Master of Trinity College, Cambridge, where Charles went in 1967, thinks however that it was there that he really began to "grow up". With the exception of a term spent at the University College of Wales in Aberystwyth immediately preceding his investiture as Prince of Wales in 1969, Charles was at Trinity until 1970. Initially, he studied archaeology and anthropology, later reading modern history. He went on a number of archaeological "digs", wrote a light-hearted essay for the student magazine *Varsity*, played the cello in the college orchestra, joined an acting group called the Dryden Society and appeared on stage in a variety of burlesque roles which would probably not have amused Queen Victoria – as a Victoria lecher, a cello-playing pop star ("the best plucker in the business") and a weather forecaster plodding about the stage in a gas-mask and frogman's flippers. He spent his vacations fishing and shooting, skiing, sailing and playing polo. He quickly proved himself a good shot, an even better fisherman and able to sit a polo pony better than his father even if he lacked some of his father's dash and daring in actual play.

In his free time from Cambridge he also learned to fly. He learned at RAF Oakington, but because there was too much cloud there on the day, made his first solo flight at RAF Bassingbourn. That was in January, 1969. In 1970 he obtained a grade A licence as a private pilot and also took his seat in the House of Lords, though he did not make his maiden speech, in support of a recommendation to set up urban parks and recreation areas, until four years later. From March to August 1971, having secured his Bachelor of Arts degree at Cambridge and undertaken a number of royal chores – representing his mother at Fiji's independence celebrations, visiting Australia, New Zealand, Japan, France, Canada and the United States (where he was labelled "charming, sexy and adroit") – he went to RAF College Cranwell as an unpaid flight lieutenant for a conversion course on jet aircraft. A parachute drop was not an obligatory part of the course. Nevertheless he made one, jumping from an Andover flying at a height of 1,200 feet over Studland Bay. His feet caught briefly in the parachute rigging – "a hairy experience" Charles recalls – but did not become entangled and he was hauled out of the water safe and sound. At the end of the course he received his RAF "wings". The report which accompanied them said that he had excelled at high-speed aerobatics and would make an excellent fighter pilot. Instead, still following in father's footsteps, he went into the navy.

Following a six-week graduate officer's course at Britannia Royal Naval College, Dartmouth, he flew to Gibraltar to join the guided missile destroyer *Norfolk* as a sub-lieutenant. He served with *Norfolk* from November 1971 to July 1972. From July-November 1972 he was at *HMS Dryad*, a naval shore establishment, taking courses there and at *HMS Dolphin* in communications, navigation, bridgework and gunnery. He served briefly with the coastal minesweeper *Glasserton* before joining the frigate *Minerva*. He was aboard *Minerva* for six months except for a brief interruption when he served with *HMS Fox*, a survey ship. He qualified for his watch-keeping and ocean navigation certificates and earned promotion to lieutenant. Following a further navigation course at *HMS Dryad* and a flight deck officer's course at *HMS Osprey*, he flew to Singapore to join another frigate, *Jupiter*. Returning to Britain in November 1974, he decided to train as a helicopter pilot and went to RNAS Yeovilton in Somerset, where he not only qualified on helicopters but won the award for the best pilot on the course. He also took a Royal Marines commando course and, following some advanced flying training, was assigned to 845 Naval Air Squadron for a spell of sea-going duty in the Western Atlantic and West Indies aboard the commando ship *Hermes*.

Inevitably, royal duties punctuated his naval career from time to time. In 1973, while serving aboard *Minerva*, he opened the newly-restored Prince of Wales Bastion on St Kitts and also represented his mother at the independence celebrations in the Bahamas. His helicopter conversion course was interrupted by a flight to New Zealand to attend the funeral of Prime Minister Norman Kirk. A month later he found himself attending independence celebrations in Fiji before going on to inaugurate the Anglo-Australian telescope at Siding Spring,

Australia. While in Australia he also addressed a joint session of the
New South Wales Parliament. In 1975 there was a trip to Katmandu
for the coronation of King Birendra of Nepal. There was a visit to
Ottawa and Canada's North-West Territories, where he dived under
the ice at Resolute Bay, some 600 miles inside the Arctic Circle, and a
visit to Papua New Guinea for more independence junketing.

Whenever and however he grew up, grow up he certainly had, matur-
ing from a shy and nervous small boy into a confident and likeable
Prince of Wales who went round kissing pretty girls and, judging by his
parachute jump and Arctic Circle diving exploit, was prepared to try
almost anything at least once. Naval flying he found, in his own words,
"Very exciting, very rewarding, very stimulating and sometimes
bloody terrifying."

He served with *HMS Hermes* from March–June 1975. Next came a
junior staff officer's course at the Royal Naval College, Greenwich, and
a mine warfare course at *HMS Vernon*, after which he found himself in
command of his own ship. It was hardly the latest thing in fighting
ships. It was a small (153 feet from stem to stern) woodbuilt twenty-
year-old minehunter, *HMS Bronington*, based at Rosyth.

Charles was just twenty-eight in December, 1976, when he left the
navy after five years' service in order to play a full princely part in his
mother's Silver Jubilee celebrations the following year. Among other
things, he launched a Silver Jubilee fund to raise money for youth projects which ended up with nearly £16 million in the kitty. He now had a
country home of his own (*see* Chevening) and everyone wondered when
he was going to get married. To the general disappointment of the
public and perhaps the particular disappointment of several seemingly
eligible young ladies, Charles himself, though freely confessing that he
had already been "in love" more than once in his life, seemed in no tearing hurry to enter into the bounds of matrimony.

PRINCE EDWARD

The Queen was only a few weeks short of her thirty-eighth birthday
when she gave birth to her fourth child on March 10, 1964. But at whatever age, she was clearly delighted at the prospect of renewed motherhood, as family photographs of mother and baby in bed together
revealed – though not until four years later when they somehow found
their way into newspapers and magazines around the world. An experienced monarch after twelve years, she could afford to interrupt her
morning paperwork to spend a few minutes playing with the new baby.
Each evening, her work done, she would make her way upstairs to the
nursery to bath him, feed him and tuck him up for the night. Of an

afternoon, she would take him for an airing in the palace gardens in the old-fashioned high-bodied pram carefully preserved from the arrival of her first-born, Prince Charles. But there were no outings with his nurse into London parks, such as attracted the attention of photographers and sightseers when Charles was a baby.

The new baby, third in line of succession to the throne (*see* Succession), was christened Edward Antony Richard Louis, Antony being the name of the Queen's brother-in-law, Lord Snowdon, and Louis the name of Prince Philip's uncle, Earl Mountbatten of Burma. As has been the case of each royal child in turn, Edward began his education in the palace schoolroom. When brother Andrew, four years older, went off to boarding school, the Queen arranged for Edward to have the company of other children in the schoolroom, among them Princess Margaret's daughter, Sarah, and Princess Alexandra's son, James. There were, in addition to lessons, riding sessions in the royal mews, swimming in the palace pool and visits to an army sports ground to be indoctrinated in the British pursuits of football and cricket.

There was a short spell at a day school in London where Edward, a quiet youngster with the fair hair and blue eyes of all the royal children, took part in a school concert which his mother went along to watch and merited an award on prize-day as the child "making most effort". Then it was off to join brother Andrew at Heatherdown, a boarding school some seven miles from Windsor, and, later, to follow him to Gordonstoun. His first experience of public life came at the early age of fourteen. Visiting Canada with his parents for the 1978 Commonwealth Games, he planted a commemorative tree at Lloydminster and, in the company of his father, made the 3,300-feet descent of the world's biggest potash mine at Cory, Saskatchewan.

PRINCE AND PRINCESS MICHAEL OF KENT

Except for the occasional item in the gossip columns, Prince Michael of Kent, cousin to Queen Elizabeth II, had largely contrived to escape the glare of the public spotlight until his 1978 marriage to a Catholic, and one whose previous marriage had been annulled, suddenly found him making headline news.

Youngest of the three children of the late Duke and Duchess (Princess Marina) of Kent – the present Duke of Kent is his brother and Princess Alexandra his sister – Michael was a war-time baby born on July 4, 1942, only seven weeks before his father was to be killed in an air crash. He was christened Michael George Charles Franklin, the last name in honour of America's President Roosevelt, a close friend of the Kents and one of Michael's godparents.

After schooling at Eton, where he was in the college cadet force, he went to the Royal Military Academy at Sandhurst and from there into the 11th Hussars. Off-duty spells were to be filled with sporting adventure. He has done a 65-second lap on the Brands Hatch circuit in a Formula 3 racing car, crewed the winning entry in a power-boat race, taken part in the Transatlantic Air Race and injured himself in a four-man bob-sled crash. On his thirty-second birthday he was fined £50 and banned from driving for three months for exceeding the speed limit in his Ferrari. He was doing 110 m.p.h. at the time.

In the army he rose to the rank of major and moved to the Ministry of Defence. It was while working there in 1978 that he renounced his right of succession to the throne (*see* Succession) – he was sixteenth in line – in order to marry the Baroness Marie-Christine von Reibnitz, a thirty-three-year-old Catholic, following the annulment of her previous marriage to merchant banker Tom Troubridge. The Queen's consent under the Royal Marriage Act (*see* Marriage) was sought and given. At the same time it was stated that any children of the marriage would be brought up as Anglicans. It was this statement which caused all the fuss and bother that followed.

In order to attract a minimum of publicity, the couple had planned to marry outside Britain, in the Schottenkirche, a Roman Catholic church in Vienna. But the statement about any children being brought up as Anglicans resulted in the prompt intervention of Pope Pius VI, who refused permission for the marriage to be solemnized in a Catholic church. A statement issued from the Catholic Archbishop's House in Westminster said merely that the Pope's refusal was because "the couple were unable to satisfy the conditions laid down by the Catholic Church when asked to celebrate a marriage between one of its members and a Christian from another Church," but the Catholic Information Office in London elucidated further. The future religious upbringing of any children was the "central problem" which had led to the Pope's decision, it said, adding that Prince Michael's undertaking to bring up any children as Anglicans "renders ineffective the undertaking offered by the Catholic to do all in her power to baptize and bring up the children as Catholics."

In the event, Vienna Town Hall became the venue for the marriage, a civil ceremony lasting barely ten minutes on June 30, 1978. Princess Anne, Michael's brother and sister, the Duke of Kent and Princess Alexandra, and Earl Mountbatten of Burma, were among the guests. To enable the bride to set a personal religious seal on the marriage, by attending a private Mass the following day, bride and groom spent their wedding night apart.

On April 6, 1979, Princess Michael of Kent gave birth to a son, Lord Frederick Michael George David Louis Windsor.

PRINCE PHILIP

Though he no longer arouses the degree of controversy that once buzzed so frequently around his now balding head, the Queen's husband is still apt to speak his mind bluntly upon occasion, saying those things he feels need to be said in the national interest and sometimes, in doing so, coming close to entering those political arenas into which the Royals are no longer supposed to venture. But because he is who he is, his views have seldom made the real impact they have sometimes merited. Too often the content of what he says is, and always has been, fogged by the fact that he is the Queen's husband. Controversy stems less from what is actually said than from who has said it.

In a sense, Philip has perhaps been unfortunate that he was born into an age when politicians, not princes, were increasingly to carry the real clout. Like his own son Andrew, he was by way of being an "afterthought" baby, born nearly seven years after the youngest of his four sisters. He was born on June 10, 1921, on the island of Corfu, in a villa which was a good deal grander than its rather suburban name of *Mon Repos* might suggest. He comes down from the house of Schleswig-Holstein-Sonderburg-Glücksburg, a grandson of the Danish prince who became King George I of the Hellenes, a great-great-grandson of both King Christian IX of Denmark and Queen Victoria. His mother was a Battenberg, daughter of that Prince Louis of Battenberg who was later 1st Marquess of Milford Haven (*see* Earl Mountbatten of Burma) and Princess Victoria, granddaughter of Queen Victoria.

Sadly, Philip's mother, Princess Alice, was born deaf. Despite this handicap, she could speak both English and German by the time she was twenty. Later came Greek, though at the time of her third wedding ceremony – civil, Protestant and Greek Orthodox – to Prince Andrew of Greece she mis-lipread some of the priest's phrases and, initially at least, gave the wrong responses.

Philip's Danish-born grandfather had been installed on the Greek throne after Queen Victoria had turned down that somewhat doubtful honour on behalf of her own son, Alfred, Duke of Edinburgh. So Prince William of Denmark, brother of the Princess of Wales who was later Queen Alexandra, became King George I of the Hellenes, only to be assassinated at the 1913 victory parade in Salonica which followed the Balkan War. He was succeeded by his son Constantine whose wife was a sister of the German emperor, and the pro-German attitude of this royal couple during World War I saw Constantine driven from the throne. His second son, Alexander, took over, while the father sought refuge in Switzerland. So did his brother Andrew together with his wife, the former Alice of Battenberg, and their four small daughters. Philip was not yet born.

Then in 1920 there occurred one of those strange incidents which change the course of history. Alexander was bitten by a pet monkey and died from blood poisoning. The result was a plebiscite which restored Constantine to the throne. Andrew and Alice, she was now pregnant again, returned to Greece with him.

Hardly had they settled again in their villa on Corfu than Greece was at war with Turkey. The expectant father was despatched to the battle front as lieutenant-general commanding the Third Army Corps. His son Philip, Prince of Greece and Denmark, sixth in the line of succession to the Greek throne, was born while he was away.

The war with Turkey ended in the defeat of Greece, the slaughter of 40,000 Greek troops and the sacking of Smyrna. In the turmoil which followed Constantine was again ousted from the Greek throne and his place taken by his eldest son as King George II. Prince Andrew returned to Corfu, to his wife, daughters and newly-born son. He had barely had time to remove his uniform before he was summoned to Athens. He was required, it was said, to give evidence at the courts-martial being carried out by the revolutionary junta which really ruled Greece at the time. But instead of giving evidence, he found himself arrested, charged with negligence and desertion.

His wife immediately journeyed to Athens to appeal to her husband's cousin, the Greek king. But there was nothing he could do. In a desperate last-minute attempt to save her husband from execution, Philip's mother appealed for help to her many royal relatives throughout Europe, among them Britain's King George V. George V promptly ordered a British agent, Commander Gerald Talbot, to Athens to negotiate Prince Andrew's release. And in case that did not work, he also ordered the Admiralty to dispatch a British cruiser to the spot.

Three ex-premiers, two former government ministers and the Greek commander-in-chief had already been tried and executed when the cruiser *Calypso* arrived on the scene. Mindful of how a British fleet had bombarded Athens only five years earlier, the revolutionary tribunal, though declaring Prince Andrew guilty, did not sentence him to death. Instead, he was stripped of his military rank and Greek nationality. Under the unspoken threat of another British bombardment, the revolutionary leader, Theodoros Panaglos, personally drove Prince Andrew and Talbot to the port of Athens and put them aboard the cruiser. From Athens *Calypso* sailed to Corfu to pick up the royal couple's children. Cabins and bunks were quickly made available for Philip's four sisters. But warships are not normally fitted out with cots for eighteen-month-old babies. As a result, Philip sailed into exile in a cot hastily improvised from a well-padded orange crate.

After a brief stay in England, Prince Andrew and his family settled in France. Royal relatives rallied round to help. King Christian X of

Denmark made the stateless Andrew a Danish national. Andrew's brother, Prince George of Greece, who had married the wealthy Princess Marie Bonaparte, made a lodge available in St Cloud, in the Rue de Mont Valerien. There was help too from another brother, Prince Christopher of Greece, and his wife Nancy, widow of the American millionaire, William B. Leeds, and from the Milford Haven-Battenbergs in Britain. From time to time also a little money trickled through from family holdings in Greece.

At the age of six Philip was sent to the Country Day and Boarding School in St Cloud, where his fellow-pupils were mainly the children of American diplomats and businessmen resident in Paris. Their American antecedents rubbed off on him. He learned to speak English with an American accent, to swing a baseball bat and utter American-style football chants. School fees were stiff, but Uncle Christopher and his American wife, Aunt Nancy, saw to those. At this stage of his young life Philip's upbringing was an anomalous one. Vacations were spent with royal or near-royal relatives in various parts of Europe. Yet the clothing in which he went to school was sometimes patched, he had no raincoat to wear when it rained, and had to save his pocket-money a long time before he had sufficient to buy his first bicycle.

Most people who know that Earl Mountbatten of Burma is Philip's uncle, not his father, also picture him as Philip's mentor in boyhood. In fact it was Mountbatten's elder brother, George, having succeeded his father as Marquess of Milford Haven, who took over responsibility for the boy's upbringing when he journeyed to Britain at the age of nine. In company with George's son, David, Philip was sent to the Old Tabor School at Cheam in Surrey. He made good progress there, winning prizes for French and history, shining at soccer and proving himself both the best diver and the best high-jumper of his day. Vacations were spent sometimes with royal relatives in Europe, sometimes with the Milford Havens at Lynden Manor, sometimes at Kensington Palace with his maternal grandmother, the Dowager Marchioness of Milford Haven, and sometimes with his parents in Paris.

Within a short space of two years his four sisters had all married German princelings, a fact which was to cause problems later when he himself married the then Princess Elizabeth at a time when the wounds of World War II still smarted in both Britain and Germany. Sophie, youngest of the sisters, was only sixteen when she married Prince Christopher of Hesse (who later died in a World War II air crash after which she married Prince George of Hanover); Cecilie married the Grand Duke George of Hesse; Margarita, the eldest, married Prince Gottfried of Hohenlohe-Langenburg; while Theodora married Berthold, Margrave of Baden.

Their daughters married, their young son being looked after by relatives in Britain, Philip's parents drifted apart. They lived separately for a time in Paris. Then Princess Alice followed her daughters to Germany while Philip's father drifted south to Monte Carlo, where he was to enjoy many a glass of champagne and the company of many a pretty woman until his death in 1944.

At the age of twelve, Philip, though he would have preferred to have remained in Britain, found himself shunted across to Germany, to continue his education at the unorthodox school which educationalist Dr Kurt Hahn had established in 1920 in a group of ancient monastic buildings at Schloss Salem, ancestral home of the Margraves of Baden on the shore of Lake Constance. The school had been founded under the patronage of Prince Max of Baden. His son Berthold had been educated there and had subsequently married Philip's sister, Theodora, thus completing the chain of circumstance which resulted in the rootless Philip entering upon an élitist Germanic educational programme which started with a quarter-mile run and a cold shower before breakfast proceeding by way of studies, sports and such physical chores as concrete mixing and cinder raking to a compulsory rest period during which good books were read aloud, evening homework and setting-up exercises before retiring for the night. However, he was not to remain there long. The Nazis were now in power in Germany and eager to use Salem for their own purposes. At the time Philip arrived there Dr Hahn was already in prison as "an enemy of the state". Prince Berthold obtained his release and, wisely, he fled from Germany to re-establish his unorthodox educational régime at Gordonstoun in Scotland. With life in Germany becoming ever more unpredictable, Philip's sister hastily packed him off in Dr Hahn's footsteps.

Under Hahn, he became, in a sense, one of the founders of Gordonstoun, then only a small community of a few score boys and masters who, in addition to studies and sport, also undertook the actual physical work of converting the school buildings and constructing new ones. Among other things, Philip helped to build a pig-sty.

At Gordonstoun he made good, though not brilliant, progress, particularly in mathematics, geography, French and German. He played for the school rugby team, took part in the Scottish schools' athletic championships, and captained the hockey and cricket teams. He became a colour bearer (prefect) and eventually Guardian (head boy or school captain). His imagination fired by his Uncle George's tales of the sea, more than anything he loved messing about in boats. He went to sea with the local fishermen, and acted as cook and lamp-trimmer on a trip to Norway aboard a three-masted schooner, renamed *Prince Louis* in honour of his Battenberg grandfather, which the school had acquired.

At the age of fifteen he returned briefly to his native Greece, to attend ceremonies marking the restoration of the monarchy (the king had abdicated the year after Philip and his parents sailed into exile). His father was in Greece too for the occasion and, when Philip mentioned his love of the sea, suggested that he should stay on in Greece and enter the Greek Nautical College. But Philip preferred Gordonstoun.

That same year of 1936 Philip was also summoned to Hahn's study to be given the tragic news that his sister Cecilie, her husband and their two small sons, Louis and Alexander, had all perished while on their way to London to attend the wedding of Prince Louis of Hesse to the Hon. Margaret Campbell-Geddes. Flying through fog, their aircraft had crashed into a factory chimney in Ostend.

Two years later came news of the death of Uncle George who had acted *in loco parentis* for so many years. Philip's cousin David succeeded his father as Marquess of Milford Haven while "Uncle Dickie" – Louis Mountbatten – took over the responsibility for Philip's welfare. He was quickly to become the biggest single influence in his life.

His years at Gordonstoun nearing their end, Philip toyed briefly with the idea of joining the Royal Air Force. But his old love of the sea proved decisive and in the spring of 1939, shortly before his eighteenth birthday, he entered the Royal Naval College Dartmouth as a cadet. After taking a cram course with a naval coach, he came sixteenth out of the thirty-four would-be naval officers who took the entrance examination at that time. Then, as now, he was a good talker and scored 380 marks out of a possible 400 in the oral examination. In the final report he brought away with him from Gordonstoun Dr Hahn had this to say:

"Prince Philip is universally trusted, liked and respected. He has the greatest sense of service of all the boys in the school.

"Prince Philip is a born leader, but will need the exacting demands of a great service to do justice to himself. His best is outstanding; his second best is not good enough.

"Prince Philip will make his mark in any profession where he will have to prove himself in a full trial of strength."

Philip had been at Dartmouth only a few weeks when, amidst an outbreak of the inevitable spit and polish, King George VI paid a sentimental return visit to the naval college where he too had once been a cadet. With him were his wife and their two young daughters, Princess Elizabeth, then just turned thirteen, and Princess Margaret, not quite nine. A combination of circumstances was to bring Philip and Elizabeth together.

Philip's Uncle Dickie accompanied the royal party as the king's naval aide-de-camp. Philip himself, perhaps because of his relationship to the Royals, was selected to act as Captain's messenger for the period of the king's visit. Then there was a twin outbreak of mumps and chicken-pox among the cadets. Because of this, it was thought unwise for the king's young daughters to attend a service in the cramped confines of the college chapel. The result of all this was that Philip's uncle suggested to the Queen that his nephew might help to entertain the girls while their parents were in chapel.

Accounts of what followed differ. Philip and Elizabeth may have played with a clockwork train set in the house of the Captain of the College (Admiral Sir Frederick Dalrymple-Hamilton) and may have enjoyed croquet on the lawn, Philip may or may not have jumped over a tennis net (Marion Crawford, Elizabeth's governess, mentions the incident in her memoirs, though Philip himself does not recall it), but there is no doubt that for two days they were almost constantly in each other's company. Philip showed the two girls round the college, had lunch and tea with them and is said to have scoffed an inordinate amount of shrimps followed by a banana split.

When the royal yacht *Victoria and Albert* sailed again, all the cadets who were not down with either mumps or chicken-pox piled into a collection of small craft – rowing boats, sailing boats, motor boats – to escort the Royals out to sea. As the distance between yacht and shore widened the king had a signal flown ordering them to turn back. All did so except one. A single boat with a solitary oarsman continued to follow the yacht until considerable bawling through a loud-hailer persuaded him to turn back also. The oarsman was Philip (for further details of romance and courtship *see* Queen Elizabeth II).

Six weeks later Britain was at war with Germany for the second time in many people's lifetimes. The following January, after winning a £2 book token and the King's Dirk as the best cadet of his term, Philip was posted to the battleship *Ramillies* and found himself shepherding Australian and New Zealand troops to Egypt. He would much have preferred to be in the thick of things. But no sooner had the *Ramillies* reached Alexandria than he was transferred to the cruiser *Kent* and then to the *Shropshire*, another cruiser engaged in convoy duties. With Greece still neutral, the British Admiralty did not want a Greek prince, which was what Philip still was, getting too involved in the action. There were trips ashore and there were girl friends. There was a spell at a shore station in Colombo. But, for Philip, there was no actual fighting. There was a spell of leave and a visit to Athens, where he saw his mother and other relatives, but not his father. Indeed, he was never to see him again.

Sir Henry "Chips" Channon, that twentieth-century Samuel Pepys, was in Athens at the same time. He met Philip's aunt, Princess Nicholas, at a cocktail party. "He is to be our Prince Consort and that is why he is serving in our Navy," he noted in his diary. It would seem to have been a somewhat premature observation, but the first part of it has certainly turned out to be true.

The Italian invasion of Greece in October, 1940, ended Greek neutrality. Now it did not matter so much if a Greek prince was killed aboard a British warship, and a degree of string-pulling found Philip transferred to the battleship *Valiant*. It was aboard *Valiant* that he took part in the Battle of Cape Matapan which virtually put paid to the Italian fleet. Three Italian heavy cruisers, two six-inch gun cruisers and two destroyers were wiped out; a brand-new battleship and another destroyer were seriously damaged. The British fleet suffered no material damage and did not sustain a single casualty. The battle took place on the night of March 28, 1941, with Philip in charge of searchlights on the engaged side. "Thanks to his alertness and appreciation of the situation we were able to sink in five minutes two eight-inch gun cruisers," reported Rear Admiral Sir Charles Morgan. Admiral Sir Andrew Cunningham, Mediterranean commander-in-chief, mentioned him in despatches and his native Greece awarded him the War Cross. Philip himself was later to describe the battle as being "as near murder as anything could be in wartime".

With the Germans joining in the invasion of Greece, the *Valiant* served as an escort when the destroyer *Decoy* ferried Philip's cousin, King George II, to safety in Egypt. While others of the Greek Royal Family also fled the country at the same time, Philip's mother did not. She stayed on in Athens, setting up a small orphanage for children whose parents had been killed in the war.

Philip was still aboard the *Valiant* when it took part in the battle for Crete. Hit by two enemy bombs, it managed to withdraw under cover of darkness and was back in Alexandria when the destroyer *Kipling* arrived there with survivors from its sister-ship *Kelly*, among them Philip's Uncle Dickie. In June, 1941, around the time of his twentieth birthday, along with other midshipmen due to take the examination necessary to become sub-lieutenants, he returned to Britain. Even that, in wartime, was a good deal less simple than it sounds. With the Mediterranean now at the mercy of German aircraft, the group had to journey down the east coast of Africa in a troopship to Durban and there transfer to another troopship sailing for Canada to pick up troops for Europe. At Puerto Rico the Chinese stokers jumped ship and Philip and his mates had to substitute for them in the ship's boiler room, for which temporary duty he later found himself the recipient of a certificate as "a qualified coal trimmer".

Back in Britain, he passed the necessary examination and was promoted to sub-lieutenant on February 1, 1942. Simultaneously he was posted to the *Wallace*, a destroyer engaged on convoy duty in the Channel and North Sea. Later that year, on promotion to first-lieutenant, he became second in command of the *Wallace*. First-lieutenant aboard the *Lauderdale*, another destroyer in the same squadron, was a breezy young

Australian named Michael Parker. The two became close friends and Parker was later to become Philip's private secretary until the complications of his personal life obliged him to tender his resignation.

The following year saw *Wallace* helping to provide cover for the Canadian landing on Sicily. Then it was back to Britain for a re-fit and that Christmas found Philip invited to Windsor Castle where he sat between King and Queen to watch Princess Elizabeth, legs gleaming in silk tights, play the title role in an amateur production of *Aladdin and his Wonderful Lamp*. That the two of them would eventually marry appears to have been taken rather for granted on the Greek side, though by no means on the British, and Philip's cousin, George II of Greece, raised the question with Elizabeth's father when they met each other at the London wedding of King Peter of Yugoslavia in March, 1944. King George VI was somewhat taken aback. He liked Philip well enough, regarding him as a young man who "is intelligent, has a good sense of humour and thinks about things the right way", but his daughter was still not yet eighteen and he regarded her as far too young to marry. "Philip had better not think any more about it for the time being," he told the exiled Greek king.

Philip was transferred to the *Whelp*, fresh off the stocks, and sailed to join the 27th Destroyer Flotilla in the Far East. Michael Parker was there too aboard the *Wessex*, and the pair of them saw action off Burma and Sumatra. There were also some convivial periods of shore leave in Australia, including a day at the races when Press and public clamoured to know which was the prince. "The one with the beard," said Philip, indicating Parker and having shaved off his own beard at the time.

With the end of the Japanese war, Philip was briefly transferred to Admiral William Halsey's flagship, *USS Missouri*, to witness the Japanese surrender in Tokyo Bay. Early in 1946 he arrived back in Britain again to find himself posted first to *HMS Glendower*, a training establishment at Pwllheli in Wales, and subsequently to *HMS Royal Arthur*, a similar establishment at Corsham in Wiltshire, as an instructor. He bought himself an MG sports car for trips to London to see Princess Elizabeth who he was now courting assiduously, though rumours of their betrothal were promptly denied by Buckingham Palace. Indeed, over the next twelve months, they were to be denied several times.

That summer he was invited to join the Royal Family at Balmoral, a visit for which he found himself rather ill-equipped. Philip himself has said that he was one of a generation who "started the war in nappies, spent the next few years in uniform and when peace broke out found myself without any other clothes." He also had very little money, but he managed to borrow a tuxedo in which to join the Royal Family for dinner each evening.

On December 3, 1944, his father died of a heart attack and Philip
found himself making a trip to Monte Carlo to wind up his affairs.
There was a small enough inheritance of personal possessions, including his father's ivory-handled shaving brush and a suit he had altered to
fit him. Presumably he wore it when the Royals invited him to Sandringham that Christmas.

Philip and Elizabeth had long ago come to the sort of romantic
"understanding" which results in marriage. But her father still would
not give permission for a formal announcement of their betrothal. The
reason was partly, though only partly, political. Philip at that time, for
all his British upbringing, was still technically a Greek citizen. Or was
he? The 1701 Act of Settlement, in passing the succession to Britain's
throne to the descendants of Sophia of Hanover (*see* Succession), also
endowed them with British nationality. And Philip, through his great-
great-grandmother, Queen Victoria, was surely among Sophia's many
descendants. But no one seems to have thought of that at the time. Not
even Philip himself. He had already sought the permission of his cousin,
George II of Greece, to renounce his Greek citizenship and his right of
succession to the Greek throne. That permission had been given while
Philip was still serving in the Far East. On his return to Britain he had
applied for British naturalization, not at the time to facilitate marriage
to Princess Elizabeth, but simply so that he could continue serving in
the Royal Navy with a permanent peacetime commission. But naturalization, in those immediate post-war years – and especially for someone
so close to the Greek throne – was a slow process.

It had still not come through when the Royal Family sailed for South
Africa on February 1, 1947. It materialized finally while they were
away and was chronicled in the *London Gazette* on March 18: Mountbatten, Philip; Greece; serving officer in His Majesty's forces; 16 Chester
Street, London SW1.

The name Mountbatten had been arrived at only after considerable
discussion, though one would have thought it would have been an
obvious first choice. The King had offered to make Philip a Royal Highness, a style he had declined to bestow on the Duchess of Windsor (*see*
Duke and Duchess of Windsor). But Philip, having just ceased to be a
prince of Greece, wanted no fresh title, at least not at that time. He
preferred to be simply a plain lieutenant. But Lieutenant what?
Lieutenant Schleswig-Holstein-Sonderburg-Glücksburg was clearly
unpractical. The College of Heralds harked back to the Dukedom of
Oldenburg, which was also in Philip's family tree, and suggested the
anglicized version of Oldcastle. Then the Home Secretary, Chuter Ede,
perhaps having in mind that Philip's Uncle Dickie had just accepted
the socialist Government's request to become Viceroy of India, had the
not very original idea of Mountbatten and Philip accordingly took the

adopted name of his mother's family.

The Royal Family returned from South Africa in May and on July 10 came the long-awaited betrothal announcement. There still remained the muddle of Philip's religious status. Although he had worshipped as an Anglican ever since joining the navy, Philip had been baptized into the Greek Orthodox Church. So prior to his marriage on November 20, 1947, he was formally received into the Church of England at a private ceremony arranged by Dr Geoffrey Fisher, Archbishop of Canterbury, in the chapel of Lambeth Palace. And the day before he married, the king elevated him to the style of Royal Highness with the triple title of Duke of Edinburgh, Earl of Merioneth and Baron Greenwich; he also gave him the Order of the Garter. The King was apparently under the impression that by giving his future son-in-law the style of Royal Highness he was also making him a Prince. In fact, he was not, though Press and public alike, under the same misapprehension as the King, were consistently to refer to him as "Prince Philip" from then on. It was left to Queen Elizabeth II, five years after she became queen, on February 22, 1957, to rectify her father's inadvertent omission and make her husband a Prince.

Philip's new royal style had come too late for any amendment to be made to the order of service, and his name was printed as Lieutenant Philip Mountbatten, RN. He was married in naval uniform and wore the dress sword which had once belonged to his grandfather, Prince Louis of Battenberg. His cousin David, Marquess of Milford Haven, was his best man.

Philip's mother was a guest at the wedding. His three surviving sisters were not. As the war with Germany was still fresh in so many British minds, it was felt that it would be indiscreet to invite relatives, however close, with German husbands.

Philip, at that time, had a desk job at the Admiralty which was to be frequently interrupted by the necessity to accompany his wife on provincial tours and other public engagements. To supplement his pay as a naval officer, Parliament voted him an allotment of £10,000 a year. He was later to be placed on half pay by the navy so as to have more time to devote to royal duties, among them the presidency of the National Playing Fields Association which he took over from Uncle Dickie.

However, by the time Princess Anne was born, Philip was back on full pay; back at sea. He returned to active service in October, 1949, and from then until July, 1951, with the exception of leave periods, he was either at sea or in Malta, to where his wife flew several times to be with him. In July, 1950, he was promoted to the rank of lieutenant-commander and that September he was given command of the frigate *Magpie*.

But career-wise, Philip's time was fast running out. With the King's health deteriorating, Princess Elizabeth was required to deputize for her father on a tour of Canada and a visit to the United States. Her husband must necessarily go with her. In Malta, however reluctantly, Philip packed his uniform, his water-skis, his spear gun. "It will be a long time before I want those again," he said.

The Canadian tour and US visit, though there were a few rough patches, were amazingly successful overall. With the King's health showing little sign of improvement, it was arranged that his daughter and son-in-law should again deputize for him on a similar tour of Australia and New Zealand. To this end, in January, 1952, they flew out of London yet again. They had travelled no further than Kenya when news overtook them of the King's death (*see* King George VI).

With his wife's accession to the throne, Parliament gave Philip an increased allowance of £40,000 a year, subject to tax (*see* Tax). One of the Queen's early acts of monarchy, in October, 1952, was to sign a royal warranty in which she accorded her husband "Place, Pre-eminence and Precedence next to Her Majesty", thus ranking him ahead of the small son who was heir apparent to the throne. The Regency Act of the following year – November, 1953 – saw him appointed as Regent in place of Princess Margaret in the event that the Queen should die while her son and heir was still a minor. Earlier that year, the coronation (*see* Coronation) had brought Philip a reunion with his surviving sisters. World War II, it was felt, was now sufficiently in the past for them to be officially invited to Britain along with their German husbands. In fact, his eldest sister, Princess Margarita, had already visited Britain, if only semi-privately, to stand as godmother to Princess Anne when she was christened. In the years following the coronation, all three sisters, with their husbands and families, were to slip in and out of Britain frequently on visits to their brother and his wife. And Philip, from time to time, would fly to Germany to see them, sometimes taking Charles and Anne with him. But not his wife. As Queen, it was felt that she could not yet visit Germany and it was not until her state visit of 1965, nearly eighteen years after she married Philip, that she finally found herself free to visit her sisters-in-law in their own homes.

Those early years of the Queen's monarchy were not easy ones for Philip. He was forced to stand by while his wife reverted to her father's name of Windsor (*see* Name) for herself and the two children. Not for another eight years, just before the birth of Prince Andrew in 1960, was the hyphenated name of Mountbatten-Windsor to be adopted and then it was to be many more years before it was clear to whom it applied.

While a king's wife becomes queen on her husband's accession, with her own particular sphere of work and influence, a queen's husband, as Philip was quickly to discover, does not become king or even prince consort. For Philip, at a time when his wife was busier than ever with a whole new monarchical world of interest, there was too little to do and far too much time in which to do it. What Philip could do, he did energetically and conscientiously enough. The trouble was that there was not enough work for a man of his energy nor enough responsibility for a man of his character. He was, for instance, appointed chairman of the Coronation Commission, but it was really the Duke of Norfolk, as hereditary Earl Marshal of England, who headed the set-up and did the real work. Both to fill in time and because he saw it as part of the royal future, Philip learned to fly, starting with a Chipmunk at White Waltham in 1953. He also tried, with rather less success, to jerk monarchy into the twentieth century. He had more success in reorganizing and modernizing his wife's private estates at Sandringham and Balmoral. But publicly he lived in his wife's shadow, accompanying her on provincial progresses and on her 1953–4 six-month world tour.

While he may have had no desire to be another Prince Albert, who was virtually King to Victoria's Queen, while he may have had no wish to pry into prohibited constitutional areas (like the contents of the Queen's boxes), Philip did want to be something more than merely the second royal handshake along the line. Cautiously at first he began to feel his way towards a position of his own; to say things of his own. All the reward he received initially was a good deal of criticism in the newspapers, some of it unfair. His first big attempt to go solo in the royal sphere, his trip to Australia to open the 1956 Olympic Games followed by visits to such far-flung British outposts as the Falkland Islands, St Helena, Ascension Island and the Trans-Antarctic Expedition, resulted only in rumours of a "rift" between him and his wife. "It is quite untrue that there is any rift between the Queen and the Duke of Edinburgh", retorted an unprecedented royal statement from Buckingham Palace.

Ignoring rumour and criticism alike, Philip continued to go his own way and do his own thing. Gradually, bit by bit, he carved a special niche for himself in the set-piece of monarchy, widening its scope by going where the Queen herself cannot easily go, concerning himself with those fields – such as science and technology – in which she might be expected to have only a minimum of interest. By saying things it would be undiplomatic for her to say herself, he was to become more and more the true mouthpiece of Britain's monarchy.

Gradually, more and more patronages and presidencies accrued to him, starting with Admiral of the Sea Cadet Corps, Member of the Council of the Duchy of Cornwall, Ranger of Windsor Great Park and Patron of the Amateur Boxing Association in 1952, adding Captain General of the Royal Marines, Colonel of the Welsh Guards, Hon. Colonel of the University of Edinburgh Training Corps, Admiral of the

Royal Canadian Sea Cadets, Colonel-in-Chief of the Royal Canadian Army Cadets and the Royal Canadian Regiment, Commander-in-Chief of the Royal Canadian Air Cadets, Patron of the British Council for the Rehabilitation of the Disabled in 1953, and so on year by year until today he is patron, president or honorary member of well over five hundred clubs, organizations and public bodies. The full range of his presidencies and patronages, colonelcies, chancellorships and chairmanships, governorships and trusteeships would today occupy something like a full yard of closely-printed column inches in the average tabloid newspaper. They range from being colonel-in-chief of around a dozen British, Australian, Canadian and New Zealand regiments to membership of the Sydney University Tiddly-winks Society, membership of the Porcupine Rod and Gun Club at Timmins, Ontario, and being a deputy sheriff of Harris County, Texas.

Today, he regularly puts in a fourteen-hour day on princely duties, travels an average 75,000 miles a year in carrying out 250–300 official engagements and making some eighty, sometimes controversial, speeches. All this, in addition to accompanying his wife on all her state visits abroad and her Commonwealth tours as well as on most of her provincial progresses in Britain, makes him far and away the most travelled prince in history. So much so that one newspaper, one year, topped an item about his return home with the headline: PRINCE PHILIP VISITS BRITAIN.

Trips to Germany from time to time, mainly to visit British troops stationed there, also enable him to keep in touch with his surviving sisters. Theodora, the eldest, fifteen years his senior, died in 1969. When his mother was taken ill in Germany he flew out to bring her back for medical treatment in Britain. After a spell in hospital she went to live with her son and daughter-in-law at Buckingham Palace, where she too died in 1969.

Whatever criticisms may still be directed at Philip at times, not even the most republican socialist denies his capacity for hard work, his passion for the Monarchy and his enthusiasm for the Commonwealth. The degree to which the Monarchy has rid itself of some of its more cobwebby traditions and stepped out more boldly into the twentieth century has been in no small measure due to him. It was due to him that the royal children, starting with Prince Charles, shed their traditional tutors and governesses and were brought up in the real world. It was his idea too to bring part of the royal picture collection out of the confines of Buckingham Palace and Windsor Castle each year and put on public display in the Queen's Gallery. He was also the prime mover behind, if not the original instigator of, the Television film *Royal Family*. Intellectuals may have scoffed at it as "Corgi and Bess", but the general public loved it. He has urged his wife, the Queen, out of her

earlier shyness to an extent where she can indulge in, if not always actually enjoy, public walkabouts. He has made her occasional public
speeches less prissy and more down-to-earth. But perhaps his most successful innovation has been his Duke of Edinburgh Award Scheme.
Launched in the early years of his wife's monarchy with the object of di-
verting the energies and enthusiasm of young people into a challenging
programme of worthwhile activities, it has involved well over a million
youngsters over the years and has spread outwards from Britain to
more the twenty-five Commonwealth countries. "It has probably done
more for people than anything else I have been involved in," Prince
Philip has said.

PRINCES OF WALES

The heir to the throne does not automatically become Prince of Wales
at the moment of birth. The title is bestowed on him at the monarch's
discretion, usually when he has been somewhere between nine and seventeen years of age, though some monarchs have been quicker in this
respect than others. The future George IV, for instance, was given the
title when he was only seven days old and the future Edward VII when
he was a month old. And some monarchs have not bothered to bestow
the title at all. Indeed, the very first Prince of Wales, when he became
King Edward II, appears not to have created his own son Prince of
Wales in turn – certainly there is no documentary record of it – though
he did make him Earl of Chester and Duke of Aquitaine. Henry VIII
similarly withheld the title from Jane Seymour's son who became
Edward VI.

According to legend, the title of Prince of Wales came into existence
when Edward I, as a sop to the rebellious Welsh, mounted the battlements of Caernarvon Castle with his new-born son in his arms and
cried, "I give you a Prince of Wales born in your own country." Unfortunately, legend does not quite square with the known facts. Edward
did not begin building Caernarvon Castle until 1283 (though there was
previously a Norman stronghold there) and the structure was still
unfinished half a century later. So there would hardly have been any
battlements to mount when that first Prince of Wales was born in 1284.
A few courses of masonry, perhaps. Moreover, that first Prince of Wales
was not actually given the title until 1301, when he was certainly no
babe in arms, and the act of creation would seem to have taken place at
Lincoln, not Caernarvon.

Historians are similarly inclined to dismiss the story of how *Ich dien*
(German for "I serve") became the traditional motto of the Princes of
Wales and three white ostrich plumes their traditional crest. But the

story is perhaps worth re-telling for all that. It was after the battle of Crécy. Edward III and his heir, the Black Prince who never lived to become king, were touring the battlefield when they came across the body of John, the blind King of Bohemia. Around the dead king lay the bodies of his knights, the bridles of their dead horses still linked together in the protective circle the knights had formed in a vain attempt to safeguard him. So impressed was the youthful Black Prince that he immediately decided to adopt the dead king's motto and adapt his eagle's wing coat of arms into a feathered crest for the Prince of Wales. Whatever the truth of the story, it is a fact that at the time of his death in 1376 the Black Prince had two coats of arms (*see* Arms) – his war shield and what was known as his "shield of peace". On the "shield of peace" were painted three white feathers and the motto *Ich dien*.

And while historians may scoff at legend, politicians are not above making use of it if it serves their political ends, as the wily and imaginative Lloyd George made use of the Caernarvon Castle legend concerning the first Prince of Wales. With an eye to the Welsh vote, he suggested that a royal visit to Wales following the coronation of George V should also be used to "revive" the ancient investiture ceremony at Caernarvon.

Until that "revival", it is doubtful if there had ever been an investiture at Caernarvon. The first Prince of Wales, though he was born in Snowdonia, was invested at Lincoln and subsequent investitures took place at Westminster. In Georgian and Victorian times an actual ceremony of investiture was considered unnecessary and the one masterminded by Lloyd George was the first for nearly three hundred years.

All of which did not prevent the Welsh "wizard", once having obtained royal approval to the scheme, throwing himself into things with characteristic exuberance. He even taught the young Prince of Wales and future Duke of Windsor one or two suitable Welsh phrases for the occasion, among them *Mor o gan yw Cymru is gyd* (All Wales is a sea of song).

The Prince himself was considerably embarrassed by the whole business, the more so because he found himself having to dress for the occasion in an outfit which consisted of white satin breeches and a mantle and surcoat of purple velvet trimmed with ermine. "A preposterous rig", he labelled it and worried about what his cadet friends at Dartmouth would think of him.

"Your friends will understand that as a prince you are obliged to do certain things that may seem a little silly," his mother, Queen Mary, said soothingly.

Windsor was unmarried and childless at the time he became King Edward VIII and the title lapsed temporarily. The brother who succeeded him as George VI, though married, had no son and in 1944, when his eldest daughter celebrated her eighteenth birthday, Pwllheli Town Council petitioned the King to create her Princess of Wales instead. But the title of Princess of Wales, as the King pointed out, was reserved for the wife of a Prince of Wales and so could hardly be bestowed upon a daughter.

Caernarvon similarly petitioned Elizabeth II, soon after her accession in 1952, to create her son Charles Prince of Wales. He was not quite four at the time and his mother thought him too young. However, she did bestow the title upon him when he was a schoolboy at Cheam, on July 26, 1958. Because she was recovering from an operation for sinusitis at the time, she had been compelled to abandon a proposed visit to Cardiff to attend the Commonwealth Games. Instead, she recorded an announcement that she was creating her son Prince of Wales and gave it to her husband, Prince Philip, to relay to the crowd on the closing day of the Games.

"When he is grown up," her recorded message concluded, "I will present him to you at Caernarvon."

Charles was duly invested as Prince of Wales in the grounds of Caernarvon Castle on July 1, 1969. In a television age, it was perhaps inevitable that the ceremony, masterminded this time by the Queen's brother-in-law, the Earl of Snowdon, resplendent in a self-designed, zip-fronted outfit in hunting green, should have come close to being a television spectacular complete with state trumpeters, the Household Cavalry, the Yeomen of the Guard and a contingent of Welsh Druids. The actual investiture took place on a pexi-glass royal rostrum surmounted by a pop-art version of the Prince of Wales feathers. But at least Charles was saved from wearing the sort of "preposterous rig" the Duke of Windsor had been obliged to wear in his day. As Colonel-in-Chief of the Royal Regiment of Wales, it was felt quite in order for him to dress in regimental No. 1 blues.

According to a public opinion poll, 76% of the Welsh people were heartily in favour of staging an investiture ceremony. Unfortunately, a small proportion of the remaining 24% proved every bit as belligerent as the rebellious tribesmen of Edward I's day. There were not a few bomb incidents in the lead-up to the occasion and in the Denbighshire town of Abergele, in the early hours of investiture day, two would-be bombers succeeded in blowing themselves up with their own bomb.

To ensure that no bombs marred the actual ceremony, a boom was strung across the water approach to Caernarvon Castle, helicopters patrolled overhead and minesweepers out to sea, and the four thousand guests invited to witness the ceremony had their picnic hampers and handbags searched.

Despite this, the moments of actual investiture, when Charles knelt before his mother to take the same vow of allegiance that his father had taken at the coronation, when she buckled on his sword, placed a £3,000 diamond and emerald coronet on his head, draped a velvet mantle about his shoulders, slipped a ring on his finger and placed a sceptre in his hand, were extremely moving.

The ceremony of investiture concluded, the Queen led Charles in turn to the balcony of St Eleanor's Gate, to the King's Gate and to the Lower Ward of the castle, at each place presenting him to his Welsh subjects as "my most dear son".

Thus Charles was invested as the twenty-first Prince of Wales since the far-off days of Edward I. The complete list is:

NAME	QUALIFICATION	CREATED
Edward (Edward II)	Son of Edward I	1301
Edward (Black Prince)	Son of Edward III	1343
(Died 1376)		
Richard (Richard II)	Son of the Black Prince	1377
Henry of Monmouth (Henry V)	Son of Henry IV	1399
Edward of Westminster	Son of Henry VI	1454
(Died 1471)		
Edward (Edward V)	Son of Edward IV	1472
Edward	Son of Richard III	1483
(Died 1484)		
Arthur	Son of Henry VII	1489
(Died 1502)		
Henry (Henry VIII)	Son of Henry VII	1503
Henry	Son of James I	1610
(Died 1612)		
Charles (Charles I)	Son of James I	1616
Charles (Charles II)	Son of Charles I	1630
James (Old Pretender)	Son of James II	1688
(Died 1766)		
Styled Prince of Wales but exiled, along with his father, in infancy.		
George (George II)	Son of George I	1714
Frederick	Son of George II	1727
(Died 1751)		
George (George III)	Son of Prince Frederick	1751
George (George IV)	Son of George III	1762
Albert Edward (Edward VII)	Son of Queen Victoria	1841
George (George V)	Son of Edward VII	1901
Edward (Edward VIII, Duke of Windsor)	Son of George V	1910
Charles	Son of Elizabeth II	1958

PRINCESS ALEXANDRA AND THE HON ANGUS OGILVY

Princess Alexandra, the Queen's tall and always cheerful-looking cousin, is one of those mildly unfortunate people – Princess Alice, the widowed Duchess of Gloucester, is another – who have to make one batch of presents a year suffice for two. Christmas Day is also her birthday. Born on December 25, 1936, daughter of the late Duke and Duchess of Kent, her mother being the former Princess Marina of Greece, she was christened Alexandra Helen Elizabeth Olga Christabel.

The death of her father when she was only five hit the Kent family hard, both emotionally and financially. While they were not impoverished by ordinary standards, their circumstances were certainly reduced by royal standards. Alexandra's childhood clothes were made relatively cheaply by the village dressmaker and summer holidays, with her widowed mother and two brothers (*see* Duke and Duchess of Kent *and* Prince and Princess Michael of Kent), were often spent at small, inexpensive seaside hotels.

Nevertheless, she was educated at Heathfield, one of the more fashionable girls' schools, after which she went to France, where she stayed at the home of le Comte de Paris while studying the piano and modern Greek and improving her conversational French. Life quickly resolved itself into a round of secondary royal duties which took her to many different countries, as, for instance, when she represented the Queen at the independence celebrations in Nigeria. In return for all this, while her name never appeared on the Government's official royal payroll, she did receive an unspecified allowance funnelled through her cousin, the Queen. Throughout her early twenties the gossip columnists were consistently trying to "marry her off" to this or that European princeling. In the end, however, it was a London businessman she married, the Honourable Angus James Bruce Ogilvy, second son of the Earl of Airlie.

Born September 14, 1928, Eton educated, Ogilvy served in the Scots Guards before embarking on a career in the City of London. The extent of his success is shown by the fact that at the time of the couple's betrothal he was a director of twenty-nine different companies.

Unlike Lord Snowdon, he evinced no desire to retreat from public view as the day of the wedding approached, but continued to go back and forth to his office in Old Broad Street as usual. Indeed, he was at his desk the day before the wedding, despite the fact that he had been kept up until 4 a.m. that morning by a reception and ball at Windsor Castle.

The Queen put herself out to host the many European royals who flocked to Britain for the wedding. While she entertained them with the reception and ball at Windsor, it was her husband's novel idea to pile a miscellaneous assortment of kings and queens, princes and princesses, counts and margraves, into a couple of buses for a mystery tour of the countryside around London, including a stop for a pub lunch at the Hind's Head Hotel in Bray.

The wedding took place at Westminster Abbey on April 24, 1963. The bride's brother, the Duke of Kent, flew home from Hong Kong where he was based with his regiment to give her in marriage and Princess Anne was the chief bridesmaid. The couple set up home in Thatched House Lodge in Richmond Park. Their first child, James Robert Bruce, was born on February 29, 1964 – a leap-year baby – and a daughter, Marina Victoria Alexandra, followed on July 31, 1966.

In 1976 Angus Ogilvy found himself at the heart of what became known as "the Lonrho affair" when the report of two Department of Trade and Industry inspectors accused the company of defying Britain's policy of sanctions against Rhodesia by maintaining investments in that country. Ogilvy had in fact resigned his directorship of Lonrho in 1973. Nevertheless, he found himself slated in the report for "either supporting or recommending or acquiescing in" certain actions of the company. Although insisting that the comments and conclusions of the report were alike "unfair and unjust", Ogilvy promptly resigned from all his other directorships. With no way to effectively clear his name, it was, he said "the only honourable thing to do".

PRINCESS ALICE, COUNTESS OF ATHLONE

Very few people, surely, could lay claim to having witnessed both the Diamond Jubilee of Queen Victoria and the Silver Jubilee of Victoria's great-great-granddaughter, Elizabeth II. Princess Alice, Countess of Athlone, did. In 1897, as a girl of fourteen, she took part in her grandmother's jubilee procession through London, sharing a carriage with Prince Philip's mother. Eighty years later in 1977, at the ripe old age of ninety-four, she witnessed the jubilee celebrations of her great-niece, the present Queen. In between those two dates she also attended no fewer than four coronations, those of Edward VII, George V, George VI and Elizabeth II.

Princess Alice was born at Windsor Castle on February 25, 1883, the daughter of Queen Victoria's youngest son, Leopold, Duke of Albany, and Princess Helen of Waldeck-Pyrmont. Her brother, Charles Edward, Duke of Albany and later Duke of Saxe-Coburg-Gotha (he died in 1954) was born on July 19, 1884, but by then their father, who suffered from haemophilia (*see* Haemophilia), had himself been dead nearly four months.

In 1904, at St George's Chapel, Windsor, she married Queen Mary's brother, Prince Alexander of Teck, who was to become Earl of Athlone when the family followed King George V's example of adopting British names and titles during World War I (*see* Name). They had three children, May (later Lady May Abel-Smith), Rupert who died following a car accident in France in 1928, and Maurice who died in infancy.

Princess Alice accompanied her husband to South Africa where he was Governor-General from 1924–30 and similarly to Canada where he held the same post from 1940–6. Since his death in 1957, she has lived in an apartment at Kensington Palace (where her husband was born) on a small official stipend.

PRINCESS ANNE AND MARK PHILLIPS

Labelled "The Royal Family's own little gift to Republicanism" by one newspaper writer, Princess Anne, the Queen's second child and only daughter, shares with her aunt, Princess Margaret, the somewhat doubtful distinction of being the family's most controversial character. With two notable exceptions – when she won the European eventing championship and when she was on the receiving end of a would-be kidnap attempt – recent years have seen her cast regularly as the "black sheep" in the non-stop serial of royal life. If some people might regard this merely as type-casting, Anne herself does not. "There are always people around waiting for me to put my foot in it," she has said.

Anne Elizabeth Alice Louise was born at Clarence House on August 15, 1950. Brother Charles was not quite two at the time. Her father, Prince Philip, was still in the navy, based on Malta, but home on leave at the time of the birth. Following her mother's accession to the throne eighteen months later, the family moved to Buckingham Palace where the two children had their own apartment of day nursery and night nurseries and their own small staff of nanny, under-nanny and footman. While Nanny Lightbody took care of Charles (*see* Prince Charles), Anne was looked after by Mabel Anderson – known to her by the childhood diminutive of "Mamba" – whom she employs today to look after her own son at Gatcombe Park (*see* Gatcombe Park).

Initially, the relationship between Anne and her elder brother was very much that which existed between Princess Margaret and her elder sister in childhood, with Anne wanting to copy everything her brother did and Charles encouraging or reprimanding her as his twenty-one months' seniority seemed to require. But as she grew old enough to join him for lessons in the palace schoolroom under governess Katherine Peebles, Anne was quickly to develop as "a more forceful child". She had "a much stronger, more extrovert personality", Miss Anderson remembers.

Considered still too young in 1953 to witness the coronation ceremony (though her brother did), she had to be content with watching her mother's departure for Westminster Abbey from an upstairs window of Buckingham Palace. However, the following year she was thought old enough to join Charles aboard the then new royal yacht *Britannia* (*see* Yacht) for a voyage to Tobruk and a reunion with their parents at the end of the Queen's six-month Commonwealth tour.

Childhood upbringing at Buckingham Palace, with weekends at Windsor and holidays at Balmoral and Sandringham, was in the royal tradition, relatively secluded and cosseted. From an early age Anne displayed a passion for horses – Charles at the same age was somewhat nervous of them – and was later to develop a riding ability which not only rivalled that of her mother, herself no mean horsewoman, but included something of the dash and daring her father displayed on the polo field in his younger days. She was both high-spirited and determined. She was once caught trying to lead her pony up the steps at Sandringham with a view to re-mounting at the top and surprising the rest of the family by riding into the Saloon. Unfortunately – or perhaps fortunately – the pony declined to co-operate. There was another occasion, riding full tilt at Balmoral, when she failed to notice a line stretched between two trees for the purpose of airing linen. It caught her across the body and whisked her from the saddle. Shaken but undeterred, she scrambled to her feet, brushed herself down, remounted and rode on.

With the departure of Prince Charles for boarding school, the paths of brother and sister began to diverge. For Anne, private lessons continued in the palace schoolroom with two other small girls, Susan Babington-Smith and Caroline Hamilton, the daughters of a banker and company director respectively, for company. To afford her further contact with other children, a palace Brownie pack was formed and met once a week. There was also a dancing class shared with five other small girls, piano lessons from Hilda Bor and French lessons from a visiting tutor.

She was chief bridesmaid at the wedding of the Duke of Kent in 1961 and again at the wedding of his sister, Princess Alexandra, in 1963. Later that same year, at the age of thirteen, she followed Charles to boarding school, to Benenden in Kent, a girls' school few people had heard of until the Queen selected it for her daughter. Her headmistress there was Elizabeth Clark. At Benenden, in addition to lessons, Anne found herself making her own bed and taking her turn at such light chores as emptying the wastepaper baskets and waiting on table at mealtimes. She did well at Latin and French, but had something of a struggle, as Charles did also, with the intricacies of mathematics. She had piano and dancing lessons, did pottery, played lacrosse and tennis, a game in which she had had some prior coaching from Dan Maskell. Enthusiasm for riding continued undiminished and with her ability consistently improving she took part in a number of gymkhanas as a member of the school team.

While at Benenden she passed her O-levels in six subjects and also gained two A-levels. However, her schooldays over, she had no wish to go on to university as brother Charles had done. What she wanted to do was carry on with her riding. "It's the one thing I can do well and can be seen to do well," she reportedly said.

But a princess can hardly make a career of riding. Instead, at eighteen, with an official allowance of £6,000 a year, Anne found herself launched on a career of royal chores, presenting leeks to the men of the Welsh Guards on St David's Day, visiting children's homes and youth clubs, launching a tanker and naming a hovercraft, presenting the trophies at the Cup Final and Wimbledon. Initially, she was like a fresh breeze blowing through the musty protocol of the royal round, with everyone waiting eagerly and delightedly to see what she would come up with next. Visiting the Road Transport Training Centre, she climbed behind the driving wheel of a double-decker bus. At a police cadet school she slewed a patrol car round a greasy skid-pan. Visiting the 14th/20th Hussars, of which she is Colonel-in-Chief, at their base in Germany, she not only drove a massive Chieftain tank but fired a sub-machine gun from the hip with all the aplomb of Modesty Blaize. It was all new and novel and people loved her for it.

Then, all at once and for no apparent reason, it all went wrong, and in countries where people do not genuflect to the Royals to quite the degree that they do in Britain, people were quick to say so. A visit to Canada saw her labelled "sulky". In Australia, where she is said to have sworn in public, she was called "impatient". Did she swear? "I may have done," Anne said, frankly. In Kenya she was termed "arrogant", and in the United States she was tagged with a whole string of critical adjectives: "snobbish, pouting, spoiled, bored, sullen and disdainful". Even in Britain, after a brush with photographers at the Burghley horse trials, she was referred to, more mildly, as "unco-operative".

But all was immediately forgiven her when she won the European Three-Day Event at Burghley in 1971. While it was by no means her first riding success – her sitting-room at the palace was already liberally besprinkled with rosettes – it was easily her biggest. And achieved in unusual circumstances.

She was not long out of hospital where she had had an ovarian cyst removed. As a result, she did not qualify for inclusion in the British team, though Mark Phillips, who she was later to marry, did. Undeterred by the fact that hands and leg muscles alike had slackened during her spell in hospital, she submitted an individual entry for the championship, as she was qualified to do. "She has a steely determination," her trainer, Alison Oliver, was to say after Anne had won. This she demonstrated in private in the weeks following hospitalization, hardening her hands with endless games of deck tennis aboard the royal yacht and toughening her legs by tramping up and down Scottish mountainsides during a family stay at Balmoral. Competing against the pick of international riders, official teams from Britain, France, Italy, Russia and Ireland, she led the championship all the way on Doublet, a chestnut gelding bred by her mother. At the end of the dressage section she was already in the lead. In the cross-country section, she took risks and cut corners (literally) to return the best time, contriving to avoid what might well have been "a dangerous fall" – the words are Alison Oliver's – at one obstacle which found Doublet struggling to get out of the water and up the steep, slippery bank beyond. In the show-jumping section she cleared all twelve fences without incurring a single penalty point. Sadly, Doublet, the horse on which she achieved so much, was later to injure a leg while being exercised and had to be destroyed. Anne attempted to repeat her championship victory on another horse in 1975 in Germany, this time as an official member of Britain's all-girl team, but just failed, finishing second to her teammate, Lucinda Prior-Palmer.

By then she was married. Her first meeting with Mark Phillips, then a lieutenant in the Queen's Dragoon Guards, son of middle-class parents – his father, Peter Phillips, was a director of the Walls food firm – was at the end of 1968, at a palace reception for members of the British Olympic squad, among them the eventing team which had won a gold medal in Mexico City. Mark was the team's reserve rider. They continued to run into each other on subsequent equestrian occasions, including that 1971 championship which Anne won, though Mark had twice beaten her previously. Rivalry led to friendship which turned to romance. After engagement rumours had been several times denied, their betrothal was officially announced on May 29, 1973. They were married in Westminster Abbey on November 14 that same year, coincidentally Prince Charles' twenty-fifth birthday.

For some curious reason, the wedding ceremony was classed as "private" by Buckingham Palace. Nevertheless, there were some 4,000 police on duty in London that day, five military bands played for the benefit of the crowds, the 1,600 wedding guests included twenty-five members of foreign royal families, and the Queen loaned the newlyweds the royal yacht for a honeymoon cruise. The only slight drawback was that the yacht boasted no double bed. That small problem was overcome by lashing two single beds together.

For Mark there was no princely title or royal dukedom as a result of marriage, though the Queen did appoint him as one of her personal aides-de-camp. So Anne became the Princess Anne, Mrs Mark Phillips. The army promoted him to the rank of captain and he was posted as an instructor to the Royal Military Academy Sandhurst, where he and Anne lived in Oak Grove House, a five-bedroomed Georgian property which they rented for £8 a week. Mark's army pay at that time was around £2,800 a year. Anne had more. As a married princess, her official allowance was increased to £35,000 a year.

For Mark, military duties were interrupted, as Philip's naval duties had been in the early years of his marriage to the then Princess Elizabeth, by the necessity to accompany his royal wife on a number of official occasions, including tours of Australia, New Zealand and Canada. He acquitted himself well. Those who had hoped that marriage would mellow Anne were sometimes disappointed, however. She remained as unpredictable as ever, often charming, sometimes prickly. In Canada with Mark she was again classed as "snobbish" on one occasion. In Australia, when a photographer called out, "Look this way, love," she is said to have snapped back, "I am not your love. I am Your Royal Highness." Even in Britain, after another brush with photographers at a riding event, Kenya's earlier "arrogant" was upgraded to "plain arrogant" by one newspaper.

The couple had been married only a short time when there was a violent attempt to kidnap the Princess. It was the evening of March 20, 1974. Anne and Mark were on their way back to Buckingham Palace from a charity film show when another car cut in front of them in the Mall, forcing their chauffeur to brake. An armed man jumped out of the car ahead and raced towards them. In quickfire succession, their chauffeur, Alex Callender, Anne's bodyguard, Inspector James Beaton, a policeman, Michael Hills, and a passing journalist who tried to help, Brian McConnell had been gunned down, though fortunately all were to survive the attack. The gunman wrenched open the door of the royal car, grabbed Anne by the wrist and tried to drag her out. Despite Mark's efforts to frustrate him, he might have succeeded but for the intervention of a burly Cockney, Ron Russell. He ran to aid the Princess and knocked the would-be kidnapper to the ground. Later a rambling ransom note was found in the man's pocket. Addressed to the Queen, it demanded a ransom of three million pounds for Anne, a free pardon for himself and an aircraft to fly him to Switzerland.

Stated in court to be "schizoid", the would-be kidnapper, whose name was Ian Ball, pleaded quilty to the charges against him and was ordered to be detained in a mental hospital for an indefinite period. For his part in the affair, Inspector Beaton received the George Cross while Ron Russell and police-constable Hills were each awarded the George Medal. Alex Callender, Brian McConnell and Peter Edmonds, another police-constable, were each awarded the Queen's Medal for Gallantry while Glenmore Martin, another passing motorist who also stopped to help, received the Queen's Commendation for Brave Conduct. The citation for all seven, read out during the course of an investiture ceremony at Buckingham Palace, stated that all had "displayed outstanding courage and a complete disregard for their own safety". Anne was made a Dame Grand Cross of the Royal Victoria Order and her husband a Commander of the same Order.

For the first few years of marriage Anne and Mark seemed more interested in riding horses than in having children. It was not until they had been married four years that their first child, a boy weighing 7 lbs 9 ounces, was born on November 15, 1977, in St Mary's Hospital, Paddington. Had his father been a son of the Sovereign, the baby would have been born a prince. But because relationship to the Sovereign was through his mother – daughter, instead of son, of the Sovereign – he was born without a title, the first royal child to be born a commoner for something like five centuries. And although he was born fifth in line of succession to the throne (*see* Succession) (a position from which he can be ousted by any children born to Anne's three brothers, Charles, Andrew and Edward), his grandmother, the Queen, saw no reason, in this increasingly egalitarian age, to change the situation by bestowing a title upon him.

On emergence from hospital, Anne stayed briefly with her parents at Buckingham Palace before moving into Gatcombe Park, the country home in Gloucestershire the Queen had generously provided for her daughter and son-in-law. On December 22, with her husband and baby, she returned briefly to the palace so that the baby could be baptized by Dr Donald Coggan, Archbishop of Canterbury. The child was given the names of Peter Mark Andrew. Mark is of course his father's name while Peter is that of his paternal grandfather and Andrew is the name of one of Anne's brothers as well as having been borne by Prince Philip's dead father.

At around the same time came news that Anne's husband was quitting the army. He did not feel that there was much future for him in military life, his father explained, adding, "For fairly obvious reasons he is not able to get some of the regimental soldiering that he would have needed for command." In the autumn of 1978, his army career now behind him, Mark embarked on a year's course at Cirencester agricultural college designed to turn him into a gentleman farmer with the ability to run the Gatcombe Park estate.

PRINCESS MARGARET AND LORD SNOWDON

If his elder daughter, Elizabeth, was the serious and dutiful one King

George VI saw as being the natural successor to his crown, then his younger daughter, Margaret, was undeniably a "fun" child. Vivacious and warmly affectionate, she was the one who brightened her parents' lives with her non-stop chatter and laughter. Her father, with his firm regard for the sanctity of family life, would no doubt have been very distressed, had he lived, by much of what has happened since the "fun" child grew up.

Princess Margaret was born at Glamis Castle, the Scottish family seat of her mother's family, the Earls of Strathmore and Kinghorne, on August 21, 1930. Her parents were then still Duke and Duchess of York. One of her uncles was Prince of Wales and her grandfather, gruff old King George V, was on the throne. But for her grandfather, she would have been named Ann; he didn't like the name. So Ann Margaret was changed to Margaret Rose. "She's not really a rose," objected sister Elizabeth from the lofty pinnacle of her four years. "She's only a bud."

Throughout the years of childhood and teenage, the elder sister was to treat the younger one very much as a "bud", fussily protecting her, chiding and admonishing her when necessary. She must not laugh so loudly or at the wrong things; must be quieter; must not wriggle and so draw attention to herself at this or that wedding. And throughout the years of childhood and teenage, Margaret was to come to lean more and more on the elder, more serious sister, looking to her for guidance, encouragement, help, relying upon her in all sorts of ways.

Even as children the two sisters were as different as chalk from cheese. Elizabeth, almost from the age when she could first toddle, was punctual and punctilious, tidying her clothes neatly at bedtime, writing dutiful thank-you notes for Christmas and birthday gifts, even sorting her sweets into carefully counted piles to be eked out day by day. Margaret, by contrast, was always quick to stuff her sweets into her mouth in sticky handfuls. Despite their very different natures, the two of them had a close and warm relationship and it is interesting, if pointless, to speculate on how different life might have been for Margaret if her elder sister had not fallen in love with Philip at so young an age or if their father had lived longer. As it was, romance, marriage and public duty – the need to deputize for her sick father – combined to switch Elizabeth's thoughts in other directions and Margaret was robbed of her companionship and guidance. And, to a large extent, lost without them.

In a sense, all that has happened to Princess Margaret since had its roots in the family's 1947 tour of South Africa. By going to South Africa, George VI had hoped to ease some of the tensions and reconcile some of the differences in that country, at that time still a member of the Commonwealth. The tour proved an exceptionally arduous one during which the King, his health already beginning to fail, lost seventeen pounds in weight. His wife worried about him while his elder daughter pined for Philip, back in Britain. All three had their own public engagements to fulfil. Only Margaret was largely uncommitted and sometimes at a loose end. A member of the King's entourage was given the task of ensuring that she didn't get too bored. His name was Group Captain Peter Townsend.

Margaret at the time was not yet seventeen. Townsend was thirty-three, a married man with a wife and two small sons living in a grace-and-favour cottage on the royal estate at Windsor. His involvement with the Royal Family had first come about in World War II when the King conceived the idea of surrounding himself with able young men who had distinguished themselves in combat. Townsend was among the first of these war-time temporary enquerries. He was born in 1914 and on February 3, 1940, had the distinction of destroying the first Heinkel bomber ever shot down over England. He flew his Hurricane with 43 Squadron and later commanded 85 Squadron. At the time he first went to Buckingham Palace he had eleven enemy "kills" to his credit and had been decorated with the Distinguished Service Order and the Distinguished Flying Cross and Bar. He had also lost a big toe, amputated after he himself was shot down in the summer of 1941, and married Rosemary Pawle, nineteen-year-old daughter of a brigadier. Their first son, Giles, was born the following year.

Townsend's initial appointment to the King's staff was for a mere three months. But the King took a liking to him and the appointment was extended . . . and extended . . . until it had lasted nine years. In 1945 when Peter and Rosemary Townsend had their second son, Hugo, the King was one of the godparents. To an extent, it could be said that, more and more, the King treated him as one of the family. So, from the time of the South African tour, did Margaret. To her, he was, at first, like an older brother.

Later in 1947 he accompanied her when she carried out an official visit to Belfast. The following year he was with her on a visit to Amsterdam. In 1949 and again in 1950 he piloted aircraft entered in her name in the King's Cup Air Race. In 1950 too he was appointed Deputy Master of the Royal Household. On a less official basis, he was often with Margaret when she went out riding at Balmoral and elsewhere. So their friendship ripened, with the King too ill, and the Queen too worried about her husband, to notice what was happening.

Elizabeth's betrothal and marriage to Philip found Margaret robbed of the sisterly companionship and guidance on which she had relied for so long. To fill the gap, she turned more and more to Townsend. Her father's death resulted in her sister becoming heavily preoccupied with the new-found duties of monarchy while her mother was deeply absorbed in grief. Needing someone with whom to share her own grief in her father's death, again Margaret, only twenty-one at the time, turned to Townsend.

At the time of the King's death Townsend's wartime marriage to Rosemary Pawle had already broken down. Ten months later, in December, 1952, newspapers briefly reported: "Group Captain Peter Woolridge Townsend, an Extra Equerry in Waiting to the Queen, was granted a decree nisi in the Divorce Court yesterday on the grounds of misconduct at a London hotel in August, 1951, by his wife, Cecil Rosemary. Mr John Adolphus de Laszlo, an export merchant, was cited as co-respondent."

In normal circumstances, divorce at that time, because of the moral attitudes of the day, might well have meant resignation from royal service, even for an innocent man. But circumstances, in the aftermath of the King's death and his daughter's abrupt accession to the throne, were hardly normal. Moreover, the former Queen who was now the Queen Mother was as fond of Townsend as her late husband had been. So when at Easter, 1953, along with her younger daughter, she moved to Clarence House in order to free Buckingham Palace for the new Queen and her family, she took Townsend with her as her Comptroller. It was as her Comptroller that Townsend planned the tour of Southern Rhodesia, including a visit to the Rhodes Centenary Exhibition in Bulawayo, which the Queen Mother and Margaret were to make. He was to have gone with them. But before the time of departure arrived, newspapers around the world, following the obvious and somewhat indiscreet attachment Margaret had shown to Townsend at her sister's coronation, were full of romantic speculation concerning the Queen's sister and the World War II fighter ace.

Even before this, Elizabeth was already aware of her sister's love for Townsend and her wish to marry him. But with Margaret still under the age of twenty-five, the cobwebs of the Royal Marriage Act (*see* Marriage) meant that she could marry only with her sister's formal consent as Queen. This placed Elizabeth in a quandary, for she was now not only Queen, but, as Queen, also head of the Church of England which was – and is – strongly opposed to divorce (though it appears to make exceptions at times). The only way out was if her consent was political rather than monarchical, given on the express advice of the prime minister. A subsequent prime minister, Harold Wilson, ten years or more later, was prepared to oblige when the Queen's cousin, the Earl of Harewood, wished to re-marry following his divorce (*see* Earl of Harewood). Winston Churchill, in 1953, was not. For the Queen to consent to her sister marrying a divorced man, however innocent, could be "disastrous", he felt.

But if the Queen could not give her consent to marriage, neither could the situation be simply allowed to drift. The consensus of advice the Queen received from Churchilll and the "old guard" of royal aides she had inherited from her father was that Townsend should be sent away. As a result, instead of going to Southern Rhodesia with Margaret and her mother, Townsend remained behind to accompany the Queen and her husband on a visit to Northern Ireland. By the time Margaret returned to Britain he was in Brussels, air attaché at the British embassy there. He had been given a choice of three postings, Singapore, Johannesburg and Brussels, and had picked the last as being nearest to both Margaret and the two young sons of his failed marriage.

Separation lasted two years during which time they saw each other only once. That was in July, 1954, when Townsend returned secretly and briefly to Britain for a reunion at Clarence House. It was that same year, coincidentally, in Brussels, that he first met Marie-Luce Jamagne, the Princess Margaret "look-alike" he was subsequently to marry. At the time of that first meeting he and Margaret were still in love; still hoped to marry. While, except for that brief reunion at Clarence House, they could not meet, they wrote to and telephoned each other often. Occasional guarded interviews with Townsend kept the romantic story alive in the newspapers. "I came here because the situation was impossible for us both," he was quoted as saying. In the discreet tradition of royalty, Margaret said nothing.

In August, 1955, Margaret celebrated her twenty-fifth birthday. Under the Royal Marriage Act, she was now of an age to marry without her sister's consent provided Parliament raised no objection. Seven weeks after her birthday Townsend returned to Britain. Margaret travelled south from Balmoral, where she had been staying with others of the family, the same day. They met the following day at Clarence House, and nearly every day after that. They spent the weekend together in the Berkshire countryside, at the home of Mrs Jean Lycett Wills, a royal cousin.

By now, Anthony Eden had succeeded Churchill as prime minister, but the advice Elizabeth received from both him and her own royal advisers was still the same. As Queen, she could not consent formally to her sister marrying a divorced man. Sympathetic though she might feel towards the couple, she felt she could not fly in the face of her advisers nor disregard her own position as head of the Church of England. If Margaret wanted to marry, she would have to do it without the Queen's consent. And that, if she did not want Parliament to object, would mean renouncing her right of succession to the throne – she was third in line at the time – and forgoing her royal allowance.

The situation was put squarely, if sympathetically, to Margaret at a weekend she spent with her sister and Philip, but without Townsend, at Windsor Castle. Dinner for the three of them ended with Margaret in tears.

Margaret was also to see the Archbishop of Canterbury, Dr Geoffrey Fisher (later Lord Fisher of Lambeth), but by then she and Townsend had already come to their decision to part. Their love for each other, though it had survived two years of separation, was perhaps not strong enough to embark upon a future in which they would be forced to live on his income alone and perhaps, like the Windsors, even in "exile". They spent one more weekend together, this time at the country home of Lord Rupert Nevill and his wife Anne, an American on her mother's side. On Monday, October 31, Townsend called again at Clarence House, this time to say goodbye.

That evening came Margaret's "statement of renunciation". It was issued by the Princess, but the words were those which Townsend had drafted for her.

"I would like it to be known that I have decided not to marry Group Captain Peter Townsend. I have been aware that, subject to my renouncing my rights of succession, it might have been possible for me to contract a civil marriage. But mindful of the Church's teaching that Christian marriage is indissoluble and conscious of my duty to the Commonwealth, I have resolved to put these considerations before any others.

"I have reached this decision entirely alone, and in doing so I have been strengthened by the unfailing support and devotion of Group Captain Townsend. I am deeply grateful for the concern of all those who have constantly prayed for my happiness."

Within the comparatively short space of two years it seemed as if those prayers for Margaret's happiness were destined to be answered. By that time she had already met Antony Armstrong-Jones, an up-and-coming young photographer whose portraits of the Queen and Prince Philip were issued at the time of their 1957 tour of Canada. Born in 1930, he was the same age as Margaret, the grandson of a knight, the son of a countess (even if his mother did not become Countess of Rosse until after parting from Tony's father) and the brother of a *vicomtesse*. Margaret's romance with Townsend had been played out in the fierce glare of the public spotlight and she wanted no repetition of that. So, initially, she and Tony courted in secret. He would visit Royal Lodge, Balmoral and Sandringham in his guise of royal photographer. When they went to the theatre together, seats were booked in the names of Norman and Ruby Gordon. Ruby, a sister of the Queen's "Bobo" Macdonald, was Margaret's personal maid. Margaret was escorted to and from parties by a helpful long-time friend, Billy Wallace, stepson of the American-born Pulitzer prizewinner, Herbert Agar. But it was Tony she danced with while she was at the party. There were also secret romantic meetings at a Thames-side cottage which Tony borrowed from a journalist friend.

In December, 1959, at the Hôtel de Ville in Brussels, Townsend married Marie-Luce Jamagne. Two months later, on February 26, 1960, came news that Margaret too was to marry someone else. In the words of the official announcement: "It is with the greatest pleasure that Queen Elizabeth the Queen Mother announces the betrothal of her beloved daughter The Princess Margaret to Mr Antony Armstrong-Jones, son of Mr R.O.L. Armstrong-Jones, QC, and the Countess of Rosse, to which the Queen has gladly given her consent."

They were married in Westminster Abbey on May 6, 1960. Prince Philip gave the bride in marriage and the eight bridesmaids included Princess Anne. The guest list varied from dukes and earls, princes and princesses on the bride's side to theatrical designers, model girls and the young airline hostess the bridegroom's father had recently made his third wife. The Queen lent the newly-weds her royal yacht to serve as a honeymoon base for visits to Trinidad, Tobago, Antigua and Dominica. Margaret's allowance was increased from £6,000 to £15,000 a year, and £65,000 was spent on renovating a twenty-one-room apartment at Kensington Palace as their future home.

For a time married life was happy enough. Margaret supported her new husband staunchly in his wish to continue his photographic career – he took a job as "artistic adviser" to *The Sunday Times* – and he dutifully accompanied her on a variety of public engagements. She also understood and supported his initial desire not to be encumbered with a title, though he finally accepted one, becoming Earl of Snowdon just prior to the birth of their first child, David Albert Charles, who thus became Viscount Linley when he was born on November 3, 1961. A daughter, Sarah Frances Elizabeth (Lady Sarah Armstrong-Jones) followed on May 1, 1964.

Sadly, Margaret's new-found happiness was not to last. The gossip columns began to hint at marital disagreements. Husband and wife drifted more and more apart, Snowdon taking off on prolonged photographic and filming expeditions while Margaret took refuge in the luxury villa she had built for herself on the island of Mustique, on a plot of land given to her as a wedding gift by her long-time friend, the Hon. Colin Tennant. Several times, in 1967, 1970 and again in 1975, there were rumours of impending divorce. Each rumour was quickly denied, either jokingly by Lord Snowdon or officially by a royal spokesman. But hardly had the latest 1975 rumours been denied than Margaret was again flying out to her hideaway home on Mustique for another holiday with Colin Tennant and his wife Anne, one of the princess's ladies-in-waiting. Also in the party was a young man sixteen years Margaret's junior, Roderic Llewellyn. She called him "Roddy".

A few months later, in March, 1976, came news that Margaret and

Snowdon were to separate. It was a civilized arrangement in the modern tradition, Margaret would have custody of the children and Lord Snowdon would have access to them for holidays and suchlike. Margaret would go on living at Kensington Palace, but there would be a financial settlement to enable Snowdon to find another home for himself elsewhere in London.

So once again Margaret found herself confronted with the necessity to pick up the pieces and start trying to build herself a new life. And this time it was not simply in the aftermath of a disastrous love affair, but of a broken marriage. And she was no longer an unattached princess in her twenties, but a woman in her forties, mother of two children. She threw herself into an extended round of public duties, including a tour of Tunisia designed to boost Britain's flagging export trade. Lacking a husband, she sometimes had her son, now nearly fifteen, along as escort. She could hardly be seen in public with Roddy Llewellyn. But the two continued to meet in private.

The Queen invited both her sister and the husband from whom she was separated to the party she gave to celebrate her fiftieth birthday in 1976. Husband and wife were also together, their daughter Sarah sitting between them, when their son was confirmed at Windsor, afterwards sitting at the same table for a family lunch. But if separated husband and wife continued to remain "good friends", there was to be no reconciliation and on May 24, 1978, in the Family Division of the High Court, the princess who was once thwarted in her desire to marry a divorced man, was herself – ironically – divorced. The case was one of a batch of twenty-eight dealt with simultaneously and in two minutes it was all over. Margaret's divorce was granted, with her husband's consent, on the grounds that they had been separated for two years and the marriage had irretrievably broken down. At the time of the hearing Margaret herself was convalescing from an attack of hepatitis and gastro-enteritis.

A little over six months later, on December 15, Lord Snowdon married again, taking as his second wife Lucy Lindsay-Hogg, a television researcher some elven years his junior who had herself divorced her first husband in 1971. She first met Lord Snowdon two years later and the following year worked as his production assistant during the six weeks he spent in Australia filming an episode for the BBC television series *The Explorers*.

In contrast to the television spectacular of his earlier union to Princess Margaret, Snowdon's second wedding was an unglamorous affair in the local register office at Kensington. No dukes or earls (apart from Snowdon himself) present on this occasion; and no members of the Royal Family. Neither, to protect them from the inevitable publicity, did the Snowdon children attend. There were only four friends of the couple as witnesses, no formal reception afterwards and no honeymoon. Instead, after a quiet weekend together, it was work as usual for both Snowdon and his new wife, now sharing the title of Countess of Snowdon with Princess Margaret.

PRIVY COUNCIL

About once every two weeks during the course of the average Parliamentary session – perhaps twenty times a year in all – the Queen presides over a meeting of the Privy Council. The name has its origin in the small, tight circle of loyal advisers with which monarchs once surrounded themselves, though its functions go back even further than that, to the Witan – or Circle of Wise men – of Saxon times. William I, after conquering England, continued the old Saxon custom as a sop to the defeated and in time what had once been the Witan became known as the King's Privy (or Private) Council.

With the shift of political and executive power from Monarch to Cabinet, the myth of monarchical power was retained – and still is – by causing all members of the Cabinet to be sworn in also as members of the Privy Council. Thus the Cabinet, in theory at least, is merely a committee of the Privy Council. "Pure mumbo-jumbo", the late Richard Crossman, Lord President of the Council in Harold Wilson's government, styled the proceedings after witnessing the spectacle of new members taking up a wrong position, crawling to the correct one on their knees and knocking a book from the table at which the Queen was standing in the process.

Mumbo-jumbo or not, "The Queen's Most Excellent Majesty in Council" still concludes treaties, mobilizes the armed forces in times of emergency and declares war. It is also the combination of Queen and Privy Council which, technically, summons or dissolves Parliament, hands out seals of office to newly-appointed government ministers, grants royal charters to professional, educational and charitable organizations, grants – or refuses – permission to marry to those in line of succession to the throne, and appoints sheriffs. The appointment of sheriffs still takes the form of pricking a parchment roll with a bodkin in accordance with a tradition dating from the days of Elizabeth I. It is said that the first Elizabeth was sewing in the garden when the roll was brought to her. Having no quill handy, she used her bodkin instead. Her namesake does the same today.

Because appointment to the Privy Council, which carries the right to use the prefix "Right Honourable", is for life, the once small, tight circle of wise men has today swollen to a total of 300–350. It includes all Cabinet ministers and ex-ministers, the Lords of Appeal, the

Archbishops of Canterbury and York, some members of the Royal Family (Prince Philip and his uncle, Earl Mountbatten of Burma) together with ministers, ex-ministers and other distinguished citizens of the Commonwealth. But the only time they all, or nearly all, gather together is when they swear allegiance to a new monarch on the death of the old one. Because Elizabeth II was out of the country when her father died, the Privy Council had to meet twice when George VI died. The first occasion, on the day of the King's death, was to proclaim the new monarch. The second, following the Queen's return to London, was to hear her declaration of accession. However, this second meeting took the form of the Accession Council which also includes dignitaries like the Lord Mayor of London who are not necessarily members of the Privy Council.

A normal Privy Council meeting consists of only a handful of members. Three is a minimum and it is left to the Lord President of the Council to decide who shall attend. Meetings are generally held in the 1844 Room at Buckingham Palace (*see* Buckingham Palace), but can be anywhere the Queen happens to be at the time. In 1955, when the Queen in Council was required to declare a state of emergency because of a rail strike, she was staying at Balmoral. So a Privy Council was held there. The following year there was a Privy Council aboard the royal yacht *Britannia* so that the Queen could give consent to the marriage of Captain Alexander Ramsay, a great-great-grandson of Queen Victoria, to Miss Flora Fraser. Another time, that same year, it met at Arundel Castle, home of the Duke of Norfolk. The Queen was there for the races when it became necessary for her to sign a proclamation mobilizing army reservists at the time of the Suez crisis. There have been meetings of the Privy Council in New Zealand, Australia and Canada when the Queen has been travelling in those countries. Canada, incidentally, has its own Privy Council while Australia and New Zealand both have roughly equivalent bodies known in each case as the Executive Council.

Traditionally, no one sits at a meeting of the Privy Council. Even the Queen herself remains standing. While she personally signs proclamations, as she did at the time of Suez, she does not sign the much more frequent Orders in Council. She simply listens while the Lord President of the Council reads them out, utters the one word "Approved" and the Clerk of the Council does the signing for her.

QUEEN ELIZABETH II

Those who would see the birthplace of Queen Elizabeth II will search in vain for the splendid Georgian mansion, London home of her maternal grandparents, which once stood at 17 Bruton Street. Like much else in London, it fell victim to wartime bombing and a bank now occupies the site. Only a plaque in the entrance hall recalls the fact that "here was born on April 21, 1926, the Princess Elizabeth who was to become Queen Elizabeth II."

It is sometimes said that the baby who is now Elizabeth II was born by Caesarean section. The assumption, based on a medical bulletin following the birth, would seem to be erroneous. She was born at twenty minutes to three in the morning. The bulletin, issued just over seven hours later and signed by the attendant physicians, Henry Simson and Walter Jagger, stated: "The Duchess of York has had some rest since the arrival of her daughter. Her Royal Highness and the infant Princess are making very satisfactory progress. Previous to the confinement a consultation took place at which Sir George Blacker was present, and a certain line of treatment was successfully adopted."

Whatever else it may have involved, that "certain line of treatment" was not a Caesarean section, as was made clear by an authoritative statement circulated by the Press Association the following day. According to this statement:

"The wording of Wednesday morning's bulletin appears to have given rise to some misunderstanding and natural, but absolutely unnecessary anxiety. The phrase 'a certain line of treatment' led to considerable speculation from which the possibility of a Caesarean or other operation was not excluded. Nothing of the kind was intended to be implied or was the case in fact."

Nothing, surely, could be more categorical than that.

The baby's parents, the Duke and Duchess of York, had been married some three years at the time of the birth (*see* King George VI *and* Queen Elizabeth, the Queen Mother). "Our happiness complete", a delighted father wrote to his father, King George V. As the daughter of a king's son, she was born a Royal Highness, Princess Elizabeth of York. Her birth also altered the line of succession to the throne (*see* Succession). Until then, the King's four sons – the Prince of Wales, the Dukes of York, Gloucester and Kent – had been next in line followed by the King's daughter, Princess Mary, and her two sons. But now the new baby interposed herself to become third in line after her father and his elder brother, her Uncle David, the Prince of Wales.

Those privileged to see the baby in the days immediately following her birth were struck by two things, her "large dark-lashed blue eyes" and her "tiny ears". On May 29 she was baptized in the private chapel at Buckingham Palace. Like the baby's birthplace, this too was to be destroyed by bombs during World War II and the Queen's Gallery with its annual display from the royal picture collection now stands on the site. The ceremony was conducted by the then Archbishop of York, Dr Cosmo Lang, and the baby was given the names of her mother, great-grandmother and grandmother respectively – Elizabeth Alexandra Mary. Grandfather George V wondered at one time whether her great-great-grandmother's name, Victoria, should perhaps be included also, but finally decided that it didn't matter. Like everyone else in the family, her grandfather was to call her "Lilibet" in the future. He was one of her sponsors at the christening ceremony. The others were her grandmother, Queen Mary, her maternal grandfather, the Earl of Strathmore, two aunts – Princess Mary and Lady Elphinstone – and a great-uncle, the Duke of Connaught, surviving seventh child of Queen Victoria.

Lilibet's young life was eminently secure, cosseted, contented. Her nurse was the selfsame farmer's daughter who had nursed her mother before her, Clara Cooper Knight, known as Alla in the family. For the first few months of her life, until her parents acquired a home of their own at 145 Piccadilly in 1927, the baby's upbringing was divided between 17 Bruton Street, London home of her maternal grandfather, and Glamis Castle, his Scottish seat, where a sister, Margaret Rose (*see* Princess Margaret and Lord Snowdon), was to be born four years later.

Following Margaret's birth, with Mrs Knight now preoccupied with the new baby, a young nurserymaid named Margaret Macdonald was promoted to look after four-year-old Elizabeth. So began a friendship which was to survive both the years and difference in station. Margaret Macdonald – "Bobo" to the Queen, a name originating with the excited boo-booing which occurred during childhood games of hide- -and-seek – was born the daughter of a railway worker in a small Scottish hamlet. Today, as the Queen's dresser, she has her own suite of rooms at Buckingham Palace and is the privileged holder of the Royal Victorian Order, which the Queen bestowed on her.

Another person who was to have not inconsiderable influence on the character of the young princess entered her life when she was seven. This was her governess, Marion Crawford, another Scot. Under Miss Crawford, she learned English grammar and literature, history and geography, music and drawing. Special attention was paid to her handwriting after her grandfather, George V, had urged that she should be taught to write "a decent hand". She also learned arithmetic, though grandmother Queen Mary thought she was unlikely to need much of that. Canon Crawley, a member of the chapel of St George's Chapel, Windsor, gave her religious instruction and there were lessons in conversational French from the Vicomtesse de Bellaigue.

Her character formed quickly, patient and painstaking, a rather serious little girl who was soon taking it upon herself to help keep her more volatile younger sister in order. Weekends were spent at Royal Lodge, Windsor, which King George V had given to her parents. He also gave his small granddaughter a Shetland pony so that she could learn to ride. She was soon as enthusiastic about horses as other small girls are over dolls, and at one time she and her sister Margaret had a collection of thirty toy horses "stabled" on the landing at 145 Piccadilly.

She was a bridesmaid when her uncle, the Duke of Kent, married the elegant Princess Marina of Greece in 1934 and again the following year when another uncle, the Duke of Gloucester, married Lady Alice Montagu-Douglas-Scott. Earlier that same year, when her grandparents celebrated the Silver Jubilee of King George V's monarchy, she accompanied her parents to a commemorative service at St Paul's Cathedral. She also drove with her grandparents through the cheering, flag-waving London crowds and made her first appearance on the Buckingham Palace balcony. Less than a year later, still not yet ten, she was dressed in mourning to attend the lying-in-state and funeral of the king she knew as Grandpapa England.

Out of respect for the dead king, her dancing lessons were discontinued for the six months of court mourning which followed his death. But swimming lessons were all right, it seemed, and both she and Margaret qualified for their life-saving certificates. Uncle David was now King Edward VIII, her father was first in the line of succession and she came next.

Initially, of course – at least as far as the general public was concerned – there was no reason to think that she would ever inherit the throne. Edward VIII could reign for years and years, and would presumably marry and sire children to supplant both her and her father. It didn't work out like that, though the growing crisis which led to the abdication (*see* Duke and Duchess of Windsor, *and* King George VI) was largely above her young head. By odd coincidence, she was doing a history lesson on the day (December 10, 1936) and at the time her uncle signed his Instrument of Abdication. However, she understood sufficient of what was happening to remark "That's Mummy now, isn't it?" when she glimpsed a letter addressed to "Her Majesty the Queen" on a side table in the hall at 145 Piccadilly.

At the age of ten, she was now Heiress Presumptive to the throne (only "Presumptive" because it was not completely beyond the bounds of possibility that her parents could yet have a son who would rank ahead of her in the line of succession [*see* Heir Apparent/Heir Presumptive *and* Succession]), thought there was at the time some query as to whether, in the event that the new King had no male heir, his two daughters would inherit the throne jointly. Indeed, a question was asked in Parliament as to whether the Government proposed to amend the Act of Settlement, which lays down the line of succession, in order to clarify the situation.

"There is no need," the Home Secretary said in reply to the question. "His Majesty's Government is advised that there is no doubt that in present circumstances Her Royal Highness The Princess Elizabeth would succeed to the throne as sole heir."

That settled, the task of training her for future monarchy began in earnest. As a first move, her father devised a special picture book in which the significance of the coronation ceremony was made clear to her. She was taken along to attend one of the rehearsals for the ceremony and for the ceremony itself was outfitted with a small coronet, a lace and silver dress with a short train, an ermine-trimmed cloak and silver sandals. To accord with her new status as Heiress Presumptive, Parliament granted her an annual allowance of £6,000 (which would rise to £15,000 on her twenty-first birthday).

Her educational schedule was broadened to include lessons in Latin and German as well as French, and the history of the United States along with that of Britain and Europe. Tennis was introduced to ensure she enjoyed sufficient exercise and, by stages, her pocket money was raised from one shilling to five shillings a week. Her grandmother, the regal and indefatigable Queen Mary, took her on educational visits to various museums – the British, the Science and the Victoria and Albert to Westminster Abbey and the Tower of London, Hampton Court and Greenwich Palace, the National Gallery and the Wallace Collection, the Royal Mint, the Bank of England and the postal sorting office at Mount Pleasant. Her father took her along with him to various public functions, as when he opened the National Maritime Museum at Greenwich and witnessed a march-past of Boy Scouts at Windsor. A special palace troop of Girl Guides (the 7th Westminster Company) was formed to give her some contact with other girls of her own age. She was taught a short speech in French with which to greet President Lebrun of France when he arrived in London to attend her father's coronation.

Most of this she took in her childhood stride, though the move from the homely compactness of 145 Piccadilly to the more impersonal vastness of Buckingham Palace perturbed her somewhat. She longed, she said, for a secret tunnel so that she could creep back to her old home to sleep at night. She was slightly upset too that her father was now so preoccupied with monarchy that he had little time to play with her. "I do wish Papa didn't have to see all those people," she lamented on one occasion. "It would do him more good to play with us."

Young though she still was, she carried out occasional small royal duties, cutting the cake at a tea for disabled ex-Servicemen, presenting the rosettes at the National Pony Show and taking the salute at a rehearsal for the Aldershot Tattoo. When she was twelve she began travelling back and forth to Eton College at the start of a five-year course in constitutional history from the college's vice-provost (later provost, then Sir), Clarence Henry Kennett Marten. It was planned at that time that she should later go to university, but World War II was effectively to put a stop to that. She was thirteen that summer of 1939 when she accompanied her parents on a visit to the Royal Naval College at Dartmouth and an encounter with the eighteen-year-old Prince Philip which was later to lead to courtship, betrothal and marriage (*see* Prince Philip). For the future Queen Elizabeth II it was love at first sight.

She was in Scotland, on holiday with her parents, when World War II erupted. The King, of course, was required back in London. His wife travelled south with him, leaving Elizabeth and Margaret at Birkhall, a property on the Balmoral estate. For Elizabeth, lessons with Miss Crawford continued much as usual though constitutional history had now to be learned by correspondence. She played her small part in Britain's war effort by knitting woollies for the troops, though her knitting left a good deal to be desired. So, to the despair of that excellent needlewoman Queen Mary, did her needlework.

There was some suggestion that she and Margaret should take sanctuary in Canada, but their parents did not agree to this. Instead, after short spells at Sandringham and Royal Lodge, they were moved to the comparative safety of Windsor Castle, its stout walls sandbagged for added protection, and with a special company of Grenadier Guards to watch over them.

Once settled in Windsor, Elizabeth resumed her studies in constitutional history, knitted more woolly "comforts" for the troops, wrote letters to members of the royal staff who were now in the Services, helped to collect scrap metal to build more aircraft for Britain and took part in anti-gas drills. Meticulous, and even slightly prim, as she was, she insisted on "dressing properly" before descending to the safety of the castle dungeons when there was a night-time air raid alert. Worried by these delays, those in charge of her had siren suits made which she and Margaret could slip on quickly over their nightwear.

Christmas brought a card from Philip, now serving with the navy. She had omitted to send him one and wrote a letter instead. So began a correspondence which was to become increasingly romantic with the passage of the war years. Later the two of them exchanged photographs. That first-ever photograph from Philip, youthful and uniformed, his hand raised in salute, continues to occupy a place of honour on the Queen's desk today. The one she gave him in exchange was signed with the pet name of Lilibet.

In 1940, at the age of fourteen, she made her first broadcast. "All we children at home are full of cheerfulness and courage," she said. "We are trying to do all we can to help our gallant sailors, soldiers and airmen, and we are trying too to bear our share of the danger and sadness of war. We know in the end that all will be well."

In 1942 she was confirmed in the private chapel at Windsor Castle. To mark her sixteenth birthday that year she was given her first official appointment, as honorary Colonel of the Grenadier Guards. There was a birthday march-past at which she took the salute in a pleated skirt and woollen jacket. She also went along to the local labour exchange in Windsor to register for war service as required by the war-time National Service Act. She listed her education as "Private", answered "No" to the question of whether she was attending evening classes and wrote down "Girl Guides" as the youth organization to which she belonged. Soon after, however, girl guiding gave way to Sea Rangers with a mock-up ship's bridge for weekly drill. The Princess was "bo'sun" of the starboard watch.

Amateur pantomimes at Christmas provided annual light relief to the monotony of those war-time years and in 1943, when she was seventeen, looking extremely fetching in a short tunic and silk tights, she played the title role in *Aladdin and His Wonderful Lamp*. Margaret had the part of Princess Roxana. One of the small, hand-picked audience who watched the show was Prince Philip. Elizabeth had prevailed upon her parents to invite him to spend part of his leave at Windsor.

On her eighteenth birthday she was granted her own armorial bearings and standard. She was also given her own car, a Daimler, and had her first lady-in-waiting, Lady Mary Strachey, who also acted as her private secretary.

At eighteen, in the event of her father's death, she could succeed to the throne in her own right with no necessity to have a Regent to act for her. But by one of those curious anomalies of the British constitution, until she was twenty-one she could not serve as a Counsellor of State (*see* Counsellors of State) to deputize for her father on his war-time visits to

QUEEN ELIZABETH II. *Above*: After their wedding, Princess Elizabeth and the Duke of Edinburgh wave to the crowds gathered below from the balcony of Buckingham Palace. *Below left*: The Queen looking as radiant as ever, and Prince Philip, in Jubilee Year. QUEEN ELIZABETH, THE QUEEN MOTHER. *Below right*: The Duchess of York with her husband, the future King George VI, in 1925.

QUEEN ELIZABETH, THE QUEEN MOTHER. Posing for a photograph with her daughter, her son-in-law and two grandsons, Prince Andrew and Prince Edward (1976). QUEEN VICTORIA AND PRINCE ALBERT. With their nine children, photographed at Osborne in 1857. (*Left to right*) Prince Alfred, Prince Albert, Princess Helena, Princess Alice, Prince Arthur, Queen Victoria holding Princess Beatrice, Princess Royal, Princess Louise, Prince Leopold and the Prince of Wales.

RACING AND HORSES. The Queen watching an exciting finish to the Derby in 1978. ROYAL LODGE. "Entrance Front of His Majesty's Cottage" (Royal Lodge). Lithograph published by Ackermann, 1824. SANDRINGHAM. One of the Queen's private residences as seen from the lake.

SILVER JUBILEE. *Above*: During one of her 1977 Silver Jubilee walkabouts, the Queen chats with twins in the Pilgrim Choir. *Below*: The Queen and Prince Philip leaving Buckingham Palace in the Gold State Coach to drive to St Paul's Cathedral for a Service of Thanksgiving.

THRONE. *Above left*: At the State Opening of Parliament in 1976, the Queen reads "the Speech from the Throne" in the House of Lords. Most leading authorities agree that this is the true throne. *Above right*: The Throne Room at Buckingham Palace – the two Chairs of State stand beneath an elaborate canopy of red velvet with golden fringes. TRAIN. The ornate interior of Queen Victoria's saloon.

TRAIN. The lounge area of the Queen's new saloon – a great contrast to that of Queen Victoria (*see previous page*).

TRAVEL. *Above*: New Zealand, 1963. The Queen leaving Parliament Buildings with the Prime Minister (the Rt. Hon. Keith Holyoake) after the State Opening. *Left*: In Kaduna during a royal tour of Nigeria, 1956.

TROOPING THE COLOUR. Her Majesty the Queen with Prince Philip (*centre*) and the Duke of Kent (*right*) at the Trooping the Colour ceremony, June 1972. They are wearing black armbands for the Duke of Windsor. WINDSOR CASTLE. The Round Tower, floodlit during the Festival of Britain in 1951.

WINDSOR CASTLE. Another view of the castle – a painting by John Piper.
YACHT. The royal yacht *Britannia* sails under Tower Bridge at the end of the
Commonwealth tour of 1953-54 after the Coronation. On board were the Queen and
Duke of Edinburgh with Prince Charles and Princess Anne, who had gone out to
the Mediterranean to meet them, and Sir Winston Churchill.

the battlefronts. Her father saw the oddness of this and promptly requested an amendment to the necessary Act of Parliament. He wanted her, he said, to have "every opportunity of gaining experience in the duties which would fall upon her in the event of her acceding to the throne." The Act was amended and three months after her birthday she found herself deputizing for him while he was away in North Africa and Italy.

At eighteen she was also liable for military service or some type of war work. Her father thought that her royal responsibilities constituted war work enough. Certainly there were plenty of royal duties for her, visits to Wales and Scotland, visits to British, Canadian and US air bases, dinner with the Commonwealth prime ministers when they forgathered in London. She became president of the National Society for the Prevention of Cruelty to Children, made her first public speech (to the governors of the Queen Elizabeth Hospital for Children) and launched the battleship *Vanguard.*

She herself wanted to do more, but it was some time before she could bring her father round to her own way of thinking. It was not until March, 1945, a month before her nineteenth birthday, that she finally got her way and was given an honorary commission as second-subaltern in the Auxiliary Territorial Service. As such, she was driven back and forth from Windsor each day for a course in driving and vehicle maintenance at No. 1 Mechanical Transport Training Centre, Camberley.

She was in uniform when she appeared on the palace balcony with her parents and Winston Churchill on VE Day. Royal chores increased apace in the aftermath of war. Dressed in the unflattering, fashionless clothes of the period – pleated skirts, woollen jumpers, boxy jackets, thick stockings and flat-heeled shoes – she visited Scotland with her parents to attend a thanksgiving service in St Giles' Cathedral, visited Wales to inspect Girl Guides, toured Northern Ireland where she launched the aircraft carrier *Eagle,* reviewed a parade of army cadets in Hyde Park and took the salute at a passing-out parade at the Royal Military Academy. She became president of an increasing number of organizations, among them the Red Cross, the Royal Life Saving Society and the Student Nurses' Association. She also "starred" in a film designed to bring her more into the public eye, *Heir to the Throne.*

With Philip's return from war service in the Far East, they began to meet with increasing frequency. Coppins, the country home of Philip's cousin, the widowed Princess Marina, afforded them the occasional opportunity for romantic privacy such as they could not find at Buckingham Palace or Royal Lodge. They dined and danced at the Bagatelle Club and went several times to the theatre together. They saw the American musical *Oklahoma!* when it opened in London as well as the Ivor Novello show *Perchance To Dream.*

Her parents invited Philip to stay at Balmoral in the summer and at Sandringham over Christmas. For all that, her father seemed reluctant to consent to their betrothal. This was partly due to a father's natural caution, a desire to feel that his daughter was quite sure of her feelings. But it was also perhaps due to a degree of possessiveness. George VI was always slightly possessive where his elder daughter was concerned. In childhood, when she was first learning to ride, the young Elizabeth had fallen into a habit of quoting her groom Owen as the ultimate authority on everything. It was always "Owen says this" or "Owen says that." Even this childish trait had offended her father to the extent of retorting "Why ask me? Ask Owen" on one occasion when she asked him something. So, in those immediate post-war years, he seemed extremely reluctant to consent to his daughter's betrothal. However, by the time the family sailed for South Africa early in 1947 it was understood that Elizabeth and Philip were unofficially engaged even if there was still no formal announcement.

The four months of the South African tour included her twenty-first birthday, at that time the recognized coming-of-age for young people. From Government House on her birthday she made her broadcast of dedication:

"I declare before you all that my whole life, whether it be long or short, shall be devoted to your service and the service of the great Imperial Commonwealth to which we all belong. But I shall not have the strength to carry out this resolution unless you join in it with me, as I now invite you to do. I know that your support will be unfailingly given. God bless all of you who are willing to share it."

She did not write the speech herself. Her father's private secretary composed it for her. But the words struck such a responsive echo that her eyes filled with tears of emotion when she first read it.

Philip became a naturalized British citizen during her absence in South Africa and following her return came a formal announcement from Buckingham Palace on July 8: "It is with the greatest pleasure that the King and Queen announce the betrothal of their dearly beloved daughter The Princess Elizabeth to Lieutenant Philip Mountbatten, RN, son of the late Prince Andrew of Greece and Princess Andrew (Princess Alice of Battenberg)." Prior to that, at that year's annual Trooping the Colour ceremony, the Princess had ridden in the traditional position of the Prince of Wales, a position previously taken (since there was no Prince of Wales) by her uncle, the Duke of Gloucester.

She and Philip were married in Westminster Abbey on November 20, 1947. The bride wore a wedding gown of satin encrusted with pearl and crystal. It had been designed by Norman Hartnell who went to some pains to ensure that the silk he used had been spun by Chinese Nationalist silkworms rather than ex-enemy silkworms from Italy or Japan. Such are the oddities which result from war. He also took considerable precautions to ensure that no fashion "pirate" copied the bridal gown in advance, whitewashing his workroom windows, locking the design patterns in a safe each night and having the workroom manager doss down on a camp-bed in the same room.

Princess Margaret was chief bridesmaid at the wedding. The other bridesmaids were Princess Alexandra, then not quite eleven, Pamela Mountbatten, Diana Bowes-Lyon, Margaret Elphinstone, Lady Caroline Montagu-Douglas-Scott, Lady Mary Cambridge and Lady Elizabeth Lambert. The wedding guests included the King and Queen of Denmark, the Kings of Norway, Rumania and Iraq, the King and Queen of Yugoslavia, the Queen of the Hellenes, the Princess Regent and Prince Bernhardt of the Netherlands, the Prince Regent of Belgium, the Crown Prince and Princess of Sweden, Queen Helen of Rumania, Queen Victoria Eugénie of Spain, the Count and Countess of Barcelona, Prince Jean and Princess Elizabeth of Luxembourg and the Duchess of Aosta. Various people thought variously that the bride looked "calm and composed", "pale but lovely", "radiant" and "beautiful but sad". The wedding ring was fashioned from a gift of Welsh gold.

The King gave his daughter in marriage. He was, as he wrote to her later, "So proud of you and so thrilled at having you so close to me on our long walk in Westminster Abbey." But he was also, as he confessed in the same letter, conscious as the ceremony ran its course of having "lost something very precious".

Following a honeymoon at Broadlands, the country mansion at which Philip's uncle, Mountbatten of Burma and his bride had also spent their first night, and at Birkhall in Scotland, the newly-weds took a short lease of a country house at Windlesham Moor, near Sunningdale, later moving into Clarence House (*see* Clarence House) which had been renovated for them at a cost of £55,000. Now that the Princess was married Parliament increased her annual allowance to £40,000 with an additional £10,000 for Philip.

Because Clarence House was not yet ready for them, their first child, Prince Charles, was born at Buckingham Palace. Their second, Princess Anne, was born at Clarence House. Initially, her father did what he could to prevent too much royal work falling upon the shoulders of the daughter who was now also a wife and mother. "There will be enough for her to do later," he said. But as his own health steadily declined, so the burden on her necessarily increased. Between flying visits to Malta, where Philip was then based with the navy, she deputized for her father at the annual Trooping the Colour ceremony, and helped with hosting state visitors like President Auriol of France, the King of Norway, and the King and Queen of Denmark. With Philip, she flew to Canada to carry out a 16,000-mile royal tour which the King's health would no longer permit him to carry out in person. With her she took a large sealed envelope which she was instructed to open "only in the event of the death of His Majesty". In it were directions as to what she must do in the event that she suddenly found herself Queen.

She did not have to open the envelope on that Canadian trip. But the King was suffering from cancer and the inevitable was only a matter of time. On February 6, 1952, at the age of twenty-five, in Kenya, en route to Australia and New Zealand to carry out another royal tour on her father's behalf, she suddenly found herself Queen Elizabeth II.

At the time she became Queen she was wearing slacks and a shirt, and perched high in the branches of a wild fig tree in the Aberdare Forest. As a break in the long journey to Australia and New Zealand, she had been spending a few days at the Sagana hunting lodge which had been a wedding gift to her from the Kenya Government. Her perch in the fig tree was due to a desire to see something of the wild life of the area, elephant and rhino, water-buck, hyenas and baboons. She spent the night of February 5–6 in a small rest-house built into the branches. When she went to sleep that night her father still lived and she was still Princess Elizabeth. When she awoke the following morning, she was, though she did not yet know it, Queen Elizabeth II.

The news reached her in a roundabout way. A news flash from Reuters concerning the King's death was passed to Granville Roberts, a reporter for the *East African Standard*. Roberts told Lieutenant-Colonel the Hon. (later Sir) Martin Charteris, private secretary to the new Queen, who chanced to be lunching at the same hotel in Nyeri at the time, and, at his request, also telephoned Philip's secretary, Michael Parker, at the hunting lodge. Parker told Philip when he and the Queen, as she now was, returned from the Aberdare Forest and Philip broke the news to his wife. It was then around two o'clock in the afternoon, local time, some three hours ahead of Greenwich.

Once she had recovered from the first shock of her father's death, the new Queen dealt with a telegram from London which had finally managed to reach her over the solitary telephone line which linked the hunting lodge with the outside world. Among other things, it asked by what name she wished to be known.

"My own, of course," she said. "What else?"

She flew back to London that same day, boarding the aircraft in one of the light summery dresses which was all she had with her. Her mourning outfit, always a part of royal luggage, was already on board the liner *Gothic* in which she should have sailed from Mombasa for Australia and New Zealand. However, a refuelling touch-down in North

Africa enabled a telegram to be sent to London as a result of which a second mourning outfit was taken to the airport to meet her aircraft on arrival. She changed aboard the aircraft and then descended its steps to be greeted by her Uncle Gloucester, Philip's uncle, Mountbatten of Burma and the man who was now her prime minister, Winston Churchill. "This is a very tragic homecoming," she murmured.

Awaiting her at Clarence House was the first of the inevitable dispatch-boxes, her father's title – "The King" – still gold-lettered on the leather lid. The following morning, in St James's Palace, she made her Declaration of Accession. About 175 members of the Privy Council were there to hear her say:

"By the sudden death of my dear father, I am called to assume the duties and responsibilities of Sovereignty. . . .

"My heart is too full for me to say more to you today than that I shall always work, as my father did throughout his reign, to uphold constitutional government and to advance the happiness and prosperity of my peoples, spread as they are the world over.

"I pray that God will help me to discharge worthily this heavy task that has been laid upon me so early in life."

New brooms sweep clean. New monarchs want to tackle everything. So it was, initially, with Elizabeth II. She received government ministers, and countless others, in audience; read the small print of countless state papers until her eyes ached; sat for portraits; undertook provincial progresses, and, following her coronation, (*see* Coronation) a series of state visits and Commonwealth tours, including her round-the-world tour of 1953–4 (*see* Travels). That tour alone ate up six months of her time. She delegated nothing, or very little. Everything had to be done personally and in painstaking detail. Just as her great-grandfather had insisted on signing army appointments personally and her grandfather had insisted on handing out World War I decorations for bravery personally, so she insisted on personally signing the scores of photographic portraits of the new monarch sent out to British embassies and military units and Commonwealth governments. There were so many that royal aides suggested using a rubber-stamp facsimile of her signature. She turned down the idea, saying, "It would not be the same."

As well as being Queen, she was, of course, also the mother of two small children. In addition to all else she had to do or felt she ought to do, she somehow found the time to be with them for perhaps half an hour after breakfast each morning, while the end of each day's work found her popping up to the nursery to play with them, read to them, help bath them and tuck them in bed for the night. At her request, Prime Minister Winston Churchill readily agreed to alter the time of his regular Tuesday evening audience, at which he updated her on political matters, so as not to interfere with this nursery visit. At weekends and on holidays she spent nearly all her available time with the children.

So hectic was her life at this stage that the authoritative medical journal *The Lancet* cautioned against the dangers of trying to do too much. "Of late," it stated in an obvious reference to the death of her father, "the medical profession has become more and more aware of the physical price paid by those subjected to too frequent or continuous strain of the kind nowadays imposed on royalty." It urged that "by deliberate decisions taken in advance Her Majesty's health and vitality will be protected from her hereditary sense of duty."

Despite the fact that no such "deliberate decisions" were taken, the Queen's health did not suffer. On the contrary, she seemed positively to thrive on a diet of hard work and royal duty. Only for a few months during 1957 and 1958 did her normal good health and vitality desert her temporarily. Returning from another visit to Canada and the United States, she was plagued by a succession of recurring colds. She was down with a cold in the October and again in the December of 1957, again and again – in January, April and June – in the first half of 1958. She was taken ill yet again in July during a tour of Scotland and the North East and forced to return to London, leaving Philip to complete the tour on his own. Her physicians identified the sinuses as being the root cause of the trouble and these were irrigated under local anaesthetic.

In 1959, during another tour of Canada, she again had to take briefly to her bed and leave her husband to go it alone. Her Canadian tour would not normally have been too much for her but for the fact that, following a gap of nine years since the birth of Princess Anne, she was again pregnant at the age of thirty-three. Her third child, Andrew, was born in 1960, followed by a fourth, Edward, in 1964.

Largely through the influence of Prince Philip, she contrived to make a few small changes in the pattern of monarchy. Perhaps the most important of these was her decision to send her children to school, something no previous monarch had ever done. On a less personal level, she scrapped some of the more outmoded monarchical ceremonies, such as the annual presentation of dewy-eyed débutantes, and introduced new ones more in keeping with the age, like a series of informal lunches for guests ranging from politicians to pop stars, from trade union bosses to actresses and athletes. In 1957, following a successful, if somewhat nervous, television début in Canada, her Christmas Day broadcast in Britain, a tradition inherited from her father and his father before him, was televized for the first time (*see* Television). Two years later came the television film *Royal Family* in which she "starred".

If television stardom has been limited so far to a one-off film, Elizabeth II has assuredly shown herself to be a true monarch of the jet-age, taking advantage of modern air travel to go further and faster than any other monarch in history (*see* Travels). Most years she has undertaken a Commonwealth tour or state visit to some foreign country, sometimes more than one. Each year, in Britain, she undertakes a number of provincial progresses, gives four or five garden parties (with a larger guest list than in her father's day) and perhaps the same number of luncheon parties, holds some six or seven investitures and around twenty meetings of her Privy Council, has more than twenty meetings each year with successive prime ministers, and gives several hundred other audiences to Cabinet ministers, Commonwealth representatives, ambassadors, archbishops and the like. There are visiting heads of state to be hosted and entertained, receptions given and Parliament to be opened. She normally goes to the Derby as well as to Ascot, perhaps to the Cup Final or Wimbledon, and to other such hardy royal annuals as the Chelsea Flower Show, the Royal Tournament, the International Horse Show, the annual Cenotaph service of remembrance and the British Legion Festival at the Albert Hall. She may go to a Royal Variety Show, a Royal Film Show or visit the BBC as she did to watch an episode of *The Good Life* being video-taped. In Scotland there is the Braemar Gathering to be attended and a stay at Holyroodhouse with another garden party and perhaps an installation or service of the Order of the Thistle. Each day there are the contents of her boxes to peruse and correspondence to be dealt with.

Her life is governed to a large extent by the clock and the calendar. Except when she is on her travels, the same time each day will find her, if not doing exactly the same thing, then much the same kind of thing. An average day at her palace home finds her rising at eight o'clock and leafing through the newspapers over breakfast. Breakfast finished, she goes through to the sitting-room which also doubles as her study (*see* Buckingham Palace). Before starting work for the day she usually telephones her mother just down the road at Clarence House for a brief mother-and-daughter chat. That done, she settles to a morning's work at her desk. Her most important task is tackling the contents of the leather-bound dispatch-boxes which have plagued successive monarchs for generations. Going through them, Cabinet papers, Foreign Office telegrams, communications from Commonwealth governments, some requiring her formal approval, others for information only, takes her not less than forty-five minutes and maybe longer (*see* Monarchy). There is her private secretary to be seen, and perhaps the deputy or assistant private secretary also; correspondence to be sorted and dealt with. Her official correspondence is voluminous – invitations to this and that, letters appealing for help, letters simply expressing loyalty and affection, and, very occasionally, crank letters and those which threaten her life. Routine letters are dealt with by the private secretary and his staff, those from children are passed over to the duty lady-in-waiting to be answered, and those on matters of public concern are sent on to the appropriate government department with a request that they be looked into. Later in the morning may come a series of Audiences or a meeting of the Privy Council.

The afternoon can bring a visit from her hairdresser (usually on Monday), perhaps a spatter of public engagements in or near London, perhaps a visit from one of her fashion designers and his assistants so that she can try on the outfits she will be wearing for some Commonwealth tour or state visit months ahead. Failing all of those, there is perhaps the Master of the Household (to discuss staffing problems or matters of repair or replacement) or the Keeper of the Privy Purse (to discuss finances) to be seen. She undertakes few evening engagements these days, preferring to leave those to her energetic husband. But the first thing she does when she returns to her sitting-room after dinner is glance at her desk to see if anything fresh has come in since she last looked at it around five. If it has, she deals with it. Only when that is done does she relax totally, usually kicking off her shoes to sit with her feet up while reading the evening newspapers, tackling a crossword puzzle – one of her favourite diversions – or, if there is anything on which appeals to her, watching television. Bed is usually around half-past ten.

It is a curious anomaly that the more the power of monarchy has decreased in recent decades, the more the work-load of successive monarchs has increased. Elizabeth II's work-load might have proved insupportable, leading to the breakdown in health feared by *The Lancet*, but for the help of her family and relatives. Her husband has shouldered a large part of the burden. Her eldest son has grown up to play an increasing part. Princess Anne helps out too, as does sister Margaret. The Queen Mother, who once seemed as though she might withdraw entirely from public life, continues to do rather more than her fair share. The Gloucesters and the Kents help out more often than many people realize.

One day not long ago (the actual date does not matter, for the same sort of thing happens often) found the Queen receiving two High Commissioners, a newly-appointed ambassador and a retiring member of her own staff in her audience room at Buckingham Palace at the same time that her husband was speech-making during an industrial tour of the Midlands, and her eldest son was airborne in the direction of Wales where he was to open a new hospital. Also on the same day the Queen Mother was arranging to visit a cattle show in East Anglia, Princess Alice of Gloucester was attending a flower festival, her son and daughter-in-law, the Duke and Duchess of Gloucester, were naming a new ship, and Princess Alexandra of Kent was finalizing plans to open some new almshouses.

A century after Walter Bagehot, the Victorian historian, first visualized it, his "family on the throne" concept has finally come about. Bagehot envisaged it resulting from the marriage of Queen Victoria's eldest son to Princess Alexandra of Denmark. Because Victoria never really trusted her eldest son, because she liked to keep things very much in her own hands, it never happened. Now, under Victoria's far less autocratic great-great-granddaughter, it has.

For Victoria's great-great-granddaughter, the years of monarchy have not all been easy-going. If there has been no major political dilemma to resolve as there was in her grandfather's day, no world war to survive as there was in both his and her father's day, there have been not a few lesser dilemmas and some strident criticism. If the more personal criticisms of Lord Altrincham who later became John Grigg ("the personality . . . of a priggish schoolgirl") and Malcolm Muggeridge ("royal soap opera . . . a sort of substitute or ersatz religion") are now well in the past, there has been more recent criticism of a more trenchant sort, in Canada over the role of the monarchy there, and in Britain over the mounting cost of monarchy (*see* Civil List) in an era of seemingly non-stop inflation. So far, Elizabeth II has contrived to ride out such rough patches with dignity by the traditional royal method of lying low and saying nothing.

By 1977, when she celebrated her Silver Jubilee (*see* Silver Jubilee), that eager young Princess who found herself unexpectedly succeeding to the throne in February, 1952, had matured into an experienced monarch. That same year also saw her graduation to the role of grandmother and found her resorting to the aid of spectacles in order to read the speech with which she opened Parliament. Under Philip's influence she had also conquered her inherited shyness, once so noticeable, to the extent where she could indulge in smiling walk-abouts among the cheering crowds who thronged to see her and accept the bruised posies thrust at her by excited children. If she no longer rules Britain in the sense that her medieval forebears once did, she proved again that year – and has continued to prove since – that she can reign with charm and dignity.

QUEEN ELIZABETH, THE QUEEN MOTHER

To most people she is more simply and more affectionately known as the Queen Mum. As far as can be traced, this more down-to-earth title was first applied to her in an article by a former royal servant which was published in an American magazine in 1961. It quickly crossed the Atlantic to Britain and has stuck ever since. A public opinion poll in 1978 ranked her only fourth in popularity among the Royals, with her daughter, the Queen, grandson Charles and son-in-law Philip ahead of her, but such polls, as general election results have shown, are frequently wide of the mark. What other member of the Royal Family gets a "Happy Birthday" salutation from the general public each year?

Whatever the degree of the Queen Mother's public popularity, there can be little doubt of her effect upon the Royal Family itself. More than anything else, it was her marriage into the family which changed it into the close-knit unit of today . . . a family held firm, as her elder daughter has said, by a web "of family relationships between parents and children, grandparents and grandchildren, cousins, aunts and uncles".

For generations prior to that marriage there had consistently been a wide gulf of misunderstanding between successive British monarchs and their heirs. Among the first four Georges, fathers and sons roundly abused each other. Queen Victoria never quite trusted the son who became Edward VII and certainly, while she lived, did not permit him to play his full and proper part in public life. George V openly admitted, "I was frightened of my father", and George VI, though he never said so, was certainly frightened of his.

But between George VI and the daughter who was to succeed him as Elizabeth II there was never anything but love, trust and understanding. And much of the credit for that lies in the calm, soothing, warmly affectionate nature of the woman he married. "My dear wife", he always called her, while the Duke of Windsor, at the time of his abdication, was to refer with wistful envy to the "matchless blessing" of his brother's happy home life.

The Queen Mother was fifty-one when her husband died in February, 1952. She was born on August 4, 1900, ninth of the ten children of Lord and Lady Glamis, later the Earl and Countess of Strathmore and Kinghorne. Much has been made of her Scottish ancestry. But if her father was Scots, her mother was English, the former Nina Cecilia Cavendish-Bentinck, and she herself was born in England, at St Paul's Walden Bury in Hertfordshire, though she was christened in Scotland, at Glamis Castle, the lowland stronghold of her father's family since the fourteenth century.

On her mother's side, the Queen Mother's ancestry goes back to Henry VII and the girl he married, Elizabeth of York, daughter of Edward IV. Through her father, she is descended from Sir John Lyon, who in 1372 married the widowed daughter of Scotland's King Robert II. Lyon became Bowes-Lyon as a condition for inheriting the wealth of George Bowes, a Durham industrialist whose daughter Eleanor married the ninth earl. In fact, under the strict terms of his will, the family was required to change its name from Lyon to Bowes and did so for a time.

The Queen Mother was accordingly named Elizabeth Angela Marguerite Bowes-Lyon. From 1904, when her father inherited the earldom, she was mainly brought up at Glamis with its many relics of Bonnie Prince Charlie and his ill-fated rising of 1745, including the watch he left under his pillow when he was forced to flee in haste. She was brought up in the care of a devoted nurse, Clara Cooper Knight (later to become nurse also to the future Elizabeth II) in an old-world country atmosphere of home-baked bread, milk fresh from the cow, home-brewed potions for coughs and colds, and, as she grew into her teens, home-made beauty lotions. The childhood days which she shared with her brother David, born two years later, were very different from and much happier than those of the boy she would one day marry (*see* King George VI).

She met him first, though they were then far too young for romance, in 1905 when they were both guests at a children's party in London where the Bowes-Lyon family spent much of its time so that father could attend the House of Lords. It was because of this that the youngest-but-one child spent two terms at a London day school before being privately educated under a succession of governesses.

During World War I, when Glamis Castle became a convalescent home for the wounded, she helped out as an unpaid auxiliary. One of her brothers, Fergus, was killed in the war, at Loos, and another, Michael, was reported killed but later discovered alive in a German prison hospital. She was eighteen when the war ended, a lively petite girl, fond of dancing and with a "quite delicious" sense of humour. Accordingly, there was no shortage of eager suitors, among them, after they had renewed their childhood acquaintance at a small private dance given by Lord Farquhar, the Duke of York, second son of King George V. That year and again the following year he was a guest at Glamis. On one of his visits the Countess was ill in bed and her daughter deputized as hostess. It was then that Bertie, as he was called, knew that he wanted to marry her.

Initially, however, Elizabeth Bowes-Lyon was not at all sure that she wished to marry him . . . or, rather, marry into the Royal Family. If she did, she said, she feared that she would "never again be free to think, speak or act as I really feel I should think, speak and act." It was not until the third time he proposed to her – in January, 1923, as they strolled among the trees at St Paul's Walden Bury one Sunday morning while the rest of the family were in church – that she finally accepted. (For further details of their courtship *see* King George VI.)

They were married in Westminster Abbey on April 26, 1923, their honeymoon being somewhat marred by the fact that the bride went down with whooping cough. With marriage, she became Her Royal Highness the Duchess of York, fourth lady in the land after her husband's mother, Queen Mary, his sister, Princess Mary (later Princess Royal) and his grandmother, the widowed and eccentric Queen Alexandra.

Lacking a home of their own, they lived for a time in Chesterfield House which was loaned to them by Princess Mary and her husband, the then Viscount Lascelles, and their first child was born at the London home of the bride's parents in Bruton Street (*see* Queen Elizabeth II). In 1927, following a royal tour of Australia and New Zealand which compelled them to leave their year-old baby daughter behind them, they moved into 145 Piccadilly, a tall, narrow house which they rented on a ten-year lease.

Here the Duchess of York, as she then was, set about creating the same sort of warm, happy family life which she herself had known in childhood, a sanctuary for her husband from the royal duties which, because of his stammer, he found such a trial. She was helped in this by the fact that they did not actually live over the shop, as it were. Instead, her husband had an office almost round the corner in Grosvenor Crescent. Naturally they had servants, but the Duchess herself supervised the meals to ensure that they conformed with the diet the Duke had been obliged to follow since being invalided out of the navy. He, for his part, always made the late-night cocoa they sipped at bedtime.

The birth of a second daughter, Margaret Rose, in 1930 completed the family unit. It was the Duchess' own wish that her second child should be born at Glamis and Princess Margaret thus became the first royal baby to be born in Scotland since the year 1600.

While she was often required to leave her small daughters in the care of "Alla" Knight while she herself toured Britain with her husband during those depressed years of the 1930s, the five years which followed Margaret's birth were to rank among the happiest of her married life. This was especially true of weekends spent in the relaxed atmosphere of Royal Lodge at Windsor after George V gave it to them in 1931. Much has been written of how her husband toiled and laboured to bring the overgrown garden there back into cultivation. Less well-known is the fact that it was his wife who first tempted him to the task, seeing it as a healthy antidote to his often desk-bound way of life. Similarly, despite the public attention to which they were often subject outside their home, she did her best to bring her daughters up as down-to-earth and unspoiled as she had been herself.

She was ill with her second attack of influenza in a year – there had been a previous one when George V died – at the time of the abdication and her husband's unexpected accession to the throne. Her husband telephoned her from Royal Lodge with the news that his brother

David had signed the Instrument of Abdication (*see* Duke and Duchess of Windsor *and* King George VI) and she was in bed when her mother-in-law, Queen Mary, arrived at 145 Piccadilly to pay her respects to the new Queen Consort. Even so, she provided firm support for her nervous and uncertain husband at this time which was to bring so great a change in their lives. Time and again he paid tribute to her support. "With my wife and helpmeet by my side, I take up the heavy task which lies before me," he told his Accession Council. He referred to her again – ". . . supported as I shall be by my dear wife" – in his reply to a message of loyalty from Parliament. Further proof of his feelings for her and his consciousness of the debt he owed her came on his forty-first birthday later that year when he conferred upon her the Order of the Garter.

With her elevation from Duchess of York to Queen it was as though she underwent a metamorphosis. Prior to her husband's accession, though accompanying him on innumerable royal duties, she had tended to cut a rather subdued figure for all her natural vivacity. Now, suddenly, she became radiant, changing her hair-style, dressing more colourfully, sporting more jewellery. A new crown, the first to be fashioned in platinum, was made for her to wear at the coronation she shared with her husband. Following upon his own coronation, she knelt on a faldstool under a canopy held by four duchesses – Norfolk, Buccleuch, Rutland and Roxburghe – to be anointed in turn with holy oil. The new crown, in which the Koh-i-Noor diamond gleamed, was placed on her head and the ring once worn by Elizabeth I slipped on her finger.

Nowhere was the new Queen more popular in those early years of her husband's reign than in Canada and the United States when she went there with the King in the summer of 1939. "You're a great Queen-picker," one grizzled US senator told the King, while the eight-year-old daughter of Harry Hopkins, adviser to President Roosevelt, after glimpsing the Queen in her crinoline and tiara, was sure she had actually seen "the Fairy Queen". Her elegant deployment of the parasol made that gadget all the rage among the ladies of Virginia. "The British Re-Take Washington", one US newspaper headlined its report of the royal visit, while in New York, where the royal couple visited the World Fair, they were surprised, on attending Sunday service, to hear prayers for the King and Royal Family said in an American church. They stayed with the Roosevelts in their Hyde Park mansion and from the close friendship formed between the two couples stemmed the lease-lend supplies which were to prove so valuable to Britain during World War II.

When the President's wife, Eleanor, subsequently paid a war-time visit to Britain, a grateful and delighted Queen surrendered her own bedroom to her. It was similarly due to her in no small measure that so many European royals – Queen Wilhelmina of the Netherlands, King Haakon of Norway, King Peter of Yugoslavia and the Grand Duchess of Luxembourg – were made so comfortable in Britain when the spread of war forced them into exile. Both with her husband and on her own, as World War II ran its grim course, she visited war factories and hospitals, and toured areas devastated by German bombing. When her husband left Britain on secret visits to troops on overseas battlefronts, she deputized for him. When Buckingham Palace was bombed her reaction was typical. "Now I feel I can look the East End in the face."

Just as the early years of her husband's monarchy had been clouded by threats of war, so the post-war years were to be marred by threats to his health. Impossible though she knew it was to go against his obstinate sense of duty, she did her best to persuade him to work less, rest more. Her first reaction when her husband died, like that of Queen Victoria before her, was to withdraw from public life. Like Queen Victoria too, she sought to keep her husband's memory alive. Queen Victoria had had Albert's bedroom left just as it was when he lived. Similarly, the widowed Queen Elizabeth kept her husband's desk at Royal Lodge just as it was in his lifetime, complete with his leather blotter, silver inkstand and travel clock, and his favourite photographs, including one of herself in the days he had first known her and others of their daughters in childhood.

She spent much of the first year of widowhood in Scotland. She stayed for a time at Dunnet Head with an old friend of childhood days, Lady Doris Vyner, and it was while there, out motoring one day, that she came across the ruined Castle of Mey (*see* Castle of Mey). She thought at first of restoring it and retiring there. But though she did buy it and restore it, in the end she did not retire. Public demand was too great and her own love of public life too strong. Even in Scotland in those early months of her widowhood she carried out the occasional royal duty, speeding the 1st Battalion of the Black Watch (whose Colonel-in-Chief she had been since 1937) on its way to Korea and unveiling the commando memorial at Lochaber.

To make way for her daughter, the new Queen, she moved out of Buckingham Palace and into Clarence House. Her younger daughter, Margaret, in the throes of her romantic attachment to Peter Townsend, went with her. With the death of Queen Mary shortly before the coronation in 1953 – "the kindest, dearest mother-in-law" – she became the Queen Mother.

She took charge of Prince Charles, then only four years old, when he was taken to Westminster Abbey to witness his mother's coronation. Between her and Charles there has always seemed to be a special bond, perhaps because he was the first of her grandchildren, perhaps because in many ways he reminds her of his grandfather, her dead husband.

"One of those extraordinarily rare people whose touch can turn everything to gold," Charles himself affectionately terms her in his foreword to Godfrey Talbot's biography.

She helped to look after both Charles and Anne, as well as deputizing for their mother, the new Queen, while Elizabeth and Philip were away from Britain on their six-month round-the-world tour of 1953–4. Following their return, she herself again visited Canada and the United States. Not for the first time, or the last, Britain's dockers were on strike. But so warm is the affection inspired by this remarkable woman that a bunch of them risked being labelled "scabs" by turning out in secret to get her luggage aboard the liner named after her and which she herself had launched in 1938. In the United States she had a warm reunion with her old friend, Eleanor Roosevelt, as well as meeting up with another old friend of war-time days, President Eisenhower. She visited not only Washington, but New York and the reconstructed colonial township of Williamsburg in Virginia, addressed the English-Speaking Union and received an honorary degree as Doctor of Law from Columbia University. In Canada she visited Ottawa and Quebec, where she was hailed with shouts of "*Vive la Reine*".

Keeping busy, as she did, helped speed time's inevitable cure. By the time Queen Elizabeth II, with Philip and the children, cruised the coast of Scotland in the royal yacht in 1955 she was ready to show them her restored Castle of Mey. But now she looked upon it as merely a holiday home instead of a place of retirement. In 1956 she was at Aintree to see her horse Devon Loch run in the Grand National, Britain's premier steeplechase. It seemed she was on to a certain winner. Starting second favourite at 100–7, Devon Loch cleared the last of thirty stiff jumps a full fifteen lengths ahead of the nearest challenger. With the winning post little more than fifty yards ahead, victory seemed assured and a great roar went up from the crowd. Perhaps startled by the tremendous volume of sound – and subsequent medical examination could find no other explanation for what happened – Devon Loch suddenly sprang into the air as though trying to clear one more non-existent fence and landed spread-eagled with jockey Dick Francis still in the saddle. By the time it regained its feet it had been passed by every other horse still in the race.

More concerned for horse and jockey than over the result of the race, the Queen Mother hurried to the paddock to enquire after them. To those who commiserated with her in not achieving what had seemed a certain victory she responded with a philosophical smile and shrug of the shoulders. "That's racing," she said. "There'll come another time."

Unlike Queen Victoria, she did not continue to grieve for her husband throughout the long years of widowhood which stretched ahead.

Or if she did, it was in private. But neither did she have any thought of marrying again, and few things have upset her so much as when an American newspaper published a story saying she was contemplating marriage to her Treasurer, the late Sir Arthur Penn. She was in Africa at the time and promptly issued a statement in which she castigated the report as "complete and absolute nonsense". Indeed, it is said that the statement was a good deal milder than the words she actually used.

Except for a few weeks at a time when ill-health intervened, there was to be no slackening of pace in her public life. Indefatigably she continued as Commandant-in-Chief of all three of Britain's women's services as well as the Women's Royal Australian Air Force, Colonel-in-Chief of a dozen regiments in Britain, Australia and Canada, president or patron of some three hundred organizations, visiting festivals, hospitals, universities, including the University of London which she has been known to visit as many as ten or twelve times a year in her role as Chancellor. While only a few of these – like the King's Lynn Festival, the Royal Schools of Music and the London Gardens Society – echo her own personal enthusiasms, she has an appetite for life which makes her interested in everything. And because of her zest for life and love of people, she has continued to perform the most boring and mundane royal chores – like planting a tree or laying a foundation stone – as though each time is the first one.

She has continued to travel extensively, to Canada, Australia and New Zealand, France and Germany, and a score of places besides. In 1958 she became the first of the Royal Family to fly round the world. The following year African nationalists planned a boycott when she visited Kenya. But the boycott quickly melted away under her charm and appeal.

But warm and charming though she is, and has always been, it was a long time before she could bring herself to forgive the Duke of Windsor for abdicating the throne and thus compelling her duty-conscious husband to assume the role of King which neither he nor she ever wanted. Throughout the years of her husband's reign she would not agree to meet Windsor and pointedly had an engagement to take her away from Buckingham Palace whenever the King was expecting his brother. Nor did she visit her brother-in-law – though her daughter, the Queen, did – when he entered the London Clinic for eye surgery in 1965. It was to be another two years before her attitude melted at all, and then only to the extent of accepting a peck on the cheek from the Duke and a polite handshake from the Duchess when the couple visited London for the unveiling of a memorial to Queen Mary, the Duke's mother.

In 1966 there was concern for her own health when a medical check-up revealed a partial obstruction necessitating abdominal surgery. She was three weeks in hospital and it was a measure of her immense popularity that get-well cards and letters of good wishes streamed in at a rate which sometimes exceeded one thousand a day. Once recovered, however, she resumed public life at a pace which was not to slacken until around her seventy-fifth birthday and then only marginally – dropping from an average of three to two public engagements a week.

Her life of public service by then had already extended to over half a century in which more than one wheel had come full circle. When she visited Devonport in 1970 for the re-commissioning of the *Ark Royal*, for instance, she could look back on the fact that she herself had launched that same famous aircraft carrier more than twenty years before. In 1978, in tribute to her long years of stintless service, she was accorded the unprecedented honour of being the first woman ever appointed as Lord Warden of the Cinque Ports, a traditional and now honorary post dating back to the days of William the Conqueror.

With her furs and pearls, her cartwheel hats and crinoline gowns, the Queen Mum, however an opinion poll may assess her popularity, is nearly everyone's idea of the archetypal Royal . . . smiling yet stately, warm and dignified at one and the same time. Yet warm and smiling as she is in the flesh, it is curious to note that she is not particularly photogenic. She mentioned this fact once to royal photographer Cecil Beaton. Determined to do her justice on this one occasion at least, Beaton subsequently submitted a set of proofs which he had skilfully retouched. To his surprise, they were returned with an equally skilful diplomatic note: "Very nice, but they're not me." She did not want people thinking that she had come through her years on earth unscathed, the Queen Mother added.

QUEEN VICTORIA AND PRINCE ALBERT

In the popular imagination, Queen Victoria is largely remembered as the autocratic, black-clad "widow of Windsor" which she became after the death of her beloved Albert. But she was not always like that. As a young monarch, she was vivacious and impulsive. There was no question in those days of "We are not amused." She was very easily amused and laughed a lot. She was also, according to one of her contemporaries, "immensely seductive" to look at, and especially when glimpsed on horseback.

She was born at Kensington Palace on May 24, 1819. Her parents were Edward, Duke of Kent, fourth son of George III and the widowed Princess of Leiningen (the former Princess Victoria of Saxe-Coburg) whom her father had hastily married after being brusquely informed that funds would be cut off if he did not play his part towards ensuring the succession to the throne (*see* Lineage). Three months later, on August 26, a son was born to Princess Louise, wife of Princess Victoria's brother, Ernest, Duke of Coburg. He was christened Albert Francis Charles Augustus Emmanuel.

Victoria herself, though everyone remembers her by the name she took as Queen, was christened Alexandrina Victoria. When she was born, her grandfather, George III, was still on the throne. With her father and three uncles ahead of her, she was only fifth in the line of succession. But by the end of the following January her father was dead. So was the unfortunate George III and the gouty and painted Prince Regent reigned as George IV. Now she was third in line. In 1827, when she was eight, one of her uncles, Frederick, Duke of York, died and she moved into second place. And when, three years later, George IV died and his brother succeeded him as William IV, she became heir to the throne. She had just celebrated her eleventh birthday.

This was exactly what her ambitious mother had always hoped for and from then on the young Victoria was brought up to regard herself as the future queen. While her Saxe-Coburg cousin, Albert, at the same age, was noting in his diary, "I intend to train myself to be a good and useful man", she was being taught French, German, Italian and Latin as well as English, history and philosophy, drawing, dancing, singing and how to play the piano. Her mother carted her round Britain on a number of "royal" progresses which considerably offended her uncle, William IV. With the exception of an elder half-sister, Anne Feodorowna, the child of her mother's first marriage, she had no companions of her own age. Lacking playmates, she made do with dolls instead, collecting them as enthusiastically as her great-great-granddaughter was later to collect toy horses. At one time she had 132 of them.

She was still a child when she started the first of the series of journals (or diaries) she was to keep so painstakingly all her life. She showed early signs too of the indefatigable letter-writer she was to become. Her principal correspondent, at this stage, was her uncle, King Leopold of the Belgians, and it was through him that she first met her Saxe-Coburg cousins, Albert and his brother, Ernest. Just as her great-great-granddaughter, at the tender age of thirteen, was to know love at first sight, so did Victoria at seventeen. Elizabeth, at thirteen, may not necessarily have connected love with marriage. Victoria did, and from then on her letters to Uncle Leopold in Belgium urged a course of studies she thought Albert should be prevailed upon to follow so that he would, in time, make a suitable Prince Consort.

She had just turned eighteen that early morning of June 20, 1837, when the Lord Chamberlain and the Archbishop of Canterbury galloped through the darkness from Windsor Castle to Kensington Palace with news that William IV was dead. She was fast asleep in bed when they arrived. At six o'clock they roused her. She took off her nightcap, slipped a cotton dressing-gown over her nightdress, draped a shawl about her shoulders, put on her slippers and came downstairs to learn that she was now Queen Victoria.

Her mother had previously been appointed to act as Regent in the event that she succeeded to the throne before the age of eighteen and took the appointment so seriously that she even slept in the same room at night. But Victoria was now eighteen and determined to be queen in her own right. She promptly banned her mother from the queen's bedroom and, indeed, refused to see her at any other time except by appointment.

Parliament voted her a Civil List annuity of £375,000 a year out of which she quickly paid off the long-outstanding debts of her dead father. She doted on her first prime minister, Lord Melbourne, seeing in him a combination of the father she had never known and the husband she had not yet married, to such an extent that the crowd hailed her with cries of "Mrs Melbourne" as she was driven up the course at Ascot one year. When he resigned in 1839, she wept.

Initially, she detested Melbourne's successor, Sir Robert Peel, who got off on the wrong foot by demanding that she should dismiss her ladies of the bedchamber because they were Whigs and replace them with Tories. The young Queen flatly refused and won the confrontation. However, later, under Albert's influence, she came to see Peel as a great prime minister.

She was twenty when Albert and brother Ernest arrived for a second visit in October, 1839. In pursuit of that childhood ambition to make himself "a good and useful man", Albert could now speak three languages, English, French and Italian, in addition to his native German. He was equally an accomplished artist and musician, and excellent horseman and dancer. He was also undeniably handsome – "beautiful" was the word Victoria used in a letter to Uncle Leopold.

On the sixth day of the brothers' visit Victoria sent for Albert to wait upon her in the Blue Closet. There she told him that "I thought he must be aware why I wished them to come here and that it would make me too happy if he would consent to what I wished."

They were married in the Chapel Royal at St James's Palace on February 10, 1840. The honeymoon at Windsor was limited to three days, because, as she told Albert, "I am the Sovereign and that business can stop and wait for nothing." They were, nevertheless, as she confided in her journal, three days of "heavenly love and happiness".

Victoria said once that she "dreaded" childbirth. But in those days she could hardly avoid it. Their first child, a girl, arrived later that same year of marriage, on November 21. Others followed at more or less regular intervals. Altogether, they had nine children. They were:

Victoria, born in 1840, the Princess Royal who married Germany's Crown Prince; Albert Edward (1841), who followed his mother on the throne as King Edward VII (*see* King Edward VII and Queen Alexandra); Alice (1843), who married Prince Louis of Hesse; Alfred (1844), the dissipated Duke of Edinburgh who married the Grand Duchess Marie of Russia and later became Duke of Saxe-Coburg and Gotha; Helena (1846), who married Prince Christian of Schleswig-Holstein; Louise (1848), who married the Marquis of Lorne, later Duke of Argyll; Arthur (1850), who became Duke of Connaught and married Princess Louise of Prussia; Leopold (1853), the unfortunate haemophilic (*see* Haemophilia) who married Princess Helen of Waldeck-Pyrmont; and Beatrice (1857), who married Prince Henry of Battenberg. If only one of these – Victoria, who became Empress of Germany – actually ended up by marrying into monarchy, the grandchildren were to fare rather better. One became Empress of Russia while others married the kings of Spain, Sweden, Norway, Greece and Rumania while a great-granddaughter became Queen of Yugoslavia.

Though Albert is best remembered today as the Prince Consort, they had in fact been married some seventeen years before his wife accorded him that title. Initially, he found the going no easier than Prince Philip was to find it just over a century later. Harder, in fact. His naturalization as a British citizen caused a deal of controversy and Parliament cut his proposed £50,000 a year allowance to £30,000. For the first two years of their marriage, much as she doted upon Albert, Victoria kept her royal privileges jealously to herself. "I am the husband, not the master in the house," poor Albert moaned. However, an attempt on her life by a feeble-minded youth, who discharged a pistol at her as she drove up Constitution Hill, caused her to re-assess their relationship. She appointed Albert to act as Regent should the necessity ever arise. Soon he was acting also as her private secretary, household major-domo and political adviser. He pensioned off the Queen's long-time confidante, Baroness Lehzen, reorganized the palace and instituted economies. In a very short time he had saved £200,000, enough to buy Osborne House on the Isle of Wight as a hideaway royal home. They pulled down the original house and erected the imposing mansion of today in its place. However, like Windsor, it proved too easily accessible to the public and in 1848 they discovered an even more remote retreat, Balmoral (*see* Balmoral).

Victoria adored Albert to the extent of experiencing pangs of jealousy if anyone else, even one of their own daughters, was conceded too much of his time. On his side, married relationship was cooler. He thought her hasty and quick-tempered and was constantly sending her little notes in which he urged her to try to control her "fidgety nature". More and more she permitted him to take over the reins of monarchy. He stood beside her when she received ministers in audience, read the dispatches which were sent to her and even drafted answers for her to sign. He began to see himself as Britain's unofficial foreign secretary, a role in which he and Viscount Palmerston, when he became prime minister, did not always see eye to eye. He became the self-appointed patron of both the army and the navy, and the army training centre at Aldershot was largely his creation. The Great Exhibition of 1851 was his idea also, as was the vision of the vast Crystal Palace in Hyde Park which eventually housed it. Even elm trees were enclosed within the huge glass structure. But Albert had overlooked one thing. Where you have trees, there you also have birds and their nests. Bird droppings proved to be such a nuisance they threatened to ruin the exhibition until that veteran campaigner, the Duke of Wellington, suggested to the Queen, "Try sparrow-hawks, Ma'am." The birds and their droppings quickly disappeared and the exhibition became such a success that it was visited by six million people and made a profit of £250,000. Queen Victoria herself visited it nearly every day from its opening in May until she went on holiday in late July.

Together, Victoria and Albert made a formidable royal team. If he saw himself as her unofficial foreign adviser, she herself liked to have a finger or two in ministerial appointments and was quite prepared to duel with Parliament over who should control the Indian Army. Like Albert, she was a considerable innovator and anything new appealed to her immensely. Her 1843 visit to France was the first time a reigning British monarch had visited a foreign one since the days of Henry VIII and the Field of the Cloth of Gold, and marked the start of the state visits of today (*see* Travels). With the spread of the railways, she was quick to have her own royal train. She helped to set childbirth on a new course when she resorted to chloroform for the birth of Leopold in 1853. In 1856 she instituted the Victoria Cross, which takes precedence over all other decorations, as the supreme award for gallantry. The inscription "For Valour" was her own suggestion and she personally presented the first sixty-two medals, cast from guns captured in the Crimea, at a review in Hyde Park.

Then tragedy struck. In 1861, following a visit to Cambridge to sort out the unhappy matter of their eldest son's entanglement with Nellie Clifden, an actress, Albert, already suffering from insomnia and rheumatism, contracted what was at first thought to be no more than a chill. William Jenner, the royal physician, was called in. He sought a second opinion from Dr (later Sir) James Clark. They agreed that there was no cause for alarm; it was simply gastric fever. In fact, Albert had typhoid, one of the great killers in that age of poor sanitation. Yet another physician was called in as his condition worsened, his speech becoming rambling and incoherent. All to no avail. On December 14, with his wife clutching his hand, his daughter Alice on the other side of the bed, his eldest son and another daughter, Helena, at the foot, the Prince Consort died at the age of forty-two. The eldest son who later became Edward VII was there only because sister Alice had sent him a secret telegram. Blaming her husband's illness on all the worry their son had caused them through his affair with the Clifden girl, Victoria herself had refused to send for him.

Hysterically distraught over her husband's death, she had to be almost carried from the room. For hours she lay sobbing on a sofa in the Red Room and for the rest of her long life never quite recovered from the shock of losing Albert. So great was her initial grief that at night she continued to take his night-shift to bed with her. She had his room photographed so that it might always be preserved just as it was in his lifetime, and had herself and the children photographed in a group surrounding his bust. She erected statues and memorials to him all over the place. Fond of singing and dancing as she had always been, it was to be five years before anyone heard her sing again and nearly twenty before she danced once more.

She retreated into seclusion, hiding herself away at Osborne and Balmoral. She refused to appear in public; would not even receive her ministers. When the Privy Council met, its members were forced to group themselves in an adjoining room while the clerk relayed the Queen's words to them through a partly open door. She witnessed her eldest son's marriage to Princess Alexandra of Denmark in St George's Chapel from the half-darkness of Catherine of Aragon's closet and would not attend the wedding luncheon which followed the ceremony.

It was not until five years after Albert's death that, very reluctantly, she consented to open Parliament again. She dressed all in black, including a black veil and skull-cap, for the occasion. That year, equally reluctantly, she started giving garden parties again and resumed her visits to art galleries and museums. Visits to hospitals and prisons accorded more with her grief-stricken frame of mind. More than anything, she would like to lead "a private life, tending the poor and the sick", she said. This later became a veiled threat to abdicate which she used as a stick to beat her ministers if she did not get her own way. For, despite grief, she still knew her own mind as much as ever. She refused to let her son Alfred accept the throne of Greece when it was offered to him and it went instead to her Danish daughter-in-law's brother, Prince William. Most of her time continued to be spent in seclusion, though in 1863 she did visit Germany in an unsuccessful attempt to reconcile the King of Prussia and the Emperor of Austria.

The following year, in an attempt to woo her away from her state of professional widowhood, her favourite Highland servant, the hard-drinking, rough-spoken John Brown, was brought south from Balmoral. The ploy succeeded only too well in that it resulted in rumours that she and Brown had secretly married. Certainly she favoured him above everyone else and permitted him liberties she would instantly have denounced in anyone else. Not even her closest relatives, let alone any other servant, would have dared call her "Wumman", as Brown did. Her eldest son disliked Brown intensely and was extremely indignant when the marriage rumours reached his ears. The rumours also disturbed the Queen's ministers. But despite his rudeness to her and his continued heavy drinking, the Queen herself was always quick to defend "poor, good Brown", and when he died, at Windsor in 1883, she had a plaque to his memory installed in the royal mausoleum at Frogmore, a granite seat dedicated to him and a statue of him erected at Balmoral.

With the arrival on the scene of William Gladstone as prime minister, she retreated again into the seclusion from which she had so recently begun to emerge. In 1869, the first year of his premiership, she moved directly from her hideaway home on the Isle of Wight to her other hideaway home at Balmoral and, by doing so, contrived to appear only once in public. That was to open the new Blackfriars Bridge. She disliked Gladstone immensely, complaining that he spoke to her as though addressing a public meeting. She disliked him even more after the delay in dispatching a relief force to Khartoum and largely blamed him for General Gordon's death. Disraeli, who contrived to flatter her, she liked enormously and quickly came to rely on him as she had once relied on Albert and, before him, on Lord Melbourne. Under Disraeli's influence, she again began to emerge from seclusion, even taking holidays abroad though she had by now abandoned all idea of lording it over Europe through the marriage alliances of her children. It was on her insistence that a Bill to control experiments on animals was introduced into Parliament, and the King of Prussia's assumption of the title Emperor gave her the idea of becoming Empress of India, which she was proclaimed in 1876.

The first thing she did when Gladstone returned to power in 1880 was to inform him curtly that foreign policy was on no account to be changed. Disliking him as she did, it is hardly to be wondered at that she objected strongly to some of the things contained in the Speech from the Throne which she was obliged to read when opening Parliament. "A disagreeable person – half crazy", she said of her prime minister behind his back and continued to keep in touch with his predecessor, Disraeli, now Lord Beaconsfield, until his death in 1881.

Following the death of John Brown, she appointed a young Indian, Abdul Karim – known as the Queen's Munshi – as her personal servant. Under his influence, she became more and more pre-occupied with her Indian Empire and there were quickly the same disagreements with her family and ministers over the Munshi as there had earlier been over John Brown.

To celebrate her Golden Jubilee in the June of 1887 she paid one of her rare visits to Buckingham Palace. Fifty royalties attended a luncheon in her honour and she consented to ride to a thanksgiving service at Westminster Abbey in an open landau. But not in her crown and robe. Instead, she wore a bonnet of white lace decked with diamonds. The jubilee celebrations included other drives, garden parties, receptions, fireworks, a review in Hyde Park, a naval review at Spithead and, perhaps inevitably, yet another statue to the dead Prince Consort. "The most perfect success", the Queen termed it all.

By September 23, 1896, she had reigned a day longer than any previous British monarch, beating the record previously held by the unfortunate George III. The following year, on June 22, she celebrated her Diamond Jubilee with a drive through London, her head shaded by a parasol of black Chantilly lace presented to her by the House of Commons. Ahead of the royal carriage marched a column of troops drawn from all parts of her vast Empire, Lifeguards and Dragoons, lancers from Australia and cavalry from New Zealand, Sikhs and Cypriots, Dykas, Hausas and Fijians; a column so long that the first few ranks were already passing Buckingham Palace while the Queen still sat at breakfast. Guns boomed in Hyde Park and at night beacons blazed on 2,500 hilltops. The Queen was seventy-eight now and tears ran down her ageing cheeks as the London crowd roared its loyalty.

"They are kind, so kind," she murmured.

The closing years of her life, and the outbreak of the Boer War in 1899, brought a resurgence of her old spirit. Her eyesight was failing now and she was compelled to wear glasses in public (as she had been doing in private for more than twenty years), but she was busier than ever, reviewing troops, visiting hospitals, dispatching tins of chocolate and parcels of woollens to her troops fighting in South Africa. Exhausted by all she did during the day, she was unable to sleep at night. Yet she continued with a spate of public duties such as she had not undertaken since Albert died. At the age of eighty, moved by the gallantry of Irishmen fighting in South Africa, she even insisted on visiting Ireland for the first time in nearly forty years. She created the Irish Guards and decreed that Irish soldiers should wear the shamrock on St Patrick's Day.

Of the war in South Africa, she said, "We are not interested in the possibilities of defeat. They do not exist."

On December 18, 1900, she went again to Osborne and its memories of Albert. By January 13 she found that she could no longer continue the last of the series of journals she had kept so painstakingly for sixty-nine years. On January 18 her children were summoned to her bedside. Her German grandson, Kaiser William II, heard the news and came as well. At half-past six on January 22, 1901, with her Pomeranian Turi snuggled up on the canopied bed at her feet, with her children and grandchildren around her, she died.

"Queen dead. Queen dead," the reporters who had gathered outside the gates of Osborne House yelled from their bicycles as they pedalled furiously towards Cowes in an endeavour to be first with the news.

She was buried in white, her wedding veil over her face, as she had long ago decreed in readiness for that reunion with Albert which she firmly believed awaited her in death.

RACING AND HORSES

The 1979 flat-racing season opened in Britain with Queen Elizabeth II still cherishing a personal ambition unrealized after more than a quarter of a century as an owner and breeder of thoroughbreds. Through all that time she has hoped for nothing so much as to emulate her great-grandfather and breed a Derby winner. Edward VII bred two, Persimmon and Diamond Jubilee. His third Derby winner, Minoru, was leased.

Britain's monarchs have been breeding horses since the distant days of Alfred the Great when the horse was a necessity both for fighting and speedy messenger work. Richard I sent stallions back to Britain to lend speed to the royal breed after finding himself out-run by the nimble steeds of his Arab adversaries. But he was still thinking in terms of warfare, not sport. Even Henry VIII, when he first established the royal paddocks at Hampton Court, was more concerned with raising horses for hunting rather than racing.

The first monarch to attempt the establishment of a true racing thoroughbred line was James I. He bought the Markham Arabian in 1616, but failed to found a lasting male line with it. Charles II, who started a stud at Tutbury in Staffordshire after the Hampton Court paddocks had been closed down by Cromwell, acquired a number of Arab mares and also encouraged the importation of stallions, among them the Byerly Turk. Similar encouragement on the part of William III was also responsible, in part at least, for the arrival in Britain of the Darley Arabian. William re-opened the Hampton Court stud and his sister-in-law, Anne, when she succeeded to the throne, both expanded it and founded Royal Ascot (*see* Ascot). George II's son, the Duke of Cumberland, bred the celebrated Eclipse. George IV, as Prince Regent, won the Derby with Sir Thomas only eight years after it was first founded, though the first royal Derby winner actually bred at the royal stud – Moses in 1822 – was owned by his brother, the Duke of York.

The death of William IV saw the stud again dispersed, but it was reformed in 1850 at the instigation of Queen Victoria's husband, Prince

248

Albert. The Derby winner Orlando was one of the stud stallions and the stud fee in those days was a mere fifty guineas. One of the royal colts, Sanfoin, won the 1890 Derby, the filly Memoir won the Oaks and St Leger, while Memoir's sister, La Flèche, won the Oaks, St Leger, One Thousand Guineas and could have won the Derby if her jockey had ridden a less shocking race. But none of these victories were in the royal colours. Queen Victoria, though she broke the window of the royal box at Ascot one year in her excitement over a close finish, was not the racing enthusiast her great-great-granddaughter is. Instead, she had the royal stud yearlings auctioned off each year at Hyde Park Corner.

However, her son who later became Edward VII was passionately devoted to both breeding and racing. He established his own stud at Sandringham and nearby Wolferton. The first of his mares to achieve fame was Perdita II. Her three colts by St Simon – Florizel II, Persimmon and Diamond Jubilee – all had successful racing careers. Persimmon won the 1896 Derby, the St Leger and the Ascot Gold Cup while Diamond Jubilee won the 1900 Derby, the Two Thousand Guineas and the St Leger. Florizel II subsequently sired the 1901 Derby winner Volodoyovski and Persimmon sired the filly Sceptre which won every classic race except the Derby.

Feola, a yearling bought by George V in 1934, was to prove an important acquisition to the royal stud. Second in the One Thousand Guineas and third in the Oaks, she went on to found one of the world's most influential thoroughbred families. Her daughters have included the classic winner Hypericum, the dams of Round Table, Aureole, Doutelle, Above Suspicion and the Argentinian champions Sideral, Siderea and Sagittaria, and the grand dams of Highclere and Ben Marshall. On the male side, her descendants have included not only Aureole and Round Table, but Vaguely Noble, St Paddy, St Crespin III, Vienna and Baldric.

As a girl of twenty Elizabeth II was at Newmarket to see her father's horse Hypericum win the One Thousand Guineas, her interest in racing having been previously aroused by teenage trips with her father to view Big Game and Sun Chariot, the thoroughbreds he leased from the National Stud. A wedding gift from the Aga Khan gave her an opportunity to enter racing on her own account. The wedding gift took the form of a filly appropriately named Astrakhan, which notched up a win and two placings in four races but proved also to have weak forelegs and a trick of choking on her own tongue.

As a princess, Elizabeth also had a half-share with her mother in a nine-year-old steeplechaser named Monaveen which they bought from Lord Mildmay for £1,000. Monaveen won four races, netting £3,000 in prize money, and was placed fifth in the Grand National. But the Queen Elizabeth Chase the following year resulted in a broken leg and

Monaveen had to be put down. The future Queen was so distressed by the incident that she promptly abandoned steeplechasers entirely, though her mother has continued to race them with a considerable degree of success.

As Queen, following her father's death, Elizabeth took over the nine horses he had had in training together with five more leased from the National Stud, and continued to race them in the traditional colours of the Sovereign, purple, scarlet sleeves, gold braid, black cap with gold tassel. Since then she has twice been leading owner, in 1954 and 1957, and has twice come second, in 1958 and 1977. She has twice come second in the list of winning breeders, in 1957 and 1977 (when she was also the leading British breeder) and once third, in 1958.

The first time she was leading owner was largely due to Feola's grandson, Aureole. Ever since she had helped feed him when he was no more than a week-old colt the Queen had felt that here was a chestnut to rival her great-grandfather's Derby winners. But Aureole proved himself a highly unpredictable animal, sensitive to the slightest touch. He snapped at her once when she offered him an apple. Another time only a frantic shout of "Look out, Your Majesty!" enabled her to side-step just in time to avoid a lashing hoof. Her hopes that he would provide her with a royal victory in the coronation year Derby were dashed when he was unsettled by a good-luck pat from a passing racegoer and finished second to Victor Sassoon's Pinza. The following year it was a different story. He won four races that year, including the Coronation Cup, the Hardwicke Stakes and the King George VI and Queen Elizabeth Stakes to make her leading owner with a total of £40,993 in prize money. So excited did the Queen become as Aureole took the lead in the race named after her parents a furlong and a half from home that she hopped excitedly from foot to foot and yelled encouragement at the top of her voice.

Her great-grandfather had a larger-than-lifesize bronze statue erected at Sandringham to honour Persimmon. The Queen did not go quite that far. But she did have a small statuette of Aureole fashioned to grace her sitting-room at Windsor.

Aureole became the royal stud stallion, siring a succession of top-class thoroughbreds until his death in 1976, among them St Crespin III, winner of the Prix de l'Arc de Triomphe, the Derby and St Leger winner St Paddy, and St Leger winners Aurelius and Provoke. He was champion British sire in both 1960 and 1961 and altogether his offspring were to win over one million pounds.

On the track Aureole's 1954 successes were followed by a stream of royal winners extending over a period of six years. Pall Mall won the Two Thousand Guineas before going on to a successful stud career in Ireland. Doutelle, after a successful racing career, joined Aureole in the royal stud and sired such outstanding thoroughbreds as Prétendre, Fighting Ship and Canisbay before coming to an untimely death after only four seasons at stud. Alexander, Miner's Lamp, Restoration and Sierra Nevada were other important winners while the filly Almeria was not only the leading staying filly of her generation but was later to breed some high-class winners for the 1970s, notably Magna Carta and Albany.

If it was Feola's grandson Aureole who was largely responsible for the Queen being winning owner in 1954, it was another of Feola's descendants, her great-granddaughter Highclere, who two decades later was to become the first filly trained in England or Ireland to win over £100,000 in a year, winning the One Thousand Guineas in England and the Prix de Diane in France. The Prix de Diane alone contributed nearly half of the £186,782 the Queen won that year.

The Queen was at Chantilly to see her filly win in 1974. She was not at either the Oaks or the St Leger in 1977 to see another of her fillies, Dunfermline, perhaps the best racehorse ever to carry the Queen's colours, celebrate her Silver Jubilee for her with wins in both races. The desire to welcome Prince Andrew back from Canada kept her from one and the necessity to play host to Prime Minister James Callaghan at Balmoral from the other. However, both wins brought her the additional satisfaction of knowing that they stemmed from following her own instinct.

It all started when the yearling filly Stroma came up for sale at Doncaster in 1956. The Queen does not normally buy yearlings, but she "fell in love" with Stroma and bought her for the relatively low price of 1,500 guineas. Stroma became the dam of Canisbay (who later became a leading sire in Italy) and of the filly Strathcona. When the time came to breed with Strathcona, the Queen felt that Jim Joel's Royal Palace, though not held in specially high regard as a sire by all breeders, was "exactly right" for her. The result of bringing the two together was Dunfermline, who was to end her racing career as the best filly in Europe.

The Royals are often said, not always accurately, to be "expert" this or "a natural" that. But as Dunfermline has proved, the Queen really is an expert in the matter of breeding thoroughbreds. And, as they quickly found out on one occasion when she went racing in Australia, she knows her blood lines "right back to Eclipse", which is going back more than a couple of centuries.

Dunfermline's 1977 victories helped to make the Queen leading British breeder that year with a total of £151,001 won in England by horses bred at the royal stud. The Queen herself had sixteen winning and placed horses, while a further win was notched up by a horse she had sold as a yearling. In addition, two other horses won races abroad, bringing the grand total of royal-bred winnings to £174,998.

The studs at Sandringham and Wolferton, which are managed for the Queen by Michael Oswald, normally house a stallion apiece – Bustino is currently at Wolferton and until recently the Irish Derby and St Leger winner Ribero was at Sandringham – and about twenty mares (inevitably the number varies from time to time). Among the mares, the main families represented are those of Feola, Avila and Young Entry, though Canisbay's dam Stroma and Blenheim's dam Malva are also represented. The yearlings are kept at Polhampton, some two miles from Kingsclere. The Queen visits the studs whenever she is at Sandringham and calls at Polhampton to take a look at the yearlings whenever she visits her trainers, Ian Balding at Kingsclere and Major Dick Hern at West Isley. Her third trainer is William Hastings-Bass at Newmarket, a handy stopping place en route to Sandringham. Her racing manager is Lord Porchester.

Hampton Court is used these days to accommodate horses from the royal mews as well as the Queen Mother's young horses and steeplechasers resting for the summer. The Queen Mother keeps a small number of mares, five at the last count, to breed hurdlers and steeplechasers and has a small but successful string of jumpers in training with Fulke Walwyn at Lambourn. Since 1952 she has won over three hundred races.

In addition to thoroughbreds, the Queen also breeds event horses – she bred Doublet, the horse on which Princess Anne won the European championship, and Columbus – and carriage horses (*see* Coaches and Carriages) as well as polo ponies and Highland, Fell and Haflinger ponies.

REIGNS

The longest reign in British history was that of Queen Victoria. She was a month past her eighteenth birthday when she succeeded to the throne and reigned for 63 years 216 days. She was also the longest-lived monarch, being 81 years 243 days of age when she died at Osborne House on the Isle of Wight on January 22, 1901.

The next longest reign was that of the unfortunate George III. He reigned for 59 years 96 days (though in name only towards the end, his son acting as Prince Regent) between 1760 and 1820. He also ran Victoria close in the matter of age, being 81 years 239 days at the time of his death.

The third longest reign was that of Henry III – 56 years from 1216 to 1272.

The shortest reign in history was that of the youthful Queen Jane

(Lady Jane Grey). She was proclaimed Queen on July 10, 1553, and is variously recorded to have reigned for 9, 13 and 14 days before being ousted by Mary Tudor.

The youthful Edward V was king for only 77 days from April 9 to June 25, 1483, before being deposed – and possibly murdered – by his uncle, Richard III.

Among the early Saxon kings, Edmund Ironside ruled for approximately 210 days only – history is not certain of the exact dates – in 1016, while Harold Godwin reigned for only 281 days between seizing the throne on January 5, 1066 and his death at Hastings on October 14.

Edward VIII (Duke of Windsor) reigned for 325 days, technically from five minutes to midnight on January 20, 1936, when his father died, to December 11, the day Parliament ratified his Instrument of Abdication.

Anne of Cleves, fourth wife of Henry VIII, served the shortest spell of any Queen Consort. Henry, unkindly labelling her "a Flanders mare", married and divorced her all in the space of 184 days.

The youngest monarch was Henry VI. He was an infant of nine months when he succeeded his father, Henry V, on September 1, 1422.

The oldest monarch to succeed to the throne was William IV. He was only two months short of his sixty-fifth birthday when he became king in 1830.

William died from cirrhosis of the liver. So did George IV. An earlier William – the male half of William and Mary – died from pneumonia after being thrown from his horse and fracturing a collar-bone. Edward IV died from gluttony. At the age of forty-two he was so fat he could hardly walk. Before him, King John is also said to have died from gluttony, from eating too many peaches.

And many a monarch has died violently. Edward the Martyr was assassinated. Harold Godwin was hacked to pieces at Hastings. William Rufus was shot with an arrow, accidentally or otherwise, in the New Forest. Richard the Lionheart died from gangrene after being wounded by a crossbow bolt. Edward II was murdered – viciously disembowelled with a red-hot iron – while imprisoned in Berkeley Castle by his wife and her lover. Richard II was murdered at Pontefract Castle. Henry VI was almost certainly murdered. Twelve-year-old Edward V and his younger brother both vanished into the Tower of London and were never seen again. It was over 150 years before their remains were discovered, buried in a wooden chest ten feet below ground, and re-interred in Westminster Abbey. Richard III was slain at the Battle of Bosworth. Sixteen-year-old Jane Grey was beheaded, along with her young husband, after being deposed by Mary Tudor. Charles I was also beheaded, saying as he walked to the scaffold in Whitehall in 1649, "I go from a corruptible crown to an incorruptible crown where no disturbance can be.''

Queen Anne was the monarch to have the most children. She had seventeen (and some historians say eighteen). Edward I had sixteen legitimate children (plus a few bastards) and George III had fifteen. Illegitimate offspring are harder to pin down, but Henry I would appear to have had at least twenty, and possibly twenty-two, by six mistresses.

RELIGION

Queen Elizabeth II is not only Head of the Commonwealth, but also supreme head of the Church of England, as Britain's monarchs have been since Henry VIII broke with Rome in his desire to divorce Catherine of Aragon, wed and bed Anne Boleyn in her place and, hopefully, sire a son. But just as the powers of Britain's monarchs have become curtailed in recent centuries, so have those of the Defender of the Faith. It is still the Queen's prerogative to appoint archbishops and bishops, but she does so these days on the advice of the prime minister who in turn, at least as far as the appointment of bishops is concerned, takes the advice of the Archbishop of Canterbury and, if a northern see is involved, of the Archbishop of York also.

It was as head of the Church of England that the Queen, opening the first Parliament of her reign in 1952, made the declaration of faith which her grandfather, George V, amended in 1910 from the much less liberal declaration laid down by the 1689 Act of the Declaration of Rights. The Queen's 1952 declaration was in this form:

"I, Elizabeth the Second, do solemnly and sincerely in the presence of God, profess, testify and declare that I am a faithful Protestant, and that I will, according to the true intent of the enactments which secure the Protestant succession to the Throne of my Realm, uphold and maintain the said enactments to the best of my powers according to the law."

It was her position as head of the Church of England, so rigidly opposed to divorce, which placed her in such a quandary over Princess Margaret (*see* Princess Margaret and Lord Snowdon) and, as much as anything, prevented her from acceding to her sister's wish to marry Peter Townsend.

From childhood the Queen was brought up in a religious atmosphere, in a home in which Bible stories were read as a matter of course. Later she was given religious instruction by Canon Crawley, a member of the chapter of St George's Chapel, Windsor, and was confirmed just before her sixteenth birthday.

Today she continues to attend church as regularly as she did in childhood. Even on holiday at Balmoral she goes regularly each Sunday to the nearby church at Crathie, while at Sandringham she attends the church of St Mary Magdalene in Sandringham Park with its many reminders of her great-grandparents, Edward VII and Queen Alexandra. Unlike so many of her subjects, she continues to regard Christmas as an essentially religious festival and continues the royal tradition of exchanging gifts on Christmas Eve so as to leave the morning of Christmas Day free for church.

ROYAL LODGE

While her elder daughter and son-in-law adjourn to the regal vastness of Windsor Castle at weekends, the Queen Mother retreats to the pink-washed intimacy of Royal Lodge on the edge of Windsor Great Park, approximately midway between her daughter's castle and Virginia Water. Her late husband, the then Duke of York, once planned to write a book about Royal Lodge. He had already done the research – or, rather, had it done for him – and was all set to commit pen to paper when his brother's abdication found him with more important things on his mind. As a result, the book was never written.

His research revealed that the Lodge was once the residence of Thomas Sandby, draughtsman to George II's third son, "Butcher" Cumberland, and his artist brother, Paul Sandby. It was called Lower Lodge in those days to distinguish it from nearby Great Lodge in which Cumberland himself lived. George IV took it over as a country home in his days as Prince Regent, enlarging and embellishing it at the same time that he was remodelling Windsor Castle. It was George IV, after he became King, who first styled it "Royal Lodge" on his notepaper.

William IV, when he succeeded his brother on the throne, began pulling it down. Queen Victoria looked at what remained and thought of rebuilding it, but finally bought Osborne instead. For almost a century it was virtually unused by the Royals until George V gave it to his second son, York, in 1931. His eldest son, the Prince of Wales who later became Duke of Windsor, was already settled nearby in another "Butcher" Cumberland relic, Fort Belvedere.

Just as he always insisted that Sandringham should be called precisely that and not "Sandringham House", so George V stipulated that the Yorks' new home should be called not simply Royal Lodge, but The Royal Lodge. Today, however, it is known once more as Royal Lodge. It was in a sad state when the Yorks took over and they set to work to restore it. The large forty-foot-long drawing-room (known, like the one at Sandringham, as "the saloon") with a Sir Thomas Lawrence portrait of George IV above the fire-place, the octagon room and the wine cellar beneath are today all that remain of the original structure. It was the Yorks who added the wings on each flank. Throughout the years of the 1930s, the York parents, helped later by their growing daughters, toiled together in the sixteen-acre grounds (later increased to around ninety acres), turning an overgrown wilderness into a pleasant garden. While the Duke slashed away at weeds and overgrown shrubs, the Duchess, as she then was, created new flower borders and rose gardens.

"That really is my garden," the Queen's father was to say later. "I made it."

Here at weekends, surrounded by corgis, labradors and budgerigars, they lived a graciously rural life. Once they were old enough, Elizabeth and Margaret were given their own small plots to seed and weed. Also in the grounds they had their own straw-thatched, cream-walled miniature house, a gift to Elizabeth on her sixth birthday from the people of Wales. Named *Y Bwthyn Bach* (The Little House), the gift was rather more than a doll's house, though it has sometimes been referred to as such. With a twenty-two-foot frontage, and eight feet deep, completely furnished and equipped right down to electricity, plumbing and working radio, it was built to just the right scale for two small girls, though visiting grown-ups found themselves forced to negotiate its rooms on their hands and knees.

Royal Lodge remained a favourite weekend retreat for the family even after the Yorks became King and Queen. Encouraged by his wife to look upon it as an antidote to monarchy, the King would commandeer everyone in sight – wife, daughters, equerry, valet, butler, chauffeur and bodyguard – and issue them with billhooks and pruning knives for a positive orgy of slashing and trimming with the resultant huge, smoky bonfires.

The King's daughters lived briefly at Royal Lodge during the early part of World War II, until German air raids compelled them to be moved to the greater protection of Windsor Castle. In the immediate post-war years, Philip, at the time he was courting Elizabeth, was a frequent visitor. The young lovers walked the royal corgis in Windsor Park, played croquet on the lawn and swam together in the green-tiled pool.

Since the death of her husband, the Queen Mother, as she now is, has continued to use Royal Lodge as a weekend retreat, her husband remembered by the leather blotter, silver inkstand, travelling clock and family photographs which have continued to stand on his desk as they did in his lifetime.

SANDRINGHAM

Sandringham, an imposing red-brick mansion stuffed with the accumulated knick-knacks and travel souvenirs of successive reigns, set amidst the pines and heathland of the Norfolk coast just over one hundred miles from London – the surrounding estate extends to something like 17,000 acres – has been a hideaway home for the Royal Family since the days of Queen Victoria, though she herself never actually lived there or owned the place.

The Queen's grandfather, George V, used to say, "I have a house in London, but a home at Sandringham." His son, her father, could say with equal pleasure that "at Sandringham I can forget for a little while that I am King." Elizabeth II, though she goes there less often than her father and grandfather did – her father was born and brought up there – feels much the same. At Sandringham, moving around in comfortable tweeds and stout shoes, her hair held in place by a head-scarf, walking her dogs, attending meetings of the local Women's Institute, she is more lady of the manor than Queen of England.

Sandringham, like Balmoral, is her private property, not an official state residence. It first came into the possession of the Royal Family in 1861 when Queen Victoria and Prince Albert paid £220,000 out of the accumulated revenues of the Duchy of Cornwall to buy it for their eldest son, the Prince of Wales who was later Edward VII, in the hope that it would help him to steer clear of big city temptations. In fact it did nothing of the sort. Bertie, as he was known in the family, was quick to invite various delectable temptations, Lillie Langtry among them, to join him at Sandringham from time to time.

Edward VII loved Sandringham, as his son, grandson and great-granddaughter were to love it in turn. He remodelled it, adding a billiards room, a bowling alley and a smoking room on the oriental lines of one he had seen in Turkey. Then he tore down what he had remodelled and rebuilt the whole place from scratch, creating the present warm brick building with its *porte-cochère* giving direct access to the main drawing-room or "saloon" as he called it (and as it is still known). The

257

vast amount of money he poured into house and estate alike did much towards helping to keep him almost permanently in debt.

In his day, Sandringham was a regular rabbit-warren of small rooms (some of which the present Queen has recently demolished) between which male guests would tiptoe at night in panting anticipation as they played the favourite indoor game of the Edwardian upper classes – hunt-your-bed-partner. Under Bertie's ownership, life there was almost one continuous house party. Regularly each Monday and Friday a train from London – known as "The Prince of Wales special" – would pull into the station at King's Lynn, some eight miles away, with a fresh batch of guests to be ferried out to the "big house" in a cavalcade of carriages, horse buses and luggage brakes. Male guests spent their days massacring pheasants and partridges, an exercise which started promptly at quarter past ten (it was really quarter to ten, but, to get his guests going, the Prince always kept the clocks half an hour fast) with a parade of beaters in smocks and gamekeepers in suits of green velveteen. Under Bertie's supervision, as many as two thousand birds would be slaughtered in a day. While the men were out shooting, the ladies of the house party gossiped, wrote letters and changed their clothes four times a day, for breakfast, lunch, afternoon tea and again for dinner. For dinner, up to thirty people would sit down to a meal which could easily extend to a dozen courses. Afterwards would come billiards or bowls, whist, poker or baccarat, dancing to the music of a barrel organ and endless high jinks and practical joking.

Under George V, life at Sandringham was very different. The early part of his married life was spent mainly in the cramped confines of York Cottage (*see* King George V and Queen Mary) while his father continued to occupy the main house. Five of his six children were born there. With the death of Edward VII, Sandringham's night-club role was at an end. His son, though he continued the shooting parties and the tradition of "Sandringham time", was far too moral ever to countenance the sort of skylarking house parties to which his father had been so addicted. To George V, as to the son who succeeded him, Sandringham was more a sanctuary, a refuge from the cares of monarchy, easily accessible from London when things became too much for them. Christmas at Sandringham, in particular, was to be part of the royal tradition for many years. It was from Sandringham that George V made his first Christmas broadcast and his granddaughter, Elizabeth II, her first Christmas television broadcast.

Through successive reigns Sandringham has played an important part in the life of the Royal Family. Queen Victoria hurried there in 1871 when her eldest son contracted typhoid and was thought to be dying. He recovered, however, as a plaque in the nearby church of St Mary Magdalene testifies. It was placed there by his wife, then Princess of Wales, "To the glory of God – a thanksgiving for His mercy."

Their eldest son, Albert Victor, Duke of Clarence, did die there, from pneumonia in 1892, a bare seven weeks before he was due to have been married. The brother who married his *fiancée* and succeeded him as heir to the throne also died there, though not until 1936, after twenty-six years of monarchy as King George V. His son, in turn, George VI, was to die there in 1952, and it was to Sandringham and her widowed mother that the new young Queen hurried as soon as the formalities of monarchy had been completed in London.

The tradition of "Christmas at Sandringham" continued during the early part of her reign and was then abandoned for a number of reasons, though she still goes there for New Year, usually staying on into early February, and for shorter visits, mainly connected with the royal studs (*see* Racing and Horses), at other times of the year. Her mother too uses the house as a convenient base from which to attend the nearby King's Lynn Festival each summer.

At one time Elizabeth II had ambitious plans for remodelling and renovating Sandringham. The first stage of the operation, involving the demolition of 91 of Sandringham's 361 rooms, had already been completed when soaring inflation – the original estimate of £100,000 quickly doubled itself – caused the project to be brought to an abrupt halt. Instead, the Queen decided to join the increasingly long line of stately home owners who these days, for a small fee, open the doors of their mansions to the paying public.

SHOPPING

Britain's is not one of the so-called "bicycling monarchies" of some Scandinavian countries where monarchs contrive to move among their subjects on an ordinary everyday basis. For the Queen to go anywhere, once the fact is known, is sufficient for the photographers to home in and crowds to gather in force. For this reason, she seldom goes shopping. And on the rare occasion that she does go, it is usually early in the morning, by special arrangement with the store concerned, before there are too many other shoppers about. In the weeks leading up to Christmas she may make one or two quick gift-buying forays of this nature, perhaps to a store like Harrods, perhaps to the Lord Roberts Workshops. Such pre-Christmas excursions, plus the very occasional visit to the Hartnell showrooms (just across from where she was born in Bruton Street) to see the latest collection, are the limit of her public shopping.

For the most part, shopkeepers and others go to her. Or send to her. The top designers responsible for creating the Queen's clothes will send along designs and samples of material for her consideration. Rayne, who make her shoes, will send a selection from their latest range. Others send catalogues for her to peruse or samples of their wares from which she can make a choice.

A minimum of three years as supplier to the Queen can bring a shopkeeper one of the coveted royal warrants. With the warrant goes the right to display the royal arms outside the trader's premises, on his vehicles and notepaper, and in his advertising. There must, of course, be no blatant advertising; no nonsense like "The Queen Wears A LaLolla Girdle" or anything like that. Moreover, each warrant is strictly limited to the goods and services it specifies and the royal arms may be displayed only in that connection. Thus, a firm awarded a royal warrant as "Purveyors of Tomato Sauce" can display the royal arms on its sauce bottles, but not on, say, the cans of baked beans it also happens to produce.

As with so many other aspects of Britain's royalty, no one knows for certain exactly when the first royal warrant was issued. Something of the sort was already in existence as far back as the days of the first Elizabeth and by the days of Charles II the system was in full swing. In fact, the "Merry Monarch" was not above accepting what is today known as "slush money" from a trader in exchange for a royal warrant, while his bosomy mistress, Nell Gwyn, took advantage of the system to reward old friends and repay old debts.

Edward VII, a monarch with a gargantuan appetite, seems to have scattered his royal warrants around like so much confetti. He had only to take a passing fancy to someone's pies or buns to hand out yet another royal warrant, as happened in the case of a theatrical landlady named Mrs Forscutt after the King had sampled one of her hot, buttered muffins while hanging around backstage at a theatre. Strongman Eugene Sandow was similarly favoured. He held a royal warrant as the King's physical training instructor.

Today, the whole business is run by the Lord Chamberlain's department (*see* Household) on a more regular basis. Over the years of her monarchy Elizabeth II has issued something in excess of seven hundred warrants, the exact number varying slightly from time to time as new names are added to the list or old ones die off or go out of business. Warrant holders range from such world-famous names as Rolls Royce and Fortnum and Mason to small village stores in places like Ballater, near Balmoral, and the area around Sandringham. Between them, they cover the whole range of requirements of a monarch who not only has a staff of several hundred to feed in London but two large private estates to run into the bargain, from manufacturers of farm equipment and suppliers of electric cable to jewellers, hatters and the firm which cleans and mothproofs the royal furs. Royal fashion designers figure prominently in the current list of warrant holders along with the royal hairdresser, milliners, shoemakers, perfumers and the firms which make Elizabeth's favourite brands of mint chocolates and toilet soap. The list includes suppliers of dog food for the royal corgis and labradors, makers of racing silks for royal jockeys, laundries, florists, butchers, bakers and chemists as well as such oddities as livery makers and sword cutlers, suppliers of nosegays and gold leaf, two Scottish firms which turn out bagpipes, a purveyor of potted shrimps and one on the island of Orkney who markets honey.

While some of the royal warrant holders are comparative newcomers in the field, there are others who have held successive warrants through several generations. Garrard & Co., for instance, who hold a warrant as Crown Jewellers and send a small batch of expert craftsmen along to the Tower of London from time to time to clean and, if necessary, repair the royal regalia, have held royal warrants issued by various monarchs over the course of two and a half centuries, starting with the Prince Regent. Robert Jackson & Co., until 1979, had been supplying the Royals with their groceries since the days when the Prince Regent finally became George IV, while Fortnum & Mason received their first royal warrant in 1834 though they would appear to have been supplying various monarchs long before that. Or if not, they certainly have the distinction of having been founded by one of Queen Anne's footmen whose start in business came from selling candle-ends and other royal perks which gravitated his way.

Most royal warrant holders, naturally, are based in Britain. However, a few firms in other countries have also been honoured with royal warrants, among them a distiller of cognac and several champagne houses in France, a liqueur producer in Copenhagen, a producer of aromatic bitters in Trinidad and a whisky distiller in Ontario.

Prince Philip issues his own warrants. His list is considerably shorter than that of his wife, nudging a mere sixty names at the last perusal. To a considerable extent, the list reflects the man, echoing his interest in sport and technology . . . manufacturers of sound recording equipment, postal systems and power filing systems, rifle makers, marine photographers and suppliers of polo sticks (though he himself no longer plays the game) along with hairdressers, tailors, hatters and tie-makers. He goes a long way for his shoe polish, seemingly. The firm which holds the princely warrant for it is located in Melbourne, Australia. The Queen Mother also has her own list of warrant holders, longer than her son-in-law's if considerably smaller than her daughter's. The two hundred names on her list include more than two dozen in Scotland and a cheesemonger in Orkney.

SILVER JUBILEE

The 1977 Silver Jubilee of Elizabeth II gave Britain its biggest splash of colour since the Coronation and served, briefly, to enable the country to forget its continuing economic problems. Almost the whole nation either joined in or cashed in on the celebrations – as well as a few million foreign visitors – although there were a few who protested that the money outlaid on flags, bunting and other decorations could have been better spent on more deserving causes. The Queen herself said from the outset that she wanted the celebrations to be held "without undue expenditure". If Parliament took her at her word, at least up to a point, not everyone else did. Some, indeed, were almost recklessly spendthrift. Portsmouth, after originally budgeting to spend only £12,000 to host the Queen on the occasion of her jubilee visit, ended up paying out £225,000, including £9,438 spent on a fibre-glass replica of the crown standing fourteen feet high.

The Queen's 1977 Silver Jubilee was only the second of its kind. Her grandfather, George V, celebrated his in 1935; that was the first. Neither her father nor her great-grandfather reigned long enough to have one. Her great-great-grandmother, Queen Victoria, reigned more than long enough, but could not find it in her heart to head any sort of celebration when her husband had died only the previous December. So she waited another twenty-five years for her Golden Jubilee. And before Queen Victoria, no one seems to have bothered.

The actual anniversary of the Queen's accession to the throne is February 6, but the weather in February is hardly conducive to outdoor celebrations. Nor would the celebrations serve as a tourist attraction at that time of year. So it was decided to hold the British end of the celebrations in June and the Queen spent her actual anniversary weekend quietly at Windsor.

Because of this, the islanders of Western Samoa were the first to have an opportunity to celebrate when the Queen flew in on her way to Australia and New Zealand. From Samoa the royal yacht took her to Tonga and Fiji for more celebrations followed by two weeks in New Zealand and three in Australia where she managed to squeeze in a visit to every state. There were also visits to Tasmania and Papua New Guinea.

Back home in her absence, preparations for Britain's own celebrations went on apace with manufacturers stepping up output in readiness to flood the market with souvenir mugs, plates, goblets, spoons, ash trays, pillboxes, bookmarks, book ends, tea-caddies and anything else they could think of. The Cooperative Wholesale Society, worried by the vast amount it was spending on a jubilee promotion scheme spread throughout six thousand stores, saw trouble ahead if anything happened to the Queen or a member of her family and the whole thing was suddenly called off. As a back-stop, it decided to insure the lives of Elizabeth and her family for a cool one million pounds. That brought another worry. "We thought at first it might be classed as treasonable," explained a spokesman for the firm, "but found that it was not."

Once their fears of treason had been allayed, other big-spending outfits were quick to take out similar insurances on the lives of the Royals. To help get Britain in the true celebratory spirit, a brewery in Devizes filled ten thousand bottles with specially-strong Queen's Ale. Other brewers were quick off the mark with Silver Jubilee Ale, Silver Sovereign and Tolly Royal, while Newcastle Breweries, not to be outdone, reminded ale drinkers that though 1977 might be the Silver Jubilee of Elizabeth II, it was the Golden Jubilee of their Newcastle Brown.

The Post Office issued a set of jubilee stamps which some people thought "uninspiring" and the Royal Mint churned out jubilee crown pieces, some of which were soon selling at three times their face value of twenty-five pence. Madame Tussaud's mounted a new group of royal waxworks which some critics thought looked like "a cross between Barbi dolls and Thunderbirds" and the Poet Laureate, Sir John Betjeman, wrote the verses for a special jubilee hymn. Malcolm Williamson, Master of the Queen's Music, expressed himself as well pleased with Betjeman's effort. Not everyone agreed. Nicholas Fairbairn, Member of Parliament for Kinross and West Perthshire, castigated them as "pathetic . . . banal, a ninth-rate piece of child's verse".

Prince Charles launched a Silver Jubilee fund designed to raise money for youth projects. It ended up with £7,200,000 in individual donations and a further £8½ million from trusts, foundations and industrial concerns. However, the organizers of some fund-raising events were upset to find themselves being asked to pay Value Added Tax if their efforts raised more than £7,500.

Congratulatory letters and cards began streaming in to Buckingham Palace, including one card which measured an outsize ten feet by five feet and required five people to manoeuvre it through the palace gates. On one day alone there was an inundation of 3,500 cards and letters and by the time things quietened down again a total of over 100,000 had been received.

Celebrations in a tourist-packed London included a thanksgiving service attended by the Queen in St Paul's Cathedral followed by a walkabout in the City of London, a "river progress" along the Thames, a bonfire and fireworks at Windsor, and the traditional Trooping the Colour ceremony. "Great going, Liz!" said a banner in the crowd. There was also a Buckingham Palace banquet for Commonwealth heads of state and two royal tours of London were to follow. Elsewhere loyal subjects celebrated with their own bonfires, street parties and the presentation of commemorative mugs to schoolchildren. An art teacher in Leamington Spa painted a twenty-five-foot high portrait of the Queen on the side wall of his house. Determined to go one better, a taxi driver in Norwich and a school meals worker in Bulwell, Nottinghamshire, both had their hair dyed a patriotic red, white and blue.

Thirty thousand delighted recipients found themselves the proud possessors of Silver Jubilee medals, though no one seemed to know on exactly what basis their names had been selected. There were gala performances of ballet and opera, special exhibitions and military band performances. The Queen, as well as going to Ascot that year of 1977, went also to the Derby, one of the England-Australia cricket matches and to Wimbledon where, by fortunate coincidence, she saw Britain's own Virginia Wade win the ladies' singles. She reviewed British troops in Germany, the Royal Navy at Spithead and the Royal Air Force at Finningley, where the Secretary for Defence, Frederick Mulley, had the misfortune to nod off while sitting beside her. "A momentary lack of attention," he explained. The naval review, due to Government cutbacks, was the smallest in memory and even the Queen herself could not resist commenting on the slimmed-down air force she reviewed. "At my coronation review 640 aircraft took part," she said. "Today we shall see only 137 in the air."

Prior to the celebrations in London, the Queen, after the fashion of the first Elizabeth, had made royal progresses through Glasgow, Dundee, Aberdeen and Edinburgh. Despite the upsurge of Scottish nationalism, she was "completely taken aback" by the enthusiastic loyalty of her Scottish subjects. Later came similar progresses to other parts of Britain: Lancashire and Merseyside, with Manchester getting a day of its own; Gwynedd, West Wales and Swansea; South Wales and Cardiff, Suffolk and Norfolk, Humberside and Yorkshire, the North East, the West Midlands, Derbyshire and Nottinghamshire, Devon and Plymouth, Cornwall and Avon. Long before it was all over, the Queen was looking pale and strained. Altogether, she travelled some seven thousand miles through Britain's provinces, but unlike the first Elizabeth, she did not bankrupt those who played host to her. Instead, she had either the royal yacht or her new royal train (*see* Train) to serve as a base for eating and sleeping.

"I was crowned," she said in one early jubilee speech, "Queen of the United Kingdom – Great Britain and Northern Ireland." And despite threats from the IRA, she was determined that Northern Ireland should not be left out of her jubilee celebrations. Her Jubilee, she said, would not be complete without a visit to the people of Northern Ireland "who have suffered and courageously borne so much". And in August, in defiance of the IRA threats, she went there. In the event, fears for her safety went unrealized even if her visit did not go off completely without incident. Coincident with the visit there was a fresh outbreak of street violence in Belfast and Londonderry. In Belfast a bomb exploded. So did another in Crossmaglen. A British army officer and an IRA gunman were alike shot and injured. However, all this was many miles away from where the Queen was smilingly accepting flowers from schoolchildren, handing out awards for courage and bravery, talking with widows, nurses and members of the Peace Movement, unveiling a commemorative plaque and watching a youth festival in which 1,800 youngsters took part.

A further IRA threat that a bomb had been planted on the spot did not deter her from visiting the new University of Ulster at Coleraine. Indeed, the threat seemed only to harden her determination and, as though to demonstrate this, she had not only her husband but her son, Prince Andrew, then seventeen, with her on the second day of her visit.

Security precautions, of course, were on a massive scale. There was no royal walkabout such as featured in her visits to other parts of her kingdom. Her public appearances were restricted to relatively safe, easily protected areas such as the new university at Coleraine and the grounds of Hillsborough Castle. She lived aboard the royal yacht and was flown in and out of Hillsborough and Coleraine by helicopter, arriving only after buildings and grounds had been thoroughly checked by bomb experts and sniffer dogs. Helicopters, though Philip and Charles use them regularly enough, are normally considered too unsafe a form of transport for the Queen herself. But on this occasion the odds against a helicopter crash were considered preferable to the risk of a sniper's bullet on the ground.

Just as she had preceded the home celebrations with visits to Australia, New Zealand and elsewhere, so the Queen followed them with visits to yet more parts of her Commonwealth, to Canada, the Virgin Islands, the Bahamas, Antigua and Barbados. The 3,686-mile flight back from Barbados to London took her exactly 3 hours and 42 minutes. It was the first time she had flown supersonically in Concorde.

STAMPS

The value of the present-day royal stamp collection defies calculation. Its value was already put at over one million pounds more than a quarter of a century ago and inflation, if nothing else, has increased that figure several-fold since then.

It owes its origin to two princes of very different character. One was Queen Victoria's somewhat raffish son, Alfred, Duke of Edinburgh, who became interested in stamp collecting after a visit to the De La Rue printing works in 1856, and many of the earliest stamps in the collection were first collected by him. The other was the Queen's grandfather, the prince who became the gruff and essentially moral George V. He started collecting at the age of twenty-five while serving in the navy. He was helped on his way by fellow collectors who, learning of his interest in philately, gave him 1,500 stamps as a wedding gift in 1893. He was also helped by his father, then Prince of Wales, later Edward VII, who bought Uncle Affie's collection for him.

George V was mainly interested in British and Empire stamps. So enthusiastic was he that in 1904 he paid £1,450, a large amount at that time, for one of the world's rarest specimens, a 2d Post Office Mauritius. He had the advantage that he was sent specimens of all new stamps issued by either the Post Office or the Crown Agents and from 1910 he was also sent specimens of all stamps registered with the Universal Post Office in Berne. However, these were of less interest to him and he passed them on to the Royal Philatelic Society.

So enthusiastic was he that at one time he devoted three afternoons a week to his collection and at his death in 1936 it already filled 325 albums. Among his most prized specimens were the earliest of all stamps, a penny black issued in 1840, a block of four 2d blue issued the same year, a Trinidad stamp issued privately in 1847 as well as 1d and 2d Trinidad stamps of the first official colonial issue, 1d and 2d stamps issued in New South Wales in 1850, a 12d black issued in Canada in 1851, a 2d issued in Van Diemen's Land (now Tasmania) in 1855, a 4d British Guiana (now Guyana) stamp of 1856, a one shilling Newfoundland of 1857 and a 4d Ceylon of 1859, though most of these earlier stamps probably originated in the Prince Alfred collection which had been bought for him by his father.

If neither the present Queen nor her father have shown the same almost passionate interest in stamps that her grandfather had, they have nevertheless been sufficiently interested to keep it up-to-date and to plug gaps in the collection when the opportunity has presented itself.

SUCCESSION

The order of succession to Britain's throne (*see* Heir Apparent /Heir Presumptive) is decreed by the Act of Settlement of 1701. It was passed by Parliament at a time when William III reigned alone and childless following the death of the wife with whom he had previously shared the throne.

Next in line to William at that time was the sister-in-law who eventually became Queen Anne. The second daughter of James II by his first wife, Anne Hyde, she was, while William still reigned, Princess Anne of Denmark. Fertile though she had proved herself to be, by 1701 Anne had no children either. Of the seventeen to which she had given birth, all but one had failed to survive infancy while the one who did, Prince William, Duke of Gloucester, had died at the age of eleven.

Anxious not to have any of James II's Catholic offspring by his second wife, Mary of Modena, on the throne, Parliament decided upon the Act of Settlement. This harked back to James II's grandfather, James I, and his other line of descent. James I's daughter, Elizabeth, had married Frederick, Elector of Hanover. By that time, Elizabeth was long since dead. But her daughter, Princess Sophia lived and had succeeded her father as Electress of Hanover. By the Act of Settlement, Parliament awarded the throne, at such time as William III and Queen Anne were both dead, to Sophia and "the heirs of her body", carefully adding the all-important phrase "being protestant".

Almost frenetic in its determination to have no more Catholics on the throne, Parliament went further. The Act of Settlement not only decreed that "whosoever shall hereafter come into possession of this Crown" must be a communicant member of the Church of England, but, to make assurance doubly sure, totally banned from the throne anyone who was "or afterwards should be reconciled to, or should hold communion with the see or church of Rome, or should profess the popish religion, or marry a papist".

It was because of the Act of Settlement of 1701 that the Queen's cousin, Prince Michael (*see* Prince and Princess Michael of Kent), in 1978, then sixteenth in the line of succession, found it necessary to renounce any claim to the throne before marrying the Baroness Marie-Christine von Reibnitz, a Catholic. However, he did not renounce the right of succession of any children he might have by her, unlikely though it was, with so many others in line ahead of them, that any of those children would ever actually become king or queen. It was because of this, because of a statement that any children would be brought up in the Church of England, that Pope Paul VI intervened to ban the couple from marrying in a Catholic church.

In the event, the marriage took place in Vienna town hall and remarks about religious "dogma" made by Prince Charles in an address to the Salvation Army Congress on the same day were interpreted, rightly or wrongly, as criticism of the Pope's edict. In consequence, the Prince's remarks brought a stinging rebuke from the Archbishop of Glasgow, the Most Revd. Thomas Winning. He labelled the Act of Settlement "an anachronism" and called for its repeal. It constituted "a terrible slight to Catholics", he said in a radio interview. "As though a Catholic monarch would be a danger to the British Isles or Commonwealth."

James II's leanings towards Catholicism resulted not only in the Act of Settlement, but also in a quaint royal custom which was to persist for over two centuries until the Queen's father finally called a halt to it in 1948. The custom had its origins in the birth to James's second wife, Mary of Modena, of the baby son who has come down in history as the Old Pretender and whose 1715 bid for the throne ended in failure. The baby's birth, in 1688, was followed immediately by a rumour that it was not a royal child at all, but a changeling which had been smuggled through the labyrinthine passages of St James's Palace in a warming-pan. False though the rumour was, it was widely believed at the time. The fact that there had been witnesses in plenty to the birth made not a scrap of difference. After all, it was said, the witnesses were mainly Catholic and who in their right minds would believe a Catholic?

Parliament accordingly decided that it would send its own representative to witness any future birth in the Royal Family. It was, after all, merely a question of adding one more person to the crowd which crammed royal delivery rooms in those days. The Royal Family, initially, wanting no more nonsense about changelings, was in full agreement. But Albert of Saxe-Coburg, when he married Queen Victoria, was not. It was on his insistence that Parliament's witness found himself obliged to wait in an ante-room from where he could be quickly summoned to view the newborn babe once delivery had been effected and feminine proprieties observed. In this modified form, the custom continued down to the reign of King George V.

When the present Queen, leader in the line of succession among George V's grandchildren, was born at 17 Bruton Street in 1926, the Home Secretary of the day, Sir William Joynson-Hicks, was in close attendance and privileged to view the baby immediately after birth. But four years later, when Princess Margaret was born at Glamis Castle, things went badly wrong.

The task of authenticating that royal birth fell to another Home Secretary, J. R. Clynes. Over-zealous in his determination to do his duty, he arrived in Scotland far too early. "I always told him to come up when he was sent for," Elizabeth's father, the Duke of York, lamented to his mother, Queen Mary.

No one wanted the Home Secretary kicking his heels at Glamis for an indefinite period. The Dowager Countess of Airlie came to the rescue, whisking him away to stay with her at Cortachy Castle.

For two weeks the over-zealous Clynes kicked his heels at Cortachy. On the evening of August 21 he was just sitting down to dinner when a telephone call summoned him post-haste to Glamis. He drove the eight miles there through a downpour of rain and was rewarded with a glimpse of the new baby fast asleep in her crib. This he deemed sufficient to send an official announcement of the birth, as custom required, to the Lord Mayor of London and the Governors-General of the Commonwealth.

However, the whole business proved so nerve-wracking to the baby's father, a man of retiring, sensitive nature, that later, when he became King and his elder daughter, in turn, was expecting her first child, he decided to do away with the whole business.

"The attendance of a Minister of the Crown at a birth in the Royal Family is not a statutory requirement or a constitutional necessity," he announced in a royal statement. "It is merely the survival of an archaic custom, and the King feels it is unnecessary to continue further a practice for which there is no legal requirement."

Since then, starting with the birth of Prince Charles, successive Home Secretaries have been content to wait by their telephones for the news of any new royal birth to be passed to them.

The present order of succession to the throne is as follows:

The Prince of Wales
Prince Andrew
Prince Edward
Princess Anne and her son, Master Peter Phillips
Princess Margaret and her children, Viscount Linley and
    Lady Sarah Armstrong-Jones
The Duke of Gloucester and his children, Alexander,
    Earl of Ulster, and Lady Davina Windsor
The Duke of Kent and his children, George, Earl of St
    Andrews, Lord Nicholas Windsor, and Lady Helen Windsor
Lord Frederick Windsor (son of Prince Michael of Kent)
Princess Alexandra and her children, James and Marina Ogilvy

Princess Alexandra's younger brother, Prince Michael of Kent, would have preceded her and her children in the line of succession had he not renounced his right to the throne in order to marry a Catholic. However, because he did not include them in his renunciation, any children he and Princess Michael have rank ahead of Princess Alexandra and her children, though after Michael's elder brother, the Duke of Kent, and his children. Provided, of course, as the law stands, that their religious upbringing is a Protestant one in accordance with the Act of Settlement.

TAX

As Monarch, Queen Elizabeth II is exempt from paying tax on both her Civil List allowance (*see* Civil List *and* Duchy of Lancaster), calculated these days to do no more than meet the expenses of monarchy, and on her personal assets, a fact which is a sore point with Parliament's left-wingers. Nor is Prince Philip, unlike the average British husband, responsible for paying tax on his wife's income, a fact for which he is no doubt deeply grateful. And just as the Monarch does not pay tax in life, so the Monarch's estate is not liable to capital transfer tax (successor to the old "death duties") at death.

However, there are one or two small areas of taxation where the Queen does stump up. Under the Crown Private Estates Act of 1862 she is liable for rates and similar taxes on her private estates of San-dringham and Balmoral. And on those rare occasions when she is given something privately while on her foreign or Commonwealth travels – as distinct from gifts bestowed on her officially in her capacity as Monarch – she will pay Customs duty on it on her return to Britain.

Just as the Queen is exempt from paying income tax, so, to a degree, is her son and heir, Prince Charles. His Duchy of Cornwall income (*see* Duchy of Cornwall) reaches him tax-free. However, he voluntarily surrenders fifty per cent of it to the Exchequer in lieu of income tax. His predecessor, the late Duke of Windsor, did much the same in his days as Prince of Wales and Duke of Cornwall, but only to the lesser tune of thirty per cent.

But while the Queen's exemption from tax extends also to her personal assets, at least to a large extent, her son's does not. He is taxed in the normal way on any personal income or property he may have.

Others of the Royal Family – Prince Philip, the Queen Mother, Princess Anne, Prince Andrew, Princess Margaret – have no exemption. They are liable to tax on their state annuities as well as on any private income they may have. Prince Philip once likened his own position to that of a self-employed businessman. However that may be in other respects, he and the other Royals do not complete the detailed end-of-year tax returns required from other self-employed people. Instead, royal aides agree with the tax authorities to what extent the various Civil List allotments will be regarded as being the expenses of the job. There is no way of knowing how much or how little is written off in this way in each particular case, the tax affairs of the Royal Family being treated as confidentially as those of anyone else. But in the case of Prince Philip, it is not unreasonable to assume that his expenses, which include the salaries and expenses of his aides, are fairly substantial. The same is presumably true of the Queen Mother, Princess Anne and Princess Margaret.

TELEVISION

Queen Elizabeth II was quick to realize that she was reigning in an age dominated by television and it was largely at her own insistence that television cameras were permitted to eavesdrop so completely on her coronation ceremony. Even so, it was to be more than five years after her accession before she was finally lured into appearing on television in an individual capacity. This was in 1957 when, after turning down an earlier suggestion that her Christmas Day radio broadcast should be turned into a live television broadcast, she finally agreed to appear on television during a tour of Canada.

A preliminary run-through at Buckingham Palace prior to departing for Canada can hardly have been termed a success. She was extremely nervous and it showed. In Canada there was a second run-through, with the Queen nudging off her shoes in an attempt to relax more. The results were better than at Buckingham Palace, but she was still visibly tense and apprehensive as the seconds ticked away towards the actual telecast. Prince Philip, watching on a monitor screen, decided to send her a personal message.

"Tell the Queen to remember the wailing and gnashing of teeth," he said, cryptically.

His words were relayed to the Queen, who apparently understood what they meant and smiled delightedly. She was still smiling at the remark, completely relaxed all at once, when the red light came on and she was on television.

So successful was that début in Canada that, returning to Britain, she was ready to agree to a Christmas Day telecast. But when Christmas Day came, nerves came back. The thought of appearing live on television at three o'clock in the afternoon robbed her of her appetite and she left her Christmas lunch only half-eaten.

Prince Philip's cryptic message to the Queen in advance of her Canadian telecast may have been an echo of his own appearance on television earlier that same year. Returning from a four-month, 39,000-mile trip aboard the royal yacht which had included visits to survey teams in the Falkland Isles and a stop-over with the Trans-antarctic Expedition, he appeared on television as anchor-man of a pro-gramme about the trip entitled *Round The World In Forty Minutes*. Television being less stereotyped in those days, he was permitted to over-run by fifteen minutes. "Overtime, as usual," he commented, grinning.

Since then, both the Queen and her husband have continued to appear on television from time to time, the Queen regularly on Christmas Day (though this is now video-taped in advance) as well as in occasional documentaries concerned with royal art or royal horses, and both had "starring" roles in the television film *Royal Family*, screened in 1969. Largely Prince Philip's idea, *Royal Family* was made at a cost of £150,000 (recouped from its sale for American showing) and involved forty-three hours of filming, later distilled down to 110 min-utes, spread over seventy-five days. However much a few critics may have reacted against it, it went down well with the public. Viewing figures were twenty-three million the first time it was shown in Britain and fifteen million for the repeat, though some may have been watching it for the second time.

With this example to follow, it is perhaps not surprising that Charles should have become almost a Prince of the Television Age. His first ap-pearance was in 1975 when he "starred" in a film called *Pilot Royal* which dealt with his life as a naval helicopter pilot. He even scripted and directed a short sequence himself, a sort of Charlie Chaplin vig-nette with Charles (Wales, not Chaplin) as a little airman who could do nothing right.

Since then, he has appeared on Britain's television screens as inter-viewer in a programme about Welsh heritage, commentator for a tour of Canterbury Cathedral, link-man in a sociological series and in a debate with Alistair Cooke concerning the merits of his great-great-great-great-great-grandfather George III, who Charles thinks is a much misunderstood monarch. He also took the part of George III in a non-television dialogue recording of the scene between the King and John Adams, America's first ambassador to Britain (the part of Adams was taken by Elliott Richardson, former US Ambassador to Britain), which formed part of the 1976 American Bicentennial Exhibition at the National Maritime Museum.

As viewers, the Royals, like most people who lead full and active lives, are necessarily selective. The Queen's viewing is usually confined to evenings or weekends, and only then if there is something she par-ticularly wishes to see, though she will sometimes use television to watch a race in which one of her own horses is running if she cannot be there in person. She watched her horse Dunfermline win the 1977 Oaks on television. She enjoys watching equestrian programmes – show jumping and eventing – as well as other sporting occasions, such as the Olympic Games or World Cup, in which Britain is competing internationally. She likes a play with a plot to it, some of the top comedians and a really good situation comedy series. Programmes to do with her own family or royal history, like *Edward VII* or *The Six Wives of Henry VIII*, naturally intrigue her. One episode of *Edward VII*, which she could not watch at the normal time, was video-taped so that she could catch up with it later and, some years ago, she even changed the time at which she and Philip normally sit down to dinner so that they could watch *The Life and Times of Lord Mountbatten*, a series about Philip's Uncle Dickie.

THRONE

The only throne in the Throne Room at Buckingham Palace is the crimson and gold state throne once occupied by Queen Victoria. Her great-great-granddaughter, Elizabeth II, does not use it and these days it languishes in an alcove to one side. The Queen sits instead on what is known as a Chair of Estate. Two such chairs – the second for Prince Philip – stand side by side on a dais. Made specially for the coronation, they are of lime and beech gilded with gold leaf, of seventeenth-century design, with arms, back and cushion upholstered in rose pink and gold damask. The back of the Queen's chair is embroidered with her royal cypher – EIIR.

Nor are either the Coronation chair in which the Queen sat to be crowned or the Chair of Homage, which was used towards the end of the coronation service and is now in the Throne Room at Windsor Castle, her true throne. The Chair of Homage, like the Chair of Estate, was specially made for the 1953 coronation and to similar design. The Coronation chair is much older. Edward I had it made around 1300–1 to house the Stone of Scone (also known as the Stone of Destiny) on which Scotland's monarchs were once crowned and which he looted from Scone Abbey when he barn-stormed through Scotland with his army in 1296.

So where and what is the Queen's throne? Most leading authorities agree that the true throne is that which the Queen occupies in the House of Lords of the Palace of Westminster when she reads what is known as "the Speech from the Throne" at the opening of each new Parliament (*see* Opening of Parliament). Surmounted by a Gothic oak canopy, it was designed by Augustus Pugin when he was employed by Sir Charles Barry from 1836–43 to do the detailed drawings for the new

Houses of Parliament.

Also in the Throne Room at Buckingham Palace are the two chairs made for the coronation of the Queen's father, two more used by her mother during the course of the same coronation ceremony, and, in addition to Queen Victoria's state throne, two elaborately carved and gilded chairs made for the Throne Room of George IV. There are two more extremely throne-like chairs in the palace ballroom. These were made for the coronation of Edward VII and Queen Alexandra.

TRAIN

In addition to being given a new Rolls Royce to mark her 1977 Silver Jubilee, Queen Elizabeth II was also rewarded with a new royal train . . . or, rather, a set of ten air-conditioned coaches (with two more held in reserve) which had been specially built or converted for her over a period of three years, with furniture and fittings which she and Prince Philip (advised by Sir Hugh Casson) had personally selected.

The Queen's personal saloon, 75 feet long and 9 feet wide, has double doors opening on to the platform. Inside is an entrance vestibule, a lounge, a bedroom and bathroom for the Queen, with another bedroom and bathroom for her dresser. It has a ceiling in antique white, cream walls, slate-blue carpeting and blue and white curtains patterned in raindrops.

The lounge is furnished with a settee in pale blue and two easy chairs, one in matching pale blue and the other in jasmine yellow. For working purposes there is a cream-topped desk and a chair in natural beech. There are wall lights and a radio, and a telephone link can be speedily established wherever the train stops. The bedroom contains a divan bed with storage space beneath, a bedside table with a telephone on it, a dressing-table with a triple mirror and a fitted wardrobe with a full-length mirror.

Prints of historic royal train journeys hang on the walls. One shows Queen Victoria, Prince Albert and their children entraining for Scotland in 1852 while another, even earlier, shows Queen Victoria journeying from Cambridge to London in 1847.

In fact, Queen Victoria made her first-ever train journey on June 13, 1842, travelling from Windsor to Paddington on what was then the new Great Western line. She was, as she noted in her journal "quite charmed with it". So charmed that she promptly ordered her own royal train. As today, it consisted of a series of coaches converted into drawing-rooms and bedrooms, but fitted and furnished in the ornate Victorian fashion of quilted ceilings, curtain-hung walls and gilded furniture. In it she travelled not merely between Windsor and London, but south to Gosport (in order to reach Osborne House on the Isle of Wight) and north to Ballater (for Balmoral).

Today, kitchen and restaurant facilities enable the Queen to eat while travelling. Her great-great-grandmother could equally have done so, but preferred to stop when it was time to eat. At Perth Station and elsewhere special rooms, equipped with her own china, silver and table linen, were maintained for her benefit.

Prince Philip's saloon on the new royal train is designed so that it can be used either in conjunction with other coaches or on its own. For that reason, it has its own all-electric kitchen able to provide a meal for up to ten people and complete with its own refrigerator-freezer unit. Kitchen apart, it is built on very similar lines to the Queen's personal coach. It has a lounge which can be used also as a dining-room, a bedroom and shower room for Philip, and a bedroom and bathroom for his valet. The lounge is brown-carpeted with curtains in green hopsack. A two-seater settee and a single easy chair are grouped around a coffee table while a selection of five upright and chrome chairs enable the leather-topped writing desk also to serve as a dining-table. The bedroom contains a divan bed and a small fitted wardrobe with a built-in dressing-table. An electric pump ensures that the shower generates sufficient water pressure.

There is, in addition to the two main saloons, another saloon coach, a dining-car for the Royals, a restaurant-car for their aides, a coach providing both working and living accommodation for the Queen's Private Secretary and others, a combined sleeping coach and power generator, another sleeping coach, a coach providing both further accommodation and further kitchen facilities, while yet another coach, built originally in 1955 for the royal children, has been adapted and modernized to be used by others of the Royal Family or their aides.

There are, in addition to the two main saloons, another saloon coach, a a train has been made up from these new royal coaches (normally berthed at Wolverton in Buckinghamshire), the resulting train is completed with one of British Rail's standard diesel or electric locomotives.

TRAVELS

It was perhaps prophetic of the new era in monarchy which lay ahead that Elizabeth II, in Kenya (en route for Australia and New Zealand as deputy for her sick father) when news of her accession reached her, should spend the first day of her reign driving along the eighteen miles of dirt road which linked the royal lodge at Nyeri with the airfield at Nanyuki, flying the three hundred miles from Nanyuki to Entebbe in

Uganda in an unpressurized Dakota belonging to East African Airways, and then switching to an Argonaut operated by what was then the British Overseas Airways Corporation for the 4,000-mile haul back to London.

It was certainly a fitting start for a reign which was to witness royal travel on an unprecedented scale. After only seven years of monarchy, she was, it was said, already the most travelled monarch in Britain's history, and by now, though there are unfortunately no accurate figures to prove it, she must surely be the most travelled woman in the world. No one, not even her aides apparently, has taken the trouble to keep a check on her total mileage over her years of monarchy, but individual figures here and there are impressive. Her round-the-world tour of 1953–4 encompassed 43,618 miles. Then there was 18,000 miles in Canada in 1959 when she was pregnant with Andrew, 15,000 miles to India, Pakistan and Nepal in 1961, another 18,000 miles to Brazil and back in 1968, 25,000 miles covering Malaysia, Singapore, Brunei and the Seychelles in 1972, and a staggering 56,000 miles taking in thirteen countries during her Silver Jubilee year of 1977. All this in addition to countless provincial progresses around the United Kingdom.

In the air, she has experienced everything from the bumpiness of that 1952 unpressurized Dakota to the supersonic smoothness of Concorde. On water, she has voyaged in everything from *HMY Britannia*, the luxurious royal yacht (*see* Yacht), to a rubber dinghy and a Venetian gondola. On land, she has journeyed in everything from an armour-plated limousine to a gilded chariot drawn by forty-eight hefty Brunein warriors. She has found herself obliged to eat with her fingers at a feast given in her honour in Tonga and experimented with chopsticks in Singapore. She couldn't manage them and was finally compelled to fall back on using a spoon. She has sampled hot-dogs in Chicago, raw fish in Fiji, green tea in Japan (a slight grimace suggested that the flavour did not appeal to her) and *coco-de-mer*, the supposedly "forbidden fruit" of the Garden of Eden, in the Seychelles. She has watched American football in the United States, sheep-shearing in Australia and must have lost count of the number of "war dances" she has witnessed on various islands. She has been serenaded with cowhorn trumpets, noseflutes and the drone of conch shells. And everywhere she has gone she has been showered with gifts, from spears, boomerangs, animal skins and a barkcloth bedspread to mink coats, diamond brooches and emerald bracelets.

But phenomenal though her travels have been, her husband has surpassed her. In addition to accompanying his wife on all her state visits and Commonwealth tours, Prince Philip has undertaken so much travelling on his own account, often piloting his own aircraft or briefly taking over the helm of the royal yacht – there was one particularly hectic spell in 1963–4 when he visited twenty-five different countries in a jam-packed nine months – that he must have come close to doubling her mileage. But with this small difference. Because British passports are issued in her name, the Queen does not need one. Philip does.

Royal travel on today's mammoth scale had its beginnings in the days when the late Duke of Windsor was a fair-haired, blue-eyed Prince of Wales. And the shape of things to come was already to be seen as far back as 1931 when he switched from trains to 'planes for a tour of South America. Before that, because travel itself was a lengthy business, royal journeys were mainly restricted to Britain. Queen Victoria would occasionally visit her relatives in Germany or take the title of Countess of Balmoral for incognito holidays in France and Italy, but that was as far as she went. Her eldest son travelled more widely, even getting as far as India on one occasion, but as much for pleasure as anything else in his days as Prince of Wales, though later, as Edward VII, he also paid state visits to Italy, France, Sweden, Norway and Italy.

State visits go far back into history. Perhaps the most famous of all time was in 1520 when Henry VIII visited Francis I of France, an occasion which because of the opulence of its setting has become known as the Field of the Cloth of Gold. Today's state visits are less opulent, more stereotyped. They last, usually, no more than three days. The programme consists of a public welcome and a state drive through the capital of the country being visited, a state banquet given by the monarch or president of the country with a reciprocal banquet, usually at the British embassy or aboard the royal yacht, on the Queen's part, a visit to the ballet or opera and perhaps some sightseeing on a cultural and historic level. If a foreign monarch or president pays a state visit to Britain, the procedure is reversed with the Queen playing host. There is also an exchange of gifts between the two heads of state. When Elizabeth paid her first visit as Queen to the United States she took with her for President Eisenhower a pair of porcelain parula warblers, birds indigenous to the south-east United States and a walnut and calf-hide table under the glass of which was a map of the D-Day landings.

When it comes to foreign travel, Elizabeth II is by no means a free agent. Henry VIII's state visit to France may have been his own idea. His twentieth-century counterpart goes only where the government of the day decrees. It is because of the way her official visits reflect the foreign policy of the British Government that it was twenty years after World War II before Elizabeth II was able to visit her sisters-in-law at their homes in Germany. It was even longer, thirty years after the war, before she went to Japan. She has not been to South Africa since she became Queen, though she spent her twenty-first birthday there as a princess. Neither has she yet been to Spain or Russia (though Philip has) although she has been to communist Yugoslavia. On the other hand, she has been several times to the United States and France. However, the British Government has no say when it comes to visiting those countries of the Commonwealth of which she is also Queen. That is a matter between her and the Commonwealth country concerned. Visits to such Commonwealth countries may be for a specific purpose, such as attending the 1976 Olympic Games in Canada, or may involve a prolonged whistle-stop tour enabling her to see and be seen.

Even the mere three days of a state visit can involve months of planning and preparation. A Commonwealth tour can be more than a year on the drawing-board and end up with a printed schedule running to some 300–400 pages on which her every movement is charted minute by minute. So detailed was the planning for one tour of Australia that even the few seconds it would take her to walk from a luncheon table to the door of the luncheon room had been included. Noticing this, the Queen inquired impishly whether it would throw the whole schedule completely out if she happened to feel like a second cup of coffee after lunch.

From her point of view, a royal tour is no relaxing holiday trip. During the course of her 1953–4 Commonwealth tour she opened seven Parliaments, held eleven investitures, attended fifty balls, banquets and garden parties, 135 receptions, unveiled three memorials, made four broadcasts, planted six commemorative trees, laid seven wreaths, watched twenty-seven children's displays, made 157 speeches, sat through 276 more, received 468 gifts and bouquets, and shook hands with a staggering 13,000 people.

Plans for each tour or visit are drawn up by the country concerned and then submitted to the Queen for her approval. She goes through them personally and, as her joke about a second cup of coffee illustrates, studies every detail. In consequence, she will sometimes come up with an improving suggestion. Ahead of one United States visit, for instance, she spotted that it would be after dark when her aircraft landed in Washington. Surely a daylight landing would enable people to see her better, she suggested, and the change was made.

Once a draft schedule has been approved, an advance party of royal aides, usually including one of her private secretaries, the Master of the Household and a top detective bodyguard, travels the route ahead of her to check the timing, security arrangements and take a look at the accommodation being provided. Inevitably, they find themselves showered with countless questions from those who will be hosting or meeting the Queen. Does she like caviar? No. Oysters? No. But she does like a large flat-topped desk at which she can work between engagements and a full-length mirror in which she can survey herself from head to toe before going out. What sort of pillows does she like? No worry, she will bring her own.

It is not only her own pillows that the Queen takes with her when she flies out from London on each fresh trip. She also takes along her own toilet soap, a hot-water bottle in case the nights are chilly, a canister of her favourite tea and her own electric kettle, a supply of both bottled Malvern water (as a precaution against possible stomach upsets) and barley sugar (which she finds a useful antidote against nerves and travel sickness). She also takes along her movie and still cameras. She is a keen photographer, though her husband perhaps rates as a more expert one, and the travel movies she has taken over her years of monarchy – Everest from the air, Sydney harbour, the New York skyline, the Taj Mahal, elephants hauling logs in Thailand, the hot springs at Rotorua in New Zealand, the colour of maple trees during the Canadian fall and the ceremony of Buddha's Tooth in Sri Lanka – will one day rank historically alongside the journals her great-great-grandmother, Queen Victoria, kept so industriously.

Then there are clothes for the several changes a day which are required of her. Evening and other gowns are packed in two large portable wardrobes, leather-covered and mounted on wheels to make for easier handling. A banquet usually means a bulky, lavishly-embroidered state gown specially made for the occasion and this requires a leather trunk to itself to avoid undue creasing. Matching trunks hold other dresses and suits, coats and furs. A portable chest of drawers, also covered in blue leather and mounted on wheels, holds essentials like gloves and handkerchiefs, nightdresses, lingerie and pantihose. There are also matching hat boxes and shoe boxes. A crocodile dressing-case holds the thirty-piece set of silver gilt brushes, combs, hand-mirrors and cosmetic containers which was one of her wedding gifts. Another case, of unusual shape and inherited from Queen Mary, contains her parasols and umbrellas.

And all this is still only a fraction of the baggage that accompanies the Queen whenever she travels. After all, she does not, cannot, travel alone. Her entourage seldom numbers less than thirty, ladies-in-waiting and at least one equerry, private secretaries and a Press secretary, physician and hairdresser, dressers, pages, a maid (for the ladies-in-waiting), pages, footmen, clerks and detectives, to say nothing of Prince Philip's private secretary, his valet, equerry, detective. Plus politicians as the occasion may require.

All these, of course, have their own luggage. Then there are gifts and honours to be distributed as the trip progresses, medals and decorations, gold cufflinks and jewelled brooches, framed photographs and powder compacts embossed with the Queen's EIIR cypher, something for everyone from the top brass who will be hosting her to cooks, chauffeurs and maids at each stopping place. Then there are such miscellaneous items as the gold cutlery and Victorian dinner service she took with her to France in 1972 in order that she might give a suitable reciprocal banquet for President Pompidou at the British embassy. Her luggage on that occasion weighed almost a ton. Rather more – something like six tons – had to be shunted ashore for her 1975 visit to Mexico. And a staggering twelve tons was hauled around Australia and New Zealand during her 1953–4 world tour.

Despite the meticulous advance planning and preparations for the Queen's travels, it is perhaps inevitable, because of the magnitude of each separate operation, that things should go slightly wrong from time to time. In New Zealand, on one occasion, there was considerable consternation among the royal staff when the Queen's jewel case went missing for several hours. It had been inadvertently loaded on to the wrong aircraft. In Washington her staff were unable to locate the canister containing her own supply of tea and had to make shift with White House tea-bags. In Yugoslavia she landed at Dubrovnik to find no one waiting to greet her. The reception committee had moved on to Titograd under the impression that her aircraft was being diverted there. In Nigeria a commercial refrigeration plant was installed in the royal bedroom to lower the temperature. It worked only too well and plunged the bedroom almost to deep-freeze level. Fortunately, the fact was discovered and rectified just prior to the royal arrival.

Of course, the Queen travels in considerable comfort, in the lap of luxury even (*see* Yacht, Flying, Train *and* Cars), and her itinerary is planned to allow her spells of rest and relaxation. Nevertheless her days are filled with a succession of almost non-stop public engagements which often tend to be somewhat repetitive in content. But if she is ever bored, it must not be permitted to show. If she is strained or tired, that should not show either, though very occasionally it does. Inevitably there are times when she is either bored or tired or both. It could hardly be otherwise when her days on tour involve hours of walking and standing, seemingly endless handshakes – in Washington once she found herself having to shake hands with a staggering succession of over two thousand people – and the necessity to constantly smile, smile, smile. Over the years, of course, she has developed a few tricks of the royal travel trade to ease the situation. For instance, though she will take several dozen pairs of new shoes with her on a major Commonwealth tour, she usually ends up wearing the same few pairs, those she finds especially comfortable, over and over. HAS THE QUEEN ONLY ONE PAIR OF SHOES? a newspaper headline in Australia inquired once after an observant reporter had spotted this. She wears gloves to prevent her right hand being rubbed raw with incessant handshaking and has devised her own special form of handshake to avoid her fingers being crushed, though even this was not proof against the over-hearty hand-shake from a professional sheep-shearer who was presented to her during the course of one Australian tour and she could not quite restrain a wince of pain as her hand was totally engulfed in his huge mitt. Aboard her train, between stops, the Queen will rest her legs by taking off her shoes and sitting with her feet up. Prince Philip has developed the Churchillian ability to cat-nap for a few minutes at a time. And royal waves from the window of train or car are usually executed with a minimum of effort, the elbow being cushioned on an arm rest.

TRAVELS – QUEEN ELIZABETH II

As Princess Elizabeth:

1947   South Africa (with her parents and Princess Margaret)
1948   France
1949   Malta (as the naval wife of Prince Philip)
1950   Gibraltar, Greece, Malta (twice), Libya
1951   Italy; Canada and the United States
1952   Kenya (en route to Australia and New Zealand when word reached her of her father's death)

As Queen:

1953–4 Commonwealth tour of Bermuda, Jamaica, Fiji, Tonga, New Zealand, Australia, Ceylon, Uganda, Malta and Gibraltar. Also visited Libya on way back
1955   Norway
1956   Nigeria; Sweden. (Also cruised Mediterranean with Prince Philip and Princess Alexandra)
1957   Portugal; France; Denmark; Canada and the United States, where she addressed the United Nations
1958   Netherlands
1959   Canada and the United States
1961   Cyprus, India, Pakistan, Nepal, Iran and Turkey; Italy and the Vatican (including an audience with the Pope); Ghana, Liberia, Sierra Leone and The Gambia
1962   Netherlands (semi-private visit for the silver wedding celebrations of Queen Juliana and Prince Bernhard)
1963   Australia, New Zealand, Fiji and Canada
1964   Canada
1965   Ethiopia and Sudan; West Germany
1966   Caribbean tour, including Guyana (then British Guiana), Trinidad and Tobago, Grenada, St Vincent, Barbados, St Lucia, Dominica, Montserrat, Antigua, St Kitts-Nevis-Anguilla, British Virgin Islands, Turks and Caicos Islands, the Bahamas and Jamaica; Belgium

1967   Canada; West Germany (to review the Royal Tank Regiment); Malta
1968   Brazil, Chile and Senegal
1969   Austria; Norway (unofficial visit with Prince Philip and the children)
1970   Fiji, Tonga, New Zealand and Australia (stopping in Canada and Hawaii en route); Canada
1971   Canada; Turkey
1972   Thailand, Singapore, Malaysia, Brunei, Maldive Islands, Seychelles, Mauritius and Kenya; France; Yugoslavia
1973   Canada (twice); Australia
1974   Cook Islands, New Zealand, Norfolk Island, New Hebrides, British Solomon Islands, Papua New Guinea and Singapore; Indonesia; France (one-day visit to see her filly Highclere win the Prix de Diane)
1975   Bermuda, Barbados, the Bahamas and Jamaica; Mexico, Hawaii, Hong Kong and Japan
1976   Canada (Olympic Games); United States; Finland; Luxembourg
1977   Western Samoa, Tonga, Fiji, New Zealand, Australia and Papua New Guinea; Canada, the Bahamas, West Plana Cay (private), Little Inagua Island (private), British Virgin Islands, Antigua, Mustique (private) and Barbados
1978   Canada; West Germany
1979   Kuwait, Bahrain, Saudi Arabia, Oman, Qatar, United Arab Emirates; Denmark

TRAVELS – PRINCE PHILIP

Note: The following are travels Prince Philip has undertaken on his own account. They are additional to accompanying the Queen to countries she has visited as listed in the preceding schedule.

1950   Middle East, Turkey, Gibraltar plus courtesy calls on King Ibn Saud and King Abdullah of Jordan (while still serving in the navy)
1952   Finland, Norway and Sweden; France; Malta
1953   West Germany*
1954   France and West Germany*; Canada
1955   Malta and the Mediterranean; West Germany (twice)*; Denmark
1956   Mediterranean and Gibraltar (Combined Fleet operations);

* Frequent West German visits mainly to visit British forces.

Seychelles, Ceylon, Papua New Guinea, Malaya, Australia (Olympic Games), New Zealand, Chatham Islands, Deception Islands, South Shetland Islands, Falkland Islands, Tristan da Cunha, St Helena, Ascension Island, the Gambia and Gibraltar

1957　West Germany*

1958　West Germany (twice)*; Belgium; Canada

1959　India, Pakistan, Singapore, Sarawak, Brunei, North Borneo (later Sabah), Hong Kong, the Solomon Islands, the Gilbert and Ellice Islands, Christmas Island, the Bahamas and Bermuda; Ghana

1960　Malta and Switzerland; West Germany*; Canada and the United States

1961　West Germany*; Tanganyika

1962　British Guiana, Venezuela, Colombia, Ecuador, Peru, Bolivia, Chile, Paraguay, Uruguay, Brazil and Argentina; Canada and the United States (twice); Australia; Italy (private); West Germany*

1963　United States (funeral of President Kennedy); Kenya (private), Zanzibar and Sudan

1964　Greece (funeral of King Paul); Iceland; Malawi; Greece (wedding of King Constantine and Princess Anne-Marie of Denmark); Malta; Mexico, Galapagos Islands, Panama, Trinidad and Tobago, Grenada, St Vincent, Barbados, St Lucia, Dominica, St Kitts, Montserrat, Antigua; West Germany*; France; Belgium; Morocco

1965　Saudi Arabia, Pakistan, India, Singapore, Australia, Sarawak, Brunei, Sabah (formerly North Borneo), Malaya, Thailand, Nepal, Pakistan, Bahrain and Greece; Italy (twice); France (twice); West Germany*; Switzerland; Belgium

1966　United States (Miami, Houston, Texas, Dallas, Palm Springs, Chicago, Los Angeles and New York) and Canada; Netherlands (for the wedding of his nephew, Prince Karl of Hesse); Norway; West Germany (twice)*; Jamaica; Argentina; Monaco; Italy; France

1967　Iran; Australia; France (twice); Netherlands; Italy; Canada (twice)

1968　Australia and New Zealand; Mexico (Olympic Games); Ethiopia and Kenya (semi-private); France; West Germany; Canada and the United States; Switzerland

1970　France; United States (Cape Kennedy); Finland; Italy; West Germany (twice)*; Belgium

* Frequent West German visits mainly to visit British forces.

1971   Galapagos Islands, Easter Island, Picairn Island, Cook Island, Samoa, Fiji, New Hebrides, Solomon Islands, Bougainville, New Guinea and Australia; West Germany (twice)*; France; Hungary; Iran; Sweden.

1972   Denmark (funeral of King Frederik); Kenya; West Germany (four times, including one private and once for the Olympic Games); Liechtenstein (private); Holland (private); Belgium.

1973   Hungary, Yugoslavia, Iran, Afghanistan, India, Thailand, Singapore and Australia; West Germany*; Portugal; Denmark; Russia (Kiev and Moscow); Sweden (funeral of King Gustav); Bulgaria; New Zealand and Australia; Belgium; Luxembourg (private).

1974   New Zealand and Australia; France (twice, one for memorial service for President Pompidou); Switzerland (twice); West Germany (twice, one private) and Austria (private); Canada and the United States; Belgium.

1975   Belize, El Salvador, Honduras, Costa Rica, St Lucia and Grand Turk Island; Poland; Morocco; Netherlands; West Germany*; Spain (accession of King Juan Carlos I); Belgium.

1976   Liechtenstein (private); Canada; Netherlands; Mexico; West Germany (twice, one private); Belgium.

1977   Afghanistan; Saudi Arabia; Monaco; Algeria; Germany (private); Canada; Jamaica; Belgium.

1978   Canada (three times); Liechenstein (private); Luxembourg (private), Germany (four times, one private); Hungary; USA (three times), Puerto Rico; France.

* Frequent West German visits mainly to visit British forces.

TROOPING THE COLOUR

Like so many of Britain's royal traditions, the origins of Trooping the Colour are lost in the mists of time. Some military historians say that it began with the Duke of Marlborough in the seventeenth century. To sober up his men for the day's battle, they say, he would have them rousted out at the crack of dawn to stand yawning and swaying on parade while the regimental colours were trooped through the lines. While he may well have done so, the custom – though perhaps not the ceremony – of Trooping the Colour was already well established long before that with no more reason than to enable troops to recognize their own colour and rally around it in battle.

King George II was the first monarch to attend the ceremony on Horse Guards Parade, the parade ground which occupies the site of what was once the Palace of Whitehall. Indeed, it was George II, the last British monarch actually to lead his troops in battle, and his soldier son, "Butcher" Cumberland, who first conceived the idea that the men of each regiment should be dressed alike (uniformly in fact, from which the word "uniform" for military dress is derived). The Horse Guards ceremony became an annual one to commemorate the king's birthday, a practice which continued throughout the reigns of George II, George III and William IV. It was with Queen Victoria that the idea of the monarch having two birthdays – actual and monarchical – appears to have started. Her birthday was on May 24, a convenient good-weather date for what had become known in official circles as the Monarch's Birthday Parade, but the Queen, especially in her younger days, much preferred to celebrate her birthday in private. To accommodate her, official celebrations were switched for the first time in 1843 – to July 6 – and to various dates in summer thereafter.

The practice of the monarch having two birthdays, real and official, continued with Edward VII. He would have preferred it otherwise, but his real birthday, November 9, was hardly a reliable one for weather. It was more likely to be fine on George V's birthday, June 3, and during his reign the ceremony was held on or very near the correct date. But problems arose again with George VI, whose actual birthday was on December 14. He switched the ceremony to the second Thursday in June, a practice his daughter continued when she succeeded him on the throne. But the increasingly huge influx of sightseers each year caused such traffic congestion that parts of London were brought virtually to a standstill. So in 1959 it was decided to hold future ceremonies on a Saturday. Today it is usually the second Saturday in June, though it can be either the first or the third should the Queen's other engagements require it.

Her real birthday on April 21 is celebrated privately and quietly. Her official birthday, whatever the date of the June Saturday selected in a particular year, is celebrated with a spectacular parade – Trooping the Colour – and the firing of royal salutes in Hyde Park and at the Tower of London. The park salute is fired by men of the King's Troop of Royal Horse Artillery, resplendent figures in their hussar-style uniforms and plumed headgear. It was the Queen's father who gave them the name when he visited their barracks in 1947, personally crossing out the old "Riding Troop" name in the visitors' book and substituting the new one. When Elizabeth ascended the throne it was suggested they should be renamed "The Queen's Troop" in her honour, but she preferred them to retain the name her father had given them. At the Tower of London the salute is fired by the Honourable Artillery Company, a unit of part-time volunteers. The HAC had its origins in a royal charter granted by Henry VIII in 1537, which makes it one of the oldest military units in the world and the parent company of the Honourable

Artillery Company of Boston, Massachusetts, an offshoot formed by four of its members who emigrated to America in 1638.

The Birthday Parade starts at 10.45 a.m. when the Queen, accompanied usually by Prince Philip and the Prince of Wales, rides out of Buckingham Palace and along the Mall on Burmese, the horse she was given in 1969 by the Royal Canadian Mounted Police. A back-up horse, Centennial, also given to her by the Canadians, is ridden by Prince Charles. She is accompanied also by the massed bands of the Household Cavalry and a Sovereign's Escort of either Life Guards in their white breeches, scarlet tunics, chromium-plated cuirasses and nodding white plumes (the plumes are actually strips of whalebone) or of the Blues and Royals (Royal Horse Guards and 1st Dragoons) in their blue tunics and red-plumed helmets. Both outfits had their origins in the aftermath of the Civil War, the Life Guards coming from cavaliers who had fought for the king while the Horse Guards came from the Cromwellian army. Today both share the honour and duty of providing a mounted escort for the Monarch on ceremonial occasions.

An expert horsewoman who first learned to ride in childhood, the Queen normally rides astraddle. But for the annual Birthday Parade she reverts to the more femininely elegant side-saddle posture, a fact which necessitates a brief refresher course each year in the royal mews. She dresses in keeping with the occasion, in a skirted riding habit, military tunic and tricorne hat, the plume in the hat varying from year to year according to which particular regiment of foot guards will be trooping its colour that year (*see* Changing the Guard). A white plume means the Grenadiers, red is for the Coldstream Guards, blue for the Irish and white and green for the Welsh Guards. Should there be no plume in the Queen's hat it means it is the turn of the Scots Guards.

She arrives on Horse Guards Parade exactly as the clock strikes eleven, though it would perhaps be more correct to say that the clock strikes eleven as she arrives at the parade ground. To ensure that the Monarch is never late, even though it is impossible to time a ceremonial horseback ride to the nearest second, a man is stationed in the clock tower to delay the hands a little if necessary. But Big Ben, booming in the parliamentary distance, sometimes gives the game away.

Over the years the ceremony of Trooping the Colour has been refined into a highly ritualistic drill display which the men of the Guards Division claim is without equal anywhere in the world. Other members of the Royal Family, preceding the official parade in their carriages, watch usually from a window above the central arch as the Queen rides through the arrow-straight lines of guardsmen, inspecting them before taking her place at the saluting base. The beating of the Drummer's Call by a solitary drummer – exactly as drummers were once used to relay orders to troops in battle – is the signal for the regiment whose turn it is to start trooping its colour. It is the Queen's colour with its displayed battle honours, not the regimental colour, which is lowered in salute and trooped in slow time by the colour ensign and escort.

Then, with bands playing, the entire Guards Division flows into movement, giving a dazzling and immaculate display of quick (116 paces to the minute) and slow (65 paces to the minute) marching before forming up behind the Queen and following her back to Buckingham Palace where she stations herself at the main gates to take a final salute as the Guards march past.

WINDSOR CASTLE

Windsor Castle is both the largest surviving castle in Europe and the oldest of Britain's palaces still in regular use as a royal home. Each year the Queen spends Christmas there with her family around her. Each year, in June, she invites royal relatives and personal friends to join her there for a house party coinciding with Royal Ascot (*see* Ascot). Equally, she continues the royal custom of transferring herself and her court from Buckingham Palace to Windsor for around four weeks over Easter, though not for the same reason which kept her medieval forebears constantly moving back and forth between their various palaces.

In medieval times, lacking any real system of food distribution, monarchs and their followers were obliged to move house once they had devoured all the food in a particular locality. The Queen's present-day move to Windsor for Easter is simply to give herself a break, though it is not entirely a holiday. While there she continues to carry out a few public engagements and also gives a number of what are known as "dine and sleep" parties for ministers and ambassadors. About a dozen people are entertained at each party, arriving around half-past six in the evening, sitting down to dinner with the Queen, staying the night and departing again after breakfast the following morning.

Windsor's massive fortress also serves the Queen in the nature of a weekend cottage to which she and her husband retreat each Friday afternoon. To this end, they have created a comfortable private apartment for themselves overlooking the sunken garden, no easy task when you are dealing with a medieval castle with corridors wider than many a country lane. However, there are also advantages, as the Queen's father discovered. Wishing to install an extra bathroom on one occasion, he found it possible to tuck it comfortably into the actual thickness of one of the walls.

The castle is some twenty-three miles from London, its towers and battlements dominating a chalk mound just south of the Thames. It was William the Conqueror, at the same time that he was constructing the original Tower of London, who first transformed the Saxon hunting lodge which once stood on the site into a timber-built fortress with the idea of safeguarding London against possible attack from the west. His son, William Rufus, used Windsor simply as a fortress and prison, but Henry I held court there. Henry II, first of the royal Plantagenets, replaced timber with stone, and Henry III began the construction of the mighty Round Tower which today dominates the thirteen-acre site.

Edward III had the notion of using Windsor as a palace as well as a fortress. Henry VI founded nearby Eton College and Edward IV built the graceful St George's Chapel to which the Knights of the Garter (*see* Order of the Garter) still repair each year for their service of re-dedication. Henry VIII built the main gateway which bears his name and his daughter, Elizabeth I, added what is now the library. Charles II rebuilt the magnificent range of state apartments while George III, too, did much towards restoring the castle in which he was to live out his last tormented years in a blind world of his own. But more than anyone else it was that gluttonous and spendthrift monarch, George IV, who was largely responsible for the interior of Windsor as it is today.

George IV had the dream of turning Windsor into something that would outshine even Versailles. Parliament voted him £300,000 for the work, but he ended up spending three times as much. At one time his architect, Jeffry Wyatt, had as many as five hundred men, craftsmen and labourers, toiling away there. The result, among other things, was the magnificent suite of red, green and white drawing-rooms and the Grand Corridor, 550 feet from end to end, in which George could display his vast magpie collection of paintings, furniture, busts, bronzes and porcelain (*see* Furniture and *Objets d'Art and* Picture Collection).

A large part of the royal picture collection is still housed at Windsor along with the royal archives and the royal library. Also at Windsor, and on view when the castle is open to the public, is the Queen Mary's doll's house. Designed by Sir Edwin Lutyens and first shown at the Great Empire Exhibition of 1926, it bears the same resemblance to an ordinary doll's house as *HMY Britannia* does to an ordinary yacht. A miniature country mansion (built to a scale of 1 in 12), it is elegantly fitted and furnished down to the smallest detail. Some seven hundred paintings and drawings adorn the walls, many of them by famous names. Sir William Orpen painted the portraits of George V and Queen Mary which hang in the drawing-room, Sir William Nicholson painted the one of Elizabeth I which hangs in the library, while the miniature portrait of the then Prince of Wales (later Duke of Windsor) on horseback is by Sir Alfred Munnings. Famous names abound similarly on the spines of the specially written, leather-covered miniature volumes which fill the library shelves – Arnold Bennett and Sir James Barrie, Hardy, Conrad and Kipling. Even Conan Doyle wrote a special Sherlock Holmes adventure for inclusion. The one-inch bottles in the cellar are filled with real wine of fine vintage, Château-Margaux 1899 and Château-d'Yquem 1874, and everything that should work does work, electric lighting, lift, and door locks. Clocks tick, lavatories flush, baths gush water and the gramophone plays. Even the knife-grinding machine in the kitchen will actually grind miniature knives. And housed in a drawer in the base is a pull-out garden complete with trees (which fold flat when stowed away), shrubberies, flower beds and even birds, butterflies and snails.

YACHT

Her Majesty's yacht *Britannia* bears about as much resemblance to an ordinary yacht as Buckingham Palace does to the average house. In fact, it is more a floating palace than a yacht, intended not so much to get Elizabeth II about the world in this age of jet aircraft as to enable her to throw receptions and banquets when she reaches her destination.

Monarchs back to the days of Henry VIII, and possibly even as far back as Alfred the Great, have had their own flagships. But it was the pleasure-loving Charles II who first saw how much a yacht could add to the joys of royal life. So with the restoration of the monarchy, the first royal yacht – as distinct from flagship – was created from the coal brig in which Charles had earlier made good his escape to France.

The idea caught on. George IV, in the days of his Prince Regency, built himself a yacht named *Royal George* and the young Queen Victoria later inherited this along with various other trappings of monarchy. But the *Royal George* was dependent on sails and the wind and, as a result, had to be towed all the way when Victoria voyaged to Leith in 1842. She was not a monarch to stand for that sort of embarrassment in the new age of steam and promptly ordered herself a steam yacht of such power that it easily outdistanced its naval escort on its very first voyage. For Victoria, of course, there could be only one name for a royal yacht – *Victoria & Albert*.

Over her long period of monarchy, Queen Victoria had three successive royal yachts, one a paddle steamer, all with the same name. The last of the three, built in 1899, proved to be rather unstable due to the fact that the plans for it had been borrowed from the Tsar of Russia and there was some confusion between metric and imperial measurements. Because of this, Queen Victoria herself never actually used it and her son, Edward VII, preferred to use the smaller *Alexandra* after he had had it built in 1907. Nevertheless, *Victoria & Albert*, though it was hardly used except for naval reviews, remained the official royal yacht. By the 1930s it was not only unstable, but virtually unseaworthy, and George VI planned a new yacht to be built in

1939. However, World War II intervened to halt the project and nothing further was done until 1951. By then the King's health was declining and the idea of a new yacht was revived with the idea that it would be suitable for health-promoting convalescent cruises. But by the time the work was actually put in hand, in February, 1952, the King was dead and his elder daughter was Queen.

Built at John Brown's Clydebank shipyard over a period of two years, at a cost of £2.1 million, the new *Britannia* was designed so that it could be converted for use as a hospital ship in time of war. Instead of the traditional swan bow and counter stern of previous royal yachts, it was given a modern clipper bow and a modified cruiser stern. Its statistics are as follows:

Overall length: 412 feet 3 inches (125.65 metres)
Beam: 55 feet maximum (16.76 metres)
Deep load displacement: 4,961 tons (5041 tonnes)
Gross tonnage: 5,769 tons (5,862 tonnes)
Draught: 17 feet (15.2 metres) at load displacement

It has a geared turbine engine – twin shafts – producing 12,000 shaft horsepower (8,948 kilowatts). On its trials it had a maximum speed of 22.5 knots, but this reduces to 21 knots for continuous sea-going performance. With 510 tons (518 tonnes) of fuel oil in its tanks, it has a range of 2,800 miles (4,506 kilometres) at 20 knots, 3,200 miles (5,150 kilometres) at 18 knots and 3,765 miles (5,914 kilometres) at 14 knots.

Originally, as the Queen soon found out, it had a tendency to roll in rough weather. There was a night crossing of the North Sea in stormy weather when the yacht rolled so much that the dressing-table in the royal cabin broke free of its retaining hooks. The Queen awoke with a start as the dressing-table cannoned into her bed. She climbed out of bed, donned a dressing-gown and summoned help. Members of the crew were quickly on the scene to haul the dressing-table back into place. That North Sea crossing also resulted in not a few breakages, with the result that Denny-Brown stabilizers were later fitted to counteract the yacht's tendency to roll.

With its royal blue hull and snowy-white superstructure trimmed with gold, the royal arms on its bow and the royal cypher on its stern, *Britannia* looks every inch the royal yacht it is. It is fitted out to carry both a 40-foot royal barge and a Rolls Royce as well as an inflatable raft on which a Land Rover can be ferried ashore if necessary. A section of the deck is specially strengthened for helicopter landings.

Based at Portsmouth when not required for royal use, the yacht is an independent command administered by the Flag Officer Royal Yachts, normally an extra equerry to the Queen and, as such, a member of what is known as the Queen's Household (*see* Household). It has a sea-going crew of 21 officers and 256 men. Officers serve a two-year term of duty. Half the ratings are permanent crew members while the other half, like the officers, serve two years at a time. All are Royal Navy volunteers. Despite the fact that they receive no special rates of pay and no special privileges by way of allowances or leave, there is never any shortage of volunteers for this élite crew, distinguished from the rest of the navy by virtue of the fact that they are permitted to wear their jumpers inside instead of outside their trousers, thus enabling them to display the black silk bows with which the trousers are fitted at the back. Their uniform badges are white instead of the usual naval red and they carry the identification "Royal Yacht" on their hat-bands.

At sea, to avoid the necessity for constantly saluting the Queen and others of the Royal Family, they work bareheaded. Technically, they are thus out of uniform and so the necessity to salute does not arise. They also wear soft-soled pumps to avoid disturbing the Royals during the night watches and, as far as possible, orders on the upper deck are given and acknowledged by a system of hand signals instead of the more usual shouted commands.

To descend the wide mahogany staircase which leads to the yacht's state apartments is rather like passing through the Grand Entrance of Buckingham Palace. In this section of the yacht scarcely a nautical note intrudes. Tall mahogany doors link the ante-room with the drawing-room and these can be folded back to form a single large reception hall in which the Queen, when the yacht is berthed in a foreign or Commonwealth port, can host up to two hundred guests at a time.

The dining-room can seat up to fifty-six people at a single sitting. The ebony-edged table was originally designed to seat thirty-two, but Prince Philip, after taking a train-load of aides and servants to Portsmouth to try things out at the fitting-out stage, decided that this was hardly sufficient. So removable wings were designed and constructed, enabling a further twenty-four guests to be dined when necessary. Sliding wall panels conceal a screen so that the dining-room can be used also as a cinema if required.

Items of furniture from earlier royal yachts are to be seen here and there. The drawing-room contains several pieces from the second *Victoria & Albert*, among them a satin-wood desk which belonged to Queen Victoria and a gimbal table designed by the ingenious Prince Albert. The binnacle on the veranda deck is even older. It comes from the Prince Regent's *Royal George*.

The Queen and her husband each have a private sitting-room off the ante-room. The Queen's room is softly feminine with chintz curtains and silk-shaded wall lights. Philip's sitting-room, with its teak panelling and essentially functional lighting, is more ruggedly masculine. A model of the frigate *Magpie* which he commanded in his naval days stands in an illuminated case. Each sitting-room has a built-in desk, the Queen's topped with green leather and Prince Philip's with red.

A lift links the sitting-rooms with the royal bedrooms. These are on the shelter deck, the uppermost deck of the main superstructure, between the main and mizzen-masts, their windows set high enough so that members of the crew cannot see inside if they chance to catfoot past in their soft-soled pumps. On the same deck is a wardrobe room for the Queen's clothes, together with cabins for her dresser and Philip's valet. Cabins for others of the Queen's Household and any guests are located on the main deck.

Over the years since her launching in 1954 *Britannia* has played many parts. She has taken the Queen on state visits, Commonwealth tours and private cruises. She has dropped anchor in Sweden, Denmark, Norway, sailed to the West Indies and the Galapagos Islands, to Australia and New Zealand, Iceland and Turkey, Brazil, Chile and Mexico, Ghana, Liberia and Sierra Leone. She served as a floating base from which the Queen opened the St Lawrence Seaway in 1959. The 139-foot main mast proved too tall to pass under the bridges en route and the top twenty feet had to be hinged. With Prince Philip aboard, she has ploughed as far south as the pack ice of the Antarctic. She has enabled Philip to attend naval manoeuvres and, in her war-time role as a hospital ship, has taken part in NATO exercises. She served as a honeymoon hotel for both Princess Margaret and Princess Anne in turn. A Canadian travel agency once put in a bid to hire the royal yacht for winter cruises. It is hardly necessary to say that the offer was promptly rejected.

Britannia is equipped with four radio outfits, a ship-to-shore telephone link for use in harbour, a degaussing belt for protection against mines, and spotlights to illuminate the surrounding area after dark. However, all measures proved insufficient to safeguard the yacht's white ensign during a state visit to Portugal.

The Queen, during the course of that visit, called at a Lisbon seminary which was used as a British naval base during the Napoleonic Wars. Because of this, the seminary has a traditional right not only to fly the white ensign, but to demand a new one from any visiting British ship. In keeping with tradition, the Queen offered to give the seminary Britannia's ensign.

"But we already have it, Ma'am," the rector of the seminary is said to have replied.

Students of the seminary (or so the story runs) had staged a night raid on the yacht, sneaking its white ensign and leaving the seminary's old one in its place.

Bibliography

In compiling *Monarchy and the Royal Family* we have inevitably drawn upon some of our previous books. These include *Elizabeth, Queen and Mother* (published 1964); *Prince Charles, The Future King* (1966); *The Royal Family* (USA, 1969); *The Crown and The Ring* (1972); *Bertie & Alix* (1974); *The Queen's Life* (1976); and *Charles, The Man and The Prince* (1977). It may save people time and trouble if we also say that only the last three of these are still in print.

Other works we have consulted include:

Alexandra, Queen of Yugoslavia: *Prince Philip, A Family Portrait* (Hodder & Stoughton Ltd)

Alice, Princess, Countess of Athlone: *For My Grandchildren* (Evans Brothers Ltd)

Arthur, Sir George: *Queen Alexandra* (Chapman & Hall Ltd) *Queen Mary* (Butterworth & Co. Ltd)

Battiscombe, Georgina: *Queen Alexandra* (Constable & Co. Ltd)

Benson, E. F.: *King Edward VII* (Longman Group Ltd)

Boothroyd, Basil: *Philip, An Informal Biography* (Longman Group Ltd)

Bryant, Sir Arthur: *King George V* (Peter Davies Ltd), and *A Thousand Years of British Monarchy* (William Collins Sons & Co. Ltd)

Coats, Peter: *The Gardens of Buckingham Palace* (Michael Joseph Ltd)

Connell, Brian: *Manifest Destiny* (Cassell & Co. Ltd)

Cowles, Virginia: *Edward VII and His circle* (Hamish Hamilton Ltd)

Crawford, Marion: *The Little Princesses* (Cassell & Co. Ltd)

Dean, John: *HRH Prince Philip* (Robert Hale Ltd)

Donaldson, Frances: *Edward VIII* (Weidenfeld Ltd)

Ellis, Jennifer: *Elizabeth, The Queen Mother* (Hutchinson & Co. Ltd)

Gore, John: *George V* (John Murray Ltd)

Hartnell, Sir Norman: *Silver and Gold* (Evans Brothers Ltd)

Hatch, Alden: *The Mountbattens* (W. H. Allen & Co. Ltd)

Hopkins, Phyl: *Village Royal* (Angus & Robertson Ltd)

Howard, Philip: *The Royal Palaces* (Hamish Hamilton Ltd)

Innes, A. D.: *A History of the British Nation* (T. C. and E. C. Jack)

Joelson, Annette: *Heirs to the Throne* (William Heinemann Ltd)

Jones, Mrs Herbert: *Sandringham Past and Present* (1881)

Laird, Dorothy: *How The Queen Reigns* (Hodder & Stoughton Ltd)

Lee, Sir Sidney: *King Edward VII* (2 vols., Macmillan Ltd)

Longford, Elizabeth: *Victoria RI* (Weidenfeld Ltd)
Magnus, Sir Philip: *King Edward VII* (John Murray Ltd)
Massie, Robert K.: *Nicholas and Alexandra* (Victor Gollancz Ltd)
Maxwell, Sir Herbert: *Sixty Years A Queen* (London 1897)
Michie, Allan A.: *The Crown and The People* (Secker & Warburg Ltd)
Middlemass, Keith: *The Life and Times of Edward VII* (Weidenfeld Ltd)
Millar, Oliver: *The Queen's Pictures* (Weidenfeld Ltd)
Morrah, Dermot: *The Work of the Queen* (William Kimber & Co. Ltd)
Nicolson, Harold: *King George V* (Constable & Co. Ltd)
Plumb, J. H. & Wheldon, Hew: *Royal Heritage* (BBC Publications)
Pope Hennessy, James: *Queen Mary* (George Allen & Unwin Ltd)
Smith, Brian E.: *Royal Daimlers* (Transport Bookman Publications)
Smith, H. Clifford: *Buckingham Palace* (Country Life)
Talbot, Godfrey: *Queen Elizabeth, The Queen Mother* (Jarrolds Publishers Ltd)
Terraine, John: *The Life & Times of Lord Mountbatten* (Hutchinson & Co. Ltd)
Tisdall, E. P. P.: *Unpredictable Queen* (Stanley Paul Ltd)
Townsend, Peter: *Time and Chance* (William Collins Sons & Co. Ltd)
Wakeford, Geoffrey: *Thirty Years A Queen* (Robert Hale Ltd)
Wheeler-Bennett, John: *King George VI* (Macmillan Ltd)
Windsor, Duchess of: *The Heart Has Its Reasons* (Michael Joseph Ltd)
Windsor, Duke of: *A King's Story* (Cassell & Co. Ltd)
Young, Sheila: *The Queen's Jewellery* (Ebury Press)

Index